30

JOHN MCKINLEY
and the Antebellum Supreme Court

JOHN MCKINLEY
and the Antebellum Supreme Court

Circuit Riding in the Old Southwest

Steven P. Brown

THE UNIVERSITY OF ALABAMA PRESS

Tuscaloosa

Typeface: Caslon

Cover: John McKinley (portrait by Matthew Harris Jouett, circa 1817–18); courtesy
of the Collection of the Supreme Court of the United States
Cover design: Erin Bradley Dangar / Dangar Design

∞

The paper on which this book is printed meets the minimum requirements of
American National Standard for Information Sciences—Permanence of Paper for
Printed Library Materials, ANSI Z39.48-1984.

Library of Congress Cataloging-in-Publication Data

Brown, Steven Preston.
    John McKinley and the antebellum Supreme Court : circuit riding in the old
Southwest / Steven P. Brown.
        p. cm.
    "Appendix: Justice John McKinley's Supreme Court Opinions and Dissents."
    Includes bibliographical references and index.
    ISBN 978-0-8173-1771-3 (trade cloth : alk. paper) — ISBN 978-0-8173-8626-9
(e book) 1. McKinley, John, 1780–1852 2. United States. Supreme Court—Biography.
3. Judges—United States—Biography. 4. Circuit courts—Southwest, Old—
History—19th century. 5. Politicians—Alabama—Biography. I. McKinley, John,
1780–1852. II. Title.
    KF8745.M38B76 2012
    347.73′2634092—dc23
    [B]

                                                                2012015833

Contents

Illustrations

Acknowledgments

I am grateful for the opportunity to research and write about the life of Justice John McKinley. I knew a good deal about both Justices Hugo Black and John Archibald Campbell before I moved to Auburn in 1998, but it was only upon arriving here that I learned of Alabama's first Supreme Court justice. Since that time and for reasons that have become clear to me just recently, I felt compelled to learn more about Justice McKinley.

I have been amazed at the massive amounts of information that modern technology has allowed me to uncover, considering that McKinley was a man who reportedly left behind little trace of his life. Older (and slower) research methods provided further details about his life on and off the bench. I am especially grateful for the numerous people who became intrigued with Justice McKinley themselves as they assisted with my research requests. It has been a tremendous journey of discovery for all of us in many ways.

This work could not have been completed without the support of Dan Waterman and Elizabeth Motherwell at The University of Alabama Press. Their enthusiasm and encouragement for both this and an earlier project had a greater influence on my ability to finish the manuscript for this book than they will ever know.

I appreciate the ongoing friendship and support of my colleagues in the Department of Political Science at Auburn University. My constitutional law students at Auburn continue to both teach and inspire me. I am also grateful for the faculty members and students of the Junior Statesman of America (JSA) Summer School Program at Stanford University, where much of this book was written. I am particularly indebted to the following JSA faculty for their patience and encouragement: LaTosha Bruce, Vickie

Ellis, Carl Franklin, John Howell, Dave Mazerra, Andi McClanahan, Art Peterson, Greg Phelps, Dwight Podgurski, Susan Sci, Alan Tauber, Dave Wendt, and Marina Whitchurch.

I gratefully acknowledge the assistance of the following individuals and institutions that were invaluable in helping me discover Justice McKinley: Dr. Norwood Kerr and the staff at the Alabama Department of Archives and History, Montgomery; Jennifer Blancato in the Curator's Office, Architect of the Capitol, Washington, D.C.; Dr. Leah Rawls Atkins; Liza Weisbrod, Dwayne Cox, John Varner, and Greg Schmidt of the Ralph Brown Draughon Library at Auburn University; Sheri Kohler and the staff at Bellefontaine Cemetery, St. Louis, Missouri; Benjamin Peterson at the Birmingham Public Library; the Broome County Historical Society, Binghamton, New York; Matt Sarago at the Federal Judicial Center; Jim Holmberg and the Special Collections staff at the Filson Historical Society, Louisville, Kentucky; Helen Brown, Church Administrator, First Presbyterian Church, Florence, Alabama; Russell M. Funk; Steven Smith at the Historical Society of Pennsylvania, Philadelphia; Joseph Jackson and Amber Paranick at the Library of Congress, Washington, D.C.; the Manhattanville College Library, Purchase, New York; Arlene Royer at the National Archives and Records Administration, Southeast Region Archives, Morrow, Georgia; the Phillips Library, Peabody Essex Museum, Salem, Massachusetts; Samford University Special Collections, Birmingham; Naheed Zaheer, Sarah Wilson, and the staff at the Robert Crown Law Library and the Cecil H. Green Library at Stanford University; Devon Burge, Matthew Hofstedt, and Steve Petteway, Office of the Curator, Supreme Court of the United States, Washington, D.C.; the Special Collections at Transylvania University Library, Lexington, Kentucky; the Hoole Special Collections Library at The University of Alabama, Tuscaloosa; Paul Pruitt at the Special Collections of the Bounds Law Library at The University of Alabama School of Law, Tuscaloosa; Matthew Harris, Margaret I. King Special Collections at the University of Kentucky, Lexington; the Special Collections at the Collier Library at the University of North Alabama, Florence; the Louis Round Wilson Special Collections Library, University of North Carolina at Chapel Hill; Lisa Marine and Andy Kraushaar at the Wisconsin Historical Society, Madison; and the Woodford County Historical Society, Versailles, Kentucky. I also appreciate the comments and suggestions of those who anonymously reviewed the original manuscript. I am particularly indebted to Jennifer Backer, who has once again been an extraordinary copyeditor. A portion xi

of one chapter previously appeared as an article in the *Journal of Supreme Court History*, which has graciously permitted me to use it again here.

Finally, although not a native of Alabama, I love this state and the people who call it home. I am grateful for the opportunities that living here has afforded me and my family. This book is consequently dedicated to my own Alabamians: Stewart and Rachel; to the Virginians: Rebecca and Jefferson; to the Utahns: Matthew, Stephanie, and Allison; and especially to Melanie.

JOHN MCKINLEY
and the Antebellum Supreme Court

1
The Most Prominent Man in Alabama
An Introduction to Justice John McKinley

> He was undoubtedly a man of great morality and uprightness, and deficient neither in legal learning nor in ability.
> —Mississippi governor Henry S. Foote, 1876

In 1849 the citizens of the south-central Alabama town of New Ruin renamed their community "McKinley" after one of the state's most celebrated men. A Kentuckian who moved to northern Alabama in 1819, John McKinley had no personal connection with the Marengo County town named in his honor, but his reputation as a state legislator, as a member of Congress who served in both the House of Representatives and the Senate, and as the first Alabamian to sit on the Supreme Court of the United States made his a suitable and respected name to appropriate for the growing community.[1] Boasting two schools, several churches, a vibrant business district, and several large plantations on its outskirts, McKinley, Alabama, thrived, becoming one of the largest towns in the county.

McKinley, however, never lived up to its potential. It survived a devastating fire in 1860 only to be wracked by several years of economic chaos during and immediately following the Civil War. Another large fire in 1869 dealt a final blow from which the struggling community would never recover, and the once promising town of McKinley faded into obscurity.[2] Now an unincorporated area within Marengo County with little evidence of its previous prominence, perhaps the most interesting thing about McKinley, Alabama, is how its history largely mirrored that of the man for whom it was named.

An 1821 visitor to Alabama declared that John McKinley was "reputed to be the first lawyer in the three states [of Tennessee, Alabama, and Mississippi]."[3] In 1826 a Rhode Island newspaper solemnly intoned that McKinley "is associated with the best interests of Alabama, and he has done more than any other individual . . . [for] the inhabitants of that State."[4]

Andrew Jackson, who was hardly one to offer idle praise, claimed that
McKinley "was the most prominent man in allabama [*sic*]."[5]

John McKinley's name repeatedly appears next to the major economic,
educational, and political endeavors of northern Alabama between 1819
and 1837. He successfully campaigned for and won several elections to
state and federal office and played a critical role in both the 1832 and 1836
presidential elections. Over the course of his lifetime, he cultivated the
friendships of such nineteenth-century political luminaries as Henry Clay,
Andrew Jackson, James K. Polk, and Martin Van Buren and was lauded
as a man of consequence at political gatherings throughout the South.

In 1837, after nearly two decades of vigorous political activity at both
the state and national level, John McKinley became the first Alabamian
to serve on the U.S. Supreme Court.[6] His appointment came at an especially propitious time in the history of the early Court. The legendary
John Marshall had died two years earlier, but his thirty-four-year tenure
as chief justice had elevated the Court, as constitutional scholar Henry J.
Abraham has written, from a "lowly if not discredited level . . . to a position of equality with the executive and the legislature."[7] Both McKinley
and the Court seemed poised for greater things.

Yet despite being appointed at a time in the Court's history that afforded
him the opportunity to impart a significant influence, McKinley's health,
wealth, and reputation began to plummet almost immediately upon taking his seat. Just fifty years after McKinley's death, Hampton L. Carson
would refer to the justice in his celebrated history of the Supreme Court as
"little known, even to the profession."[8] His subsequent and almost complete disappearance from public memory compelled a later Court observer
to declare with little exaggeration, "Who was John McKinley? You will
search all the compendiums of universal knowledge in your libraries in
vain to find any answer to this question. His name will not be mentioned
therein."[9] Like his namesake town, Justice John McKinley, too, had passed
into obscurity.

Yet the question of "Who was John McKinley?" still resonates. Prior
to his appointment to the Court, McKinley was a robust, well-respected,
and eminent figure who received key assignments in the public offices to
which he was elected. He was well-known and widely praised not only in
Alabama but throughout the nation. After joining the Court, however, a
caricature of McKinley emerged as a man scarcely capable of completing
his judicial duties. Any effort to discover the real John McKinley thus essentially involves researching two separate lives, with his elevation to the

Supreme Court as the dividing point between the two. There are several reasons why this notable man who moved so easily within the circles of the politically powerful in both Alabama and Washington disappeared from the public mind and memory so suddenly. Ironically, nearly all of them are related to the demands of serving on the antebellum Supreme Court.

During McKinley's tenure, the Court met in Washington for just a few months each year. After their term there was finished, the justices set off in their capacity as circuit judges to hear legal disputes throughout the United States. Few of them enjoyed their circuit-riding duties, but it was little more than a necessary annoyance for those who had limited business on their circuit dockets or whose routes were small or close to Washington and their homes.

McKinley spent his first five years on the Supreme Court as the first and only justice to preside over the original Ninth Circuit. At the time of his appointment, the Ninth was not only the largest circuit in the country, it was also the farthest from Washington and by far the most difficult to traverse. Travel throughout this circuit during the antebellum era was both hazardous and time consuming for, with the exception of New Orleans, there was simply no easy way to reach the designated court sites. It was also costly as McKinley, like all of the justices, was required to pay his own expenses.

McKinley's circuit also included a broad area of newly settled territory whose growing pains included a huge number of property disputes. The extraordinary litigiousness of the region was clearly seen in March 1838 when, after the conclusion of McKinley's first full term in Washington, the members of the Court left to confront the approximately 6,000 cases on their cumulative circuit dockets. McKinley's Ninth Circuit alone accounted for 4,700 of that total.[10] The unique challenges of the Ninth were so demanding that McKinley was ultimately forced to move back to Kentucky to take advantage of water routes there that both lessened the physical strain of riding circuit and better enabled him to return to Washington in time for the start of the Court's term.

Despite his status as an associate justice, McKinley left very little behind to remind the public of who he was once he joined the Court. He might have preserved his reputation by having his circuit court rulings compiled and printed for public consumption, as did some of his Supreme Court colleagues. Even if he were inclined to do so, the vast distances he was required to travel and the circuit court schedule he was expected to maintain would have made it very difficult to complete such a project.

If he kept letters from others or even copies of his own correspondence, they have yet to be located. He is one of just twenty-three Supreme Court justices for whom there is no collection of private papers.[11] The regular correspondence McKinley previously maintained with Henry Clay, Andrew Jackson, and others largely ceased upon his appointment to the Court. His ability to write—letters, judicial opinions, or anything else—was further hampered by his ill health and subsequent partial paralysis.

Essentially all that remains of Justice John McKinley's life are his Supreme Court opinions. He sat for nearly fifteen years but missed five full terms of the Court in Washington—three for health reasons and two others because of circuit court business in New Orleans. During that time, he authored just twenty-three majority, concurring, or dissenting opinions.[12] This relatively low output has led many scholars to opine that the most notable thing about McKinley is just how unremarkable he was. Some have even suggested that his paltry record on the bench was indicative of "someone who did not pull his weight as a Supreme Court justice."[13] In 1983 two *University of Chicago Law Review* articles underscored this notion when they attempted (with more than a trace of irreverence) to identify the single most insignificant justice in the history of the Court. Focusing solely on the number of opinions authored by the justices, both named McKinley as a serious contender for the title, although he ultimately lost out to Justice Gabriel Duval in one article and Justice Thomas Todd in the other.[14]

Modern scholars have questioned not only the quantity but also the quality of McKinley's opinions.[15] In 1935 the renowned Court scholar Carl B. Swisher observed that McKinley was "a man of moderate ability who achieved neither distinction nor notoriety."[16] Three decades later in his definitive work on the Taney Court, Swisher would render a harsher verdict when he wrote that McKinley "made no significant contribution to legal thinking in any form . . . [and left no] notable imprint on the work of the profession."[17] In Swisher's oft-quoted pronouncement, McKinley was "probably the least outstanding of the members of the Taney Court."[18]

Such characterizations are rarely questioned and thus tend to be accepted and perpetuated by modern chroniclers of the Supreme Court and its members. Those who knew John McKinley personally, however, saw a man worth remembering. Writing about McKinley in 1876, former Mississippi governor Henry S. Foote declared, "He was undoubtedly a man of great morality and uprightness, and deficient neither in legal learning nor in ability in the argument of causes, both before courts and juries. There

was much in his busy and varied career to reward the labors of some impartial and competent biographer."[19]

The impetus that ultimately led to this biography arose out of a desire
to better understand the dismissive attitude of McKinley's modern-day
critics. When this project began, there was so little published information available on Justice McKinley that the original intent was to simply
incorporate a short chapter about his life into a larger work.[20] Subsequent
research, however, revealed a fascinating portrait of a man active in the
leading legal, financial, educational, social, and political circles of his day
who clearly could not have foreseen just how quickly his name would be
forgotten by both Alabama and the nation.

The fact that he was well-known and generally respected during his
lifetime contrasts sharply with modern scholarly opinion, which paints
a mostly disparaging portrait of Justice John McKinley. In fact, the *very
limited* amount of research previously conducted on McKinley by modern
legal scholars and Supreme Court historians can be condensed into five
general conclusions. First, John McKinley's appointment to the Court can
be attributed only to the fact that he was an opportunist who conveniently
shifted his political allegiances as the occasion demanded. Second, McKinley's complaining about his circuit court responsibilities bordered on the
pathological. Third, McKinley was a very average man who was intellectually out of his league on the Supreme Court. Fourth, as a southern justice, McKinley's was a dependable states' rights vote where slavery, federalism, and other issues were concerned. Fifth, McKinley's insignificance is
demonstrated, and perhaps justified, by the fact that he has virtually nothing to show for his tenure on the Court.

This book challenges all of these conclusions. Before mentioning how,
it might be helpful to explain what the research presented here does *not*
do. It does not attempt to paint McKinley as a quiet leader on the Court in
the shadow of Chief Justice Roger Taney. It does not suggest that McKinley's few opinions were actually of far greater consequence than commonly
believed. It also does not gloss over McKinley's pride, sometimes brusque
temperament, or circuit court complaints, which were all very real com-
ponents of his tenure on the Court.

Instead this project argues that all of the heretofore accepted conclusions about Justice John McKinley are incorrect. This is the result of a more
careful study of McKinley's life than has ever before been conducted, using
archival research that has never been as readily accessible. In particular,

modern newspaper databases that allow researchers to conduct multiple word searches through massive numbers of scanned nineteenth-century newspapers open up a window onto the world of McKinley and the antebellum Supreme Court that simply was not available to legal historians of an earlier day. Thus, rather than simply perpetuating the errors, impressions, and biases of material relied upon by earlier scholars, this project provides a new assessment of John McKinley. In so doing, it also questions whether a reevaluation of other early members of the Supreme Court is in order given the technology that is now available.

While this book generally takes a chronological approach to McKinley's life and career, it stresses the following five counterarguments to the general conclusions listed above. First, McKinley's political faith was admittedly not set in stone but neither was that of many other men of his era including such notables as John Quincy Adams, John J. Calhoun, Henry Clay, and Daniel Webster. They and many others demonstrated the great fluidity of party loyalty that existed during the early nineteenth century when men routinely abandoned former political ties to rally around new principles, personalities, and politics. McKinley did indeed switch his political allegiance and was savaged for it by his rivals. However, their claim that he was an opportunist of few political convictions (a charge carelessly repeated by modern scholars) is simply not accurate. Once he converted to Jacksonianism, he remained true to its basic tenets, both on and off the bench, until his death.

Second, McKinley's vociferous concerns regarding his circuit court responsibilities were really only different from those expressed by virtually every other member of the Court in one very significant way. Other justices complained about the difficulties of their circuit duties; McKinley's were impossible to complete in their entirety.

Well before the formation of the original Ninth Circuit in 1837, many members of Congress had already called attention to the serious physical challenges that would accompany the extension of the circuit court system to the Old Southwest. The transportation infrastructure between population centers in the Deep South was so underdeveloped that even short trips were arduous, with the exception of those taken between towns that lay close to the Mississippi River. In spite of these concerns, Congress created a single circuit that included Alabama, Arkansas, the eastern portion of Louisiana, and Mississippi, all of which were among the top ten largest states in the Union at that time.

As the first and only justice to preside over this massive circuit, John

McKinley had to deal with more than just the geographical and transportation-related difficulties that existed in the wild and sparsely populated area. The congressionally mandated circuit court schedule also required him to crisscross the region within a ridiculously short time frame. Indeed, so unrealistic was this schedule that it appears that no one in Congress had ever traversed the actual route within the time constraints Justice McKinley was expected to meet before the creation of the Ninth Circuit.

With little regard for the realities of his particular circuit duties, early critics attributed McKinley's complaints to a poor work ethic or weak judicial temperament, charges that have been repeated by modern critics without careful study. Further analysis of both McKinley's words and actions reveals that his concerns for his circuit were not rooted solely in his desire to have more personal time but in his ability to actually dispense justice as well. He repeatedly argued that the citizens of the Old Southwest suffered the most by the inordinate size and compressed court schedule of his circuit. Thus, whatever complaints McKinley uttered were not his alone but those of the litigants and lawyers, causes and claims that came before him.

Faced with the reality that Congress would be slow to assist (if at all), McKinley pragmatically chose to focus his efforts on the circuit courts in Louisiana and Alabama. These sites were not only the easiest to reach, they also had far more cases on their dockets than did the courts in Mississippi and Arkansas. McKinley continued to attend to his circuit court duties as long as his health permitted, even after he became partially paralyzed. A less conscientious judge might have abandoned them entirely.

Third, Joseph Story was the undisputed intellectual star on the Taney Court, and neither McKinley nor any other member could lay claim to being his equal. That notable exception aside, McKinley could hold his own with the other justices with whom he served. The dearth of information on McKinley has led modern scholars to rely upon a select number of secondhand accounts critical of his abilities. One of the most commonly cited stems from a remark Justice Story himself made upon learning of McKinley's appointment. Other disparaging comments were made by Chancellor James Kent after McKinley rendered a controversial opinion at circuit. Entrusting a man's reputation to these few statements (even when made by individuals of such stature as Story and Kent) is unfair, particularly when the context behind such words is considered.

For example, Story admittedly cringed upon learning of McKinley's appointment to the Court in 1837, but the feelings of the Harvard-trained scholar and unrepentant nationalist may have had less to do with the legal skills McKinley honed in the rural South than his political reputation as one of Andrew Jackson's key lieutenants in Congress. Whatever Story's initial impression of McKinley may have been, the two became good friends, roomed in the same boardinghouse during the Court's term in Washington, and voted together on several of the critical issues that came before the Court.

Fourth, although McKinley was a product of the antebellum South, his voting behavior and opinions on the bench clearly demonstrate his appreciation for the power of the federal government in several important ways. He never favored the type of strong nationalism championed by Justice Story nor mounted the type of vigorous defense of states' rights as did his fellow Alabamian and successor on the bench, John Archibald Campbell. McKinley was a faithful adherent to the central tenets of Jacksonian democracy, which "insisted that the power of the federal government was limited, but . . . that the federal government was supreme within those limits."[21] His views were considerably more moderate than one might expect given his initial appointment and the subsequent caricature of his career that has been embraced and repeated by legal historians.

Fifth, the argument that McKinley's insignificance is evidenced by the few Supreme Court decisions he wrote reflects a threefold bias on the part of modern Court observers. It was these modern biases, in part, that prompted political scientist John R. Schmidhauser to advocate "a thorough reappraisal of the biographical materials relating to . . . McKinley" nearly fifty years ago.[22]

The first bias is one that favors the quantity of work done in Washington. Although far easier for scholars to tabulate, this is hardly a fair reflection of McKinley's or any other justice's efforts during the antebellum era. The Court sat there for only two to three months before it adjourned so that the justices could attend to their circuit duties where they confronted the bulk of their entire workload. The circuit was where "the Court spoke directly to the people," as Story's biographer R. Kent Newmyer has written, and the people "in turn educated the Court."[23] It was here, too, that the important issues of this formative period, including those dealing with property, commerce, and slavery, were discussed and decided by individual justices before coming to the full Supreme Court. Thus, in contrast to the modern focus on the Court's work in Washington, one clearly "senses how vital the circuits were in the business of the nation" during the antebellum era.[24] If the quantity of cases decided is to be the standard by which a justice is to be measured, then the total sum of his efforts—including the number of cases he dispensed with at circuit court—should be included.

Looking only to the number of Supreme Court cases authored by a particular justice reflects a second bias, as it fails to acknowledge the inner workings of the Court. Using this analysis, how could any of the justices who served with Chief Justice John Marshall, for example, ever be considered significant given Marshall's propensity for writing the Court's opinions himself?[25] Marshall also thought it important that the Court speak with a unanimous voice, thus discouraging the associate justices from writing concurring and dissenting opinions. Marshall's successor, Roger Taney, did not exercise a similar monopoly over the opinion-writing process, but McKinley still encountered these and many other established Court norms when he joined the Court just two years after Marshall's death.

Among these norms was the judicial conference where justices were assigned opinions to write as well as the informal discussion of cases that took place after hours in the justices' boardinghouses. Both settings were deliberative in nature and saw ideas and arguments proffered by one justice invariably work their way into an opinion written by another. The scholarly emphasis on majority opinion authorship has rightly been criticized as contributing to "an overly simplistic view of the forces that influence the decision-making process of the Supreme Court."[26] Such an analysis, as constitutional historian Earl M. Maltz has observed, utterly ignores "the interaction between nine quite different individuals, each of whom brings to bear a different combination of doctrinal and legal influences."[27] To suggest that the final opinion as authored by a particular justice is the sole evidence of that justice's influence is to ignore the reality of how the members of the Court conduct their affairs both now and during the country's formative era.

A third bias associated with focusing on the quantity of a justice's opinions is that it makes it easier to sidestep the subjective and ever-changing definition of quality, although as mentioned before, modern legal scholars have not shied away from dismissing McKinley's work on those grounds as well. Perhaps quality then should include his numerous circuit court rulings, since most of those were upheld when they came up for full consideration by the Supreme Court. Or perhaps the fact that his few decisions for the Court were well supported by his colleagues and were favorably cited for many years should be factored into a "quality" analysis.

Admittedly, none of Justice McKinley's opinions can be considered landmark in nature. He wrote nothing that conferred rights, invoked new powers, or expanded constitutional provisions. That should not be particularly surprising given the fact that the antebellum Court's docket was dominated by nonconstitutional cases. As legal scholar Mark Graber has written, "With the exception of constitutional issues associated with fugitive slaves and slavery in the territories, the Taney Court was rarely ever asked to resolve any of the numerous federal constitutional questions that excited Americans during the three decades before the Civil War."[28] The justices instead entertained a wide variety of nonconstitutional arguments on matters important to a young country including questions of jurisdiction, diversity of citizenship, property rights, maritime law, a vast array of commercial issues, and land disputes.

Of the latter, which dominated McKinley's circuit dockets, Swisher has stressed that "land was the principal form and source of wealth in the country [during the antebellum period]. . . . Nothing was more important for good government and a prosperous country than the clarification and protection of titles to land."[29] That these and other such issues are now deemed inconsequential by modern Court observers may have less to do with their original significance than the fact that the United States has simply progressed beyond the relevance of these matters.

In a similar vein, it is difficult to objectively analyze legal opinions from eras other than our own. It is not surprising that legal scholars tend to prefer the recent and recognizable over the distant and unfamiliar. The consequence of that preference, however, as political scientist Saul Brenner put it nearly two decades ago, is that "[t]oo many of our findings regarding Supreme Court behavior are time-bound" to present circumstances and biases.[30] In short, to understand both John McKinley and the antebellum Supreme Court, it is necessary to set aside modern ideas and expectations with regard to the justices and appreciate the Court for what it was and what it did during that era.

In providing the first in-depth assessment of the life and Supreme Court career of Justice John McKinley, this book begins, in chapter 2, by considering his early life and political involvement in Kentucky. McKinley's connection to one of Kentucky's founding families certainly influenced his choices, but it appears that it was his decision alone to trade his carpenters tools for law books in what would be the first of several steps that would culminate in his elevation to the Supreme Court.

Chapter 3 addresses McKinley's efforts as an early land speculator and lawyer in northern Alabama. He was nearly forty years old when he left

Kentucky, but the timing of his move could not have been better as he was able to capitalize on the "Alabama Fever" that afflicted tens of thousands who came to the region in search of rich soil and easy fortunes. That, in turn, led to his rapid entry into early state politics, which was facilitated by his association with a relatively small group of influential men who dominated Alabama's governing institutions.

McKinley's political career in Alabama state politics is the focus of chapter 4. Between 1820 and 1836 he was elected to the state legislature three times. His efforts there were not inconsequential, but McKinley always seemed to have his eye on a higher office. In 1822, for example, after living in the state for just three years, he very nearly became the third U.S. senator in Alabama history but lost that honor by a single vote in the state legislature. This chapter also reviews McKinley's private practice litigation before the Alabama Supreme Court.

Chapter 5 considers McKinley's service in the U.S. Congress as both a representative and senator. First elected to the Senate in 1826 to complete the unexpired term of Senator Henry Chambers who died in office, McKinley was an active presence on the Hill during his four and a half years of service. He was denied reelection to that office but subsequently won a seat in the House of Representatives where he became an important champion of Andrew Jackson's agenda. He was elected to the Senate again in November 1836 but did not serve as he received his appointment to the Court shortly thereafter.

McKinley's role as an associate justice on the U.S. Supreme Court is detailed in the next three chapters. Chapter 6 reviews the workings of the antebellum Supreme Court with respect to both the Court's term in Washington and the now abandoned practice of riding circuit, with particular emphasis on the considerable challenges McKinley faced as the first justice assigned to the newly created Ninth Circuit. Chapter 7 highlights McKinley's judicial career from 1837 until 1842, when Congress finally divided his circuit in half. Chapter 8 continues this narrative, from 1843 until his death in 1852, making note of how, even in failing health, McKinley continued to fulfill his judicial duties. Chapter 9 concludes with a review of the memorials and remembrances that attended McKinley's death, as well as an analysis of his contributions and judicial legacy.

Given that no collection of McKinley's private papers is known to exist, the chronicle of his life is found primarily in period newspapers and public documents in which his name, actions, and influence are extensively referenced. To these are added a limited amount of correspondence to, from, and about McKinley that can be found in the papers of other nineteenth-century leaders. In addition, accounts written by his contemporaries are included to help paint a more complete picture of the era and region in which he lived, traveled, and worked. Far from the assertion of one legal scholar that McKinley died as "a cipher . . . leaving virtually no trace," these sources cumulatively offer rich details and insights into McKinley's professional life as a lawyer, land speculator, state legislator, member of Congress, and Supreme Court justice.[31]

As mentioned earlier, this project was initially conceived as a short piece on a man who was presumed to have been a rather insignificant, if lucky, figure in Alabama and U.S. politics. Further research has instead corroborated the truth of Governor Foote's 1876 pronouncement that there was indeed much in McKinley's life "to reward the labors of some impartial and competent biographer."[32] Whether this work will be viewed as either impartial or competent remains to be seen, but it at least attempts to do justice to a forgotten figure who was once the most prominent man in Alabama.

2
Logans, Law, and Political Futility

John Rowan having removed from Frankfort to Bardstown declines further practice in Franklin and the surrounding courts. His unfinished business will be attended to by Mr. M'Kinley [*sic*], on whose attention and talents, his clients may rely with the utmost safety.

—*Western World*, 1807

Like many of his contemporaries, John McKinley may have assembled his private writings, papers, business records, correspondence, and other material into a collection that highlighted many of the details of his personal life. If such a collection ever existed, it has yet to be discovered. There are, however, a few of McKinley's personal items that offer insight into his life apart from the governmental records and newspaper accounts from which the research for this project is largely drawn. Among these are the only two portraits of the justice known to exist.

One portrays McKinley toward the end of his tenure on the Supreme Court and depicts a wizened old man with drooping eyelids wearing therapeutic double lens spectacles. His clothing and hairstyle are simple, and there is no indication of social status, wealth, or energy. This portrait tends to confirm the popular image of McKinley as a careworn and physically weak judge.

The other portrait depicts a very different person. Painted around 1817 by the celebrated Kentucky artist Matthew Harris Jouett, this picture has been frequently copied with varying degrees of fidelity to the original. It portrays an erect, ruddy-faced gentleman who is well dressed and almost foppishly coiffed. There is a hint of arrogance in McKinley's slight smile, and the overall picture clearly conveys the impression of wealth and high social standing.

This portrait corroborates existing physical descriptions of John McKinley, which are almost uniform. An 1820 account described him as a "stout, fine looking man; of easy manners."[1] Others remembered him as a "large framed man, stalwart and raw-boned."[2] He was said to have been "tall . . . ,

1. John McKinley (albumen print, circa 1850). Courtesy of the
Collection of the Supreme Court of the United States.

with a countenance that exhibited great strength of character,"[3] his "figure
robust, and [his] presence commanding."[4]

One contemporary remarked that he was "a plain, . . . quiet gentleman,
whose thoughts were sound and sensible."[5] Another, commenting on his
presence at the Supreme Court's oral arguments, described him as a "gentleman who says little, but thinks a great deal."[6] Still another recalled that
he was a man "of good feelings and simple unpretending manners."[7] Fifty
years after his death, those who knew McKinley continued to laud him as
"a man of high and noble aims, possessed of remarkable tact and energy . . .
[who] wore an habitually benevolent expression."[8]

However, not all remembrances of John McKinley were positive. One
contemporary recalled that McKinley "was a man of talent and indomitable will. He would bear no contradiction; was very imperious, and often

2. John McKinley (portrait by Matthew Harris Jouett, circa 1817–18). Courtesy of the Collection of the Supreme Court of the United States.

so overbearing as to make bitter enemies."[9] The justice was said to have possessed "a quality always commendatory—the appearance of sincerity" but also a "voice of unwonted harshness."[10] Another acknowledged that McKinley was indeed "moody and rather irritable, but very generally esteemed."[11]

Much like these portraits and descriptions, John McKinley's life was one of contrasts. He was indeed a tall and robust man in his prime who would later bear the reputation of an exhausted and sickly judge. He could be exceedingly gracious in his manners but was also easily offended, and his lack of patience could border on rudeness. He was praised throughout his political and judicial career but also vilified. McKinley was well-known for his state and national political involvement when he joined the Court but, in what is probably the greatest contrast of his life, lived long enough to see his own name became increasingly unfamiliar to most Alabamians and other Americans during his tenure on the bench.

Despite being marked by such disparities, McKinley's life evidenced at least one significant area of constancy: a remarkable personal resolve. This determination not only steered him from his carpentry trade in rural Kentucky to the U.S. Supreme Court, it also sustained him through a combination of challenges that included personal and family tragedy, political and financial reversal, repeated public humiliation, tremendous physical strain, and several health-related afflictions. The fortitude he relied upon while overcoming these repeated setbacks appears to have been inherited as relatives on both sides of his family demonstrated the same characteristic.

In an 1846 interview, McKinley recalled that his paternal grandfather and his maternal grandmother, who were siblings, arrived in Pennsylvania from northern Ireland in the early 1700s.[12] Little else is known of his paternal grandfather, also named John McKinley, other than he eventually made his way to Virginia and had a son named Andrew.[13]

John McKinley's maternal grandmother, Jane, was the second wife of David Logan. The young couple married in Ireland and subsequently immigrated to America with David's two children from his first marriage, settling first in Philadelphia and later in Orange County, Virginia. They later moved to what is now Augusta County, Virginia, where they raised a large family of their own that included a daughter named Mary. David Logan fought in the early years of the French and Indian War and held local public office as an Augusta County constable and road overseer, among other things, until his death in 1757.[14]

Mary Logan subsequently married her cousin Andrew McKinley, and it was to this couple that John McKinley was born on May 1, 1780, in Culpeper County, Virginia.[15] As noted above, there is precious little information about his father's family, but his mother possessed a family name that, along with Boone and Harrod, would become legendary in early Kentucky.

Mary's brother Benjamin was the eldest surviving son of David and Jane McKinley Logan. He served in the French and Indian War with his father and later as a member of the Virginia militia in Lord Dunmore's War (1773–74).[16] The latter conflict resulted from escalating violence along the western borders of Virginia between white settlers and the Shawnee and Mingo Indian nations. The 1774 treaty that ended these hostilities opened land south of the Ohio River for settlement, and the following year Daniel Boone led settlers through the Cumberland Gap into what is now Kentucky.

At practically the same time another group of pioneers led by Benjamin Logan entered Kentucky. They pushed farther to the southwest than did Boone and established the settlement of St. Asaph's, which later became known as Logan's Fort.[17] Logan relocated his own family there in 1776 and spent the next several years defending the settlers at Logan's Fort as well as those living in surrounding areas against Indian attacks. In doing so, he would play a key role in the political development of early Kentucky.[18]

When Virginia created Kentucky County in 1776, encompassing practically the entire area of the present Commonwealth of Kentucky, Benjamin Logan was appointed its first sheriff and an officer in the Kentucky militia. The Virginia General Assembly dissolved Kentucky County in 1780 and replaced it with three new counties. Lincoln County was the largest of these, and Logan was appointed to be the county lieutenant and again tasked with its internal defense.

Frequent and violent skirmishes with both the Shawnee and Cherokee Indians forced Logan and others who occupied the far-flung Kentucky settlements to question whether they could survive on their own without additional military support and other resources from the Virginia government.[19] Benjamin and his brother John had served in the Virginia General Assembly as delegates from Kentucky, but neither had been able to draw the attention of the legislature to the continuing violence on the western frontier.

In 1784, after receiving word of an impending Indian attack, Logan called for a December meeting of area militia leaders to be held at Danville to discuss common defense measures. Lacking the ability to raise funds, procure munitions, and formally declare war, those assembled at what became known as the Danville Convention quickly realized there was little that they could do without specific authorization and appropriations from Richmond. Accompanying that realization was the first frank discussion about the necessity of separating from Virginia. Over the next eight years, nine more conventions were held, each one more insistent than the last upon the creation of an independent state. The determined efforts of Logan and others culminated on June 1, 1792, when the Commonwealth of Kentucky, the first state west of the Alleghenies, entered the union.

As the organizer of the first Danville meeting, it was perhaps appropriate that Benjamin Logan would serve as a delegate to the convention that framed Kentucky's first constitution. He would also serve in the first Kentucky General Assembly as a representative from Lincoln County.[20] Logan ran for governor in 1796 and 1800 but was unsuccessful both times despite his status as one of Kentucky's founding fathers.

Four decades after Benjamin Logan's death, McKinley would remember his uncle as "bold, daring, and taciturn, and when he spoke it was always to some purpose."[21] Others remembered Logan's far less flattering qualities, which apparently limited his political appeal. The citizens of

Kentucky were reluctant to elect Logan to the state's highest office, in part because of his "choleric disposition and lack of education."[22] As to the former, Logan's temper was legendary. He was reportedly a "large raw-boned man" who used his frame and temperament in an "arbitrary and overbearing" manner.[23] In subsequent years, critics would use these words—virtually verbatim—to characterize his nephew.

Another of McKinley's uncles, John Logan, distinguished himself as a delegate to the Virginia General Assembly. He was elected to that body three times and participated in Virginia's 1788 convention to ratify the U.S. Constitution.[24] He was also elected to Kentucky's first state senate and later served as Kentucky's first state treasurer, a position he would hold for fourteen years.[25]

The second generation of Logans was equally possessed of the public spirit. Several of McKinley's cousins held seats in the Kentucky state legislature. The most prominent of these was William Logan, who was a delegate to Kentucky's second constitutional convention and later served as Speaker of the Kentucky House of Representatives several times.[26] He was also a U.S. senator for a short time before resigning that office to pursue an ultimately unsuccessful gubernatorial bid in 1820.

The civic-mindedness that characterized John McKinley's Logan relations can also be seen, albeit in a far more limited manner, in his own father's life. By the mid-1780s, most of Benjamin Logan's siblings and their families had relocated in or around Logan's Fort. Andrew and Mary Logan McKinley moved their family there from Virginia in 1783. In November of that same year Andrew was appointed to a two-year term as a deputy sheriff, serving under his brother-in-law Benjamin.[27] Early Lincoln Country records indicate that McKinley was assiduous in his public duties and active in many important aspects of his community as a witness to numerous wills and legal transactions and serving on several juries.[28]

Andrew McKinley had been a surgeon during the Revolutionary War, but it is not known to what extent he practiced medicine afterward, if at all. However, his professional title was commonly invoked. Early records routinely refer to "Dr. McKinley's" land where property boundaries and proposed roads within Lincoln County were discussed. Even several years after his death, the county continued to record land transactions in which tracts of "Dr. McKinley's" comprised part of the total amount of property sold.[29]

Andrew died in March 1786, leaving behind his wife, five-year-old John, and two daughters named Hannah and Betsy.[30] An inventory of Andrew's estate shortly after his death suggests that he left his family comfortable but not particularly well off. The inventory included two female slaves, several head of cattle, sheep, and horses, household furniture, many tools, and several volumes of medical books.[31]

The presence of books in his home may have encouraged young John McKinley to read and learn there since, like most people raised on the Kentucky frontier, he received little formal education. Privately organized schools found in Logan's Fort and other early settlements taught basic reading and writing, but even that education was truncated by teacher availability, external threats to the community, and seasonal conditions that either made it difficult to attend school or required students to remain at home to assist with planting and harvesting.

Formal schooling, however, was not necessary to McKinley's original career path. As a young man, he sought employment as a "mechanic"—a general term used during that era to refer to those skilled in any number of handicraft trades—and accordingly apprenticed as a carpenter. He might have made a suitable income at carpentry but abandoned that trade in his late teens, according to an 1827 sketch of his life, because he believed "he could obtain a living, in an easier manner, than by labouring with the jack plane."[32] Given his family's heritage, however, there were likely other motivating factors behind McKinley's career change.

According to the class structure that then existed on the western frontier, carpenters and others who worked for wages "were considered as of no social consequence and, as 'laborers,' ranked below even the poorest farmer in point of respectability."[33] There were consequently few opportunities for these craftsmen and laborers to overcome the limitations of their trades, which served to impede both social and political advancement.

Determined to embark upon a more respectable and lucrative career in law, young John McKinley left Logan's Fort for Louisville, some ninety miles to the northwest. He clerked first in the law offices of General Thomas Bodley and later read law in Frankfort under the tutelage of the noted Kentucky lawyer and future U.S. senator John Rowan.[34] As described by the famed legal historian Charles Warren, reading law at the time consisted of paying for the privilege of "absorbing, by study, observation, and occasionally by direct teaching . . . , the principles of the law."[35] Some mentors were more willing than others to assist their protégés with their studies, but it was largely a self-directed effort that aspiring attorneys found both frustrating and fulfilling. Two years of such study concluded with McKinley's admission to the Kentucky bar in 1801.[36]

It was in Frankfort that he received his first taste of politics, although his early political participation may have been less about public service than social status given his decision to affiliate with the Federalist Party. The Federalist Party had rapidly declined as a national political force after the presidential election of 1800 when Thomas Jefferson's Democratic-Republican Party swept most of its members from national office.[37] Ideologically the Federalist Party favored a strong and active national government, which contrasted sharply with the independent spirit of many who lived on the western and southern frontiers. It also promoted governmental policies based on mercantilism, economic development, and banking, which held little appeal for rural people and those who made their living from agriculture. Writing in 1922, Kentucky historian Charles Kerr explained that the early people of his state "had the problems and ways of thinking of frontiersmen. . . . With their characteristic impatience of restraint, they were naturally drawn to the Jeffersonian way of thinking where the least government was considered the best."[38]

In addition, the fact that the largest pockets of remaining Federalist support were located in the northeastern United States troubled many frontier voters since politicians from that region had long been suspicious and unsupportive of western expansion. In short, as Kerr understatedly wrote, "the antecedents of federalism, the character of its leadership, and it tenets generally did not endear it to Kentuckians."[39] Nevertheless, several prominent citizens in Kentucky, including McKinley's mentor John Rowan, continued to proudly support the Federalist cause, attracting tremendous resentment for doing so.[40]

The political antipathy between Kentucky's Federalists and Democratic-Republicans took various forms, including succinct toasts offered initially at public dinners and later published in area newspapers. A Frankfort newspaper, for example, published this toast in 1807: "*The Hydra of Federalism*, [may] the divinity of our independence paralyze every nerve of this political monster."[41] A writer in Lexington's most prominent newspaper, the *Kentucky Gazette*, offered a more extended insult, stating flatly, "Federalism . . . is of all political sins deemed the most *mortal*, and . . . would as effectively terminate [a man's] political respectability as a conviction of sheep-stealing would ruin his moral character."[42] Although the sheep-stealing reference may have been an exaggeration, such statements clearly reveal the limited political influence of Kentucky's Federalist Party. Yet John McKinley would join its ranks in part because of Rowan's influence and, perhaps more important, because of his Logan heritage.

The Federalists typically rejected the populist idealism of their Jefferonian rivals and were reluctant to turn governing power over to the masses until the people had proven themselves capable of assuming that responsibility. Until that time came, Federalists believed that elites who had established themselves in some form should be entrusted with the power to rule. In a state where the Logan name still cast a long shadow, McKinley may have been reluctant to relinquish the prestige associated with his mother's family. That status, incidentally, included far more than just a prominent name. Just weeks after his twenty-first birthday, for example, state tax records indicated McKinley's ownership of approximately 2,600 acres of land spread across several counties. Those same documents showed his Logan relatives in possession of tens of thousands of acres throughout the Commonwealth of Kentucky.[43]

As a young Federalist attorney in Frankfort, McKinley attended to his civic duties just as his father and Logan relatives had done. Early records show that he participated for the first time as a juror in federal court during the latter part of July 1805. During the week in which they were empaneled, McKinley and his fellow jurors considered a number of cases, including one in which they found for the plaintiff's $100.42 debt and assessed a mere penny in damages.[44] In another, they took into account Daniel Boone's well-known inability to spell in determining that property boundaries had indeed been established by the frontiersman's survey marks on a tree, notwithstanding the fact that (according to the court record) "the said tree marked 'a.f.' was by Daniel Boone, who supposed he was spelling Ebenezer Frost's name, think[ing] it began with an 'a.'"[45] McKinley served on federal juries several more times during the next year, including in November 1806 when he (peripherally) and his Federalist Party (to a much greater degree) would participate in one of the most sensational events of early nineteenth-century America.

Despite their negligible political influence within the state, Kentucky Federalists did their best to make their presence known. The apex of their efforts was the 1806 trial of former vice president Aaron Burr in Frankfort. Throughout much of that year Joseph H. Daveiss, the U.S. Attorney General for Kentucky, had sent numerous panic-filled letters to President Thomas Jefferson leveling serious, if vague, allegations that Burr (who owned land in and around Frankfort and regularly passed through the area) and others were conspiring to dissolve the United States of America by creating an independent nation in the Southwest.[46]

After receiving nothing but a single cursory response from the president, Daveiss, who was a Federalist, concluded that rank partisanship was behind Jefferson's dismissal of his concerns. He resolved to stop Burr himself and, in the process, discredit the entire Democratic-Republican establishment in Kentucky. Daveiss and other Federalist leaders began to build up their case against Burr in the court of public opinion with the support of a new Federalist newspaper in Frankfort, the *Western World*.[47] For four months the newspaper served as a forum for virtually every Burr-related rumor imaginable. Among the most serious were claims that he was planning an expedition to conquer Spanish-held land in Louisiana and Texas, eventually setting himself up as ruler over that territory. As if that were not reason enough to stop Burr, the *Western World* claimed that Burr-backed revolts throughout Central and South America would soon follow. The threatened result, it warned, would be an "empire, headed by a man of the enterprise and talents of Colonel Burr, [which would] present a phenomenon in the political history of the globe perhaps only equaled by the modern Empire of France."[48]

On November 5, 1806, Daveiss asked U.S. District Judge Harry Innes to order Burr's arrest on the grounds that he was preparing for a military expedition to Texas to make war with Spain. For evidence, Daveiss cited the fact that Burr "continued to purchase large stores of provisions as if for an army—while . . . conceal[ing] in great mystery from the people at large his purposes and projects."[49]

Judge Innes denied Daveiss's motion to arrest Burr but did order the summoning of "Twenty four freeholders . . . to be empanelled as a Grand Jury," among whom was young John McKinley.[50] When the grand jury convened on November 12, it found itself before a packed courtroom filled with citizens eager to hear the attorney general's presentation. Shortly after the proceedings began, however, and before he had presented any evidence, Daveiss unexpectedly requested that the grand jury be discharged. He informed Judge Innes that one critical witness could not be located and he did not wish to proceed without that testimony.

Burr's supporters in the courtroom ridiculed the move because Daveiss had claimed for months to have a solid case against the former vice president. Amid the jeers, Judge Innes adjourned the proceedings and Burr "was discharged to the tumultuous delight of the people."[51] Daveiss, however, was not finished. Two weeks later he won a motion to seat a second grand jury, although McKinley was not among the handful of men from the earlier panel who were again called into service. After four days of testimony and deliberation, the second grand jury declined to indict Burr.

The former vice president's more famous trial for treason would take place the following spring in Richmond.[52]

On March 5, 1807, the *Western World* ran an advertisement announcing that "John M'Kinley has commenced the practice of law in Frankfort."[53] Ever since his arrival there to read law, McKinley had worked closely and practiced with John Rowan. When Rowan subsequently moved to Bardstown, he turned his entire legal practice in Frankfort over to McKinley, vouching for his protégé as one "on whose attention and talents, his clients may rely with the utmost safety."[54] Within two years McKinley would relocate the practice to Louisville and then later to Lexington.

It was in Lexington that McKinley began to firmly establish his legal reputation. He was active not only in Fayette County courts but also in the Kentucky Court of Appeals, where he was counsel of record in several complex property disputes and frequently squared off against another young Kentucky lawyer named Henry Clay.[55] In an 1827 review of McKinley's political career, a Rhode Island newspaper observed that his practice in Lexington was so successful that "in a little period, he obtained a very handsome fortune."[56] He continued to acquire property throughout Kentucky and, according to the 1810 federal census, owned two slaves.[57]

McKinley performed legal services for many nonresident landowners as well as for some of Lexington's most prominent citizens, such as Captain Nathanial G. S. Hart (brother-in-law to Henry Clay) and Reverend James McChord.[58] McChord was a young, charismatic Presbyterian minister who announced in 1815 that he was leaving his Lexington pulpit because he had offended the leadership of the Associate Reformed Presbyterian Church. McKinley was counted among a number of influential Lexington citizens, including former U.S. senator John Pope, Joseph Cabell Breckinridge (father of the future vice president, John C. Breckinridge), and Lexington's outstanding architect, Matthew Kennedy, who persuaded him to stay.[59] Along with a handful of other local notables, McKinley was named to the building committee that financed and erected a new church especially for McChord and later added his name as one of the first signatories to the church's constitution.[60]

During this time McKinley also became acquainted with John Wesley Hunt, Lexington's most famous, and most wealthy, citizen. Hunt was already a successful merchant when he began to manufacture hempen rope for use in bagging cotton in the early 1800s. He made a fortune producing the rope and other hemp products and was reputed to be the first millionaire west of the Alleghenies. McKinley provided legal work for Hunt, and the two were business partners in several ventures, including, crucially, as will be noted later, land speculation in Alabama.[61]

As his legal work and business interests expanded, McKinley also continued to be active in party politics where, according to a contemporary account, he was "known as a Federalist in his politics, and every where [*sic*] respected as a consistent one."[62] The Burr trial had been the high-water mark for Federalists in Kentucky, but party devotees continued to engage their political opponents in both public and private.

The enduring partisanship of the day was reflected in an especially pointed toast given by McKinley in 1811 at a Fourth of July celebration in Danville. To his fellow Federalists, McKinley proposed, "Bonaparte, George III, and Thomas Jefferson—May each be appreciated by the American people, according to his desserts."[63] McKinley must have known that linking the former president with the British king and French autocrat would engender controversy in a region where Jefferson was lionized. Indeed, once the toast was reported in local newspapers, Democrats were outraged. Few offered public comment on the toast itself, but the papers published several anonymous letters critical of both McKinley and the Federalist Party.

A full three months after his infamous toast, the controversy had yet to abate. In fact, it escalated sharply with the early October publication of a particularly scathing anonymous letter in the Frankfort *Argus* that targeted McKinley. Newspapers were often used by prominent men of that era as forums for their own political views as well as for publicly addressing private slights. Piqued at the way he had been characterized in that particular letter, McKinley demanded that the *Argus* reveal the author's identity. James Johnson, a state legislator and a Democrat, subsequently allowed his name to be made public.[64]

On October 7, 1811, McKinley confronted Johnson in Georgetown, Kentucky, where an altercation between the two took place. What actually transpired is unknown (although McKinley was fined twenty dollars for his actions), but the following day large handbills appeared throughout the area purporting to state the facts of the incident. Authored by Johnson's brother Richard, who was a member of Congress, the title of the broadside alone must have mortified the proud McKinley.[65] In large, bold, black letters it declared: "M'Kinley, the Poltroon and Assassin, in his True Colors."[66]

In sensational language the broadside declared that McKinley, upon accosting James Johnson in Georgetown, had beaten him with a club until

M'KINLEY,

THEE POLTROON & ASSASSIN, IN HIS TRUE CCOLORS.

THIS scoundrel drdrank a toast on the 4th of July, comparing Mr Jefferson, the man who wrote the Declaratition of Independence, to King George the IIIll. and Bonaparte, two of the most despicable n monsters as men and Tyrants. In conseququence of this indecent, ungentlemanly and Tooory toast, James Johnson of Scott County. madele some very severe strictures upon the unprincipled scoundrel, M'Kinley, and published theem in the Argus. This poltroon called upon the editor of the Argus for the author of thee publication, and James Johnson without hesitation authorised his name to be given to this puppy as the author. It was expected that M'Kinley would call for satisfaction of James Johnson in an honorable way; but he was too well convinced that upon any principle of equality, his call would not be refused—and the dastwardly scoundrel would not bring his mind to such a trial, he remained silent and disgraced uander the strictures in the Argus.—On Monday, yesterday, the 7th inst. M'Kinley came to Georgetown with a large bludgeon, where he and James Johnson met in the court-house yeard, and after a lew words passing, an engagement took place; James Johnson conscious of his own firmness of mind, engaged the scoundrel without using any weapon, and soon disarmed him of his cane without any injury—and would have ended the combat as it should have been in a few minutes, had it not beeen for the banisters to the steps, up to the court-house door, which sustained the trembling g and affrightened M'Kinley, against the jolt it of James Johnson; The scoundrel, M'Kinley, was not willing now to contend upon equal g ground, after being deprived of his weapon, here thurst his hand into his bosom where he had it his dirk unsheathed, and made three murderouous lunges at James Johnson who had not as y yet used any unlawful weapon, who immediatelyy, upon perceiving the intention the assassim he was ready for him in way, and drew a pistol but was preven killing this antagonist for a moment, the people; when finding M'Kinley's hands he refefused to take it—but was saw he the affrighted assassin retreating into the court-houuurse, then to the Tav erns, &c.

It is proper to remmark, that one half hour after the attempt at asssassination had ended, it was not known that J James Johnson was stabbed; when one of his i neighbors told him he was stabbed in the: arm; which being examined the wound was found to be of considerable depth.—Trembliing criminal—That it was not known during the cconflict, that he wounded a man who had tooo much feeling & honor to shed the blood of a villain, who had in so cowardly a manner, atttempted to take his life. As soon as M'Kinley could conveniently get his horse, he left Georgetown. Yes, after making the cowardly and murderous attempt, he run like every other crriminal who feels himself without firmness tto meet a brave man.— As soon as it was knowm to the Johnson family, that the scoundrel had: run from town, it was concluded that one of tthe brothers should pursue him with a friend,, and demand satisfaction upon equal termss, tho' he had attempted the assassination of theeir brother, and if he would not give satisfactionn upon such terms, to take it at all events. Accordingly W m. Johnson, with Mr. Taylor, tthis friend, pursued the assassin to Lexington ;: and Mr. Taylor accordingly called on M'Kinhleye told him that Wm. Johnson was in town,, and demanded satisfaction for the outrage wwhich he had committed upon his brother, and t that he was requested to give Wm. Johnsonn an interview. Upon enquiring in what way Wm. Johnson wished to settle the matter, he wwas told, that he. M'Kinley, was at liberty to chchoose the mode of combat ; upon which the i insignificant scoundrel refused to meet Wm. JJohnson in any way, in the most positive mannner. The jury, under the riot act, fined M'KKinley $19 99.

The indignation of thhe people was great, & there seemed to be a uuniversal regret, that Jas. Johnson was preventeed from killing such a villain, after it was knnown that James Johnson was stabbed—and it iit is still the regret of many of his friends.

October 8, 1811.

3. Handbill detailing McKinley's dispute with James Johnson (1811). WHI-87419b. Courtesy of the Wisconsin Historical Society.

Johnson stripped him of his weapon. McKinley then pulled out a small dagger, lunged for Johnson several times, and stabbed him at least once. Though wounded, the heroic Johnson reportedly held his own against McKinley but finally drew his pistol to defend himself. Even then, however, he held his fire long enough for McKinley to flee. In the words of the broadside, "As soon as M'Kinley could conveniently get his horse, he left

Georgetown. Yes, after making the cowardly and murderous attempt, he run [*sic*] like every other criminal who feels himself without firmness to meet a brave man."[67]

The handbill went on to note that because the twenty-dollar fine could hardly be construed as holding McKinley accountable for his actions, Johnson's brothers had approached him and demanded that he defend his shameful conduct on the field of honor in a duel. According to the handbill, McKinley refused and thus "the poltroon and assassin" had largely gone unpunished.

Not surprisingly, McKinley had a very different interpretation of the events, and upon learning the identity of the handbill's author, he immediately challenged Richard Johnson to a duel. The latter refused, however, citing the arcane rules of dueling. In his written response to McKinley's challenge, Johnson declared, "[I]t is impermissible to fight a man in an Honorable way who has disgraced himself as Mr. McKinley has done in attempting to assassinate one of my brothers and then refus[ing] to meet one of my other brothers in equal combat."[68] When McKinley's friend and fellow Federalist Lewis Marshall volunteered to fight Johnson instead, the latter again begged off, citing inexperience with the short sword—Marshall's weapon of choice. Johnson then quickly left for Washington to attend Congress.

Neither McKinley nor Johnson was harmed physically, but the near-duel affected both of their reputations. More than a quarter of a century after the incident, McKinley's role would be mentioned in a pamphlet written by the abolitionist Theodore Dwight Weld. Calling upon his readers to "Look at the men who the people delight to honor," he disparagingly cited Andrew Jackson, Henry Clay, John Rowan, Justice McKinley, and others from the South who rushed to duel as evidence that "the savage ferocity [of southerners] . . . is the natural result of their habit of daily plundering and oppressing the slave."[69] Johnson's repeated refusals to duel and his sudden flight to Washington were also long remembered. In 1838 the *Boston Courier* gave an account of the affair and its aftermath, informing its readers that Johnson, then the vice president of the United States, came "out of the matter rather shabbily."[70]

A few months after his dispute with the Johnsons, McKinley played a much more conciliatory role as a second in a dispute that, again, played its way out in the local newspaper. On December 16, 1811, Captain Nathaniel G. S. Hart apparently made some disparaging remarks about another Lexington resident, Samuel Watson. Using the *Kentucky Gazette* as his medium, Watson questioned whether there was any truth to the rumor that Hart had called him a "scoundrel" and "assassin."[71]

Hart responded by way of the same paper and clarified for Watson that he had actually "honored [him] with the epithets of '*Coward, Villain, and Assassin.*'" He refused to retract his words and noted that if Watson wished anything more of him that their mutual friend John McKinley would "know where to find me, ever ready to do all men justice."[72]

Although Kentucky had outlawed dueling a decade earlier, the ban was a small deterrent. Kentuckians who wished to settle their disputes on the field of honor simply crossed the border to skirt the law. On January 7, 1812, Hart, Watson, and their seconds crossed the Ohio River to stage their duel in the Indiana Territory. According to the published account of the duel, after both men fired and missed, McKinley "observed that he hoped the thing would be at an end, and that the parties would return to a state of intimacy and friendship."[73] Hart said that was impossible and proposed that they shoot again. For his part, Watson said he would do whatever McKinley advised. Upon which, as the *Kentucky Gazette* recorded, "Mr. M'Kinley determined to drop the affair."[74]

On April 16, 1814, McKinley, now nearly thirty-four years old, married Julianna (Julia) Bryan in Woodford County, Kentucky. Like so much else from McKinley's early life, little is known about Julia other than she was born in Philadelphia, was twelve years younger than McKinley, and was purportedly the daughter of a prominent Pennsylvania merchant.[75]

Two months later John McKinley entered the political arena as a candidate for the first time when he permitted his name to be put forward for one of Fayette County's three seats in the Kentucky House of Representatives.[76] As a member of the Federalist Party, he undoubtedly knew that his chances of winning were remote, but he was also aware that his growing wealth and legal reputation were important electoral assets. No candidate of any party during that era could hope for success at the polls without giving the voting public what it demanded in the days preceding the election including public speeches and liquor.[77] The latter, along with a variety of other drink and food accoutrements, virtually required that candidates for public office be men of substance.

Yet even as a wealthy man with an established reputation, a disappointing, if predictable, outcome awaited McKinley as the votes for the Kentucky House seats were counted. William T. Barry, a Democratic-Republican, ultimately emerged from the crowded nine-man field with the highest number of votes. McKinley came in last, receiving just 115 votes out of the 5,500 that were cast.[78] Again, this could hardly have come as a surprise given his party affiliation. More than decade later, in an article about McKinley's 1826 candidacy to represent Alabama in the U.S. Senate, a northern newspaper recalled the difficult political conditions Federalists encountered in Kentucky. Of McKinley, it declared simply: "He was one of the leaders of the Kentucky federal party, which circumstance kept him from the enjoyment of public offices."[79]

On September 20, 1817, Robert Wickliffe, a Democratic partisan and attorney from Lexington, wrote a letter to Henry Clay in which he trumpeted the apparent finish of both the Federalist Party and McKinley in Kentucky politics.[80] "[T]he Federalist[s] are completely silenced and convinced that they are despised by the people," he wrote, "and I learn that J. McKinley Esq. will migrate down the water. He says to the Alabama."[81]

McKinley had indeed made plans to leave Kentucky but could not act upon them until after the birth of his and Julia's second child, Andrew, on October 10, 1817.[82] Within a few months, however, he began to publicly confirm the rumors of his pending departure from Lexington. He placed an ad in several area newspapers acknowledging the probability that he would "be absent from Lexington for a considerable time" and had turned his practice over to Theodore F. Talbot, formerly of New York City.[83]

Given the political realities of the time, it is likely that John McKinley would have been remembered for little more than his career as a wealthy Federalist attorney had he chosen to stay in Kentucky. In leaving that state, he consequently left behind the futility that characterized his decade-long association with the loyal—and losing—political opposition.

However, McKinley left behind more than just Kentucky politics when he departed for Alabama the following spring. Nearing his fortieth birthday, he also abandoned a flourishing legal practice in mid-career. The prominent business and social circles in which he moved would no longer be readily available to him. His Lexington home, established fruit trees, and gardens would be replaced, at least initially, by something far more rustic and uncultivated. He also left behind the heritage of his pioneering family for a largely unsettled area where the Logan name had little cachet.

While there are no extant accounts of what exactly prompted McKinley to leave all of that behind and move his young family to Alabama, one could reasonably argue that it was the very thing that had led his uncle Benjamin Logan to Kentucky in the first place: land.

3
Alabama Fever and Georgia Faction

[The site for Florence] is among the most fertile and beautiful in America. The soil is of the first grade of excellence and produces even beyond its promise. . . . The streams are clear, rapid and beautiful; and the climate confessedly among the most pleasant, salubrious and delightful in the United States.

—Cypress Land Company advertisement, 1818

The most significant incident in the series of events that culminated in McKinley's 1837 appointment to the Supreme Court occurred several years before he left Kentucky. On August 9, 1814, Andrew Jackson forced the Creek Indians to sign a treaty ceding twenty-two million acres of their land to the U.S. government, the result of a crushing defeat they had suffered at Jackson's hands five months earlier at the Battle of Horseshoe Bend. Two-thirds of the land that Jackson received on behalf of the United States lay within what is now Alabama. Coupled with subsequent cessions of Chickasaw and Choctaw territory to the north and west of the Creek land, virtually the entire present state of Alabama lay open for settlement by the time McKinley announced his departure from Lexington.[1]

The promise of land excited attention wherever it became available during the nation's pioneering era, and there were always settlers eager to move into newly opened territories. It could sometimes take decades, however, before an area was populated enough to describe it as anything other than just a "settlement." Thus, what happened on the Indian lands in Alabama was not only unexpected but unprecedented. The national contagion to own land there resulted in what historians now call the "Great Migration."[2] At the time, it was known simply as "Alabama Fever."

A combination of factors led to the extraordinary demand for the Indian cession lands in Alabama. The War of 1812 had largely checked the restless spirit that induced men and women to leave their comfortable homes and established communities for the wilderness. As historian Malcolm Rohrbough observed, "The war did not diminish interest in the land, but the physical danger posed by the English and their Indian allies held mi-

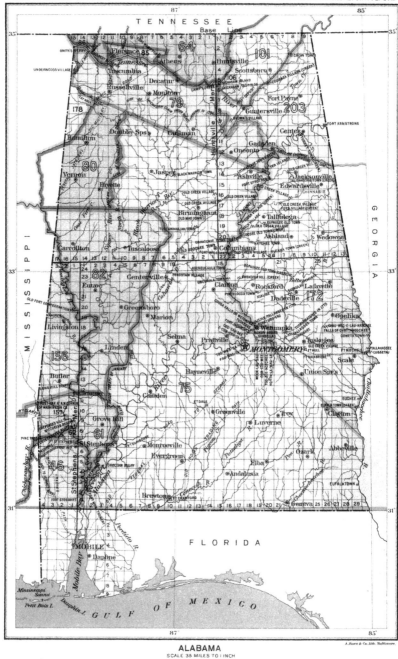

ALABAMA
SCALE 35 MILES TO 1 INCH

4. Alabama (Indian cession lands), 1902. NativeAm1902a.sid. Courtesy of the Birmingham, Alabama, Public Library.

gration and purchase within bounds."[3] However, with the war's end in 1815, the few hardy settlers who had already penetrated into Alabama were quickly joined by thousands of others now willing to hazard the postwar challenges of the frontier.

Peace also brought the resumption of trade relations between the United States and Great Britain just as the latter experienced a huge international demand for its textiles. This, in turn, increased the demand for cotton, which resulted in the doubling of cotton prices between 1814 and 1815 to just over 32 cents per pound.[4] Accompanying the soaring prices were reports that the climate and rich soil of the Indian cession lands in Alabama were exceedingly favorable to extensive cotton cultivation. As one traveler breathlessly declared, "I cannot describe the cotton fields unless I compare them to a neglected peach orchard, with branches projecting from top to bottom, with a stem about the size of a man's wrist, from eight to ten, eleven, and twelve feet high."[5]

Such statements, even after being discounted for their exaggerated claims, attracted tens of thousands of Americans to the cession lands. Whether they came with wagons full of belongings and accompanied by slaves or had all their worldly possessions fit into a hogshead that they pulled themselves, those struck by the fever were convinced that the surest path to wealth lay in Alabama.

The allure of the newly available land was so great that it was said that northern-bound travelers from Alabama could journey "for many days without being out of sight of emigrant wagons accompanied by long files of negro slaves steadily tramping southward."[6] A man from Augusta, Georgia, documented the wave of immigration he encountered as he returned home from the Indian cessions in 1816. He reported seeing "141 wagons, 102 carts, 10 stages, 14 gigs, 2 coaches, 29 droves of cattle, 27 droves of hogs, [and] 2 droves of sheep."[7] He estimated that during his nine-day trip he had passed more than 3,800 travelers, all bound for Alabama.[8]

So eager were people to stake their claim and make their fortunes in "the Alabama . . . the garden of America" that the family and friends they left behind became alarmed.[9] Writing in 1818, Johnson Taylor in Philadelphia observed, "I never saw before in this city such a notion for emigration to the westward as there is at this time. . . . Among the rest [I too have] a great idea of turning cultivator of the earth in the western part of Alabama territory."[10] In an oft-quoted letter, a concerned citizen of North Carolina declared, "[T]he *Alabama Feaver* [*sic*] rages here with great violence and has *carried off* vast numbers of our Citizens. I am apprehensive, if it continues to spread as it has done, it will almost depopulate the country."[11] He went on to warn that "this *feaver* is contagious . . . for as soon as one neighbor visits another who has just returned from the Alabama he immediately discover the same symptoms . . . [as] the person who has seen the allureing [*sic*] Alabama."[12] Farther south, a Samuel McDonald spoke of the toll the fever exacted on his fellow Georgians who abruptly left their homes and lands to move west: "Scarce any of those who are attacked by it ever recover," he wrote to his sister, "it sooner or later carries them off to the westward."[13]

A North Carolina newspaper reported serious shortages of food and supplies along the southern route between Georgia and Alabama and encouraged those afflicted with the Alabama Fever to carefully consider the costs of removing to the new territory. If the reality of such difficulties did not dissuade them, the editors opined, "we suspect the disease is incurable."[14] The paper went on to counsel would-be settlers that "the agricultural advantages [there] are not equal to those which they can obtain in many other places—The general impression seems to be, that they would be better off at home."[15] But settlers ignored such advice and continued to pour in from surrounding states and, indeed, even from overseas.[16]

Andrew Jackson was one of the few with firsthand knowledge of the area and actively encouraged the settling of the cession lands. He believed, as he put it in an 1816 letter, that "nothing [would] promote the welfare of the United States, and particularly the southwestern frontier so much as bringing into market at an early day, the whole of this fertile country."[17] Jackson saw great national promise in both the land and the revenue source that the Alabama land sales would provide for the national government. He also recognized the financial value to those who got to the Indian cessions first. It was, as one Jackson biographer put it, "a land speculator's New Jerusalem."[18]

Congress passed legislation shortly after the cessions that created survey districts and land offices in Milledgeville, Georgia, and Cahaba, Alabama, to process the sale of the public lands. In 1816, before surveying was even complete, the first Creek lands were made available for purchase and within a year the Cahaba office reported record land sales of $753,849.[19] On March 3, 1817, in response to pleas by Jackson and others that the surveying be accelerated, Congress divided the Indian cession lands along an east-west line that stretched from the Mississippi River to Georgia and created a new surveyor general position for the northern district. The land in the Indian cession became even more appealing when, on the same day, President James Monroe signed legislation dividing the Mississippi Territory nearly in half, thereby creating the Territory of Alabama. Monroe would later appoint General John Coffee, a lifelong friend of Andrew Jackson's and one of his key advisers during the Creek War, to the newly created surveyor general slot.[20]

Under the terms of the Federal Land Act of 1800, buyers of the Indian cession land could purchase property in tracts of 160 acres or larger. The land was first put up for sale at public auction and sold to the highest bidder. Property left unsold after the public auction was made available three weeks later at private sale for a minimum of two dollars an acre. One-twentieth of the total purchase price was due at the time of sale as a down payment with a full one-quarter of the entire purchase to be paid within forty days. The remaining amount plus interest would be paid in equal installments over the next three years.

While such repayment terms were well suited to those buying the minimum acreage permitted by law, the combination of available land, easy credit, and high cotton prices encouraged prospective landowners to purchase all they could—either for their own future agricultural pursuits or for a more immediate return on their investment through speculation. John McKinley came to Alabama for both purposes.

While he did not formally move to Alabama until 1819 when his and several other Kentucky families arrived in Huntsville, he did make several trips to the new territory to participate in the land sales. In November 1817, McKinley and Kentucky millionaire John Wesley Hunt formed a partnership to buy public land in Alabama. Hunt advanced $50,000 to the cause while McKinley contributed $4,400, but it was the responsibility of the latter to oversee the success of their investment.[21] The following spring, on March 12, 1818, McKinley and six other notable men formed the Cypress Land Company. The organization was actually a merger of two rival land speculation companies, one hailing from Tennessee and the other from Alabama, which were reportedly brought together by McKinley.[22]

The dreams of wealth envisioned by many of those immigrating to Alabama were fueled by both individual speculators and land companies like Cypress that bought up the best and largest tracts of land first and then resold their holdings to would-be settlers for a sizable profit. In an 1818 letter, a speculator from Virginia detailed the return he expected to see on a $600 investment in the Indian cession: "This land in four years may sell for 50 or 60 [dollars] an acre and possibly more. One thousand acres at $50 an acre will amount to $50,000. This all looks visionary but hundreds of cases have happened in this country."[23]

The unparalleled buying frenzy that accompanied the Alabama Fever and the influence of land speculators is clearly seen in records kept by the Huntsville land office. In 1817 the office recorded just over 5,600 acres sold for a paltry $11,221.[24] The following year, however, the Huntsville office found itself at the "center of [a] land mania."[25] Land west of Huntsville (where Cypress focused its efforts), which had been purchased for $2 an acre a few years earlier, now sold for $10, with some buyers paying as much as $100 an acre.[26] By the end of 1818, nearly a million acres of land had been sold by the Huntsville land office for $7.2 million.[27]

There were many land speculators in Alabama, but Cypress was the leading company in the northern portion of the territory, owing its reputation, in part, to the backing of Andrew Jackson, whom it counted among its most prominent investors.[28] Jackson's attention to the Creek lands as well as his lobbying for Coffee's appointment as surveyor general stemmed from his own interests as an ardent land speculator.

McKinley's reputation at the time might be judged by the quality of some of the six other men who served with him as trustees of the Cypress Land Company. Those selected as trustees from the Alabama group were LeRoy Pope and Thomas Bibb. Pope was a wealthy landowner with significant political influence and is regarded as one of the founding fathers of Huntsville. Bibb was one of the largest landowners in northern Alabama and would later serve as the state's second governor.

From the Tennessee group, little is known of James Childress and Dabney Morriss, but James Jackson was an Irish-born merchant who lived in Nashville. Although no relation to Andrew Jackson, James at that time was the general's principal agent and partner in several business enterprises and had made a fortune in Tennessee.[29] He would add to it by establishing a massive plantation in northern Alabama known as the Forks of the Cypress where he later raised champion thoroughbreds.

The success of the Cypress Land Company, however, lay not with the endorsement of Andrew Jackson nor with the reputations and wealth of the six men named above. Rather, it turned on its seventh trustee who was arguably the most important person in the entire enterprise: John Coffee. Cypress had an enormous advantage over the other land companies because Coffee's role in the Creek War coupled with his surveyor general responsibilities gave him a better understanding of the land than anyone else.[30]

With the benefit of Coffee's expertise, the Cypress trustees directed their attention to the area within the recently created Lauderdale County, and purchased nearly all of the land on the north bank of the Tennessee River.[31] Within weeks of the organization of their company, the Cypress trustees begin to sell shares of company stock, which eventually netted some $300,000.[32] They also began to advertise the June sale of lots in a new town they would call Florence. For the next several years in newspapers as far north as Washington, D.C., the trustees promoted the land upon which the town would rise in the confident and glowing language of speculation: "[The site for Florence] is among the most fertile and beautiful in America. The soil is of the first grade of excellence and produces even beyond its promise. . . . The streams are clear, rapid and beautiful; and the climate confessedly among the most pleasant, salubrious and delightful in the United States."[33]

In carrying advertisements for Florence and other prospective towns in the Indian cession, newspapers around the country expressed both amazement and concern. In 1818, for example, the *Richmond Enquirer* noted sarcastically, "Happy is he who owns a bend between two rivers; what pains to puff its situation; to dress it off with every advantage of health, navigation, fertility, which the most plastic imagination can supply."[34] It then went on to warn its readers in a more serious vein, "We must lay down as a rule, that where this spirit of speculation rages, some persons are to be benefitted and others to be bit."[35]

Not surprisingly, many buyers were indeed "bit" by the schemes of speculators. Those who purchased land were often bitterly disappointed to learn that the advertisements and promotions that had tempted them to buy had exaggerated the benefits or obscured the real difficulties of their property.[36] Consequently, the vision of flourishing cities emerging from the wilderness that was shared by speculators and settlers alike often never materialized.[37]

Disappointment, however, turned to despondency when the Alabama land mania abruptly ended as cotton prices began to decline during the latter part of 1818. The Panic of 1819 and the national economic depression that immediately followed saw the price of cotton dip to just ten cents per pound, shattering the dreams of wealth that precipitated the Alabama Fever. Landowners, large and small, were faced with financial obligations

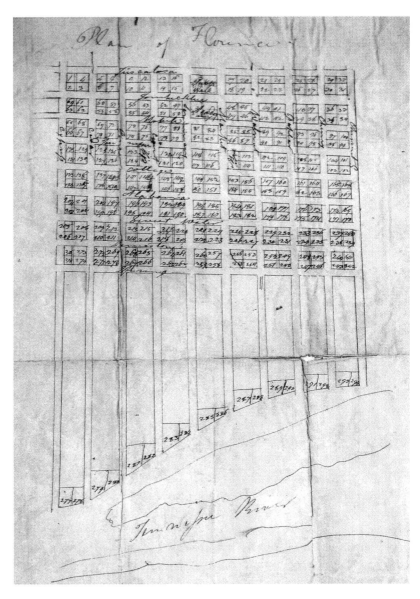

5. Proposed plan of Florence, Alabama, by John Coffee (1818). Courtesy of the *Florence (AL) Times Daily*.

that they simply could not meet. Writing to a friend in North Carolina, future Alabama senator John Williams Walker fondly recalled, "We too have had our Banks, and our days of high prices, and money-raising facilities without number, and learned to speak of thousands and tens of thousands as if they were mere sums of small change and pocket money."[38] The exhilaration of those days, Williams went on to confess, had since given way to despair: "I [now] tremble for myself and my friends, whose heads are still above water. Some are already sunk and gone. Others are still tottering—and a breach overwhelms them."[39]

Less sympathetic observers at the time argued that the greed of both speculators and buyers had secured for them exactly what they deserved. Having "got involved head over heals [*sic*] in debt," as one put it, "they have no means of extricating themselves; but must stop still and sweat for their avarice and folly."[40] A Huntsville newspaper, the *Alabama Republican*, bluntly opined, "[W]e hazard nothing in venturing the assertion that of the debt of 7 or 8 millions, which will be due at the expiration of five years, not $100,000 will <u>ever</u> be paid."[41]

Alabama was not the only state affected by the Panic of 1819, but the consequences of the economic downturn were unusually harsh there. As the southern historian Thomas P. Abernethy observed, "So great had been the influx of settlers, and so numerous the purchasers of new lands, that the entire community, merchants and farmers alike, was staggered."[42] It is no exaggeration to claim, as Abernethy did, that one result of the Panic of 1819 was to render "a larger proportion of the western population . . . insolvent than at any other time in the history of the nation."[43]

McKinley was almost certainly affected by the slump, but it is not clear to what extent. Three decades after the economic crash, a Wisconsin newspaper recalled that "[t]he whole State of Alabama was involved in the deepest distress by the bursting of the land bubble; and the Cypress Land Company felt most painfully the consequences."[44] When he renewed his partnership with John Wesley Hunt in 1821, McKinley estimated that the Alabama land he had purchased for them was worth $105,000. Four years later, he informed Hunt that the value of their property exceeded $174,000. As encouraging as those figures are, these sums may not have told the whole story even if McKinley's numbers were accurate. Almost fifteen years after they created their partnership, Hunt revealed that the crash in cotton prices might have ruined him given how extensively he and McKinley had been involved in Alabama land speculation.[45]

The land crisis would be the first in a devastating series of events that would wreak economic havoc on the region, trouble Alabamians for decades, and be the hallmark of McKinley's political activities in Congress. One positive consequence of the public land sales, however, was the staggering increase in Alabama's population over a very short period of time. The region had been Indian land in 1814, became a territory of the United States in 1817, and joined the union as a state just two years later. Squatters, speculators, and settlers all contributed to the population explosion Alabama experienced between 1810 and 1820 when the number of people living within its borders grew by more than 1000 percent, with most arriving in the region after 1815.[46] The unprecedented rapid development of the area was accompanied by a similarly mounting need for governmental institutions at both the state and local level. Like others who already possessed wealth, land, and connections in the Alabama territory, John McKinley was well positioned to participate in its governance as well.

Alabama historian Frances Roberts has pointed out that much of the most valuable land offered for public sale in Alabama was snatched up by men who would assume leadership in the economic, political, and social affairs of the new state. Significantly, many of them had already held important political positions elsewhere.[47] For example, among those who bought up large tracts of land in Alabama were Charles Tait and Bolling Hall, who had previously served Georgia in the U.S. Senate and House of Representatives, respectively. There were also future Alabama governors William Wyatt Bibb, himself a former U.S. senator from Georgia, Thomas Bibb, Clement C. Clay, and Israel Pickens, who had previously held one of North Carolina's seats in the U.S. House of Representatives. A future chief justice of the Alabama Supreme Court, Reuben Saffold, was numbered among the early large purchasers as well as future U.S. senators from Alabama John Williams Walker, Henry Chambers, and William R. King. The latter was a former member of the U.S. House from North Carolina and would later serve as vice president of the United States for a short period of time.[48]

There were many others who attracted little national attention but made contributions to the state by later serving in the Alabama state legislature.[49] So entwined were these and other men in the land, money, and politics of their era that, as Roberts noted, "[w]ere these names not listed in relationship to land purchases, they might easily be mistaken for a list of delegates to Alabama's first constitutional convention or an early listing of the territorial legislature."[50]

While people from throughout the country and even overseas flowed into Alabama, the interest of Georgians in the land to their west was particularly significant and had important political implications for both the state and John McKinley. Southern historian Albert B. Moore observed that most of the people that McKinley encountered when he moved to the territory "were not strongly politically-minded. They were too busy with work and home-building to take an active interest in politics."[51] While perhaps true generally, this characterization could hardly apply to the group of wealthy lawyers, planters, and businessmen who emigrated from Georgia to northern Alabama and established themselves as the predominant political and economic force in the state.

This group originated in Georgia's Broad River region (on its eastern border with South Carolina) where a group of Revolutionary War veterans from Virginia and their families set up homesteads in the mid-1780s. From this nucleus of families emerged a number of friendships and marriages that would form a political alliance whose influence would eventually stretch from the Mississippi River to Washington, D.C.

In 1810 McKinley's fellow Cypress trustee LeRoy Pope led a group of Broad River families and friends to a small settlement in the Mississippi Territory known as Hunt's Spring. A year earlier, Pope and a group of Georgia investors had purchased nearly half of the land in the newly created Madison County where the settlement was located. Pope proceeded to lay out a new town on the same site and christened it Twickenham, after a town in England, to the irritation of many longtime settlers in the area. Impressed with neither his money nor his property holdings, older settlers reacted sharply against Pope's renaming of their town. In the first of many battles in northern Alabama between the moneyed interests from Georgia and the common settlers, the latter were able to get the territorial legislature to change the name of the town again, this time to Huntsville.

Pope's son-in-law John Williams Walker had followed him from Broad River to Madison County and had set up a successful legal practice there. He would serve as a member and later as Speaker of the territorial legislature. When the question of statehood for the Mississippi Territory arose, he distinguished himself by vigorously opposing the admission of the entire Mississippi Territory as a state. Walker proposed instead that the territory be divided in half and encouraged his boyhood friend U.S. Senator Charles Tait of Georgia to pursue the matter in Congress.[52] Tait subsequently sponsored the legislation authorizing Alabama to hold a constitutional convention in preparation for statehood. The president of that convention, perhaps not surprisingly, was John Williams Walker. On December 14, 1819, the day Alabama became the nation's twenty-second state, Walker was selected as one of its first two senators.

Tait had served Georgia in the U.S. Senate along with another Broad River resident, William Wyatt Bibb. Bibb resigned his seat in 1816 after his constituents voiced their extreme displeasure at his vote to increase the salaries of senators. Humiliated in Georgia, Bibb looked westward to Alabama where he already owned land and where his brother Thomas had lived for several years. President James Monroe resurrected Bibb's political career when he named him governor of the newly created Alabama Territory in the fall of 1817. In doing so, Monroe relied upon the advice of his secretary of the treasury, William Crawford, himself a former senator and representative from Georgia.[53]

Crawford's position gave him considerable power over federal patronage positions, which he filled almost exclusively with men affiliated with the Georgia group. At the time of the cession land sales, the secretary of the treasury oversaw the General Land Office, which was responsible for the surveying, platting, and sale of public lands. Crawford routinely bypassed Josiah Meigs, the chief commissioner of the land agency, in determining the placement of land offices and nominating friends and associates for positions in those offices.[54]

A flagrant example of Crawford's misuse of his office to benefit his fellow Georgians can be seen in his establishment of the land office at Milledgeville, Georgia, in 1816. It was here that the best property in the central portion of the Creek cession in Alabama—river-bottom lands near the present city of Montgomery—was first made available for sale.[55] Crawford purposely located the Milledgeville office 150 miles away from the land in question to make it difficult for the squatters who had arrived in the area previously to purchase the land they had already started to cultivate. According to Roberts, "This action prevented many of the actual settlers in the Alabama Territory from bidding on these choice lands, because they were generally too poor to travel to the place of sale or to compete with wealthy men at public auction."[56]

Because of actions like these and others going back to Pope's renaming of Hunt's Spring, there was a simmering resentment against the Georgians and others like them who, by virtue of their bloodlines, friendships, or wealth, seemed to dominate the early political landscape in Alabama. As the Huntsville newspaper the *Democrat* succinctly put it at the time, the Georgians "evinced a determination to monopolize all power, and to fill every office with their own creatures."[57] This tension would serve as a backdrop to many of the key political events in early Alabama as well as to John McKinley's own political aspirations.

The population of Alabama grew so rapidly that its political institutions, both formal and informal, had difficulty keeping pace. Political parties, for example, would not be fully formed in Alabama until nearly a decade after statehood. Writing from Huntsville in 1822, Anne Newport Royall, one of America's first female journalists, declared, "[T]here are no parties here—they are all Republican. The country people, and very few of the city, know the meaning of the word <u>Federalist!</u>"[58]

Royall's reference to the absence of party in Alabama requires some clarification. First, and not surprisingly, the early settlers in the Indian cession lands had far more to worry about than party politics. As historian Theodore Henley Jack observed, the vast majority of people in the newly opened lands "were united by mutual exposure to the difficulties and vicissitudes of the wilderness; and the stress of life in a new country did not permit that leisure out of which party differences were developed."[59]

Second, and more to Royall's point, the Federalist Party's rapid disintegration after the presidential election of 1800 (and the fact that it never had much strength in the South to begin with) meant that there was really no practical alternative to the Democratic-Republican Party at that time. Thus, if an early Alabama politician were forced to declare his allegiance to a national party, he would have been "republican" essentially by default.

Third, and most important, while formal political parties had yet to be formed, there were already overlapping and shifting political alliances at work during this time. These were organized around such factors as the citizen's home state (the Georgians were generally opposed by settlers from North Carolina, Tennessee, and Virginia), geography (northern Alabama, Madison County in particular, versus the central and southern portions of the state), and wealth (the large planters versus the small farmers).[60] The boundaries defining these factions were understandably fluid, and more than one Alabama politician shifted from one group to another.

Despite the absence of formal political parties, there was considerable political tension in the state because the Georgians had essentially created, to use a modern term, a political machine. Their numbers were not excessively large, but as Alabama historian Albert B. Moore wrote, they were men "with strong personalities, experience, and unusual capacity for politics and fondness for holding office."[61] Their opponents referred to them and their political and business allies collectively (regardless of where they were from originally) as the "Georgia Faction," the "Broad River Group," the "Royal Party," or "Royalists."[62]

John McKinley's business interests and personal relationships quickly saw him identified with the Georgia Faction. Like many of those affiliated with the Georgians, he too held extensive landholdings in Lauderdale, Lawrence, Limestone, and Madison counties. He also purchased property in a number of northern Alabama towns besides Florence. In Huntsville, for example, McKinley bought a prominent half-block parcel that fronted that city's public square where the county courthouse was located and which also served as a hub for people and commerce.[63] The series of brick offices he owned there was known to locals as McKinley's Row.[64] In February 1819 he purchased one of Huntsville's most significant buildings, the Huntsville Inn, which was the site of a surprise visit by President James Monroe in June 1819 during a three-day tour through the Alabama Territory.[65] Several dozen of the city's wealthiest and most prominent citizens hosted the president at a public dinner there in his honor that was presided over by LeRoy Pope.

Pope was McKinley's primary connection to the Georgia Faction. In addition to their business relationship through Cypress, Pope and McKinley, along with James Jackson, John Coffee, and the future Tennessee senator Hugh L. White, also established and served as directors of Huntsville's Alabama and East Tennessee Steamboat Company.[66] McKinley also provided legal services to Pope's Huntsville bank, which would have serious political consequences (see chapter 4).[67]

Personal and business relationships aside, McKinley's affiliation with the Georgia Faction was central to any hope he had of holding public office. He had never won an election in Kentucky and was no longer a young man by the time he arrived in Alabama. Yet the politics of the new territory presented him and many others with the opportunity to embark upon promising political careers at midlife. Not surprisingly, his association with the Georgia Faction was quickly rewarded. On November 21, 1818, territorial governor William Wyatt Bibb appointed McKinley as chief justice of the Lauderdale County Court. This appointment came before McKinley had taken up formal residency in the state and some eight months before he was even licensed to *practice* law in Alabama.[68]

Sensing his rising political fortunes shortly after moving his family to Alabama, he excitedly wrote to John Williams Walker, a fellow member of the Georgia Faction who had recently been elected senator from Alabama: "I am at length a citizen of Alabama, and got here just in time to be run for Judge of one of the circuits [created] by the late legislature. . . . Do congratulate me on my debut."[69]

The position of circuit court judge was particularly significant at that time because Alabama's 1819 Constitution stipulated that the circuit judges were to collectively serve as the Supreme Court for the state until the legislature provided otherwise.[70] On December 14, 1819, the day Alabama was admitted into the Union as the twenty-second state, its first legislature convened to fill the five circuit court judgeships created by its constitution. Four of the five circuit positions were filled immediately, but none of the three candidates for the Fourth Judicial Circuit (Richard Ellis, Beverly Hughes, and McKinley) was able to muster a majority of the legislative vote on the first ballot. Three more ballots would be necessary before a majority of the House and Senate members eventually voted for Ellis over McKinley by a slim 37–31 margin.[71] That one so new to the state would "be run for Judge" and nearly prevail can only be attributed to McKinley's ties to the Georgia Faction.

At this same legislative session, McKinley made quick use of these new and powerful connections to push for the appointment of his fellow Cypress trustee John Coffee as a justice of the Lauderdale County Court. A week after the House elected Coffee to this position, McKinley wrote to him to explain how it happened: "I made so free with your name as to have you elected one of the justices of the county court. . . . I did this because . . . I know of no person who would be certain to be elected that was qualified but yourself."[72]

Clearly aware that his own financial interests were linked to both Coffee's reputation and the power of the Georgia Faction, McKinley went on to advise Coffee to also accept the appointment of major general for Lauderdale and Limestone counties, where both men owned significant amounts of property. "My object" in seeking this appointment, McKinley explained to Coffee, "is to keep out some electioneering bodies who have made this [their] business in the legislature."[73]

Despite this encouraging start to his political career, McKinley's prospects for continued success dimmed just a few years after his arrival in the state. The power of the Georgia Faction began to crumble with the loss of capable men like Governor William Wyatt Bibb and Senator John Williams Walker. Their untimely deaths coincided with an ever-strengthening opposition movement that capitalized on the growing distrust of the Georgia Faction's political and economic power. Ironically, the demise of the

Georgia Faction was assured by the rising political ambitions of Andrew Jackson. The man whose victory over the Creeks made possible the Alabama Fever and whose own land speculation interests were every bit as self-interested as those of the Broad River Group was now touted as the champion of the "common man" who would protect the working farmer from the abuses of the planter class that comprised the Georgia Faction.

Jackson's popularity forced politicians in Alabama to choose whether to align themselves with him or be swept aside by the massive political swell then forming throughout the Deep South. Having been affiliated with both the politically helpless Federalists in Kentucky and the once dominant but now increasingly despised Georgia Faction in Alabama, McKinley likely had an easy choice. He simply did what many other pragmatic politicians throughout the South had already done during this period of fluid political allegiances: he became a Jacksonian Democrat. Unbeknownst to McKinley, that decision would not only ensure his future electoral viability in Alabama but also result in his elevation to the Supreme Court.

4
The Politics of Political Change

> The Bar, at this place, has the character of the best in our State. . . . At the head of this, [John McKinley] stands, I am free to say, without a rival in legal attainment:—In the Supreme Court of this State, which attracts to its bar our best abilities, he occupies the same pre-eminence, and between him and the next there is a long interval.
>   —Huntsville attorney James G. Birney, 1826

Like so many thousands of others, John McKinley came to Alabama hoping to make a fortune off the land. As a lawyer, however, he also belonged to a distinct class of emigrants who continued to reap a financial windfall even after the speculative Alabama Fever had passed. On July 8, 1819, under the signature of territorial governor William Wyatt Bibb, McKinley received his license to practice law in the recently created Lauderdale County.[1] Territorial law at the time required that attorneys not only be authorized by the governor but also take the following oath in open court: "I, [full name] do solemnly swear, (or affirm,) that I will honestly demean myself in the practice as counsel or attorney: and will, in all respects, execute my office according to the best of my knowledge and abilities."[2] Any attorney who refused to abide by this oath or who in any other manner failed to uphold the obligations of his profession could be stripped of his license.

Of course, such stipulations did little to guarantee that lawyers in early Alabama were actually qualified to practice, a concern exacerbated by the large number of attorneys who moved there. The public land sales had created a lawyer's paradise, and, as the southern lawyer and humorist (and McKinley contemporary) Joseph Baldwin recalled, "Many members of the bar, of standing and character, from the other States, flocked in to put their sickles into this abundant harvest."[3]

Baldwin described the practice of law in the Old Southwest in his well-known 1853 satire *The Flush Times of Alabama and Mississippi*. In one of the few serious sketches in his book, he wrote at length about the countless opportunities for litigation that existed during the early statehood era of Alabama. The litany of legal claims derived from the fact that "many land titles were defective; property was brought from other States clogged with trusts, limitations, and uses[, and] claims and contracts made elsewhere [were] to be enforced here."[4] To these were combined "a general looseness, ignorance, and carelessness in the public officials in doing business," few statutory regulations relative to property and finance, and "universal indebtedness, which the hardness of times succeeding made it impossible for men to pay."[5] "In short," as Baldwin recalled, "all the flood-gates of litigation were opened, and the pent-up tide let loose upon the country."[6]

Attorneys of every conceivable combination of experience, education, and ethics waded into this legal tide where their efforts were far from inconsequential. Indeed, as legal historian Paul Pruitt Jr. has written, "[N]owhere were the dangers of an ignorant, undisciplined, or unethical bar greater than in Alabama and other states of the Old Southwest."[7] It was within this setting that McKinley, now forty years old with nearly two decades of legal experience behind him, built a flourishing practice and respected legal reputation prior to his elevation to the U.S. Supreme Court.

The state's newly created judicial system consisted of four tiers. Operating at the most local level of the Alabama judiciary were the justice courts. Several of these were located in each county, and each was presided over by a justice of the peace. Because they handled minor civil and criminal matters, the justice courts oversaw the bulk of all the legal work conducted in the state.

Next were the county courts, which considered additional civil claims and more serious criminal charges, as well as matters of probate. Above these were the circuit courts, which were the state's highest trial court. Circuit judges had jurisdiction over several counties and would convene court at various sites within those counties throughout the year. Early Alabama lawyers, including McKinley, also rode circuit and provided legal services in the towns where court was held. The judges and lawyers often traveled as a group, "[r]iding together from town to town, bench and bar room[ing] at available inns, 'two, four or six in the same sleeping apartment, two to a bed.'"[8]

The state's highest and only appellate court was the Alabama Supreme Court whose members, as indicated earlier, were comprised of the circuit court judges sitting en banc. The first session of the Alabama Supreme Court convened on the second Monday of May 1820 and saw the judges adopt a series of procedural rules that were largely already understood by the lawyers who came to practice in Alabama.[9]

However, there were great substantive differences between the arguments and precedents that McKinley and other lawyers invoked before the early Alabama Supreme Court. As Baldwin recalled, "Many questions decided in older States, and differently decided in different States, were to be settled here [in Alabama]."[10] The knowledge, experience, and arguments of these lawyers was thus "imported into the new country and tried on the new jurisprudence."[11]

McKinley made his debut before the Alabama Supreme Court during its second full term in November 1820. He appeared there in one of the first important cases establishing the "new jurisprudence" of Alabama. *Thomas Logwood v. President, Directors, Etc. of the Planters' and Merchants' Bank of Huntsville* pitted McKinley against the Huntsville Bank, which he would later serve as legal counsel.[12] Representing the holder of a discounted note against whom the bank had won a judgment for failure to pay, McKinley argued that Alabama's new state constitution forbade certain privileges extended to the bank by the territorial legislature in its incorporating charter. He also argued that the specific statutory provisions governing how the bank collected its debts had not been met.

With two judges recusing themselves because of personal ties to the bank, the Alabama Supreme Court rejected McKinley's first contention, holding that the charter was, in effect, a contract between the bank and the Mississippi territorial legislature, which had originally granted it. Changes to that contract, by subsequent legislative or even constitutional provisions, the court maintained, were not possible without the consent of the bank.[13] However, the court did acknowledge McKinley's second point, stressing that "wherever summary remedy is given by Statute, those who wish to avail themselves of it must be confined strictly to its provisions."[14] Both aspects of the court's opinion were frequently cited by subsequent state courts that uniformly referenced *Logwood* as one of the earliest substantive decisions of Alabama law.

Between 1820 and his elevation to the U.S. Supreme Court, McKinley appeared as counsel in dozens of cases before the Alabama Supreme Court. Most of these dealt with civil and commercial lawsuits involving contract violation, debt, recovery of payment, and estates, but McKinley also represented clients charged with voting fraud and hog stealing.[15] As his legal reputation increased, so too did his wealth and, accordingly, his prospects for public office. As mentioned earlier, the latter two were intertwined and coincided perfectly with southern electioneering practices in the 1820s.

From the late eighteenth century onward, it had been customary for American political candidates to engage in the practice of "treating" or providing food and drink for prospective voters on Election Day. Although many found the practice of "swilling the planters with bumbo" abhorrent, it was an electoral necessity and one that generally only men of wealth could afford.[16] McKinley had only dabbled in treating during his unsuccessful run for the Kentucky legislature in 1814 because there was no point in expending money and resources on an election he simply could not win. His move to Alabama, however, required him to take a more earnest look at treating. This was not only because he now had a legitimate chance of winning public office, but also because Alabamians took the social side of their politics very seriously.

By the 1820s, treating in Alabama included a variety of events, usually taking the form of political barbeques, spread over several weeks prior to Election Day. Candidates were no longer responsible for providing the food and drink on their own, but their financial assistance was necessary to help underwrite the festivities. Historian Daniel Dupre has cataloged northern Alabama's fondness for these political barbecues, noting that candidates for both state and national office "attended the events and subsidized the cost of food and drink, hoping to attract large crowds to hear their stump speeches and to persuade voters to support them at the polls."[17]

Political barbecues were a welcome diversion from the difficulties of frontier life in the Old Southwest. In addition to hearing from and mingling with the candidates, prospective voters could drink themselves sick, gamble themselves poor, and show off their dancing, fighting, foot-racing, marksmanship, and horsemanship skills.[18] They were held throughout the summer months (sometimes several in one week) prior to the August legislative elections, and local newspapers beckoned voters to each one with such eye-catching announcements as "barbecue of barbecues" and "whilst we live, we live."[19] One of the more tantalizing advertisements ran in the Huntsville *Democrat* in 1825, declaring that "a greater collection of people than has ever been seen at a barbecue in any of the southern states" would be present for the festivities.[20] To meet the demand, the ad promised that "there will not be less than ONE THOUSAND weight of meat put upon the pitt [*sic*] besides other necessities to give zest to the entertainment."[21] The best part, the ad went on to state (and the main draw for prospective voters), was that "All this will be like God's blessing, 'without money and without price.'"[22]

While understandably popular with most Alabamians, barbecues also became the target of increasing condemnation throughout the 1820s by those who questioned their political consequences. Writing under the fitting pen name "Barbecuensis," one impassioned critic complained that a candidate's fitness for office during that era was measured by a rather underwhelming standard: "The question now, is not . . . if he will enact wholesome laws and promote and preserve the peace, happiness and prosperity of the State, but if he will drink raw whiskey, eat rawer shoate, dance bare foot on a puncheon floor, . . . and pull at a gander's neck."[23]

It was within this lively electoral environment that John McKinley won his first public office. In August 1820, with the support of the Georgia Faction, McKinley was elected to represent Madison County in the state legislature. Even though he was a first-time officeholder, something of McKinley's reputation can be gleaned from the House of Representatives' journal, which recorded the official proceedings of that body when it convened at Cahaba later that year.[24] On November 6, the first day of the session, it was McKinley who offered the first resolutions in the House to elect a Speaker and a clerk.[25] The next day he and two other members were appointed to the committee that would draft the "rules of order and decorum for the government of the proceedings of th[e] House."[26]

Within a week he would be appointed to the Judiciary Committee (serving as chair), the Ways and Means Committee, and the Committee of Inland Navigation. Only two other members from the fifty delegates assembled served on as many standing committees. McKinley's other committee assignments included the Committee on Schools and Colleges and Schools and College Lands, the Committee on County Boundaries, and the curiously titled Committee on Roads, Bridges, Etc.[27] Throughout the session, he was also appointed to a number of select committees.

Other details recorded in the House journal reflect the breadth of his legislative activity during the thirty-nine-day session. Except for a one-week period when he neither spoke nor voted on any measure (and can thus be presumed to have been absent), McKinley was recognized at least once nearly every day of the session. He offered motions to permit the delegation from the newly created Jackson County to take their seats in the House, to draw up a petition to Congress seeking relief from the debt citizens of Madison and Limestone counties had incurred buying public land, to alter the Alabama circuit courts, to fix the compensation for members of the legislature, and to impose reporting requirements on county treasurers.

He also paid particular attention to issues that affected his own investments. In November 1820 he wrote to John Coffee to complain that the efforts of the men Coffee had sent to Cahaba to lobby for the selection of Florence as the seat of Lauderdale County had been ineffective. McKinley promised to guide the issue through the legislature himself and personally introduced the measure to establish Florence as the county seat. "All that can be done," he reminded Coffee, "shall be done for Florence."[28]

Throughout the record, it is clear that other members respected McKinley for his legal background, knowledge, leadership, and legislative skills, and several of the measures he introduced were passed. The only obvious defeat he suffered, interestingly enough, was his December 7 motion "that leave be given the citizens of Cahawba [*sic*] to have a party of pleasure in the hall of the House of Representatives."[29] His colleagues split their vote 24–24, which meant the measure failed.

Critics of the 1820 legislative session complained that its members had spent far too much time on matters of mostly local concern, such as the Cahaba "party of pleasure," that were designed "to secure the popularity of the individuals who introduced them" at the expense of more substantive statewide issues.[30] Perhaps the most significant failing of the legislature that session was its inability to discharge its constitutionally mandated responsibility to reapportion state legislative districts.

Alabama's Constitution of 1819 explicitly ordered that a census be conducted under the authority of the first General Assembly and charged the second session of the legislature with apportioning representation based on the results of that census. The House passed a bill to reapportion both chambers, but the Senate balked at the plan. For its part, the Senate passed a reapportionment scheme for House seats but failed to make any changes to its own districts. McKinley was appointed to the conference committee tasked with ironing out the differences. On December 20 he made a lengthy report to the House detailing the Senate's reluctance to agree to reapportionment.

McKinley informed his colleagues that the Senate's problem was not so much with reapportionment but with constitutional interpretation. The 1819 Constitution required that state senators be elected to three-year terms. Yet it also stated that after the first census was taken and for the purpose of creating staggered terms, senators were to be divided into three classes: the first group serving for one year, the second for two, and the third for three. The Senate, McKinley reported, could not agree to the portions of the House bill that created the staggered terms whereby some senators would serve less than their constitutionally mandated three-year term.[31] Unable to resolve the matter, the legislature adjourned the next day.

The following June, acting governor Thomas Bibb called the legislature back into special session with a terse reminder that, with respect to reapportionment, "both the letter and the spirit of the Constitution point to this conclusion, that the duty is obligatory and not to be dispensed with."[32] The House and Senate made considerable progress on separate bills but still could not agree upon a final plan that would apportion both houses. McKinley was appointed chairman of the conference committee overseeing the differences, but again, in his report to the House, noted the Senate's refusal to agree to any proposal in which incumbent senators served for less than three years.[33]

The matter was finally resolved the following year when both the House and Senate were successfully reapportioned. McKinley, however, was not in the legislature to help oversee the matter as he had done before. He was ineligible to retain his Madison County seat, having moved his family from Huntsville to Florence during the previous year.[34] Although he did not serve in the 1821 legislature, his name and reputation were still prominently discussed there. In a special joint session, for example, members of the House and Senate selected McKinley and eleven other men to serve on the first board of trustees for the University of Alabama.[35] Almost three years earlier, in the March 1819 act authorizing the citizens of Alabama to form a state government and adopt a state constitution, Congress had mandated that land be set aside for a "seminary of learning." The legislature formally designated the seminary as The University of the State of Alabama in 1820. The university itself would not begin operations until 1831, but the first trustees were commissioned with such responsibilities as recommending a site for the school, overseeing construction of buildings, selling land donated by Congress to benefit the university, and conferring degrees.[36]

McKinley's appointment as a university trustee reflected his own regard for education. In nearby Limestone County, for instance, he presented a tract of land to the citizens of Athens in 1822 on the condition that they "establish a suitable school house, employ a competent teacher, and establish a respectable Female Academy."[37] The gratified townspeople quickly went to work, and later that year, after purchasing an additional five acres of land, erected a building for the Athens Female Academy, which would later became Athens State University, the oldest institution of higher education in the state of Alabama.[38]

McKinley's move to Florence in 1821 coincided with the rapid growth of the young town. Unlike many other speculative ventures cultivated by the Alabama Fever, Florence actually took root. All of the Cypress trustees were interested in the area, but McKinley is purported to have purchased the greatest number of lots in the town, and he owned several properties on its outskirts.[39] Andrew Jackson also purchased several lots, established a plantation ten miles north of Florence, and visited the area regularly until the 1830s. Passing through the city in 1821, a visitor noted that just a few years removed from its founding, Florence already included a courthouse, two taverns, several commercial warehouses, and over a hundred homes and stores, with "[m]any large and elegant brick buildings already built," as well as a number of doctors and lawyers.[40] By 1826 northern newspapers would report that the town could boast of four thousand citizens as well as "numerous steam-boats and barges, in the trade between that place and New Orleans."[41]

McKinley's influence within Florence extended beyond the town's legal and economic circles. The Tennessee Valley was home to large numbers of Scotch-Irish Presbyterians, and Florence was no exception. In laying out the city, the trustees of the Cypress Land Company (who counted three Presbyterians among their number—John Coffee, James Jackson, and John McKinley) made provisions for at least one church lot. When the Florence land became available for sale in June 1818, the lot was purchased on behalf of the Presbyterians, and later that same year, the First Presbyterian Church of Florence was established. Although Methodists and Episcopalians would set up their own churches in subsequent years, First Presbyterian was the predominant church in the area.[42] McKinley was elected an elder at First Presbyterian in 1826, joining John Coffee and James Jackson in assuming leadership responsibilities for the growing church.[43] A decade later, when the church established itself as a corporate body, McKinley was the first of five men appointed to draw up articles of incorporation and a creed of faith for the church and to serve on its first board of trustees.[44]

In Florence, McKinley enjoyed his reputation as both city father and wealthy citizen and, according to a Boston newspaper, "practiced law with a high reputation." His stature there was noted by Anne Newport Royall in July 1821. Royall spent four years traveling throughout Alabama, recording her impressions of the young state and its leading citizens in letters to her lawyer, Matthew Dunbar.[45] Royall's account of McKinley, with whom she was clearly impressed, provides the earliest description of his personal characteristics and reputation in Alabama.

From Florence she informed Dunbar that the wealthiest men in the region included "General [John] Coffee, James Jackson, Esq., Major [John] McKinley, and Messrs. Simpson and Gaither."[46] The basis for Royall's reference to McKinley's military rank is unknown. State records indicate that he received a captain's commission in the Alabama state militia from the governor in October 1821.[47] He would subsequently be referred to as colonel, but the origin of that rank is also unknown.[48]

Royall gave special mention to McKinley's status and appearance: "Major McKinley lives in Florence, and is reputed to be the first lawyer in the three states. He is a stout, fine looking man; of easy manners, as all gentlemen are." She then went on to describe his home, declaring that "his dwelling contains more taste and splendor, by one half, than I ever saw in my whole life put together. . . . Every thing [sic] in the house had, to me, the appearance of enchantment. I never was in such a paradise before."[49] The McKinley home that so enamored Royall was reportedly a three-story, federal-style brick mansion located on a hill high above the Tennessee River. Together with the nearby and massive home of his sometimes law partner George Coulter (which can still be viewed today), the two mansions formed an impressive and imposing entrance into Florence when viewed from the river.[50]

Royall seemed especially taken by the McKinley children, Elizabeth, Andrew, and Mary, who prevailed on their nurse to let them enter the parlor to meet the female writer.[51] To Dunbar she exclaimed, "And the children! They are truly a pattern. . . . They were the handsomest children I ever beheld, and I was so completely fascinated by their manners, I forgot every thing [sic] else."[52]

Although Royall clearly admired McKinley and his children, she saved her highest praise for his wife, Julia: "Mrs. McKinley, the elegance of her manners, and the sweetness of her conversation, joined with her interesting children, completely disconcerted me. [She] looked as though she had dropped from above. I never was more confounded."[53] Julia informed Royall that she was originally from Philadelphia, but little else is known about her. Even in public records she is mentioned only rarely, for example, when she is listed along with John in a number of early Alabama land transactions releasing her dower rights to several parcels of land in Madison County.[54] On October 22, 1822, just fifteen months after Royall's visit, thirty-year-old Julianna Bryan McKinley died. She was buried on the family property in Florence in an elaborate crypt erected by her grieving husband.[55]

After Julia's death, and perhaps because of it, McKinley turned to a higher political prize than he had ever before sought. His reputation was now such that within just three years of his arrival in Alabama, he was

6. Julianna (Julia) Bryan McKinley.
Courtesy of the Collection of the
Supreme Court of the United States.

nominated to succeed John Williams Walker in the U.S. Senate. Walker
and William R. King had served as the state's first two senators upon admission to the Union in 1819, but Walker was unable to complete his term
because of chronic poor health and resigned his seat in late November
1822.[56] In his resignation letter to Governor Israel Pickens, Walker expressed his wish that "in the choice of a successor, the General Assembly
may fix on an individual, who, to equal zeal and devotion for the interests
of Alabama, may unite happier talents and more vigorous health."[57]

Almost immediately the Georgia Faction began to coalesce their support around John McKinley as the man possessing the requisite "equal zeal
and devotion" Walker desired. Governor Pickens, in conveying Walker's
resignation to the Alabama legislature that was already in session, expressed
his profound "regret that extreme ill health has been the cause of denying to the State, a longer continuance of [Walker's] services in that important station."[58] Regrets aside, however, Pickens was determined that the
Georgia Faction not replace Walker with one of its own.

Like many of the state's early politicians, Pickens himself had once been
affiliated with the Georgia Faction but had renounced his association with
the group just prior to running for governor in 1821. His subsequent defeat
of Georgia Faction–backed Henry H. Chambers in that contest spelled
the beginning of the end of the group's political power in Alabama poli-

tics. Coming as it did in the middle of the legislative session, Walker's resignation offered little time for Pickens and other opponents of the Georgia Faction to recruit a viable candidate for the Senate seat. They ultimately settled on Huntsville attorney William Kelly to fill the slot.

Observing the Senate race from afar was Andrew Jackson, who kept abreast of the election with the help of Sam Houston, then a newly elected member of the House of Representatives from Tennessee and a trusted confidante. In a letter to Jackson relating the details of the election, Houston noted the declining power of the Georgia Faction in Alabama and copied a long passage from an earlier letter sent to him by Anderson Hutchison (William Kelly's law partner) as evidence. Hutchison informed Houston that "[e]very possible plan had been laid, and every exertion made to have the representation prepared for Walker's resignation, so as to put in McKinley." The timing of Walker's announcement left little time for Kelly to travel to Cahaba to lobby for his nomination, but, Hutchison wrote, "he resolved to go down, and combat the matter, with the big man of the North. He got there three days before the day of election."[59]

In challenging the virtual certainty that McKinley (the "big man of the North") would be the next senator from Alabama, Kelly and his supporters were also consciously defying the power of the Georgia Faction. On December 12, 1822, the members of the Alabama Senate were invited to the hall of the House of Representatives where the legislature proceeded to select the successor to Senator John Williams Walker.[60] When all the votes were counted, John McKinley had lost by a single vote.[61]

McKinley's defeat prompted Baltimore's *Niles Weekly Register* to suggest that "the presidential election seems to have thrust itself into this matter."[62] Indeed it had, for Andrew Jackson's attention to Alabama politics generally—and McKinley's race in particular—stemmed from more than just political curiosity about the region or concern about an old acquaintance. Having already permitted his name to be put forward as a candidate for the upcoming presidential election in 1824, Jackson was quietly gauging his own support among Alabama's political elites.

In his letter to Jackson, Sam Houston noted the increasing hostility in the state toward the Georgia Faction and their patron, Treasury Secretary William Crawford, who also planned to run for president in 1824. He concluded that McKinley's loss could only be attributed to the fact that he "must have been for Crawford."[63] The implication was clear: McKinley's unexpected defeat meant the Georgia Faction's political grip on both the legislature and the state was loosening—a result that could only benefit

Jackson. As further evidence of his theory, Houston appended to his letter the following plea from a concerned citizen of Alabama: "Let me charge you, that if Old Hickory can't be President, to go for H[enry] Clay. At all events save us from <u>Crawford</u> and Georgia politics!"[64]

Jackson seemed unsure of exactly where McKinley stood politically. Writing about the Alabama election to Richard Call, a former aide during the Creek War, Jackson recounted the last-minute efforts to snatch the Senate seat and almost certain victory away from the Georgia Faction. "The plan to favor the views of the Secretary of the Treasury [Crawford] has failed," he wrote, "but it was a hard contest[.] [S]till I believe many votes were given for . . . McKinley by men not in support of the Secretary."[65] In other words, from Jackson's standpoint, the vote margin did not mean that Crawford was popular in the state. Rather, the close results could be attributed to the fact, as he later related to John Coffee, that "McKinley[,] who my friend at the city long since told me[,] was the most prominent man in allabama."[66] A vote for McKinley thus did not necessarily indicate support for Crawford.

Such a man would undoubtedly be a tremendous asset to his presidential campaign, but Jackson ultimately concluded that despite their previous business relationship, McKinley could not be relied upon politically. After Coffee expressed his concerns about James Jackson's support of McKinley in the Senate race, the fiercely loyal Andrew Jackson responded, "I have noted your remark with respect to our mutual friend. . . . [R]est assured I have, nor never had such a suspicion. . . . The friendship of James Jackson I could never doubt—he has no duplicity, but he has been deceived by McKinley."[67] Within a few years, however, Jackson would reconsider his comments about both men, becoming bitterly estranged from James Jackson and finding McKinley to be one of his most trusted political allies.

After the election, McKinley turned his attention back to his busy law practice and his considerable property holdings throughout northern Alabama. He continued to be active in civic affairs and was appointed, along with two others, to take up the fifty-dollar stock subscriptions in Florence after the state legislature authorized the creation of a company to clear the obstacles in the Tennessee River to make it navigable.[68] He also set out to find a mother for his three children.[69]

Two years later newspapers would report the February 26, 1824, marriage of forty-three-year-old "Col. John M'Kinley, of Florence, to Miss Elizabeth Armstead [sic], of Huntsville."[70] Twenty years his junior, Elizabeth Armistead was from a prominent family in Loudon County, Virginia, and cousin to John Tyler, who would later become the tenth president of the United States.[71] She bore McKinley no children but raised his son and two daughters (all of whom were under the age of nine at the time of their marriage) as her own as his business and political responsibilities kept him away from home for extended periods. She outlived McKinley by four decades, dying in 1891.[72]

The McKinleys left Florence for Huntsville in February 1825, moving into what is now known as the Howard Weeden House because it later became home to the southern poet and artist Maria Howard Weeden. Built in 1819 by Henry C. Bradford, it is listed on the National Register of Historic Places and is reportedly the oldest building in Alabama open to the public. It is also the only surviving house in which McKinley is known to have lived.[73]

In Huntsville, McKinley entered into a legal partnership with Arthur F. Hopkins, who was a well-known figure in northern Alabama, having served as Madison County's delegate to Alabama's statehood convention when he was just twenty-five years old.[74] He was also a prominent attorney who had previously squared off against McKinley in arguments before the Alabama Supreme Court and would later join that body as chief justice.[75] Their legal partnership may have originated in a mutual respect for Henry Clay, but it clearly was not dependent upon that alone. Indeed, the partnership persisted long after McKinley embraced Jacksonian principles and politics and Hopkins had become the recognized leader of Alabama Whigs, and ended only after Hopkins was elevated to the Alabama Supreme Court in 1836.[76] After leaving the bench, Hopkins represented McKinley in several legal disputes as late as 1848.[77]

Their practice extended to the county courts in Lawrence and Limestone counties, the circuit courts that covered Franklin, Lauderdale, Lawrence, and Limestone counties, and the Alabama Supreme Court. Such a partnership served many purposes, not the least of which was the facilitation of work during the time circuit court was in session. With one attorney riding circuit, the other could attend to matters closer to home. Reflecting on the legal profession in northern Alabama, James E. Saunders, another associate of McKinley's, recalled the exciting opportunities that existed during the early statehood period. "This was a favorable time for lawyers of genius and learning to rise rapidly from the ranks of their profession," he wrote, "for the construction of the statutes had been pronounced in but few cases by the court of last resort; and so there was a broad field for the exercise of the highest order of ability."[78]

That McKinley was numbered among those who practiced with the "highest order of ability" in the state might be inferred by his lucrative law practice or general references to his reputation. However, a far more explicit description of his standing was offered by Huntsville's James G. Birney in February 1826. During the previous year, rumors had circulated that Congress was about to extend the federal circuit court system to the Old Southwest. Believing that Tennessee and Alabama would be placed together in a new judicial circuit, Birney wrote to Secretary of State Henry Clay hoping to convince him that an Alabamian deserved to sit among the circuit judges who would be appointed.

Birney had lived in Alabama since 1818 but was a native of Kentucky and a friend to both Clay and McKinley. He had been a key political ally in Clay's early congressional campaigns and had become acquainted with McKinley when both were lawyers in Frankfort.[79] As a well-respected and enormously successful attorney, Birney probably deserved the appointment himself, but he recommended McKinley instead. In so doing, he offered the single best contemporary description of McKinley's legal abilities and reputation. To Henry Clay he wrote,

> My object, sir, in addressing to you this letter, is, to bring to your consideration the just and meritorious pretensions of a warm and undeviating friend of yours, Col. John McKinley, of this town [Huntsville]. An industrious and extensive practice of several years, since his removal to this Country, has added rich stores of legal science and information to a mind, with whose nature force and energy and susceptibility of high improvement, you are as well acquainted as I am, and, no doubt, better able to judge. The <u>Bar,</u> at this place, has the character of the best in our State.... At the head of this, he stands, I am free to say, without a rival in legal attainment:—In the Supreme Court of this State, which attracts to its bar our best abilities, he occupies the same pre-eminence, and between him and the <u>next</u> there is a long interval.
>
> ... And, I do believe, from the high estimation of Col. McKinley's character as a man of blameless reputation, of spotless honor, and high qualifications, that no one could be more acceptable to the community, generally, than he....
>
> ... I write this letter, sir, not knowing that it will have any, the least, weight in your consideration.... I have for [McKinley] a high

regard, it is true—but were he my bitterest enemy, I should say for him what I <u>have</u> said.[80]

The rumored circuit court extension did not materialize at that time, thus rendering Birney's recommendation moot. However, his appeal to Henry Clay on behalf of McKinley as his "warm and undeviating friend" highlighted a personal relationship that grew increasingly problematic for McKinley as he was drawn back into electoral politics.

During the latter half of 1826, McKinley's name was again put forward as a candidate for the U.S. Senate to serve out the remaining term of Senator Henry H. Chambers, who had died in office.[81] Despite the narrowest of defeats in 1822, his prospects for winning the vacant Senate seat in 1826 were seriously threatened by the combination of two powerful forces arrayed against him. The first, on the state level, was his past association with the Georgia Faction at a time when the public mood toward that group had soured. The second and perhaps even greater force that McKinley encountered was purely national in nature. He found himself in the politically untenable position as a friend of Henry Clay's in a state where Andrew Jackson enjoyed overwhelming support. Both of these forces had been present independently during McKinley's earlier bid for the Senate, but together they created a political sensation four years later.

Much of the acrimony of the 1826 Senate race can be traced to the business practices of the Planters' and Merchants' Bank in Huntsville. Predating Alabama itself, the bank was chartered in 1816 by the Mississippi territorial legislature at the prodding of members of the Georgia Faction who were serving in the legislature at that time. With LeRoy Pope as its president and other members of the Georgia Faction as directors, the bank played a key role in fueling the Alabama Fever by extending both currency and credit to those caught up in the land boom.[82] The bank's influence extended far beyond Huntsville, however, as its notes served as the primary currency for all of northern Alabama. John McKinley was not only personally close to many of the bank's principals, he also served as legal counsel to the bank through his private practice.[83]

When the Panic of 1819 brought a sudden end to the Alabama Fever, credit tightened and the paper money with which the bank had allowed debts to be paid was withdrawn, creating great tension between bank officials and members of the community who owed them money. The Georgia Faction and the bank came under additional harsh criticism for having successfully pushed a bill through the 1818 territorial legislature that removed the 6 percent interest limit that could be charged on private loans. The law was repealed the following year, but "in the meantime, numerous contracts had been made under its provisions and the interest called for ranged from 60 to 240 percent a year."[84] In one well-reported case, a loan for $4,440 resulted in one year's interest of more than $10,000.[85] To make matters worse, and following the lead of several Tennessee banks, the Planters' and Merchants' Bank suspended specie payments altogether during the summer of 1820, leaving the despairing region with little more than the rapidly depreciating currency then in use to conduct its business affairs.[86]

As mentioned earlier, the impact of the Panic of 1819 and the resulting economic depression were felt nationwide but were particularly acute for landowners in Alabama whose dreams of easy wealth conjured up by the Alabama Fever had given way to the realities of excessive land debt. It is no exaggeration to say that the entire state of Alabama was affected. When credit sales for land were abolished in 1820, purchasers of public lands nationwide owed the federal government more than $22 million; Alabama land debt alone accounted for half of this amount.[87]

As northern Alabamians strained to meet the terms of their land loans, they became increasingly wary of and even hostile toward the Planters' and Merchants' Bank. There was a growing feeling among the non-planter class that the bank was responsible for their struggles and had profited at their expense. The first political manifestation of this sentiment was the gubernatorial election of 1821 that pitted Israel Pickens against the Georgia Faction's Henry Chambers. For most voters, the election was really a referendum on banking, and Alabamians elected Pickens largely because of his support for a state-chartered bank to guard against the abuses associated with the Planters' and Merchants' Bank.

The public hostility that boosted Pickens was nursed by the *Democrat,* a Huntsville newspaper that set itself up as the voice of the common man. In an editorial written shortly after its founding, the paper fumed, "[The people know] that this Bank [has] been in the hands of a pack of shavers and extortioners, who have grown fat by grinding the face of the poor, and would have multiplied their oppressions ten fold [*sic*], but for the virtue of a few, who have fought a good fight."[88]

Andrew Wills, the editor of the *Democrat,* used his newspaper to identify both those who had "fought a good fight" against the bank and those who had not. He targeted prominent northern Alabama legislators, boasting that he could prove that they "belonged to the Huntsville party [or Georgia Faction]."[89] His damning claims were taken seriously. Indeed, so poisonous had any perceived relationship with the Huntsville bank or the Georgia Faction come to be viewed that those so designated by the paper scrambled to demonstrate their "common man" credentials.

The power of the *Democrat* and similar newspapers arose from a new spirit of democracy that permeated the South and impacted both candidates and their electioneering practices. As historian Robert J. Dinkin has noted, "[Most candidates] adapted their approach to fit the new democratic age. This was best accomplished by identifying oneself with the 'common man' and claiming to be the 'candidate of the people.'"[90] Governor Pickens's election in 1821 (after he abandoned the Georgia Faction) and reelection in 1823 provided convincing evidence of the value of this approach. Of course, if appealing to the "common man" was the ticket to electoral victory, it naturally followed that candidates would characterize their opponents as aristocratic and out of touch with the voters. According to Dinkin, "It [thus] became standard procedure to attack a rival's wealth and extravagant life-style."[91]

With the avowed purpose to use the power of the press to destroy the Huntsville bank and everything (and everyone) associated with it, the *Democrat* made constant reference to the members of the Georgia Faction as "aristocrats," "the Royal Party," and "oppressors of the poor."[92] It filled its pages "with images of manipulation and secrecy" in arguing that the Georgians, their wealthy associates, and the bank were all part of a conspiracy to defraud the common laborer and farmer.[93] In so doing, as southern historian J. Mills Thornton III has observed, the *Democrat* defined, and to some extent inflated, the power of its enemy. "What was the 'royal party' which had created the structure of all future political activity?" he asked. "We might answer, and not without some superficial validity, that it was nothing—a figment of the demented imagination of [the editors] at the *Democrat*."[94]

Yet even as its political power waned in the aftermath of Pickens's gubernatorial victories, the Georgia Faction continued to serve as a convenient foil to the interests of common Alabamians and the men who sought to govern them. "The royal party was real," Thornton continued, "as real as an irrational hatred or an unnamed fear. It was the embodiment of all the insecurity of small farmers in the midst of plantations, of the poor in the midst of plenty."⁹⁵ As one who had clearly benefited politically from his association with the Georgia Faction, McKinley thus found himself the object of intense public scrutiny when he stood for election in 1826.

As if his previous ties to the Georgia Faction were not problem enough, the 1826 Senate race also forced McKinley to grapple with his relationship with Henry Clay. Politically speaking, Clay was everything that McKinley was not. Just three years older than McKinley, Clay had already been elected to the Kentucky legislature, served twice as the Speaker of the U.S. House of Representatives, and completed two unexpired terms in the U.S. Senate—all by the time McKinley moved to Alabama. McKinley's Federalist leanings in Kentucky naturally deprived him of any real political association with Clay, but the two were more than just acquaintances, having faced off against each other in Kentucky courtrooms and sharing many common friends in Lexington. McKinley took a great interest in the meteoric political rise of his fellow Kentuckian, and in his subsequent correspondence to Clay never failed to close his letters with "Your friend, J. McKinley."⁹⁶

McKinley was an early supporter of Clay's presidential ambitions during the historic election of 1824 that pitted Clay against John Quincy Adams, Secretary of the Treasury William Crawford, and Andrew Jackson, all of whom enjoyed some support in Alabama. McKinley might have just as easily supported Crawford, the patron of the Georgia Faction in Alabama, or Jackson, who was enormously popular throughout the Deep South. Instead, he initially offered what appeared to be unequivocal support for Clay.

Responding to an earlier inquiry from Clay, McKinley frankly acknowledged in June 1823 that Jackson's presidential prospects had already generated considerable political enthusiasm in Alabama and that "[t]he contagion" of support was spreading through the efforts of Jackson's powerful friends in the state (and McKinley's fellow Cypress Land Company trustees), General John Coffee and James Jackson.⁹⁷ He then explained the challenges that lay ahead for Clay's supporters in Alabama: "Your friends here have at present a difficult part to play. . . . [W]e have deemed it bad policy to give the slightest offence to [Jackson's] friends in general as it will be very easy to turn the large majority of the people in your favour when he is out of view." McKinley knew, however, that it would hardly be easy to win further support in Alabama for Clay. As he went on to acknowledge, "[Jackson] and his warm partizans are . . . inimical both to you and

Mr. Crawford and will prefer Mr. Adams next to him. . . . From this data you may infer what your prospects are."[98]

McKinley's analysis confirmed a frustrating reality for Clay: in the four-man race for the presidency, he would be lucky to finish third in Alabama. McKinley cautioned Clay not to let this frustration spill over into the campaign, recommending that "the violence and bitterness of some of the General's friends . . . be met with temperance . . . but firmness by you and your friends." He concluded his letter by promising Clay, "As far as my little influence will go it will be exerted in your favor."[99]

However slim Clay's chances in Alabama may have been that June, his prospects had apparently dimmed even further by the time McKinley wrote to him again the following September. "Candour requires that I should state to you that at present General Jackson would get a large majority of the people of this state," he informed Clay. He sought to reassure Clay that among the state's elite, he still enjoyed wide support—at least privately. "[M]any and perhaps a majority of the most intelligent are strongly your friends," McKinley reminded him, "yet such is the influence of public opinion many of them conceal or abstain from an expression of their preference."[100] That group, curiously enough, may have also included McKinley.

One of the most interesting things about McKinley's September letter is the air of secrecy that it introduced. He begged Clay to keep their correspondence confidential so that he might, as he put it, "be the better able to <u>act and counteract</u> in the darkness which is likely to pervade future operations."[101] Looking out for Clay's best interests albeit out of public view may or may not have been McKinley's intent, but for a man who desired a future in Alabama politics, his caution was understandable. The historic bitterness between Clay and Jackson had increased considerably in the years since Clay's failure in 1819 to persuade his House colleagues to censure Jackson for seizing Pensacola, the capital of Spanish Florida, and executing two British citizens there. As tensions between the two (and their supporters) increased during the 1824 presidential campaign, so too did Jackson's popularity, particularly in the western parts of the United States. There were pockets of Clay support throughout Alabama, but, as McKinley noted in his letter, the state belonged to Jackson.

Andrew Jackson would go on to receive more popular votes than any other candidate in the 1824 presidential election (taking nearly 70 percent of the Alabama vote), but none of the four men who ran for the presidency that year received a majority of the electoral vote. In such instances, the Constitution provides that the election be determined by the House of Representatives, which subsequently selected John Quincy Adams. When Adams quickly nominated Henry Clay, then Speaker of the House, to be his secretary of state, charges of a "corrupt bargain" between the two were immediately leveled by Jackson's supporters. In Alabama, as in other parts of the country, there was a sense that Clay's influence in the House had robbed Jackson of the presidency in 1824. That embittered feeling had not yet subsided when McKinley was nominated for the vacant Senate seat two years later.

Despite having been closely identified with both the Georgia Faction and Henry Clay, McKinley entered the 1826 Senate race with some electoral advantages. As historian Albert Moore has observed, McKinley "had the benefit of an organizational backing which he had secured in his former [Senate] race and the psychological advantage of having been defeated by only one vote."[102] In addition, because he had not held elected office since 1821, McKinley was well positioned to take advantage of the political shift that had taken place within the state during the intervening five years.

While common Alabamians had long been disgruntled with the self-serving activities of the Georgia Faction, they had little recourse so long as the latter retained its political and economic domination in the state. The candidacy and ideals of Andrew Jackson, however, galvanized the opposition of the common man. Jackson's victory in all but three counties in the state in the 1824 presidential election made it clear that, at least in Alabama, it was as "dangerous as it was futile for leaders to raise their voices against him."[103] Rather than "raise his voice" against Jackson, McKinley did what many a politically pragmatic man formerly associated with the Georgia Faction had already done: he joined Jackson. In so doing, McKinley subjected himself to withering and extended criticism.

Of the little ink that has been spilled on John McKinley's life, much has been devoted to disparaging his transformation from a Federalist into a Jacksonian Democrat. Indeed, in 1850, two years before he died and long after he had abandoned electoral politics, a Boston newspaper would still cynically declare that "John McKinley trimmed his sail to the popular breeze; rendered himself useful to all parties, and was elevated to the Supreme Court of the United States."[104]

There are no extant accounts from McKinley explaining his decision to support Andrew Jackson. Viewing his switch against the backdrop of modern American politics where political party ideologies are reliably rigid and party-switching politicians are a rarity, McKinley's embrace of Jacksonian principles does indeed appear to be opportunistic and self-serving. However, such a view, commonly held by his modern critics, fails to take into account three political realities of that time: the relationship that already existed between McKinley and Jackson, the electoral reality of party politics in Alabama in the 1820s, and the generally fluid nature of partisan loyalties at both the state and national level. Each of these is considered in turn.

First, McKinley's relationship with Andrew Jackson extended beyond their mutual interest in the commercial success of the Cypress Land Company. As mentioned earlier, Jackson paid close attention to his northern Alabama land and took an active role in overseeing his property there including his significant investment in Florence. He made frequent trips to Florence to check on his business ventures and was often feted at public dinners and celebrations.[105] Given McKinley's status, it is hard to conceive of him not participating in such events and further strengthening the bond between the two. The general also utilized McKinley's professional skills to resolve several legal matters in Alabama including an 1821 dispute involving the Madison County estate of one of Jackson's nephews.[106] In short, by 1826, the relationship between the two men was established enough to convince Jackson to take an active role in McKinley's bid for the Senate despite earlier misgivings about his politics.

Second, with the demise of the First Party System, politicians throughout the country had to determine how best to transition themselves from the policies and parties of Hamilton and Jefferson to the popular if polarizing figure of Andrew Jackson. The first politicians in Alabama coalesced into separate and rival factions based on regional, familial, and financial connections, but, as mentioned earlier, they were all ostensibly Democratic-Republicans by party because there was not yet any viable alternative. The 1821 gubernatorial election was the first major challenge to the established political order in Alabama, followed quickly by the rapid political ascent of Andrew Jackson. The combination of the two gutted the Georgia Faction to the extent that by 1823, as J. Mills Thornton has noted, "there was no longer any organized effort by [this group] to extend existing social and economical power into the political sphere."[107]

The charge of political opportunism so frequently leveled at McKinley is thus unwarranted because the Georgia Faction essentially ceased to exist as a political group. Sooner or later, McKinley would have to ally himself with another political organization, just as many other notable Alabama politicians had done who previously supported the Georgia Faction, including Henry Chambers, Clement C. Clay, and Israel Pickens.[108] As historian Frank Otto Gatell gently put it, "[S]teady adherence to professed principles was *not* the hallmark of Alabama politics" in these early years.[109]

Third and perhaps just as important was the fact that the political transformations then taking place in Alabama were also occurring on the national level. Two of the most prominent examples among McKinley's contemporaries in national politics were John Quincy Adams and Henry Clay. In the course of thirty years, Adams was elected to the U.S. Senate as a Federalist from Massachusetts, successfully ran for the presidency as a Democratic-Republican, and later served in the House of Representatives as a member of the Whig Party.[110] In addition to his service in the House and Senate, Henry Clay ran for president three times: in 1824 as a Democratic-Republican, in 1832 as the leader of the anti-Jackson party known as the National Republicans, and in 1844 as a member of the Whig Party. In short, during this era there was absolutely nothing unique about even seismic shifts in political allegiances.

The swiftness with which McKinley converted to Jackson's cause, however, is noteworthy. Throughout most of 1826, McKinley appeared to be a steadfast supporter of both Clay and the Adams administration, whose every action was vilified by Jackson's followers. In a January 1826 letter to Clay, for example, McKinley predicted that there would yet be "[m]any insidious attacks upon the [Adams] administration" but opined that "firmness in the course commenced will soon disarm all but unprincipled opposition."[111] His concern may have been less for John Quincy Adams than for himself, however. In the same letter, McKinley engaged in what appears to be a thinly veiled attempt at lobbying Clay by inquiring of his old friend whether there was any truth to the rumor that Congress would soon extend the federal circuit court system to Alabama.[112] Six weeks later, James G. Birney wrote Clay with the recommendation noted earlier, which was followed just a few days later by another recommendation of McKinley to Clay by former South Carolina senator William Smith.[113]

Although he was unable to secure a judicial appointment, Clay continued to take an interest in McKinley's 1826 Senate race. In an exchange of letters with Birney later that year, Clay wrote, "I should be highly gratified to hear of the election of Mr. McKinley to the Senate, of which you say there exists a probability. The Administration would expect from him a candid consideration and an impartial judgment of public measures."[114]

Alabamians who supported Jackson, however, were not about to send anyone to Congress who would entertain "a candid consideration and an impartial judgment" of the Adams agenda. Sensing this, McKinley queried Jackson's advisers in Alabama and quietly suggested "that some concert should take place . . . among Gen Jackson's friends . . . to determine whether they will support Judge [Richard] Ellis or myself" in the race against the popular Clement C. Clay for the Senate seat.[115]

Like many other Alabama politicians, Clement C. Clay had previously been identified with the Georgia Faction, having been elected to the territorial legislature with its support.[116] He had also worked closely with McKinley while serving as a director of the despised Planters' and Merchants' Bank. He left politics to serve on the Alabama Supreme Court, from which he later resigned to resume his legal practice. By the time he reemerged as a political candidate for office, Clay had transformed himself into a champion of the people, coming out against the Adams administration and in support of Andrew Jackson. The result was that Clay, Ellis, and McKinley *all* professed their support for Jackson with varying degrees of credibility. Jackson himself was hard-pressed to know which candidate would best reflect his interests but seems to have rejected Ellis early on. Of the remaining two, he would later state simply, "[M]y friends, it appears, had not as much confidence in his [Clay's] avowals, as they had in McK[inley]."[117]

With his blessing, Jackson's supporters in the Alabama legislature quickly threw their support behind McKinley as did, curiously enough, the Huntsville *Democrat*—the same newspaper that had previously castigated McKinley and others for their ties to the Georgia Faction. The *Democrat* not only endorsed his 1826 bid for the Senate, it also pronounced McKinley a man of the people. It was a stunning reversal of opinion that was not lost on McKinley's critics.

During the fall of 1826, a competing Huntsville newspaper, the *Southern Advocate*, ran a list of names, including McKinley's, that were rumored to be candidates for the Senate seat. At that time, the paper stated, "We shall neither advocate nor oppose the pretensions of any of them. They have all filled stations of public trust, and all have acted a conspicuous part in the politics of the State."[118] A month later, however, it began to take the *Democrat* and its Jacksonian sponsors to task for their sudden show of support for McKinley.

In a series of stinging editorials, it reminded Alabamians that McKinley's politics from his days in Kentucky until the present election had never been in question and had never been in accord with that of the common man. The newspaper recalled with wonderment, "Was he a Republican in Kentucky, up to 1819, when he left that state for Alabama—and, was he so treated and considered by these new allies of his up to 1825?"[119] It reminded its readers that during the 1822 Senate campaign, William Kelly's supporters had charged that McKinley "was, and always had been a federalist."[120] "By what wonderful magic," it went on to query, "have [McKinley's] principles been changed?"[121]

The newspaper answered its own question. McKinley had not changed; it was his newfound supporters who had transformed from being "tooth and nail against Col. McKinley in 1822" to being now willing to renounce their previous perceptions and statements. "Col. McKinley is the same man now he was in 1822," the paper declared, "and . . . [either] the party who opposed him then, and charged him with being a Federalist, a usurer, etc. knew that those charges were false . . . [or a] charge which would damn a man in 1822, is a passport to office in 1826."[122]

Referring to McKinley's ties to the Huntsville bank and the detested state law that lifted interest limits on personal loans, the newspaper went on to bitterly question, "In the name of common sense, what exempts Col. McKinley from the odious name of usurer? Will his partisans deny that he loaned money at a rate of interest as high as 4 percent, a month—that he contracted for, and remorselessly exacted his 'pound of flesh?'" The writer concluded his attack on McKinley with one final, withering shot: "But I forget, he is no longer a federalist—he is no longer one of the royal party or Bank junto—he is no longer a usurer, because he has received the pardoning touch. . . . [H]e may now arise and go his way, his sins are forgiven him."[123]

The repeated references to usury were designed to highlight the fact that McKinley's firm had defended several principals associated with the Huntsville bank, as well as several other lenders, against the claims of debtors in a series of cases arising from the despised usury law. Of course, his detractors in the press conveniently made little reference to the fact that Clement Clay, their preferred candidate, had also represented the bank's interests. Indeed, even as they competed for the Senate seat, McKinley and Clay served together as co-counsel before the Alabama Supreme Court arguing that debtors could not recover interest already paid under the repealed law.[124]

The repeated accusations forced McKinley to publicly explain the political change he had undergone between his two Senate elections. Writing in the *Democrat*, McKinley claimed to have little more than a casual knowledge of the Georgia Faction: "I know nothing of the Royal party or its policy, further than I have seen the subject discussed in the newspapers, and as far as comprehended by that discussion, I have no personal or political interest in it. I had been a citizen of this state about a year before I ever heard of the existence of a party in it."[125] Although this sounds disingenuous, it was probably true. The Georgia Faction was referred to as such only by its critics. As mentioned previously, it was not even a political party per se as much as a group of like-minded men with a common socioeconomic background who used politics to protect their financial investments.

McKinley continued, "I was then informed by a friend, if I supported a particular individual for Governor, I would be considered as belonging to the <u>Georgia</u> party. What was meant by this party, I did not know, nor could my friend inform me as he was equally a stranger to its meaning or object." When the issue came to a head in his 1822 Senate race, McKinley admitted that being accused of belonging to the Georgia Faction hurt his candidacy, and he was distressed to learn that "I had no mode of denying that I belonged to any party, which was the fact."[126]

However indistinct his relationship with the Georgia Faction may have been, there was no way to obscure that fact that he had provided legal services for the hated Huntsville bank. He acknowledged this in another public letter but protested against those who thought that professional relationship should somehow disqualify him from office. McKinley wrote, "Although I have been selected by these people, as the organ of their legal right, many of them are <u>violently</u> opposed to me, as the organ of their political rights." He freely admitted the prerogative of the bank officials who retained him as counsel to oppose him as a politician and hoped that voters would allow him to make a similar distinction "between advocating a right derived, under a law, and the policy of that law, and the abuse of the power given by it." McKinley concluded by expressing his wish that "if this honorable trust is confided to me, I hope to convince even those who are most opposed to me, that my best efforts will be faithfully exerted for the good of my country."[127]

The *Democrat* gave its blessing to McKinley's statement renouncing the Georgia Faction and reminded its readers what that decision meant for McKinley personally. It attributed his previous electoral defeats to his association with the Georgia Faction, for "[w]hile their <u>pestilential</u> friendship fell upon Col. McKinley, he was <u>beaten</u> for the Bench, and for the

Senate, in spite of every exertion they could make in his favor." But once free of that connection, "his commanding qualifications were promptly rewarded by the confidence of this country."[128]

The newspaper also argued that McKinley's independence from the Georgia Faction boded well for Alabama as "[h]is talents may [now] be used for the good of the public; and not as heretofore excluded from service by the withering influence of party friendship. Powerful as his own strength always was, so long as he had to carry such a load of _riders_, he was weighed down."[129]

McKinley was also forced to issue public statements regarding his relationship with Henry Clay. In an account that was published in papers around the country, he admitted that Clay had been his first choice for president in the 1824 contest. "[B]ut I would not now support him," he went on to say, "knowing the people of this State to be decidedly opposed to him. I will therefore, if elected, to the Senate of the United States, _give Gen. Jackson my decided support._"[130]

McKinley made it clear, however, that he would also back non-Jackson initiatives such as a reduction in the patronage power of the president and internal improvements, such as those propounded by Clay, as a means of increasing national prosperity. With regard to Clay and the Adams administration generally, McKinley pledged that as a senator he would not "oppose their measures, without regard to their merits. . . . [To do so] would be more an opposition to the government than the administration of it. Such an opposition would, in my opinion, be unprincipled."[131]

McKinley's statement was praised as far north as Rhode Island where a Providence newspaper that supported the Adams administration declared, "The sentiments expressed by Mr. McKinley are so free and independent, and so consonant with the feelings of every upright mind, that we cannot refrain from recording them." It praised his willingness to work with the administration on measures important to the country as a whole while still attempting to obey the will of his constituents in Alabama. McKinley, it concluded, "is just such a man as the opposition ought to have at their head; a man that the Administration would not fear."[132]

Hailed in some circles, McKinley was condemned in others. McKinley's public repudiation of the Georgia Faction infuriated those who were still affiliated with the dwindling group. Writing after the election, the *Democrat* recalled, "This was the signal for his destruction; the blood hounds were then let slip, and he was to be hunted down, whatever it might cost." For several months his former political allies hatched schemes in which "[c]ouriers were dispatched, letters were written, and caucuses were held . . . to form a plan of operations for Col. McKinley's defeat. He was abused in the grossest manner, by some of the most notable Royalists in the State."[133]

On November 27, 1826, after all of McKinley's public renunciations and the many public and private efforts to disparage him, the members of the Alabama Senate entered the House of Representatives to select the candidate who would fill the unexpired term of Senator Chambers. When the final votes were tallied, McKinley emerged victorious over Clement Clay by a narrow 41–38 margin.[134]

In Huntsville, the *Democrat* proudly proclaimed, "Alabama could not have selected for the Senate of the United States an abler, a more faithful and an honester [*sic*] man than John McKinley. Give him an opportunity, and he will prove himself worthy of this character."[135] A Tuscumbia, Alabama, newspaper added, "From Mr. McKinley's well known talent and integrity, not a doubt rests on our mind of his rendering ample satisfaction to his constituents."[136]

McKinley left immediately for Washington to attend the second session of the Nineteenth Congress, which was already under way, taking his seat on December 21, 1826.[137] A day earlier, the *U.S. Telegraph and Commercial Herald* in Washington had touted the arrival of the Senate's newest member: "John McKinley, Esq. has been elected to supply the vacancy occasioned . . . by the death of Mr. Chambers, of Alabama. Mr. McKinley . . . is a gentleman of the first order of talents, and will, no doubt, prove an able and faithful Senator."[138]

5
Prelude to the Court
Jacksonian Devotion in Alabama and Washington

> Mr. McKinley, from [Alabama], is not duly appreciated until he is known. He bears examination well, and the better you understand his character, the better you like him.   .
> —*Baltimore Patriot*, 1830

The 1826 midterm elections saw Jacksonian Democrats increase their numbers in both houses of Congress, although they made only slim gains in the Senate. McKinley's election to that body was thus closely scrutinized by supporters of Andrew Jackson and the Adams administration as his published comments in Alabama suggested that he would work with both sides. Two days after McKinley arrived in Washington, D.C., Secretary of State Henry Clay expressed his view that the administration would benefit from the election of his old friend. "Mr. McKinley," he confidently wrote to Francis Brook, "the new Senator lately elected in Alabama, is believed to have brought with him good dispositions towards the Administration."[1]

Andrew Jackson, however, offered a very different interpretation of the election results in Alabama. As he stated bluntly in a letter to Representative Sam Houston, "Major McKinley has been elected by my political friends, and I hope he may notise [*sic*] their expectations. The major will be with you shortly, and you can soon Judge whether the confidence of the people is well founded or not."[2] Then with a nod to his political nemesis, he added, "[Henry] Clay will endeavor to wield him to his views, but I cannot believe he will succeed."[3]

Houston held his response until after McKinley's arrival in Washington, at which point he reassured Jackson that, after meeting with the new Alabama senator, "[Y]our friends here deem him—a good, and <u>true</u> man for the country! So far as I can judge, I woud [*sic*] say so too."[4]

McKinley was probably unaware of the extent to which both parties were quietly gauging his political loyalty, but he could not help notice when the same questions were asked publicly. On New Year's Day, 1827, for example, and in response to inquiries regarding McKinley's allegiance to Jackson, the *U.S. Telegraph and Commercial Herald* in Washington proclaimed, "[N]either the friends of Gen. Jackson, nor the State of Alabama, has any cause to regret the election of Mr. McKinley. . . . From our personal knowledge of his character, we are surprised to hear that such doubts exist."[5] After praising him further, the paper offered a mild warning to McKinley to consider the costs of reestablishing his political ties with Clay. Then, for the benefit of its readers who still questioned his loyalties, it concluded, "Mr. McKinley has too much respect for himself, as well as for the dignity of the station to which he has been elected, to become a factious partisan."[6]

McKinley was an active participant in the Nineteenth Congress, although there were just three months remaining in its second session by the time he arrived in Washington. His activities in the Senate consisted mostly of constituent services, such as seeking congressional assistance for individual land claims and Revolutionary War pensions. He also presented a request from the Alabama legislature for a grant of federal land to establish a school near Florence, as well as a resolution from the city of Florence seeking congressional support for a proposed road through Alabama, Kentucky, and Tennessee to connect with the National Turnpike in Ohio.

He demonstrated an appreciation for both American commerce and security by voting in favor of bills to improve trade relations with Britain and to establish the United States Naval Academy (which failed to pass the Senate at that time). In a motion that would eventually presage his own judicial career, he presented a resolution from the Alabama legislature pleading for an extension of the federal judiciary to the Deep South.[7] His voting record during this session, incidentally, closely mirrored that of John Rowan, his legal mentor and former law partner, who now represented Kentucky in the Senate.

Notwithstanding the broad variety of issues that he addressed during his first term in Congress, McKinley's overall Senate career was characterized by an almost exclusive focus on the issue of public land. Indeed, just a week after being sworn into office as Alabama's newest senator, he received his first committee assignment as one of the first five members of the newly created Senate Committee on Private Land Claims.[8] His floor statements relative to public land generally fell into one of three categories: promoting debt relief for purchasers of public land, making public lands more affordable, and the right of the states to control the public land within their borders.

On January 9, 1827, during consideration of a public lands bill, Senator John McKinley rose to speak for the first time on the Senate floor. It was a rather inauspicious debut. The *Register of Debates in Congress*, the official congressional record between 1824 and 1837, noted that while McKinley "was upon the floor, he could not forbear saying that his ill health, and the circumstance of his being a new member, had determined him not to enter upon the discussion of any subject at present, if he could avoid it with propriety."[9] Far from making a substantive statement, he merely requested that full debate on the public land measure be postponed to a later date.

McKinley's focus on public land and the accompanying issue of debt relief helped him quickly assuage any misgivings his critics at home may have had about the ability of a former member of the Georgia Faction to protect the interests of the common man. During debate on the Bankruptcy Bill of 1827, for example, McKinley demonstrated his devotion to Alabamians who struggled with debt when he took to the Senate floor to give his first major speech. The Senate was deeply divided over whether the bankruptcy provisions then under consideration to protect mercantile interests should be extended to everyone.

McKinley was adamant that individual common debtors also needed the relief provided by the bill. According to the *Register*, McKinley argued that "the system ought to be extended to all the [p]eople . . . , without regard to their degree or occupation. He wished the system, if adopted, should dispense equal justice and equal privileges to all."[10] He argued further that debt knew no class and that, while their overall debt might be much lower, the common people suffered just as much as the indebted merchant and trader. "However anxious he might be," the *Register* recorded, "to relieve the latter from the unnecessary pressure of debts beyond their power to pay, he could not agree to do so at the expense of the former."[11]

He took particular interest in debt relief for those who had purchased public land at high speculative prices but acknowledged, as he did in a January 1827 letter to the Huntsville *Democrat*, that many of his colleagues did not share the same concern. Much of the opposition in Congress to land debt relief stemmed from a belief that most of the indebted had fallen victim to their own greed and should not now be excused from their folly. McKinley reassured his constituents that his full attention "shall be faithfully exerted upon this as well as all other subjects in which Alabama is particularly interested."[12] Despite this vow, he also freely confessed that, "being a new member, and from a new state, I cannot expect to have much influence."[13]

One proposal that came before the Senate would have permitted debt-laden individuals to relinquish their property to the United States and then buy it back at a fixed cost of roughly one-quarter of its original purchase price. Many senators categorically opposed this plan because not only did it negate the existing land debt still owed to the government, it also gave settlers a preferential right to repurchase the land at a lower rate. In February 1827, McKinley arose as one of the primary speakers in support of this debt relief bill to address those critics who questioned why settlers should be given the double benefit. "[W]ith every difficulty to encounter, these settlers had improved the country," he declared, "misfortunes had forced them to relinquish part of the lands which they had purchased at high rates; and it would be neither just nor generous to refuse now to give them an opportunity of re-purchasing part of the lands they had given up."[14] His comments, and those of several others, were persuasive, and the debt relief bill passed the Senate, although the House ultimately tabled the measure when it came up for consideration there.

Later that session, McKinley weighed in on Indiana's right to control the land within her borders. Indiana hoped to construct a canal that would connect the Wabash River with Lake Erie. The land through which the canal would be constructed had been recently ceded to the United States by the Miami and Pottawatomi Indians as part of the Mississinewa Treaty of 1826, and Indiana hoped that Congress would donate the land to the state to begin the canal.

While several members of Congress debated the merits of the proposed canal itself, McKinley asked a more fundamental question: Who had jurisdiction over the ceded land, the state or the national government? According to the *Register*, McKinley argued that the land in question, already lying within the borders of Indiana, belonged to the state. The *Register* reported that McKinley wondered aloud "that gentlemen who were usually such great sticklers for State rights, should be silent on this occasion."[15] He argued that the "exclusive legislation of the United States, was confined to this ten miles square [the District of Columbia], and the Territories."[16] Congress could thus only properly dictate how the land in the District was utilized, but beyond that there was no constitutional justification for congressional regulation of the land that lay within the states. McKinley went on to warn that if Congress could regulate land "in any of the new States, they [sic] could do it also in the old ones; if they could do it in Indiana, they could do it in New York."[17] Although there were many in Congress who fundamentally disagreed with McKinley's argument, there were few willing to engage him on the topic in the waning days of the session.

McKinley returned home to Alabama when the Senate adjourned in March and was delighted to find high levels of support for his congressional efforts. He was also pleased that the personal antipathy toward him that had accompanied his election to the Senate had largely subsided. However, his election the previous November had created an entirely new controversy that enveloped northern Alabama during the spring and summer of 1827.

Just days prior to the 1826 legislative session in which McKinley was elected senator, the editor of the Huntsville *Democrat*, Andrew Wills, had sought and received permission to attend the legislature and make notes of its proceedings. In reporting the results of the Senate election, however, and consistent with the mission of his paper, Wills asserted that some of legislators who had opposed McKinley had done so because they were either part of the hated Georgia Faction or, of even greater political consequence, supporters of the Adams administration. James McClung was among those who were targeted by Wills and he proceeded to respond to the latter's allegations in a letter published in the *Democrat*.

This, in turn, led to the publication of several anonymous letters in Wills's newspaper further berating McClung, to which he also subsequently responded. The exchange of charges and refutations continued for several months until July 1827 when the *Democrat* published a letter from a "Patrick Henry." The newspaper had printed other letters attacking McClung under this pseudonym, but the latest denunciation proved too much. Believing that the unknown writer had engaged in a "gross personal attack" on his character, McClung insisted that Wills reveal the true identity of the writer.[18] Wills refused to comply, but a few days later, McClung again confronted him and demanded the author's real name so that he could address the charges directly. When Wills again declined to reveal the anonymous writer, the pair drew weapons and McClung shot the newspaper editor to death.

In reporting the event, and perhaps because it involved the loss of one of their own, the nation's newspapers bitterly denounced both McClung and the anonymous writer whose letter had precipitated the shooting. The *Daily National Intelligencer* in Washington, for example, minced no words in pronouncing, "The author of 'Patrick Henry,' who could thus permit a man to be shot, without the courage to avow himself the offender, should, if he is found out, be booted from society."[19]

McKinley's 1826 Senate race triggered the initial dispute, but his name became even more closely associated with the tragedy when it was rumored that he was actually "Patrick Henry." In a Rhode Island newspaper's account of the killing, McKinley admitted that he had provided some writings for Wills that were similar in content to the disputed letter, but he adamantly denied that he was the author himself.[20] In August 1827 he went so far as to publish a general letter to the public, which was printed in newspapers throughout the country, expressing his desire to "redeem myself from the odium which has been . . . affixed to my name" and asked both friends and enemies to "forbear from further remarks on the subject" until he could provide them with more information at a later date.[21]

It was a weak response that did little to deflect suspicion and, to some observers, only made it more obvious that he was "Patrick Henry." Northern newspapers castigated him, declaring that if McKinley "suffered an innocent man to die . . . , no odium, which the detestation and abhorrence of an insulted and indignant world can have upon him, can scarcely be sufficient to punish him."[22]

The truth of the matter was never known, as McKinley failed to provide the further information that he promised, but the affair followed him for the remainder of his life. Indeed, in announcing his July 1852 death to its readers, the *Baltimore Sun* devoted just one sentence to his fifteen years on the Supreme Court and the better part of the article to McKinley's connection to the murder of Andrew Wills.[23]

Given the controversy that had enveloped him in Alabama, McKinley surely looked forward to returning to the Senate where his efforts during the Twentieth Congress mirrored those of his freshman year. He was again appointed to the Committee on Private Land Claims as well as to the Committee on the Militia. He continued to speak out on behalf of debtors (favoring legislation, for example, that would ban imprisonment for debt) and in favor of public land reform. He was especially concerned about some of the rather arcane federal regulations governing public land in the states.

On March 25, 1828, for example, he rose to speak on behalf of a bill to allow towns in Alabama to exchange the sixteenth section of their land—public land governed by federal legislation that was to be sold with the proceeds to support education—for other land if they chose to do so. McKinley unsuccessfully argued that the sixteenth section was essentially a land lottery. Some land located in the sixteenth section was valuable, while other land, "from its sterility, was entirely useless," thus severely limiting its benefit to education.[24] In light of other floor statements that held that such an exchange would lead to a whole host of unknown problems, the Senate rejected the measure.

His most significant accomplishment that term was his bill to grant four hundred thousand acres of public land in Alabama to improve navigation of the Tennessee, Coosa, Cahaba, and Black Warrior rivers. The central feature of that legislation was the construction of a canal around Muscle Shoals. McKinley argued that because West Tennessee, Missouri, and Alabama would all benefit "from the extent and importance of the improvement proposed, it would stand among the first works of a national character."[25] However, he encountered considerable resistance from senators who were generally opposed to internal improvements and who were less than convinced that this particular land grant would serve a national purpose. To those skeptics, an exasperated McKinley queried, "Why the donations of land for universities, for a seat of Government, and for schools . . . were allowed to be for a national object" but not the Muscle Shoals canal?[26] His argument ultimately prevailed, however, and the bill passed the Senate by a 22–13 margin.

He also gave a lengthy speech encouraging Congress to permit public land that remained unsold for an extended period of time to be offered for sale at lower prices. This would not only help encourage land acquisition by those who could not afford the current minimum purchase price but also help reduce the excess of public land in the states. Opponents claimed that lowering the prices would lead to increased land speculation. As an old land speculator himself, McKinley indignantly replied, "The friends of the present land system are the last that ought to say anything about speculation. Who is the great land speculator in the country? The United States is the greatest that ever was in this or any other country."[27]

Sounding a theme that he consistently returned to during his Senate career, he declared, "[The United States] obtained from Virginia all her waste and unappropriated lands northwest of the Ohio River, under a solemn pledge to sell them for the common benefit of all the States, and apply the proceeds to the discharge of their war debts."[28] Not only had the national government disregarded that promise, he argued, but the states within which that unappropriated land lay had no authority over it "and now the lands are to be held up for high prices, to the great detriment of these new States."[29] If fear of land speculation was the only basis for refusing to sell public land at a reduced cost—land that properly belonged to the states anyway, McKinley argued—then let the "Government abandon

[the practice], and set an example of moderation, of justice, and fair dealing, by restoring to the new States their violated sovereignty."[30]

The federal government's control of the public lands in the states was an
especially sore point with McKinley. Some twenty-eight million acres of
public land lay idle in Alabama alone, and there was virtually nothing the
state could do about it.[31] McKinley voiced the frustration of many in the
newer states when he used this opportunity to underscore in great detail
his belief that the federal government really had "no constitutional right
or claim to the lands in the new States."[32] Simply put, this argument held
that none of the first states (with the exception of Virginia and Maryland,
which ceded land for the creation of the District of Columbia) had turned
over any land to the national government upon admission to the Union.
In addition, neither the early congresses nor the Supreme Court nor the
original Constitution ever conferred upon or recognized the authority of
the United States over land within the territories subsequently admitted
to the Union as states.

Both powerful and eloquent, McKinley's March 1828 speech was subsequently published in several newspapers across the country and later as
a nineteen-page pamphlet by a small Washington-area printer.[33] While
many rejected the basic premise of McKinley's argument, his views received considerable support across the nation. The *Illinois Intelligencer* pref-
aced its publication of McKinley's speech with this endorsement: "The
subject of the public lands is, assuredly, one which demands the serious regard of the friends of equal rights, . . . especially of the people of the West.
Mr. McKinley has laid the subject open with great ability . . . [and] is de-
servedly entitled to much applause."[34]

In addition to his legislative efforts this session, McKinley also kept
an eye on the upcoming presidential race that would again pit Andrew
Jackson against John Quincy Adams. From Washington, McKinley took
pains to keep his friends in Kentucky and Alabama informed about the
progress of Jackson's 1828 presidential campaign. In a January 1 letter to
John Wesley Hunt in Louisville, he wrote, "From present appearances
there is no earthly doubt of Gen. Jackson's election. The friends of the
[Adams] administration, I think, have lost all hope."[35] A month later he
would express his disgust with some of his fellow Jacksonians who, sensing an overwhelming victory in an election still nine months away, had
already thrown political caution to the wind. "Jackson constantly gains
ground notwithstanding the great imprudence of many of his friends," he
told Hunt.[36] "The people will elect him," he continued in an oft-quoted

passage, "without the aid of those who think themselves entitled to the credit."[37]

In May 1828, McKinley wrote to John Coffee to inform him of congressional actions of interest to Alabama from the just concluded session. He ended his letter with a brief reference to the Tariff Bill of 1828. Passed to protect northern industries, the "tariff of abominations" was opposed by most southern senators, including McKinley, because of the negative impact they believed it would have on cotton exports.[38] It would also serve as an early catalyst for the nullification movement in South Carolina and, as discussed later in the chapter, would impact McKinley's own bid for reelection in 1830.

Between sessions of Congress, McKinley followed up on the Muscle Shoals canal project by encouraging President John Quincy Adams to appoint government surveyors as soon as practicable and by giving other related directions to John Coffee to follow up on with the Alabama legislature.[39] He returned to the work of his law practice, which included several cases before the Alabama Supreme Court, and tended to his property holdings and other financial affairs.[40] In November 1828, just before departing for Washington, he revealed to John Wesley Hunt that both nature and competition had affected their investments. The "[cotton] crops generally are as short here as they were last year," he wrote, and "another ferry was established near Lambs Ferry on the public land by men who are worth nothing and who are carrying people across for half price."[41] He informed Hunt that the new ferry had been constructed during his time in Washington and had "injured [our] ferry so much that I have been compelled to rent it for $400."[42]

When he returned to Washington in December 1828 for the second session of the Twentieth Congress, he was greeted by an extraordinary level of activity in the capital city. Jackson's victory over John Quincy Adams a month earlier was the first defeat of an incumbent president in nearly three decades and promised substantial political changes. In this exciting and unusual political environment, however, McKinley was strangely quiet during the congressional session, saying very little from the Senate floor.

He did, however, offer one notable resolution regarding the appointment powers of the presidency. When John Quincy Adams briefly mentioned in his final State of the Union address that the king of the Netherlands had agreed to arbitrate a border dispute between the United States and Great Britain over the northeastern boundary between Maine and Canada, McKinley submitted a resolution questioning the constitutional authority of the president to unilaterally commission the Dutch monarch. In his January 1829 statement, McKinley reminded his colleagues that the Constitution requires the president to make appointments "by and with the advice and consent of the Senate." He questioned whether the Dutch king was essentially serving as a minister of the United States and thus required Senate approval for his appointment. "If he is not a minister," McKinley asked, "where and how does he derive his authority to act for the United States? . . . [W]ould a treaty, based upon the award of an umpire, be binding upon the people of the United States, if there was no power to appoint this umpire?"[43] The Senate adopted the nonbinding resolution but took no further action.

McKinley attended the inauguration of Andrew Jackson in March 1829 and described the commotion that ensued at the ceremony and immediately thereafter. Jackson's election heralded a new spirit in Washington that was fostered, for better or worse, by his "rotation in office" policy within the federal patronage system. Under this policy, Jackson removed federal officials appointed during previous administrations and replaced them with political supporters. The mass of people who came to Washington seeking jobs was thus expected, according to McKinley, but not the resulting chaos. "Such a scramble for office never was seen before as that which took place in that city after Gen. Jackson arrived there," he wrote to John Wesley Hunt. "How they have been distributed you have seen."[44] McKinley was not convinced that the president's interests had been well served by many of his appointments, telling Hunt, "[Jackson's] friends are generally dissatisfied with the distribution [of the appointments, but] I think the President in most instances is not at all to blame. His friends mislead him in many instances."[45]

McKinley called upon the new president shortly after his inauguration and just before heading home to Alabama, but as Jackson later wrote to John Coffee, they were unable to meet at that time. "I intended to have written you by Col. McKinley," Jackson said, "[but] finding me engaged, [he] left his card, and took leave, to him I must refer you for the current news here."[46]

When he returned for the Twenty-First Congress in December 1829, McKinley was immediately assigned to the Committee on Public Lands and the Committee on the Judiciary where he served with Daniel Webster and ranked second to his former law partner Senator John Rowan of Kentucky. This particular Senate session began like every other legislative session McKinley had experienced at both the state and national level, but it was profoundly different in one important way: his term would end later in the year, and McKinley would embark on his first bid for reelection to any office. McKinley's actions in Washington thus came under scrutiny like never before.

Just a month after Congress convened, perhaps at McKinley's prodding, the *U.S. Telegraph* in Washington, D.C., sought to clarify an impression of McKinley's work habits that it may have left with its readers in a previous issue. The paper announced McKinley's presence on the Senate floor in late December without noting that he had actually arrived in Washington much earlier but had taken seriously ill for several days. That apparently left a perception that McKinley had just arrived in Washington with the congressional session already well under way. "This we regret," the newspaper stated, "as we can with pleasure bear witness, that no member of either House is more punctual in his attendance, or more assiduous in the discharge of his Legislative functions, than the Senator from Alabama."[47]

The public lands—and the vast assortment of issues associated with them—continued to be a central component of McKinley's efforts in the Senate that session. One proposed measure that would have reduced the price of public land generally and even more so for land that already had settlers on it encountered vigorous opposition from northern senators. New Hampshire senator Samuel Bell, for example, exclaimed, "These settlers have taken possession of the public lands, in direct violation of the laws of the United States. . . . They are intruders—mere trespassers, who have selected and seized upon the best and most eligible of the public lands."[48]

Although Bell was technically correct in asserting that some had taken possession of this property without title, these squatters had done far more than just "seized upon the best"; they had also improved the land in the process. As historian Daniel Dupre has written, "A cleared field or a planted crop was a mark of ownership in the eyes of a squatter; his labor had altered the landscape and given purpose to the soil."[49] Ironically, the very improvements wrought by squatters that gave "purpose to the soil" also made the land much more valuable. Consequently, squatters on public lands often faced the worst possible combination of circumstances: they had cleared the land, built their homes and barns, established their crops, and then found out that the land they had improved was now too valuable for them to purchase at public sale.

Having witnessed the tireless efforts of settlers to tame the Old Southwest, McKinley was quick to defend them against Senator Bell's allegations. "I beg leave to differ with the honorable gentleman from New Hampshire, upon all of these points," he declared. "[T]hose who have settled upon the public lands . . . are not violators of law, nor trespassers. And I say further, sir, that they are meritorious individuals, because they have been the pioneers to all the new settlements in the West and Southwest."[50] McKinley reminded Bell that these lands were sometimes well under cultivation by the time the United States surveyed them and put them up for public sale. And yet the efforts of those first settlers were not appreciated but condemned. "The lands were sold from under them," McKinley continued, "which, but for the improvements they had made, and the facilities they had afforded for settling the country, would not have sold for one-half the price they bought, and, in many instances, would not have sold at all."[51] The Senate narrowly approved the measure to reduce the price of public land, but it came to the House too late in the session for that body to take any action.

For McKinley and other senators, particularly those from the newer states, concerns about specific public land sales or usage often masked a much more fundamental question: Did states have the right to determine how land within their borders was used? Those from the South and West, like McKinley, saw public land as a means of attracting settlers to their states with all the benefits that accompany population growth. Thus, he and others argued, when there were millions of acres of public land left unsold across the country, the states within whose borders that land lay should be able to do whatever they saw fit to promote settlement. The land benefited no one when left unsold.

Others senators, however, particularly those from the North or who were supporters of Henry Clay's American System were more content to use the public land as a source of revenue.[52] By retaining the land until it could be sold at a good price, the federal government could ensure a source of monies to fund internal improvements and other governmental initiatives.

The entire public land–state rights issue came to a head in December 1829 when Senator Samuel Foot of Connecticut offered a resolution instructing McKinley's Committee on Public Lands to ascertain the feasibility of temporarily limiting public land sales to existing unsold land. Southern senators immediately denounced the resolution as a deliberate attempt to impede further settlement in their states. The next month, in one of the most famous exchanges in the history of the Senate, Daniel

Webster and Robert Hayne used Foot's resolution as the starting point for their epic debate over the nature of the American republic. In doing so, they discussed not only land policy but also wages, labor, tariffs, internal improvements, sectionalism, nationalism, and slavery. Among other things, their debate presciently showed how, in a very real way, "the land question [would] became entangled with almost all of the important social problems which interested the country down to the era of the Civil War."[53]

On January 13, 1830, McKinley stood to say he was in favor of forwarding the Foot resolution to his committee. He did so not because he necessarily agreed with it, he said, but because he "was in favor of a full and fair inquiry into every subject connected with the public lands."[54] According to the *Register*, he took the opportunity to remind his fellow senators, without a great deal of humility, "that it had been his fortune . . . to be the first to advance the doctrine that the new States . . . had a right to the public lands within their respective limits, and the United States could not constitutionally hold them."[55] While McKinley may have hoped that forwarding Foot's resolution to his committee might make him appear fair minded, it had the exact opposite effect. Ignoring entirely his floor statement and the legislative tools that allowed his committee to prevent further substantive action on the measure if necessary, McKinley's political enemies in Alabama castigated his vote, interpreting it as a sign of support for Foot's resolution.

The following day, McKinley created a minor stir on the Senate floor when he offered an amendment to the pending Indian Removal bill, one of Jackson's favored pieces of legislation, to forbid the giving of secret gifts to Indian leaders during treaty negotiations. Several senators immediately arose to question whether the amendment was insinuating that bribery had been used in previous Indian treaties. Perhaps more important, they also suggested that the amendment reflected poorly on the only person empowered by the Constitution to make treaties: the president of the United States. McKinley responded that he in no way questioned the integrity of the Jackson administration and that the amendment was only meant to address presents given in secret. Still, he admitted to finding it odd "that a proposition cannot be made to appropriate money, for public purposes, under certain restrictions, without having the charge imputed to us of entertaining unfriendly feelings to the [Jackson] administration."[56] His foes back home, however, depicted his actions as an attempt to undermine the president.

McKinley offered his critics further ammunition when the Senate took up consideration of the Maysville Road project in the spring of 1830. The Maysville Road was conceived as a major north-south commercial corridor, ultimately linking New Orleans with Zanesville, Ohio, and the National Road. With construction already under way in Kentucky, supporters introduced legislation authorizing federal funds for the project. The bill received bipartisan support in the House of Representatives and passed easily. However, the Maysville Road increasingly came to symbolize the dividing line between the most devoted supporters of Jackson in Congress and everyone else.

Jackson did not resist all internal improvements, but he was quick to fight those that sought federal funding for projects primarily local in nature. The fact that the entire first phase of the Maysville Road, stretching from the Ohio border to Lexington, lay in Kentucky, the home of Jackson's nemesis, Henry Clay, made it easy for both Jackson and his supporters in Congress to oppose the project.

Indeed, when the Senate took up the measure, every senator from the South, where Jackson's popularity was the greatest, voted against it, with the exception of McKinley and John Rowan of Kentucky. Having played a critical role in defeating an earlier Maysville Road bill during the Adams administration, Rowan explained that his vote in favor of the project was compelled by strict instructions from the Kentucky legislature to support the road. For his part, McKinley believed that federal aid for internal projects requested by the states was very different from an improvement plan created by the national government and foisted upon the states. Of course, the fact that the planned road would have passed directly through Florence was perhaps an additional incentive to act against the president's wishes. Several other senators joined McKinley and Rowan, and the measure narrowly passed on May 15, 1830.[57] Two weeks later, Jackson vetoed the bill.

Although McKinley's vote on the Maysville Road and other bills drew scorn from staunch Jacksonians in Alabama and Washington, his actions were praised elsewhere. In 1830, the *Baltimore Patriot* published short profiles of each member of the Senate for the benefit of its readers and commented favorably on McKinley's independent streak. "Mr. McKinley, from [Alabama], is not duly appreciated until he is <u>known.</u> He bears examination well, and the better you understand his character, the better you like him," the newspaper declared.[58] It went on to praise him as one who "forms his own judgment and shapes his own course and would be a troublesome man to keep in the traces where party discipline was deemed expedient. He is certainly worthy of the Senate of the United States."[59]

While McKinley may have been less than enthusiastic about every piece of legislation of interest to Jackson, he was quick to defend the authority of the president. When a resolution was introduced in April 1830 questioning whether Jackson had the right to remove government officials without the consent of the Senate, McKinley arose, according to the *Daily National Journal*'s account, "and observed that he thought there should be some argument on this question by the friends of the Administration, as there had been so much said and published on the other side."[60] He quickly dispensed with the contention that the president was responsible to no one if the Senate did not check his actions by wondering aloud who ultimately restrained the Senate. He answered his own question by forcefully declaring that the president and Congress "were both responsible to the same tribunal—the people."[61] The Senate, thus, should not concern itself with trying to limit the president's removal power because "the power of removal [is] demonstrated to be exclusively in the discretionary power of the President; and if he abused it, he could only be punished by the people."[62]

He reiterated his appreciation for both state and national power the same month at a Democratic Party celebration of Jefferson's birthday. When called upon to give a toast, he responded, "The Constitution of the United States: The compact of sovereign and independent States, instituted for national purposes only; limited and specific in its powers but supreme within the prescribed sphere of its action. The powers not delegated belonging to the States exclusively."[63]

This short toast encapsulates McKinley's theory of governance both as a member of Congress and, as will be demonstrated later, as a Supreme Court justice. He was a never a states' rights absolutist. Rather, like Jackson, he recognized the authority of the national government whose power, while limited, was "supreme within the prescribed sphere of its action." State power could be invoked and exercised only after determining, by constitutional or congressional delegation, the prescribed sphere of the national government.

A few weeks later, several newspapers around the country detailed an incident that occurred shortly before the Senate adjourned involving an apparent random encounter between McKinley and a veteran of the Revolutionary War. The account is reprinted here in its entirety:

A circumstance occurred in the Senate on Wednesday last, which demonstrates most touchingly the generous feelings of that body towards the lingering survivors of our revolutionary army. A time-worn veteran, who had been waiting upon Congress for some months, had seated himself upon a sofa in the rear of the Senators, and the hour for commencing upon the orders of the day having arrived, when Mr. McKinley, of Alabama, begged the indulgence of the Senate for a few moments merely, for the consideration of a subject of interest, which he said might be dispatched without delay.

[T]he members generally manifested some impatience to proceed upon the regular business of the day. "Look," said Mr. McKinley, "upon this venerable officer of the revolutionary army. He was a captain in the continental line—was taken prisoner by the fortune of war—carried captive to England—and, after countless hardships, was restored to his native land. His claim upon the justice of his country has already been acknowledged by the other house; and he is only waiting the decision of this body for the consummation of his hopes. At this late hour of his life, at the age of 80, every day is to him a period of importance. I beg, therefore, that the Senate may waive for a few moments the consideration of other business."

[T]he effect of this brief appeal was electric; almost every member responded or manifested an amen; and the bill in behalf of the old soldier passed instantaneously through its several stages, without a dissenting voice. The war-broken patriot showed upon his countenance a feeling of happy gratification, and "went his way rejoicing."[64]

Despite the positive national press that McKinley received, his actions in Congress were often criticized in Alabama and he knew that his reelection bid would be difficult. He admitted to John Coffee in early February 1830 that he was "greatly at a loss to know what to do. My intention was when I left home to resign on my return if we shall be so fortunate as to get a suitable land Bill passed at the present session of Congress."[65] That, of course, had not happened, but McKinley was keenly aware that he could still do much good for Alabama in Washington. He just was not sure if it was worth it. As he confided to Coffee, "The great sacrifice I have to make of private interest; and the privations of my domestic comforts, certainly are strong and almost irresistible inducements, to quit a station in which I find I am to be rewarded by slander and abuse."[66]

McKinley went on to suggest that perhaps it would be better to "let someone be sent here, who will be more acceptable to the people, and who can better afford the sacrifice of interest and feeling."[67] Such a person, presumably, would find the office much more rewarding than McKinley did.

For his part, he now considered his 1826 Senate bid the "most foolish act of my life, and one by which I have, and will suffer more than all the honor of the station can possibly compensate."[68]

Three weeks later he contacted Coffee again, stating that since their last communication he had received many letters from throughout the state urging him to run for reelection. He noted too that some of these had suggested that his critics were trying "to break me down, by lying and slander, [and] have said that I dare not [run] again."[69] McKinley was a proud man and not likely to back down from such challenges. And yet he was not particularly enamored with Washington, having fulfilled his responsibilities there at considerable personal sacrifice, and desired to return home to Alabama.

His critics, he went on to explain to Coffee, "wish to have it in their power to say that, I was intimidated and thereby destroy any little influence I might exercise against what I consider one of the most unholy combinations to get possession of the power and offices of the state."[70] In short, if he refused to stand for reelection, it would look cowardly. If he did seek reelection and won then he would be obligated to split his time between Alabama and Washington for six more years with all of the accompanying ramifications for his family, legal practice, investments, and personal life. The entire prospect, as he put it to Coffee, "places me in a very awkward situation."[71] McKinley ultimately concluded to simply "leave it to my friends, the friends of the state, and more especially the friends of the present [Jackson] administration, to take such course on this subject as to them may seem best."[72] If they wanted him to run for reelection, he would.

McKinley's deference to Jackson and his supporters highlights one of the more ironic charges made by his critics. His enemies had badly twisted his record to make it appear that, in spite of Andrew Jackson's own stated desire to see McKinley reelected, he had actually impeded the president's agenda. Such allegations were politically intolerable in a state where Jackson enjoyed tremendous support.

By June 1830 and despite consistent rumblings, the only announced opposition to McKinley was from Huntsville attorney and former state legislator David Hubbard. Northern Alabama newspapers seemed astonished that anyone would actually challenge the sitting senator. The Huntsville *Democrat* stated, "[W]e think it very certain that no man can contend with [McKinley], with any prospect of success, unless his abilities are superior, and his services have been of more benefit to the people; and such an one we do not believe can, or will be found arrayed against him."[73]

Even the *Southern Advocate*, which had so vigorously condemned McKinley in 1826, could find little to criticize in his congressional efforts. "Col. McKinley has faithfully served the state of Alabama," it declared, "[and the] whole State has experienced the care of his fostering hand. . . . His services in his present station have been valuable, and we trust they are properly appreciated by our people."[74] So effusive and uniform were the newspaper praises of McKinley that it caused one exasperated Hubbard supporter to question, "If it be certain that everybody is pleased with McKinley—that Davy Hubbard stands no chance to beat him—that Hubbard is not fit for a Senator, etc., why so many writers engage, as if there was no danger?"[75]

Against what would seem to be rather long odds of victory, Hubbard went on the attack, boldly raising questions about McKinley's commitment to Jackson. He challenged McKinley's loyalty not only to the president's policies but also to the man himself. Hubbard reminded the public that fifteen years previously he had served with Jackson in the Creek War but openly wondered what McKinley had done instead of answering the general's call to arms.[76] McKinley was repeatedly forced to counter Hubbard's charges during the summer in public letters and at political rallies throughout northern Alabama.[77]

Despite the political damage it had inflicted, Hubbard's candidacy began to quietly fade by October 1830. In late November, well into the legislative session that would select Alabama's senator, a correspondent with the *Democrat* would write, "No one has been certainly fixed upon as yet, to run against Mr. M'Kinley. The fact is, no one can beat him; and I think it probable, he will have no opposition."[78] A few days later, however, McKinley found out that he would indeed have a challenger—the popular sitting governor of Alabama and his erstwhile friend Gabriel Moore.

Moore's decision to enter the race apparently arose out of personal rather than political differences with McKinley. He had previously appealed to McKinley and the entire Alabama congressional delegation to help secure a political appointment for his nephew as U.S. marshal for the northern district of Alabama. Jackson appointed an old friend and veteran of the Creek War to the position instead, and Moore blamed McKinley.

When Jackson learned that Moore had entered the Senate race, he was livid. He had personally met with the governor to explain the circumstances of the appointment, emphasizing "how faithfully both [Alabama] senators had urged the claims of young Mr. Moore."[79] Having explained his reasons for appointing another, Jackson came away with an assurance that Moore was satisfied and would not seek retribution by challenging McKinley for the Senate.[80] Although he was quick to disparage Moore ("no honest man can have confidence in him again," he declared), Jackson was more concerned about the motivation behind the governor's decision.[81] This he attributed to the efforts of his recalcitrant vice president, John J. Calhoun. "I hesitate not in believing," he confided to John Coffee, "that this has been a secret intrigue of the great <u>nullifier,</u> and after he tried to convert McKinley to his nullifying doctrines and could not, . . . set to work this secret conspiracy against Col. McKinley."[82] This was the only plausible explanation for Jackson as he believed "it was only by silent intrigue that McKinley could be beaten."[83]

The McKinley-Moore Senate race highlighted the influence of national politics and personalities in the election, but it also drew attention to the practice of pledging in Alabama. Pledging was an election-year ritual in which some candidates for the state legislature ran on the promise to vote for specific individuals in their race for the U.S. Senate.

As early as January 1830, McKinley's supporters sought to extract pledges from those running for the state legislature who, if elected to their office, would support McKinley's bid for reelection. Both leading newspapers in northern Alabama, the *Democrat* and the *Southern Advocate*, supported McKinley, but they each held very different views with respect to pledging. The *Democrat* argued that "the representative is the agent of the people: and <u>when their will is known,</u> it is his duty to act in strict accordance with it."[84]

However, the *Southern Advocate* argued that only a man truly independent of such pressures could properly act on behalf of his constituents. Pledging encouraged factions and base partisanship, it opined, and led "to bargaining, intrigue, and management[.] . . . [It] is entirely at war with the purity and simplicity of republican institutions."[85] The *Southern Advocate* seemed especially disappointed that the McKinley camp would resort to such practices. "The services of such a man [McKinley], should not be lightly estimated, nor soon forgotten," it told its readers, "and to us the thought is humiliating that his friends should . . . deem it necessary to resort to the odious method of exacting pledges."[86]

With Moore's candidacy now in full swing, McKinley sought to shore up his political support among legislators, including those who had previously pledged to vote for him. He published an address in the December 11, 1830, issue of the *Southern Advocate* directed at the members of the legislature (then in session) who would select the next senator. McKinley calmly explained his unsuccessful efforts on behalf of Moore's nephew, his controversial votes in Washington during the previous Congress, his support for Jackson, and his desire to serve if reelected. His remarks were met with a blistering set of responses from Governor Moore and his supporters.

Former Senate candidate David Hubbard, now writing in support of Moore, referred to McKinley's comments as the "EXPIRING HOWL of the POLITICAL DEMOGOGUE [sic]."[87] Lest anyone mistake his true feelings with regard to McKinley, he added, "I was opposed to his principles as a politician from his commencement in life."[88] "[I]f Colonel McKinley was a steady and uniform supporter of any one principle or opinion," he argued, "and did not manifest so strong a disposition to be any thing, and every thing, and no one thing at a time; my principle objection would be much softened down."[89] That was not the case for Hubbard and, after resurrecting both McKinley's unpopular Federalist background in Kentucky as well as his association with the Georgia Faction, he warned his fellow Alabamians, "[McKinley's] uncertain and devious course as a politician . . . ought to lead the mind of every man to pause before they render him support."[90]

An R. K. Anderson followed suit in the same edition of the paper, questioning McKinley's allegiance to the president. He linked McKinley to Jackson's despised rival when he questioned whether McKinley's Maysville Road vote made him "in principle what Mr. Clay and his friends call an 'American System' man."[91]

Governor Moore then weighed in, taking McKinley to task for referring publicly to the content of private meetings and letters regarding his nephew's unsuccessful appointment. He openly supposed that McKinley's focus on his nephew was easier than defending himself against "every other objection which has been urged against his official or public conduct."[92] As for McKinley's supposed personal connection with Jackson, Moore said that Alabamians could determine for themselves who had a better relationship with the president but quietly added, "[I]t is probable they would claim the merit for me of having been one of his old soldiers, found laboring in his ranks at the first outset, no new convert at the eleventh hour after the heat of the battle was over."[93]

McKinley and his allies vigorously protested these and other charges, but when the election was held on December 13, Governor Moore prevailed by a 49–40 vote of the state legislature. McKinley's supporters were devastated by the loss. Speaking of the people and the tactics that had

helped put Moore into office, Florence attorney Charles Savage wrote,
"[B]y this one act they have disgraced our state and I truly hope have also
caused their own downfall and that their face may be like Lucifer's never
to hope again."[94]

In a somber account of the Senate race, the *Democrat* in Huntsville
stated, "[T]here has been political juggling and maneuvering here . . . that
would disgrace even a Tallyrand [*sic*]. It appears the motto has been 'down
with him! Down with him!' perfectly regardless of the means."[95] It went on
to add the following, final tribute to Senator John McKinley: "[W]e believed and still believe, that Mr. McKinley was the choice of the people—
because he had been an able, honest, and efficient senator—because he was
hated and slandered by men, who would have adored him if they could
have used him."[96]

In Washington, D.C., the *Daily National Journal* reported McKinley's
loss in its New Year's Day editorial, freely admitting that it "regarded Mr.
McKinley as a man of respectable talents, and upright character, and [was]
induced to think that he came into the National Councils with just and
liberal political views."[97] But it also chided him for staking out positions,
few as they may have been, contrary to the will of President Jackson. The
lesson, it reminded its readers, was that "retribution sometimes follows a
departure from the course of truth and real patriotism."[98] Closer to home,
the *Tuscaloosa Inquirer* sounded a similar theme, triumphantly declaring
that "this election may be regarded as an evidence of the strong attach-
ment of Alabama to State sovereignty, and the principles of [Jackson's]
celebrated [Maysville Road] veto message."[99]

Such statements elicited a strong rebuttal from the editor of the pro-
Jackson *U.S. Telegraph* in Washington, who believed the election results
could be explained by something other than McKinley's "want of attach-
ment to the interests of the States, or to the [Jackson] Administration."[100]
It added, "We regret to see . . . such a remark, calculated to do great injustice to Col. McKinley. . . . [He] has been the able, efficient friend of
the Administration. He has been a faithful and successful advocate of the
rights and interests of his State."[101]

Despite having expressed his own ambivalence about being reelected,
McKinley was very upset by his defeat and wrote several letters to John
Coffee bitterly complaining about the national political forces that worked
against him. From Washington where he was attending his last session of
Congress in February 1831, McKinley wrote, "Calhoun took great pains
last winter to get me to support their South Carolina [nullification] doc-

trine, with a view I have no doubt to the present contest with General Jackson."[102] McKinley believed that after he refused to join the nullification camp, Calhoun began to search for someone else who could represent Alabama in the Senate. "[I]n the present state of affairs between the President and Calhoun," he explained to Coffee, "it was important for the latter to have a convenient tool like Moore in the Senate."[103]

He informed Coffee that many people, including Andrew Jackson, had urged him to run for governor in the wake of his Senate loss. Unbeknownst to McKinley, Jackson had already suggested that very thing several weeks earlier in his own letter to Coffee. In the event that Moore should actually defeat McKinley, Jackson had written, "the good people of Alabama ha[d] but one course to pursue, and that justice points to—elect Col. McKinley governor of the state."[104]

McKinley appreciated the support of Jackson and others but confided to Coffee, "I am so tired of politics, and so unwilling to engage in a bitter scene of electioneering, such I would have to encounter, that I do not feel at all disposed to engage in it. . . . If I were to consent, it could only be upon a strong appeal from the people."[105] He concluded his letter and his Senate career, appropriately enough, by informing Coffee that a debt relief bill to assist the purchasers of public lands had finally passed the Senate. "This is the last public act," he wrote, "which I will have it in my power to perform here in which the people of Alabama have a direct interest."[106]

In June 1831, McKinley supporters in Madison County held a public dinner to honor him and Representative Clement C. Clay "as a testimonial of the high respect and regard entertained by them for the eminent services of these distinguished public servants."[107] The toasts offered up on McKinley's behalf reflect both the bitterness of the past campaign and the esteem in which he was held. One participant saluted "Our guest, the Hon. John McKinley—While gratitude holds a place in the affections of mankind, his services and talents will be remembered and rewarded by the people of this State, though recently disregarded by a majority of their representatives."[108] Another proclaimed, "John McKinley, our late Representative in the Senate of the United States—He will live in the affections of his countrymen, when those who have traduced, and vilified, and supplanted him, shall have sunk 'To the vile dust from which they sprung, Unwept, unhonored, and unsung.'"[109]

Although unwilling to run for governor, McKinley was unable to fully disengage himself from Alabama state politics. He had moved back to Florence from Huntsville during his years in the Senate and was imme-

diately elected as a Lauderdale County representative to the state legislature in August 1831. More important, however, he was also unable to disengage himself from national politics. Within six months of his election
to the legislature, he again found himself at a critical moment in state history that had important national implications.

Andrew Jackson was up for reelection in 1832 and while his place on the
Democratic presidential ticket was a foregone conclusion, the vice presidential slot was not. Jackson was so outraged by the Senate's refusal to confirm Martin Van Buren as his minister to Great Britain in January of that
year (the deciding vote cast by his own vice president, John C. Calhoun)
that he selected Van Buren as his new running mate for the 1832 campaign
to spite and punish those who had fought against his earlier nomination.

He also vigorously counseled his political allies on how to deal with
those who, like Alabama senator Gabriel Moore, had opposed Van Buren.[110] Writing to John Coffee from Washington in January 1832, Jackson
advised, "I trust you and Col. McKinley will see to it . . . that your citizens
do not approve of Moores [sic] course."[111] Specifically, he encouraged them
to convene a meeting at Florence for the express purpose of condemning
Moore and calling for his resignation. That gathering, the president predicted, would then serve as a model to "be followed all over your state and
there is nothing that will destroy him here so much and so soon as such a
movement of citizens."[112]

Van Buren's selection as vice president, however, troubled many of
Jackson's strongest supporters. During his earlier confirmation battle, Van
Buren's enemies had attacked him with such ferocity that some southern
Democrats now feared that he would be a drag on the ticket. Some also be-
lieved that the political power the South enjoyed under Jackson and Cal-
houn during the president's first term would be compromised with a New
Yorker as vice president. Accordingly, southern Democrats put forward
the name of Philip Barbour of Virginia as a more suitable candidate for
the vice presidential slot. Barbour had formerly served as Speaker of the
U.S. House of Representatives and was then serving as a federal judge in
Virginia. The fact that Jackson appointed him to the latter position (and
would later elevate him to the Supreme Court in 1836) gave Barbour's supporters confidence that their efforts would not alienate the president.

In January 1832, Jackson's supporters in Alabama met at the state capitol
in Tuscaloosa to select electors as well as delegates to represent the state
at the Democratic National Convention in Baltimore the following May.
Governor John Gayle presided at the meeting while McKinley chaired the

twenty-two-member select committee tasked with recommending electors.[113] When it became apparent that McKinley's committee would recommend an electoral ticket loyal to Van Buren, several members of the state convention withdrew to create a new nominating committee to select a different slate of electors. McKinley's committee did exactly what its opponents had feared, having extracted a pledge from each of the five electors it named to vote for whomever the national party selected at the Baltimore convention.[114] Van Buren was the overwhelming favorite there and he went on to receive the nomination with more than 70 percent of the total delegate vote.

McKinley's actions at the Alabama party meeting and indeed throughout the entire election year not only reinforced his fidelity to Jackson but also brought his loyalty to the attention of Van Buren. Several times during that year, McKinley and other party leaders had quickly intervened to prevent Barbour's supporters from persuading Alabama electors to drop their pledge to Van Buren.[115]

In September, McKinley was selected to chair the proceedings of a large meeting of prominent northern Alabama citizens held at Athens. Among the resolutions adopted by the group was one of particular concern to Jackson's supporters. Based on the results of the 1830 census, Congress had allocated two additional House seats to Alabama, thus bringing the state's total number of congressional seats—and presidential electors—to seven. However, Alabama law at the time only provided for the election of five electors. With McKinley as voice, these citizens resolved that the governor and legislature "repeal so much of the existing law as may in any manner restrict the number to less than <u>seven,</u> to which our State is constitutionally entitled."[116]

The group further resolved that the citizens of Alabama be encouraged to cast their vote for the seven electors pledged to vote for Jackson and Van Buren. To do anything different, they argued, would not only be "unfriendly to the success of our cause" but also run the risk of sending the vice presidential race, in the event of an electoral tie, to the U.S. Senate where Calhoun was certain to undermine the president's choice.[117] Whatever concerns the president's supporters had ultimately proved unfounded as Jackson and Van Buren went on to prevail in the presidential contest, winning more than four times as many electoral votes as their nearest opponent, Henry Clay. As for McKinley, the presidential campaign had only further cemented his Jacksonian credentials.

When the Twenty-Third Congress convened on December 2, 1833, Alabama's two additional representatives took their seats along with their three colleagues in the House. Among their number was former senator John McKinley. He announced his intention to seek the second congressional district slot the previous March because Samuel W. Mardis, who had held the seat, was running for reelection in the newly reconfigured third congressional district. McKinley's opponent was General James Davis of Franklin.

Always keen to political developments in Alabama, Andrew Jackson was pleased to see his old friend back in the political arena. In an April 1833 letter to John Coffee, he declared, "I am gratified to learn that Col. McKinley is up for Congress. He has my best wishes for his success. He will keep the Alabama representation right."[118] Later that year, Clement C. Clay, who represented Alabama's first congressional district, reported the results of McKinley's race in a letter to James K. Polk: "In this state, as you will have seen, the elections for Congress have resulted in our favor. . . . McKinley is elected after a close contest—accounts vary his majority from 270 to 350—and it is further rumoured that his election will be contested."[119]

General Davis, however, did not contest the results and John McKinley along with former governor John Murphy joined incumbents Clay, Mardis, and Dixon H. Lewis in the newly expanded Alabama congressional delegation in Washington. Of this group, the *Mobile Patriot* proclaimed, "This presents an aggregate of talents, experience and information, that is highly creditable to the State, and places it on footing of respectability that will secure its just weight in the national councils."[120]

If Alabama could claim any power in the "national councils" because of its larger delegation, it was due primarily to John McKinley. He would serve only a single two-year term in the House of Representatives, but his impact there was arguably much greater than during his previous service in the Senate. This was due in large part to the committee assignment that he received. The Speaker of the House made the committee assignments, typically basing such decisions on party loyalty and ideological compatibility and only after determining which key members were needed on which key committees to ensure the success of preferred legislation.[121]

On December 5, 1833, McKinley was appointed to the House Committee on Ways and Means, which was then, as it continues to be, one of the most powerful committees in the House of Representatives. The committee was particularly influential in McKinley's day because in addition to its wide jurisdiction, it oversaw all tax-related measures as well as all appropriations. The committee was powerful in other ways as well because the chairman of Ways and Means during this era was also the de facto leader of the majority party.

In early 1833, after House Ways and Means chairman and former Jacksonian Gulian C. Verplanck authorized a committee report declaring the Bank of the United States to be financially sound, an infuriated Andrew Jackson determined that the committee would be comprised of his most loyal friends in the House at the next Congress. James K. Polk of Tennessee, who had been the junior member during Verplanck's tenure, was selected as the new head. To assist the new chairman, as historian Charles Sellers recorded, "five of the ablest Jackson men in the House—Churchill C. Cambreleng of New York City, Isaac McKim of Baltimore, George Loyall of Virginia, Henry Hubbard of New Hampshire, and John McKinley, a personal friend of Polk from Alabama—were assigned to the committee."[122] "The Democrats," he added, "were taking no chances."[123]

During the Twenty-Third Congress, Polk utilized his committee to not only manage the Democratic Party's interests but also promote Andrew Jackson's second-term legislative agenda in the House. Because the president lost his Senate majority in the same November 1832 election in which he was soundly reelected, the House Ways and Means committee and its Democratic members became the focal point for the president's efforts in Congress.

McKinley focused far less on issues of concern to Alabamians as a representative than he did as a senator, but he spoke frequently on a wide range of subjects that were important to the administration. Not surprisingly, he benefited in unexpected ways from his association with Jackson and Polk, two of Tennessee's most popular politicians. While returning to Alabama after Congress adjourned in 1834, for example, McKinley stopped in Tennessee to view the proceedings then under way to revise the 1796 state constitution. A Nashville newspaper reported that "[w]hen Col. McKinley (who we understand is on his way home from Washington City) visited the Hall of the Convention this morning, and was perceived among the spectators in the lobby, he was immediately, on motion of Col. [Robert] Weakley, invited to a seat within the bar of the House."[124]

In June 1834, McKinley was similarly lauded in *Paul Pry*, a pro-Jackson newspaper in Washington. In its profile of the Alabama delegation, the newspaper reported, "[The] Honorable John McKinley is by far the ablest and most gentlemanly representative from Alabama; he is a sound reasoner, and an able debater."[125]

As members of the Ways and Means Committee and sharing a determination to further Jackson's agenda, Polk and McKinley worked together closely. When John Bell unexpectedly sought and won the contest for the Speaker of the House in 1834, Polk contacted several House members, including McKinley, and asked them to vouch for the fact that Polk was to have been the Jackson administration's choice for Speaker and that Bell's actions had essentially contravened both the party's and the president's wishes. McKinley promised, "Should it become necessary to the maintenance of truth and justice for me to make a statement, I will do so without hesitation."[126]

Polk and McKinley worked with others on the committee and those in Jackson's cabinet to push the president's initiatives. In 1835, Polk wrote Secretary of the Treasury and future Supreme Court justice Levi Woodbury asking to meet with him and McKinley as soon as possible, stating, "Col. McKinley and myself are very anxious to see you upon the subject of the Senate bill."[127] They also exchanged thoughts on the upcoming 1836 presidential election. In March 1835, McKinley wrote to Polk proffering advice and strategy regarding prospective candidates for the vice presidential slot to run with Martin Van Buren. He closed his letter with reference to their wives and reminded Polk that "Mrs. M. [sic] unites with me in respects to Mrs. P. [sic] and insists on the performance of your promised visit next summer."[128]

So closely were the two affiliated that during the summer of 1834 at a public dinner in Tennessee held in Polk's honor, a round of toasts also went up for John McKinley. A J. S. Walker toasted the "Hon. John McKinley: The firm and undeviating friend of the [Jackson] Administration, and a prominent member of the Committee of Ways and Means. His public services are highly appreciated, and will be suitably rewarded by his grateful constituents."[129]

McKinley continued to demonstrate his "undeviating" friendship in a public letter on behalf of Jackson's embattled postmaster general, William T. Barry. Barry had served in Jackson's cabinet since 1829 and, by virtue of his office, controlled more patronage positions than virtually any other department. By the mid-1830s, however, it was not patronage but Barry's embarrassing mismanagement of his office, characterized by inefficient mail service and growing debt, that led to increasingly strident calls for his removal.

McKinley had known Barry since at least 1814 when the latter had soundly defeated him in his first run for public office in Kentucky. By June

1834, however, McKinley was solidly behind both Barry and Jackson. Responding to criticism of Barry, McKinley declared, "The injustice of the course pursued towards the talented and patriotic Postmaster General, is obvious to all who take the trouble to examine the subject a moment."[130] He noted that congressional expansion of postal routes coupled with little increase in governmental resources to manage these routes had indeed stretched thin the office of the postmaster general. "This circumstance is seized by the opposition," he argued, "truths suppressed, facts discolored, and a tirade of abuse poured forth on the devoted head of Mr. Barry. Will the people . . . step forward and sustain him against his enemies and the enemies of the present administration?"[131]

Such devotion earned him countless accolades during his time in the House, such as those given at a public dinner of Democrats in Alabama where he was the subject of two toasts. The first proclaimed, "The Hon. John McKinley: His services in the Senate of the United States, and more recently as a Representative in Congress, have been characterized by a devotion to the public good and to the interests of his State. We owe him our thanks and our gratitude."[132] Later in the evening, an H. M. Andrews rose and said, "The honorable and distinguished John McKinley: Our worthy Representative in Congress, true to the voice of his constituents. The high-minded course which governed him in the trust confided in him, deserves the highest mark of approbation."[133]

When the House reconvened in December 1834, McKinley offered the first resolution of the session, informing the Senate that a quorum of the House was assembled and ready to proceed to business. He also motioned that a committee of House members be appointed to prepare for the president's State of the Union address. Upon adoption of these resolutions, the new Speaker of the House, James K. Polk, appointed McKinley and Gerrit Lansing of New York to represent the House in the congressional delegation that would call upon the president and receive any communication he might send.[134]

McKinley was active in party leadership, well respected by his peers, and recognized for his loyalty to the president. It may have been this last factor that compelled McKinley, shortly after the Twenty-Third Congress adjourned in May 1835, to abruptly announce that he would not be a candidate for reelection to the House.[135] His supporters again encouraged him to run for governor, but he ultimately refused to challenge Clement C. Clay for that office.

There are no extant accounts to explain why McKinley abandoned his safe seat and the power of his House committee. However, some have suggested that he did so with an eye to eventually regain his Senate seat.[136] Jacksonians already dominated the House, holding two-thirds of its seats. In the Senate, however, just a few seats separated Jackson's party from the anti-Jackson forces that controlled that chamber. Given McKinley's loyalty to the president, the narrow defeat he had suffered in 1830, and the low stature of incumbent Senator Gabriel Moore (who was up for reelection and now deeply despised within the state), it is likely that either McKinley or Jackson or both concluded that the former could probably win back his old Senate seat and strengthen the president's support in that chamber.

Until that opportunity presented itself, McKinley resumed his legal practice. Later in the summer of 1835, McKinley and his law partner Arthur F. Hopkins were injured in a stagecoach accident near Columbia, Tennessee. A Nashville newspaper reported, "The Hon. John McKinley, of Alabama, is now in this city, having received . . . a severe injury from the overturning of the stage."[137] Ten other passengers were on the stage, but only Hopkins and McKinley were injured. The paper continued, "Mr. Hopkins and Col. McKinley both received severe, though not dangerous, contusions on the right side of their heads, from the effect of which, however, they are both rapidly recovering."[138]

Although out of Congress, McKinley had one more opportunity to influence national politics and demonstrate his devotion to Jackson as the presidential election of 1836 approached. Van Buren was the sitting vice president and Jackson's handpicked successor, but he faced growing opposition particularly from southern Democrats. As indicated during the 1832 election, some distrusted him simply because he was a northerner, assuming that his policy agenda as president would favor that region's interests over those of the South.

Others, however, had simply grown weary of Jackson's personality and browbeating tactics. Even as he insisted upon Van Buren as his successor, southern Democrats were quietly seeking a person of *their* choosing who possessed Jacksonian ideals but was free of Old Hickory's personal influence. They ultimately settled on Tennessee senator Hugh L. White, who had once been a close personal friend of Jackson's and who reportedly had even been offered a cabinet post in the administration. By 1834 White was estranged from Jackson, but his previous personal connection with Jackson as well as the general esteem with which he was held led to a groundswell of southern support for his candidacy.

The Alabama legislature declared its preference for White by passing a resolution proclaiming him to be the best qualified to succeed Jackson. To the great consternation of Jackson, several other southern legislatures did the same thing. Throughout the South, Van Buren's supporters, and even Jackson himself, spent the next eighteen months countering every pro-White movement they could find. In Alabama, as historian Albert Moore later recorded, "every inch of ground was hotly contested."[139] This forced McKinley and other Jackson loyalists to work tirelessly throughout the summer and fall of 1835 to buttress Van Buren's support there.

On December 7, 1835, Democratic Party delegates from virtually every county in the state of Alabama met in Tuscaloosa for a three-day convention to choose an electoral slate favorable to Martin Van Buren. Selecting from what was purported to be the very "bone and sinew of the country," the delegates chose seven eminent men as electors. Heading the list were the two most prominent Jackson/Van Buren supporters in the state, former South Carolina senator William Smith and John McKinley.[140] Reporting on the meeting, one partisan wrote, "The Convention . . . has had a happy effect. Van Buren will . . . certainly get the vote of Alabama."[141]

Prior to adjourning, the convention adopted a motion recommending that the state legislature rescind the White resolution of the previous session. A few days later, the efforts of Van Buren's supporters in Alabama were rewarded when the state legislature, with several newly elected representatives supportive of Van Buren, voted 48–34 to rescind its resolution supporting White. A partisan letter to the *Globe* in Washington, D.C., proclaimed, "The nomination of Judge White has been rescinded! Alabama stands 'redeemed, regenerated, and disenthralled' from the shackles of unauthorized and unconstitutional dictation!"[142]

Van Buren would go on to soundly defeat the four Whig candidates vying for the presidency in 1836, winning 170 electoral votes. He won the state of Alabama by over 4,800 votes, but only heavy turnout in the northern counties, where McKinley had focused so much of his efforts, made it possible to overcome pro-White voters in the state's southern counties. Of McKinley's role in Van Buren's victory, Supreme Court scholar Henry J. Abraham has written, "McKinley had been one of Van Buren's key managers during the presidential campaign of 1836 and was personally responsible for capturing Alabama's electoral votes."[143] Given the strength of the pro-White forces in the state, it was not an overstatement.

As mentioned before, McKinley's refusal to stand for reelection to the House of Representatives, according to some scholars, stemmed from his desire not only to help elect Martin Van Buren but also to return to the

Alabama state legislature in hopes that it "would serve as [a] springboard to reclaiming his old Senate seat."[144] If that was his plan, it worked to perfection. Voters returned McKinley to the state legislature in the August 1836 election. Reporting the statewide results of the legislative races, a Mobile newspaper wrote, "Col. McKinley too is returned from Lauderdale. We like to see such men sustained in such a crisis. It shows that the true and genuine principles of the good old republican party have not become altogether unfashionable in Alabama."[145]

It was at the 1836 session of the state legislature that McKinley met a talented young representative from Montgomery named John Archibald Campbell, who would join him on the House Judiciary Committee and who would one day succeed to the U.S. Supreme Court himself. A native Georgian, Campbell was just twenty-five years of age but already had a significant reputation. He was a prodigy in his home state, entering the University of Georgia at the tender age of eleven and graduating three years later. Campbell subsequently received an appointment to the United States Military Academy at West Point but resigned to help his family after the death of his father. He then read law for a year and was admitted to the Georgia bar in 1829, but only after a special act of the legislature permitted him to do so because he was just eighteen at the time. Campbell left Georgia for Alabama in 1830 and immediately embarked upon a successful legal practice first in Montgomery and later in Mobile.

When John McKinley died in 1852, it was Campbell who helped author a set of moving resolutions on behalf of the Supreme Court bar deeply lamenting the passing of the justice. But in 1836, as a young, ambitious, and brash member of the Alabama legislature, Campbell apparently had nothing but contempt for his older colleague. Indeed, in personal letters describing the 1836 session, Campbell singled out McKinley for particular disdain.

Recounting McKinley's arguments against a proposed bill to raise the salary of members of the Alabama Supreme and circuit courts, Campbell wrote, "Col. McKinley will move to submit these questions to people!!!! He is an unspeakably weak man. [He] quarreled all the morning yesterday on a point of order . . . [and then] apologized, explained, and disgusted everyone. I keep out of all such scrapes."[146]

Obviously not every member of the legislature felt the same way. If the proud McKinley had sensed such opposition against him personally or his candidacy to regain his Senate seat, he probably would not have permitted his name to be put forward. However, even in light of such opposition, his path back to Washington looked to be considerably easier thanks to the efforts of the incumbent senator Gabriel Moore.

In the six years since defeating McKinley, Moore's allegiance to Jackson (one of the focal points of the 1830 campaign) had been publicly called into question several times. Newspapers in both Alabama and Washington were quick to remind voters that the very doubts successfully raised by Moore regarding John McKinley's loyalty to Jackson had been realized by Moore himself.[147] He had opposed not only several pieces of Jackson's favored legislation but also Jackson's appointment of Martin Van Buren as minister to Great Britain in 1832. This elicited a call from the Alabama legislature the following year for Moore to resign, which he freely ignored. At the same time, there were less than subtle public reminders that "[h]ad Mr. McKinley, who served the people so ably and faithfully, been in the Senate, . . . Jackson [and his policies] would have been sustained."[148] Needless to say, by 1836 it was clear Moore would not be selected by the state legislature for another term.

Jacksonian Democrats in the legislature resolved to put McKinley's name forward as their candidate for the Senate since he now enjoyed a reputation as "a figure of the very first rank in the state party."[149] There was considerable debate, however, as to how to proceed with McKinley's candidacy. Van Buren supporters dominated the legislature and urged that McKinley be elected in the first days of the legislative term.

They were opposed by some in the legislature who saw in their plan an effort to try to rush McKinley into his Senate seat, assuring his election even though the popular vote from the just concluded presidential race had yet to be tallied. This caused one Whig observer from North Carolina who happened to be in Alabama at the time to write, "[C]all you this 'Republican Democracy.'—Is this Van Burenism? What, the servants of the people afraid to trust the people,—afraid to suspend for a few days, their deliberations on this important subject, until the people . . . shall speak out, and make known their wishes?"[150] He further questioned the need for such hasty action when there was virtually "no doubt of the election of Col. McKinley."[151]

John Archibald Campbell noted that there was a serious campaign to prevent McKinley from returning to Washington, led in part by Calhoun Democrats: "The nullifiers say they will beat him," he wrote, "but I do not know how in as much as sixty-six [members of the legislature] have pledged themselves for McKinley in secret."[152] While the Calhoun faction in the legislature ultimately failed to even field a candidate for the Senate seat, Alabama Whigs, in a curious twist, decided to run McKinley's well-respected law partner, Arthur F. Hopkins. Campbell pronounced that he would "infinitely prefer" Hopkins.[153]

On November 21, 1836, with the notable backing of several legislators who had supported Hugh White over Van Buren in their presidential politics, McKinley defeated his friend and legal partner Hopkins by a vote of 72–45.[154] The young Campbell was livid with the results. In a subsequent letter announcing McKinley's victory, Campbell carped, "McKinley is daily discrediting himself by the most frivolous conduct. A motion to take up a bill from the table, as a motion to print, will call for exposition of all his resources. He is a feeble man not much superior to a common Methodist preacher."[155] To this diatribe Campbell added a rather startling postscript: "I feel degraded in having voted for him."[156]

Reporting on election returns from across the country, the *Pensacola Gazette* stated, "The Hon. John McKinley has been elected by the Legislature of Alabama, a senator in Congress. Mr. McK. is an old and experienced public servant, and the choice of the state could scarcely have fallen upon a better or a fitter man."[157] The *New York Spectator*, however, was more cautious: "Mr. McKinley . . . was in the Senate when the first simoom of Jacksonianism first swept over the land, and voted against . . . some of the baser sort of the spoils men. It remains to be seen whether he has any of that sort of independence left."[158]

Somewhat presciently, a correspondent with the *Montgomery Advertiser* covering the 1836 Senate race wrote the following about McKinley: "Mr. McKinley seldom speaks, but when he does make the venture, his arguments are generally sound. From what I have seen I should judge that he would appear best in a court of justice. His mind is well-trained and his application no doubt intense."[159] Neither McKinley's supporters nor his detractors would ever have the opportunity of finding out how he would again perform in the Senate because he never had a chance to serve.[160]

On March 3, 1837, his last full day in office, Andrew Jackson received a letter from James K. Polk informing him of the passage of the Judiciary Act of 1837. It was the culmination of more than two decades of an intensely frustrating effort by representatives from the Ohio Valley and the Deep South who were finally able to get the circuit court system extended to the nine states that had been admitted to the Union since the federal judiciary was last reorganized in 1807.

Although there had long been a consensus that the federal judiciary needed to expand as new states were admitted to the Union, there were sharp disagreements in Congress as to how exactly that should be done. In particular, members argued over the role of the Supreme Court justices in an expanded circuit system. For twenty years, Congress debated a range of measures that basically fell into one of two categories: those that would relieve the justices of a portion or all of their circuit responsibilities, allowing lower federal judges to deal with the judicial workloads at circuit, and those that would add more seats to the Supreme Court as a way to deal with the growing amount of litigation found on circuit.[161]

Members of Congress from the southern and western states generally opposed the first of these, believing that the circuit court responsibilities were too important to be entrusted to district court judges who often possessed questionable legal skills. Representatives from the North, however, resisted the notion of expanding the bench with the admission of new states because the establishment of such a precedent would lead to a large and unwieldy Supreme Court as the country continued to grow. Of even greater concern to the latter were the calls from southern and western congressmen that any additional seats on the Supreme Court be filled with judges from the new states who reflected the values and concerns of the citizens in those areas. While still serving as a senator from New Hampshire, for example, Levi Woodbury (who would be appointed to the Supreme Court himself in 1845) decried the idea of geographical representation on the Court. "[This would] tend to sap the very foundation of all just confidence in lofty judicial integrity," he said, "by opening a door to that lamentable state, when judgments of a grand Judiciary of the Union may be considered as mere sectional questions, settled on Eastern or Western votes."[162]

While there were legitimate concerns associated with geographical representation on the bench, pure political calculation actually drove much of the debate. That is, expanding the seats on the Supreme Court by *any* number would allow the sitting president to make one or more lifetime appointments. For two decades, opponents of the president in Congress refused to give him that opportunity.

As finally passed by Congress, the Judiciary Act of 1837 reorganized the existing Seventh Circuit and created two new circuits: the Eighth covering Kentucky, Missouri, and Tennessee, and the Ninth, which encompassed Alabama, Arkansas, Louisiana, and Mississippi. The legislation also expanded the Supreme Court from seven seats to nine.[163]

In announcing the successful passage of the legislation in his letter to Jackson, James K. Polk stressed the importance of both geography and political ideology when filling the two new seats.[164] He submitted to Jackson the names of two men who were impeccably qualified on both counts. "I earnestly recommend the appointment of Judge [John] Catron and the Hon. John McKinley to the Bench. I know of no two men in the South or West so well qualified or who have more character before the country."[165] He added that with the addition of Catron and McKinley "the Court will be strong, and will have a decided democratic bias. Upon all the great constitutional questions, the opinions of Catron and McKinley are known to be sound."[166]

Jackson did not comply with Polk's recommendations entirely. As one of his last official acts as president, he did nominate Catron from his and Polk's home state of Tennessee. But instead of McKinley, whom Polk and several others had recommended, he nominated William Smith, a lifelong friend and former U.S. senator from South Carolina, who was then also residing in Alabama. Both were subsequently confirmed by the Senate, but Smith, who was seventy-five years of age at the time of his nomination, declined to serve.[167] On April 22, 1837, the new president, Martin Van Buren, followed up on Polk's recommendation and nominated fifty-six-year-old John McKinley to fill the vacant seat. He accepted the recess appointment and subsequently declined the Senate seat he had won the previous December in order to serve.[168]

It should be noted that this nomination hardly came as a surprise to McKinley. Indeed, that he had anticipated receiving one of the new Supreme Court appointments should Congress pass the Judiciary Act before Jackson left office was evident from a candid letter McKinley sent to Polk just two weeks after his nomination. "I had the great pleasure to receive, by yesterday's mail, your very kind letter," he wrote to Polk. "And the same mail brought me the commission of [A]ssociate Justice of the Supreme [C]ourt. So you see that your kind offices, exerted in my behalf before you left Washington, were not unavailing." McKinley confessed that he expected the bill reforming the federal judiciary to fail once again, and only realized that it had passed upon a chance meeting with Alabama representative Reuben Chapman. Chapman told McKinley that he, Polk, Representative Joshua Martin, and others had lobbied for his elevation to the Court, but Jackson had selected William Smith instead.[169]

McKinley went on to state that when he heard "that Judge Smith had declined the office, I determined never to apply for it directly or indirectly. As it came to me without solicitation, on my part, I have accepted the appointment."[170] Although McKinley was technically correct that he had never solicited the seat after Smith declined it, he had previously made it clear to several people who might have any influence over such a decision that he yearned for any seat that might become available on an expanded Supreme Court.

More than a year earlier, for example, in a February 1836 letter to Polk, McKinley had written, "You know the office of judge of the Supreme [C]ourt is the only one I ever desired."[171] He went on to acknowledge that "if the office were offered I would accept it" but cautioned Polk that should there "be the least unwillingness manifested on the part of the President to appoint me drop the matter and never mention it again."[172] A month later, he again conveyed his wishes to Polk in subtle ("Offices and appointments may gratify our ambition; but it is true friendship that alone can warm the heart") and not-so-subtle ways ("I should be very happy to have, not only the aid of the present chief justice [Roger Taney], with the President, but his approval of my appointment to the office").[173]

What benefited McKinley the most, however, was not his relationship with Polk or the recommendation of influential friends but his loyalty toward and political efforts on behalf of Jackson and, particularly, Martin Van Buren. In fact, the efforts of his political friends to secure the seat may have been unnecessary if rumors spread by Senator John Bell in 1836 were correct. Although McKinley would vigorously denounce the allegation, Bell claimed that Martin Van Buren had already promised McKinley a seat on the High Court in return for his support during the 1836 presidential election.[174] While impossible to verify, Bell's claim is certainly plausible given McKinley's reputation at the national level, his long-held desire to be on the Court, and his key support of Van Buren during the vice presidential crisis of 1832. With memories still fresh of his struggle to win support from southern Democrats during his vice presidential bid, Van Buren may well have considered the mutual benefits of promising an open seat on the Court to someone of McKinley's caliber in order to secure his support.

As much as he desired the office, however, McKinley could hardly have anticipated how joining the Supreme Court would affect his health, wealth, and reputation. The latter two began to suffer almost immediately. The Financial Panic of 1837 began during Martin Van Buren's first month in office. It was brought about, in part, by widespread speculation, particularly in the East and South. Taking out millions of dollars in loans, investors sunk their money and credit "into unproductive, uncultivated lands of the West; . . . into imaginary steamboat and river-dredging companies;

into unmarketable supplies of cotton and woolen goods; into urban real estate, and rural highways and wilderness canals."[175]

The common man who had little money with which to speculate was also affected by the Panic as a result of the rising prices of basic commodities. Barreled flour and pork, for example, nearly doubled in price between 1835 and March 1837.[176] The depression left few Americans untouched, but southerners were especially hard hit because of the sharp drop in cotton prices. Cotton had commanded seventeen cents a pound prior to Van Buren's inauguration but would dip down to as low as five cents and rarely go above ten cents a pound for the next decade.[177]

Writing to Andrew Jackson on April 14, 1837, from New Orleans, McKinley gave a stark assessment of the cotton market there. "I came here nearly four weeks ago to see to my cotton," he wrote, "fearing the dreadful commercial convulsion which has taken place. . . . Every cotton house, with the exception of four or five, has failed . . . [and] no cotton can be sold here at present—scarcely at any price."[178]

Ten days later, McKinley wrote to William Pope, a business partner in Kentucky, to express his disappointment that the latter had not accepted offers on some of McKinley's property that was for sale near Louisville. The letter suggests that the Panic had already had an impact on McKinley. He wrote, "I am sorry you did not sell as I am in great need of money. My crop of cotton I left at New Orleans on the 15th unsold, and unsalable. For there is no money there to purchase anything with. This renders it necessary I should have money from some quarter."[179] Given the low price of cotton, property was one of the few things McKinley could liquidate, and he contacted Pope again two months later. He instructed him to sell off further parcels, again imploring, "I really am in great need of money."[180]

Perhaps with reference to his upcoming circuit-riding duties, he directed Pope further in his June 1837 letter that "If a pair of large, likely, young and well broke, carriage horses could be had at a reasonable price, in part payment of the lots to be sold on credit, I would take them."[181] McKinley went on to specify that "they must be bays, well matched; and not to cost more than $400 and delivered here. Horses are very low now for cash but I have none to give."[182]

McKinley's financial woes would continue for several more years, but just as embarrassing to a proud man like him were the questions already being raised about his fitness for the Supreme Court seat to which he had been appointed. Writing to Justice Joseph Story shortly after learning about the nominations of their two new colleagues, Justice John McLean declared, "McKinley's temper is not unlike Baldwin's and Catron is full of himself."[183] The comparison to Justice Henry Baldwin might have been a compliment in an earlier day when he was a prominent and successful Pennsylvania lawyer. However, since his appointment in 1830, Baldwin's physical and mental health had seriously deteriorated. By the time McKinley joined the Court, the general impression of Baldwin was, as a contemporary put it, "that he is partially deranged at all times."[184]

Story expressed similar reservations about the two men who would shortly join him on the bench. To Justice McLean he replied, "I agree with you as to the . . . two new judges [Catron and McKinley]. An increase in numbers without an increase in strength and ability and learning is a . . . disadvantage."[185] Story confessed that he did now know McKinley, but in an oft-quoted passage he relayed to McLean that "some . . . who do know him, speak of him in very moderated terms of praise—so moderated as to leave me to the conclusion that he has not the requisite qualifications for the office."[186]

Modern scholars have repeatedly relied upon this statement as evidence that McKinley was not qualified for his seat on the Court. The problem with this assumption is that it is not known exactly to what qualifications Story was referring. If he meant judicial experience, McKinley indeed had none outside his brief appointment as chief justice of the Lauderdale County Court by the Alabama territorial governor.[187] But judicial experience has never been a requirement to sit on the Supreme Court.[188] Neither Story nor Chief Justice Taney had any prior judicial experience, and even the great chief justice John Marshall had served only three years as a judge on a minor state court in Virginia before being elevated to the High Court.

If Story was referring to intellectual qualifications to serve, McKinley admittedly had little formal education. However, this may reflect more of an "old state versus new state" bias that southern members of Congress often complained infused its way into national policymaking. Six of the justices on the bench at the time McKinley was appointed were from the original thirteen states, and Philip Barbour from Virginia was the only one of the six who had not graduated from college. The remaining three were from newer states—McLean from Ohio, Catron from Tennessee, and McKinley from Alabama—and were all self-educated or had been privately tutored.

None of the nine justices held a law degree (Benjamin Curtis, who was appointed in 1851, would be the first) but, like McKinley, had read law or apprenticed in a law office to learn their trade and had successfully practiced law prior to embarking on their respective political careers before joining the Court.[189] In short, McKinley was probably as intellectually qualified as any of the other justices with the obvious exception of the brilliant Joseph Story, who was the leading intellectual light on the Taney Court. If he was the standard of "strength and ability and learning" by which the new associate justice would be evaluated, neither McKinley nor any other member of the bench at that time would be able to measure up.

It is likely that Story's initial misgivings about McKinley had to do more with the latter's politics and connection with Andrew Jackson than his judicial skills. Story routinely lamented the "memory of departed days" as the influx of Jacksonians tilted the philosophical balance on the bench far from what it had been when he had joined the Supreme Court during the early Marshall era.[190] The *Pittsburgh Gazette,* western Pennsylvania's most prominent Whig newspaper, sounded a similar theme when it reported McKinley's appointment. His nomination, it argued, "indicates very distinctly that the jacobism of [Jackson's] Kitchen Cabinet holds its control over President Van Buren." For its part, the *Democratic Review* in Washington gleefully noted that after the appointment of Catron and McKinley, "The late renovation of . . . this august body . . . may be regarded as the closing of an old and the opening of a new era in its history."[191] From the Jacksonian perspective, as Justice Catron put it when discussing McKinley's appointment with James K. Polk, "The matter has worked itself out rightfully."[192]

In addition to those who wondered about his qualifications, there were others who wondered whether the Supreme Court was a good fit for a man who had always been involved in electoral politics. In June 1837, McKinley responded to an earlier inquiry from his friend William Pope about his nomination. "You ask whether I accept the appointment of Judge of the supreme court of the U.S," he exclaimed. "I have accepted; although the duties of this circuit will be extremely laborious. Old Judge Smith says he is the first man that ever declined that office; and I suspect he will be the last."[193]

McKinley's comment briefly notes his awareness of the demands that would accompany his circuit-riding responsibilities, something he expressed in detail in a much more serious letter to James K. Polk:

> I have accepted the appointment, although it is certainly the most onerous and laborious of any in the United States. Should I perform

all the duties of the office I shall have to hold eight circuit courts, and assist in holding the Supreme [C]ourt, and travel upwards of five thousand miles every year. These are four or five times greater than many of the judges have; and besides my expenses in attending courts alone will not be less than $1500 a year while other judges will not have to expend five hundred. These inequalities could not, I know, be canceled in the passage of the bill. But I hope for the sake of justice, no matter who may be the Judges, that some mode will be hereafter adopted, by reorganizing the circuits, adding another Judge, allowing of mileage or some other means proper in themselves to equalize the duties and compensation.[194]

He would return to the theme of this letter many times during his tenure on the Court, repeatedly calling for the equalization of the financial and workload burdens at circuit. Comparing his traveling costs to that of the other justices might seem petty, but the financial reverses McKinley had already suffered during the economic downturn coupled with the fact that the justices paid their own expenses out of pocket made for real concerns on McKinley's part.

Congress was not in session at the time of Van Buren's initial appointment of McKinley, so the president resubmitted his name to the Senate for confirmation when Congress reconvened the following September.[195] On September 25, 1837, the Senate formally confirmed John McKinley by a voice vote as the twenty-seventh justice of the U.S. Supreme Court.

6

The Burdens of Justice on the Antebellum Supreme Court

> A judge of the Supreme Court is obliged to be up at daybreak, having
> little or no time for relaxation or sleep. . . . I have seen [the judges] . . .
> barely able to hold a pen in the morning, because of the utter prostration
> of the nervous system by the labors of the antecedent nights.
> —Senator Reverdy Johnson, 1848

There are considerable differences between the modern-day Supreme Court
and its antebellum predecessor. Today's justices come under intense public scrutiny almost from the moment they are nominated to the bench. Legal scholars, news commentators, and Internet blogs report and parse not
only the justices' opinions but their off-the-bench comments as well. They
work in their own building, sit in session from the first Monday in October until the end of June, and, with the help of their law clerks and other
administrative staff, face an ever-expanding docket that now exceeds ten
thousand cases annually.[1] The Court's caseload is both varied and complex,
dealing with, among other things, local, state, and federal government actions that affect protected rights and liberties, as well as the constitutionality of statutory, administrative, and regulatory matters.

The Supreme Court that McKinley joined in 1837, on the other hand, sat
for just a few months in Washington and held oral arguments in a dreary
room located in the basement of the U.S. Capitol. The number of cases on
its annual docket remained so low, relatively speaking, that several hours
and even days of oral arguments were permitted on a single case.

In part because the Bill of Rights would not be incorporated, or made
applicable against state and local government action, for another century,
the antebellum Supreme Court considered few cases requiring constitutional interpretation. Instead it considered issues arising out of such areas
as admiralty, diversity of citizenship, property, commercial, and common
law disputes. The Supreme Court also further delineated the boundaries of
state and federal governmental authority by resolving jurisdictional questions that were critical to the development of the young nation during the
antebellum period.

The greatest difference between the nineteenth-century Court and its modern counterpart, however, involved the duties of the justices away from their Washington courtroom. Indeed, McKinley and other members of the early Supreme Court spent relatively little time in Washington, D.C., in their official capacity. There were two reasons for this and each will be discussed in detail. The first was the short duration of the Court's session in Washington. The second was the circuit-riding responsibilities that were imposed upon the justices.

When McKinley joined the Supreme Court, its Washington term lasted just two months, from the second Monday in January through the middle of March.[2] Given this short time frame, there was no need for the justices to take up permanent residence in Washington. Instead, just as most members of Congress did when that body was in session, the justices lodged in the many boardinghouses that were scattered throughout the District.[3] The relative lack of both permanent housing and residents led a British visitor to refer to early Washington as a "card-board city" that was "taken down and packed up again" until Congress and the Court reconvened.[4]

From the earliest days of the Court until the mid-1830s, the justices resided together in the same boardinghouse while in Washington. There they slept, took their meals, and discussed in a more informal manner the cases that came before them.[5] By the time of McKinley's appointment, this judicial fraternity had begun to fragment as some members started to bring their wives with them to Washington and take up residence in separate boardinghouses or hotels during the term.[6] However, several of the other justices continued to board together until 1850.[7]

The boardinghouse groupings of justices, members of Congress, diplomats, cabinet members, and others throughout Washington were known as "messes." Party, ideological, or regional considerations were some of the factors that determined where men in D.C. would board and to which mess they would belong. As historian Catherine Allgor has written, not only did the messes provide their members with an identity, they also "were hives of political activity, and discussion and coalition (or, to enemies 'cabal') took place over the dinner tables . . . [and] in the parlors."[8]

The justices' boarding arrangements varied from year to year. Justices McKinley, Catron, and McLean, for example, were housed together in the private home of a Mr. Treacle during the Court's 1841 term.[9] Three years later, McKinley occupied a boardinghouse with Justices Story and McLean when the prominent Boston attorney and author Richard Henry Dana visited them in February 1844. Dana wrote in his journal, "[Judge

Story] came down into the parlor, and brought with him Judges McLean and McKinley. . . . These judges are the pleasantest set of fellows I met in Washington."[10] They struck him as "easy and natural, and having gone thro' a heavy day's work are very glad to relax themselves."[11] Indeed, Dana recorded that during his evening with the three justices they all enjoyed "a great deal of pleasant conversation, and loud laughing."[12]

The following December, a young representative from Georgia named Alexander H. Stephens informed his brother that he was boarding at a Mrs. Carters with several other congressmen and that the twelve dollars per week she charged them for room and board "was higher than it was last fall."[13] He also mentioned that "we have . . . the Judges in our mess," noting the presence of Chief Justice Taney and Justices Story, McLean, and McKinley.[14] Stephens wrote often about the "attic nights" he spent in conversation with the justices and others who joined their mess at Mrs. Carters. Indeed, two decades later while imprisoned in the immediate aftermath of the Civil War, Stephens, the former vice president of the Confederate States of America, would again fondly recall the messes, deeming them some of the choicest experiences of his time in Congress.[15]

The justices who greeted John McKinley upon his appointment to the bench and with whom he lived and worked were a diverse group, and all were eminent men before their elevation to the Supreme Court. Presiding over the Court during McKinley's entire tenure was Chief Justice Roger Taney. Taney was a successful Maryland lawyer and politician who, like McKinley, had also once been an ardent Federalist. He abandoned that party to become a Democrat but offered only qualified support for Andrew Jackson's 1824 presidential bid. Four years later, however, he emerged as the leader of Jackson's supporters in Maryland.[16] Content with his position as attorney general of Maryland, Taney apparently harbored few ambitions for higher office. His brother-in-law, Francis Scott Key, however, unfailingly promoted him for positions in Jackson's administration. When Jackson shuffled his cabinet in 1831, he appointed Taney as attorney general of the United States.

Taney would go on to become one of Jackson's most trusted associates. In September 1833 he received a recess appointment from Jackson to serve as secretary of the treasury from which position he oversaw the rerouting of federal deposits away from the Bank of the United States to various state banks. Incensed at Jackson's actions with regard to the national bank, the Senate declined to confirm Taney's appointment, turning him out of office after just nine months of service.

Never one to let a slight go unchallenged, Jackson sent Taney's name back to the Senate the next year for confirmation as an associate justice of the Supreme Court to replace Gabriel Duvall, who had resigned from the bench because he was almost completely deaf. Instead of formally rejecting Taney, the Senate decided instead to postpone his nomination indefinitely, which accomplished the same purpose. Taney was bitterly disappointed, but another opportunity to join the Court became available when Chief Justice John Marshall died during the summer of 1835. Jackson again submitted Taney's name, this time for the chief justice slot. Taney's second nomination to the Court won easy confirmation as Jackson's supporters had taken control of the Senate in the midterm elections of the previous year.

Despite Taney's connections to Jackson and his controversial route to the Court, the justice who attracted the most public attention during McKinley's tenure was the Massachusetts lawyer and scholar Joseph Story. Kind, gregarious, and brilliant, Story was appointed to the Supreme Court by James Madison in 1811 despite having no judicial experience. Just thirty-two at the time of his appointment, he remains the youngest person ever to sit on the High Court. Story's influence extended far beyond the bench he occupied for more than three decades. While serving as a member of the Court, he simultaneously held the position of Dane Professor of Law at Harvard University where he was a beloved teacher for nearly twenty years. His lectures on a variety of legal topics were subsequently reprinted as treatises and widely disseminated. In 1832 he published his landmark three-volume *Commentaries on the Constitution of the United States,* which was the leading scholarly work on the Constitution of its day. It was translated into several languages and was regularly reprinted until the early twentieth century.[17]

Justice Smith Thompson was appointed to the Supreme Court in 1823 by James Monroe. Best known outside legal circles as one of the founding members of the American Bible Society in 1816, Thompson took an active role in that organization until his death.[18] He had been a member of both the New York legislature and New York's 1801 constitutional convention and had spent sixteen years on the New York Supreme Court. He was serving as the secretary of the navy at the time he was nominated to the Court. In 1828, without resigning his position as associate justice, he ran for governor of New York but lost to Martin Van Buren.

Justice John McLean harbored even greater political aspirations than Thompson. Appointed to the bench by Andrew Jackson in 1829, McLean was steeped in state and national politics from his service on the Ohio Supreme Court, as a member of the U.S. House of Representatives, and as postmaster general in both the Monroe and Adams administrations. In 1841 President John Tyler actively courted the sitting justice to become his secretary of war.[19] In addition, as legal historian Charles Warren noted, "In practically every campaign since his appointment to the Bench, [McLean] had been, either actively or passively, a candidate for the Presidency; . . . and he entertained and publicly expressed positive . . . views as to the entire propriety of a Judge being a candidate for that office."[20]

At various times during his career on the Supreme Court, he actively courted the Democratic, Anti-Masonic, Whig, and American parties to help him win the White House. In 1856 he even hoped to be the fledgling Republican Party's first presidential nominee but lost that privilege to the western explorer John C. Fremont. Four years later, the seventy-five-year-old justice still managed to win twelve votes on the first ballot for the Republican presidential nomination that ultimately went to Abraham Lincoln.[21] It is little wonder that Daniel Webster once complained that McLean had "his head turned too much by politics."[22]

Another Jackson appointee, Justice Henry Baldwin, nearly resigned after his first term in 1831 but went on to serve fourteen years on the bench. At the time of his appointment, Baldwin was a charismatic and successful Pittsburgh attorney who reportedly possessed the best law library in the Northeast.[23] He represented Pennsylvania in Congress from 1816 to 1822 but resigned due to poor health. Both his physical and mental health grew increasingly fragile after he joined the Court, which affected his performance on the bench and his relationship with the other justices.[24] His behavior led one scholar to characterize him as the "emotional and at times intellectually unbalanced Pennsylvanian."[25] Baldwin's condition was exacerbated by the serious financial difficulties that plagued him during the entire time he sat on the Supreme Court and that eventually caused him to sell his considerable collection of books to the Library of Congress to pay off his debts. Baldwin was utterly penniless when he died, which forced his friends to take up subscriptions to help pay his funeral expenses.[26]

Born and bred in Georgia, Justice James M. Wayne was something of a child prodigy, entering Princeton at the age of fourteen. He spent most of his life in public office, serving as mayor of Savannah and as a Georgia state legislator, state judge, and congressman. In January 1835 just as he was about to begin his fourth term in the House of Representatives, Andrew Jackson nominated him for the Supreme Court vacancy created by the death of Justice William Johnson the previous August. He spent the next thirty-two years on the Supreme Court. When the Civil War began, he ignored pleas by friends and family to return to Georgia and support the Confederate cause.[27] Instead he abandoned his Savannah home and took up residence in Washington.

Andrew Jackson nominated Justice Philip Barbour for an open seat on the Supreme Court at the same time he forwarded Taney's name for the chief justice slot in 1835. A prominent and well-respected Virginian, Barbour was active in state and national politics, serving for over a decade in Congress including one term as Speaker of the House of Representatives from 1821 to 1823. His popularity was so great that even after he was appointed by Jackson as a federal judge for the Eastern District of Virginia in 1830, he had to resist continual entreaties to reenter electoral politics although, as mentioned earlier, he did permit his name to be run as an alternative vice presidential candidate in 1832. Barbour was a favorite of all those who served with him on the Supreme Court, including those who disagreed with his judicial views, and he was deeply mourned by his colleagues when he died after less than five years on the bench.

Although McKinley was the most junior member of the Supreme Court, he was not the only newcomer when he arrived in Washington for the beginning of the Court's 1838 term. John Catron of Tennessee, who was nominated six weeks before McKinley, was the eighth member of the newly expanded Supreme Court. A self-educated lawyer, Catron built one of Nashville's most successful legal practices and was elected to the Tennessee Supreme Court, serving for twelve years, the last three as chief justice. However, in 1835, after Catron supported Martin Van Buren's bid for the presidency over Tennessee's own Hugh Lawson White, the Tennessee legislature instituted several sweeping judicial reforms, one of which abolished Catron's position as chief justice.

He returned to private practice and, like McKinley in Alabama, devoted his efforts the following year to managing Van Buren's presidential campaign in Tennessee. Catron had known Andrew Jackson for two decades prior to his nomination, having briefly served with him during his campaign against the Creeks in Alabama. On his last day in office, Jackson rewarded his old friend and fellow Tennessean with a seat on the newly expanded Supreme Court. Catron would remain on the bench for the next twenty-eight years.

The opportunity to join these eight notable men on the highest appellate court in the country may have awed McKinley at first.[28] It is highly unlikely, however, that he was overwhelmed when, as a new justice, he set foot in the Court's chambers to hear his first oral arguments. This was

not only because, like most people in Washington, he had probably visited the Court often while serving in Congress but also because the room
itself was far from inspiring. It lacked both the spaciousness of the great
hall in which the House of Representatives assembled and the richness
of the Senate's chamber. In fact, it was not even reserved for the sole use
of the Court. Early Washington newspapers contained notices for a variety of public meetings that were often convened in the Supreme Court's
chambers.[29]

First-time visitors were often startled by the unimpressive room in which
the Court sat as well as the difficulty in finding it.[30] A newspaper correspondent in 1824 declared, "In arriving at it, you pass a labyrinth, and almost need the clue of Ariadne to guide you to the sanctuary of the blind
goddess. A stranger might traverse the dark avenues of the Capitol for a
week, without finding the remote corner in which Justice is administered
to the American Republic."[31]

Touring the Capitol during his visit to the United States in 1831, the
Scottish writer Thomas Hamilton offered this assessment of the Court's
chambers: "It is by no means a large or handsome apartment; and the low-
ness of the ceiling, and the circumstances of its being under ground [sic],
give it a certain cellar-like aspect, which is not pleasant."[32] The courtroom
was redecorated in 1837 to include mahogany desks and velvet-covered mahogany armchairs for the justices and cushioned seating for spectators, but
most descriptions of the chamber during McKinley's tenure continued to
be unflattering.[33] Nearly all mirror this brief, if blunt, description from
1841: "The apartment for the accommodation of the Supreme Court is an
ill-arranged, inconvenient, and badly lighted room."[34]

As to the latter point, the only windows in the chamber were located
behind the bench and the justices' chairs and bodies partially blocked the
incoming light. A cloud of smoke from the room's oil lamps hung under
the ceiling and further contributed to the murky environment. The result,
according to one contemporary account, was that the justices' "countenances [were] therefore indistinctly seen."[35] The shape of the room and its
poor ventilation also created oppressively hot surroundings. Daniel Webster recalled the conditions that accompanied one of his appearances before the Court on December 26, 1848. "I suppose I took cold in the Court
room on Friday," he wrote. "[W]hen I finished [my arguments], the heat
was suffocating, the thermometer being at ninety. The Court immediately adjourned—all the doors and windows were opened, and the damp
air rushed in."[36]

7. Old Supreme Court Chamber.
Courtesy of the Architect of the
Capitol.

Richard Henry Dana was one of the few to note the chamber's redeem-
ing qualities, having viewed it for the first time after visiting McKinley
and other justices in 1844. Dana acknowledged that he "felt indignant, at
first, [that] the highest court of the nation should have so inferior a place."[37]
But in speaking with the justices, he found that they "liked it, as they preferred to have no crowd in the galleries for the lawyers to talk to, they are
out of the way of the idlers about the rotunda, and the room being low
saves them the trouble of mounting high flights of steps."[38]

Because there were no anterooms or offices connected to the courtroom
at the time, McKinley and his colleagues navigated the same labyrinthine
route as courtroom visitors to get to the chamber and used the same entrance. As the spectators quickly took their seats, the justices paused just
inside the room to remove the black robes that hung from wall pegs near
the door, putting them on in full view of the audience before advancing to
the bench.[39] The proceedings formally began only after the marshal cried
out, "Yea, yea, yea, yea! The Supreme Court of the United States is now in
session. All persons having business before the Court, will be heard. God
save the United States and this honorable Court!"[40]

As mentioned before, relatively few people lived year-round in Washington during this period. With the return of Congress for its annual session in December and the beginning of the Court's term on the second Monday in January, however, the population exploded and the entire city was swept up in politics. Floor debates in the House and Senate attracted large numbers of observers who viewed the proceedings as a form of political entertainment. That a large proportion of those in the crowd were female (often the wives and daughters of the lawmakers) contributed perhaps to the oratorical flourishes that politicians felt compelled to adopt.[41]

In spite of the difficulty in finding it and the dreariness of the room itself, the Supreme Court Chamber also served as a "popular and instructive place of resort to strangers visiting the seat of government," as an 1842 New York newspaper stated.[42] However, the scores of people who streamed into the courtroom did so not to see the justices but to observe the eminent counsel who argued before them. Some of the most impressive and important lawyers ever to argue before the Supreme Court did so during McKinley's tenure. These included Henry Clay, John Sergeant, and Daniel Webster, who, while simultaneously serving as leading politicians in the halls of Congress above, could also be often found arguing cases in the Court's basement chamber.[43]

The Court's small room provided a much more intimate setting for the public to observe these men than could be had anywhere else in the Capitol. When it became known that these and other lawyers of their caliber would be arguing before the Supreme Court, the justices, indeed the case itself, could become something of an afterthought, as this 1841 account from the *Cleveland Daily Herald* suggests:

> The Supreme Court Room was filled this morning to hear the argument of Mr. Webster, not given yesterday as was expected. The argument was every way worthy of Mr. Webster's reputation as the ablest Constitutional lawyer of the country. He occupied but little more than two hours, and condensed his points in a manner so compact that the Judges upon the Bench were compelled to keep themselves busy in noting the heads and strong points of his remarks. Mr. Webster may well leave the Supreme Court for a time, with such an argument behind him. It is reputation enough for one man.[44]

Notwithstanding the complete omission of the legal issues involved in its description of the case itself, this newspaper's reference to Webster's "compact" argument of two hours highlights another key distinction between the modern Supreme Court and its early predecessors. Oral arguments before the justices are now limited, with some exceptions, to thirty minutes per side. At the time McKinley joined the Court, there were no such limitations and oral arguments on important cases could sometimes take days. The landmark commerce clause case of *Gibbons v. Ogden* (1821), for example, consumed six full days, while arguments in the famous *Amistad* case (1841) required eight.[45]

It is not surprising, then, that what passed for entertainment in Washington, as least for those gathered to listen to the most famous attorneys of their day, could understandably become a chore for the justices.[46] A New York newspaper correspondent from that era explained, "Counsel are heard in silence for hours, without being stopped or interrupted. . . . The Judges of the Court say nothing, but when they are fatigued and worried by long and pointless argument, displaying a want of logic, a want of acuteness, and a destitution of authorities, their feelings and wishes are sufficiently manifested by their countenances."[47]

Chief Justice John Marshall himself gave a rare voice to the justices' feelings regarding lengthy oral arguments. After a young lawyer complimented him that he, by virtue of his position on the Court, had now reached the "acme of judicial distinction," Marshall retorted, "The acme of judicial distinction means the ability to look a lawyer straight in the eyes for two hours and not hear a damned word he says."[48]

The Court refused to formally address the problem during its first sixty years, preferring instead to advise counsel off the bench to limit their arguments. In 1849, however, a majority of the Court, including McKinley, finally adopted Rule 53, which forbade counsel from speaking for more than two hours per side without special permission from the Court.[49]

One of the factors propelling the imposition of time constraints was the dramatic increase in the Court's workload, which was exacerbated when a single oral argument consumed several days. At the time McKinley was appointed, the Court had approximately eighty cases on its docket. By 1845 the Court's docket had doubled and Congress pushed the beginning of the Court's term back to the first Monday in December to help deal with the increased caseload.[50] Further increases in the Court's docket made it impossible for the justices to adjourn in mid-March as they had traditionally done, and by 1850 the Court was deciding cases well into the last week of May.

Importantly, the justices themselves were partially responsible for their expanding caseload. The Court's ability to manage its docket was severely hampered whenever its members failed to attend to their duties in Washington. McKinley's absence from five full terms of the Court is typically and frequently noted as an example. However, he was not the only member of the Court who missed cases and even whole terms. Poor health caused Justice Story, along with McKinley, to miss the entire 1843 term, and Chief Justice Taney missed virtually all of the following term in 1844. Nearly every other member of the bench missed oral arguments at one time or another, with period newspapers usually attributing their absence (for whatever reason) to "indisposition."

The business of the Court was impeded when even a single justice went missing. Ties produced by an evenly divided eight or six-member Court were often ordered to be reargued later, re-calendared amid the growing docket of new cases. In a letter to Justice Story, Chief Justice Taney lamented the poor progress made by the Court during the 1843 term when Story, McKinley, and later Smith Thompson were all absent. "After Judge Thompson left us," he wrote, "there were only six attending, and it several times happened that we were reduced to a mere Court, from the indisposition of some one or other of [these] Judges."[51] These absences had a compounding effect, as he reminded Story, for "at the close of the session we found that we had not been able to dispose of the cases which stood for argument at the last Term—some fifteen or twenty I believe not having been reached in the call of the docket."[52]

The primary business of the Court took place after oral arguments concluded when the justices met to discuss the case. As mentioned earlier, the justices participated in informal discussions about the cases in their D.C. boardinghouses but also, more formally, at conference. Justice McLean offered this glimpse into the decision-making process that emerged from both formal and informal processes. "Before any opinion is formed by the Court," he wrote, "the case after being argued at the Bar is thoroughly discussed in consultation."[53] He explained further that, "Night after night, this is done, in a case of difficulty, until the mind of every judge is satisfied, and then each judge gives his views of the whole case, embracing every point of it. In this way the opinion of the judge is expressed."[54]

Whether or not a justice wrote a particular opinion had little to do with his awareness of and even potential impact upon that opinion in its final form. To paraphrase Joseph Baldwin's 1853 counsel to attorneys, "It is a great mistake to suppose that a [justice's] strength lies chiefly in his [pen]; it is in the preparation of the case—in knowing what makes the case."[55] In 1874 former justice John Archibald Campbell (who succeeded to the

Court upon McKinley's death) offered additional information about the influence that individual justices, including McKinley, had on the conferences of the Taney Court when he declared, "The duties of the Justices of the Supreme Court consist in the hearing of cases; the preparation for the consultations; the consultations in the conference of the judges; the decision of the cause there, and the preparation of the opinion and the judgment of the court. <u>Their most arduous and responsible duty is in the conference</u>."[56]

He went on to describe the specific process by which members of the Taney Court reached their decisions:

> In these conferences, the Chief Justice usually called the case. He stated the pleadings and facts that they presented, the arguments and his conclusions in regard to them, and invited discussion. The discussion was free and open among the justices till all were satisfied.
>
> The question was put, whether judgment or decree should be reversed, and each justice, according to his precedence, commencing with the junior judge, was required to give his judgment and his reasons for his conclusion. The concurring opinions of the majority decided the cause and signified the matter of the opinion to be given. The Chief Justice designated the judge to prepare it.[57]

Because members of the Taney Court typically did not circulate their written opinions for review before they were delivered orally in court, both formal and informal discussions gave the justices a potential voice and even a formative influence on the final ruling.[58] The majority opinion reflected the will of the Court, but it would be a mistake to assume that the influence of a given justice was limited to opinion writing alone. Justice Story himself succinctly described that influence, albeit in exasperation: "[At circuit] I speak for myself upon full research and deliberate considerations and in the exercise of my free Judgment. [In Washington] I speak for the Court, and my opinions are modified, controlled, and sometimes fettered by the necessary obedience to the opinions of my Brethren."[59]

One of the frequent criticisms leveled at Justice McKinley by contemporary legal scholars is the surprisingly small number of opinions he wrote despite serving nearly fifteen years on the Court. He authored twenty majority decisions for the Court and three written dissents. There are eleven additional instances in which he concurred or dissented without opinion or joined with another justice's concurrence or dissent.[60] Focusing on the quantity of written opinions as a measure of a justice's significance, however, is problematic, particularly during the antebellum era.

Prior to the chief justiceship of John Marshall, the majority opinion in cases that came before the Court was typically delivered in the form of a brief statement by the chief justice, but only after the other justices expressed their views in separate opinions. However, during Marshall's tenure (1801–35), such seriatim opinions ceased to exist almost entirely. Marshall valued unity and tried to promote an image of solidarity on the Supreme Court by releasing a single opinion that reflected the Court's will. More often than not, these opinions were released under Marshall's name, even if he were not the author. According to one study, Chief Justice Marshall was responsible for more than half of the 1,100 decisions the Court issued during his thirty-four years on the bench.[61]

Set beside the large number of opinions authored by Marshall, Story (288), Taney (289), and McLean (299) during their extended terms on the Bench, McKinley's small number of opinions does indeed appear small.[62] However, it was also by far the norm. Of the twenty-six justices who preceded him, sixteen wrote twenty-one or fewer opinions. Of the ten justices who wrote more prolifically, six served for at least three decades on the Court, while two more served for twenty-eight years.[63]

It is important to remember also that at the time of McKinley's elevation to the bench, John Marshall had been dead but two years, and many of the Marshall Court norms were still in place. Dissenting and concurring opinions were generally discouraged, and the chief justice played the central role in the assignment of opinion writing.[64] Chief Justice Taney did not exercise the same dominance as his predecessor but "nevertheless tightly controlled the Court and limited the opportunities of most of his Associate Justices."[65] He also did not write as many opinions as Marshall but still assigned himself "the majority of the important constitutional cases on his Court."[66]

As far as the other cases that came before the Court were concerned, Taney apparently deferred to the justices who sought opinion-writing responsibilities. Justice Benjamin Curtis remarked that during his tenure on the Court, Taney was "aware that many of his associates were ambitious of [writing opinions], . . . [a]nd these considerations often influenced him to request others to prepare opinions."[67]

Modern scholars who have been quick to criticize McKinley's low output on the Supreme Court neglect the fact that not all justices relished the prospect of writing opinions. Because of this, as University of Virginia law professor G. Edward White observed, "opinions of the Court [were assigned] to those who liked writing them. Others could concentrate simply on making decisions."[68] As McKinley's health deteriorated, he was still capable of doing the latter.

In short, all of the antebellum justices had many opportunities, in both formal and informal settings, to discuss the issues presented by and questions arising from oral arguments. Even accounting for the terms he missed because of illness and extended circuit court business, McKinley still heard and discussed several hundred cases during his tenure.[69] To suggest his influence on the Court was limited to the small number of opinions he wrote is to vastly underestimate the Court's operating norms during this era.

Those norms made for a very demanding schedule during the justices' short session in D.C. In 1848 Maryland senator Reverdy Johnson, who frequently argued before the Court during McKinley's tenure on the bench, left this detailed and revealing description of the justices' workday:

> The labors of these judges are herculean. Their physical labor breaks them down at the end of six or seven weeks. . . . They meet at eleven o'clock and hear arguments until four. They then retire to their rooms; dine at five; go into consultation almost every day at seven; sit until nine, ten, eleven, or twelve at night. In the morning generally, their opinions are prepared, books have to be examined, records are to be pored over. . . . [R]ecords of two, three, four, or five hundred pages to be gone over word by word—authorities without number, owing to the multiplicity of reports to be examined; and no judge does his duty if he does not look at everything that is exhibited before him.[70]

Over the course of several weeks, this schedule coupled with their workload affected the physical health of the justices. They were obligated, Johnson continued, "to be up at daybreak, having little or no time for relaxation or sleep . . . yet compelled to be in court at eleven o'clock—compelled to take up new cases heaped upon them continually, and forced to go through the same routine of labor from day to day until the hour of final adjournment."[71] As arduous as their duties in Washington could be, however, antebellum justices generally preferred them to those associated with riding circuit, which was their other major responsibility.

The circuit allowed the justices to hear legal disputes throughout the country. In doing so, the members of the Court, in the words of the first chief justice, John Jay, brought "justice, as it were, to every man's door."[72]

Fulfilling that ideal demanded far more of the justices' time, attention, and personal resources than did the Court's brief session in Washington. Indeed, during the Court's first decade, the justices presided over 8,358 cases at circuit while disposing of less than one hundred cases in Washington during this same period.[73] As the first and only justice to preside over the original Ninth Circuit, John McKinley, perhaps more than any other member of the Court, personified the competing demands of the Court's growing responsibilities in Washington and its circuit duties.

The Judiciary Act of 1789 created the circuit court system by dividing the country into three geographical areas that comprised the eastern, middle, and southern circuits. The law also established thirteen district courts within these circuits to consider petty federal crimes and minor cases in which the federal government was the plaintiff, among other things. The circuit courts oversaw disputes dealing with major federal crimes, diversity of citizenship, and civil suits brought by the U.S. government. They also possessed limited appellate jurisdiction over the district courts' decisions.

With original jurisdiction in some areas and appellate in others, the circuit courts were critical to the development of federal law during this era. As legal historian R. Kent Newmyer has observed, "[The circuit courts'] jurisdiction over suits between citizens of different states made them a primary forum for the growing class of capitalists doing business across state lines."[74] Their decisions not only affected the people in their circuit, Newmyer added, for "[i]f authoritatively rendered, they could influence state and national law as well."[75]

The lower federal courts were the primary source for resolving the uncertainties associated with doing business during the antebellum period. Such uncertainties arose because the "local law of many states pertaining to [business] transactions was frequently confused and lacked uniformity . . . which increased risks and hurt enterprise."[76]

In thus overseeing interstate business disputes as well as local issues regarding debtor-creditor relations and property, the federal courts helped fashion broad commercial principles that became increasingly influential in the national economy. Given the broad jurisdiction they possessed over economic and other affairs important to a young nation, it is clear that the circuit courts had a great impact upon the local citizenry. Indeed, as constitutional historian Mary K. Tachau has noted, because of the thousands of people affected either directly or indirectly by its rulings, "It is doubtful whether any other branch of the federal government acted so directly upon so many people . . . as did this segment of the federal judiciary."[77]

An additional justification for instituting the practice of circuit riding had little to do with adjudicating disputes in far-flung areas. Riding circuit during this early period was supposed to help the justices fulfill an important civic education role as "republican schoolmasters."[78] Charles Warren has argued, "It was, in fact, almost entirely through their contact with the Judges sitting in their Circuit Courts that the people of the country became acquainted with this new institution, the Federal Judiciary."[79]

Others believed that the enlightenment the justices would gain by mingling with the American citizenry would find its way into the Court's decisions. Senator William Smith (whose refusal to accept President Jackson's nomination to the Court permitted McKinley's name to go forward) had earlier argued that the justices must ride circuit lest they become "completely cloistered within the City of Washington, and their decisions, instead of emanating from enlarged and liberalized minds, . . . assume a severe and local character."[80]

Each circuit court was initially comprised of two Supreme Court justices and a district court judge, any two of whom constituted a quorum. Therein lay one of the oddities of the Court's early years: a justice who rendered a decision at circuit would have the opportunity to review his own ruling if it was appealed to the Supreme Court. Possessing far less discretionary authority over their docket than their modern counterparts, antebellum justices were able to shape their Washington docket through their circuit court actions, which included approving writs of error and/or invoking a certificate of division.[81]

Most writs of error were initiated by the claim that a state tribunal had improperly ruled on the federal constitutionality of a state statute. Those seeking the Court's review of the lower court action had to have their petition for a writ of error approved by either a judge of the state supreme court or a Supreme Court justice. The fact that the state supreme court might be unwilling to approve the writ (not wanting the U.S. Supreme Court to review one of its rulings, for example) was reason enough to seek the assistance of a Supreme Court justice sitting at circuit.

The second and much more direct method by which justices were able to bring issues to the Supreme Court was through a certificate of division. Anticipating that the justices and the district court judges with whom they sat at circuit would not always agree, Congress authorized the certificate of division in 1802 as a means of bringing an issue to the full Supreme Court to settle the difference of opinion. Such differences surely occurred, but the justices also deliberately agreed to disagree with the district judge in order to bring issues they considered important to the attention of their brethren in Washington.[82] In short, should a district judge and a Supreme Court justice reach contrary conclusions on a case before them, the justice (usually with the assent of the district judge) would authorize and approve the certificate. Antebellum justices thus had at least four ways to influence the ultimate outcome of disputes arising at circuit: by their circuit rulings themselves (that were not appealed); by granting (or denying) a request for a writ of error; by disagreeing with the district judge and thereby initiating the certificate of division process; and by considering the circuit case again when it came before the full Court in Washington.

Relatedly, circuit riding helped spread and establish early Supreme Court precedents. At one time or another, every justice was put in the unenviable position of having to uphold the precedent of the Supreme Court even when he disagreed with it. As one scholar put it, a justice at circuit "was able to develop the law in cases of first impression, but when the Supreme Court had already ruled on an issue, he was obligated, as a conscientious jurist, to follow the high court."[83]

From the earliest days of the Court's history, however, the realities of riding circuit far outweighed the lofty ideals that supported the practice. The justices not only were far from home for extended periods of time, they also had to cope with less than ideal traveling conditions and public lodging. "To add insult to injury," Supreme Court historian Maeva Marcus notes, "the justices had to pay their own expenses."[84]

In 1790, during the Court's first term, Chief Justice John Jay pled with George Washington to convince Congress to remove the justices' circuit-riding responsibilities. Two years later, the entire bench signed their name to a letter to Washington declaring, "the burdens laid upon us [are] so excessive that we cannot forbear representing them in strong and explicit terms."[85] The combined responsibility of holding two Supreme Court sessions in Washington in addition to their circuit court duties was simply too burdensome, they argued, since it required "the Judges to pass the greater part of their days on the road, and at inns, and at a distance from their families."[86] Half of Washington's Supreme Court appointees (including Jay) subsequently resigned their seats within five years of joining the Court in large part because the rigors of circuit riding made the Supreme Court unattractive in comparison to other positions that had just as much, if not more, prestige but required little travel.[87]

With the inclusion of the western states of Kentucky, Tennessee, and Ohio into the Union (which necessitated the creation of another circuit and a seventh seat on the Supreme Court in 1807), the traveling demands on the justices increased, as did their complaints. The subsequent addition of several new and much larger states in virtually every direction—Alabama, Illinois, Indiana, Louisiana, Maine, Mississippi, and Missouri, all by 1821—only exacerbated the problem.[88]

By the time Congress expanded the seven seats on the Supreme Court to nine in March 1837, it had restructured the Court's circuit duties such that each justice presided over a single circuit and attended a single session of the Supreme Court in Washington. Acknowledging the additional off-circuit responsibilities borne by the members of the Court, Congress even authorized district judges to hold circuit court in the absence of a justice. While these accommodations provided some benefit, they did little to ease the practical burdens of circuit riding.[89]

For John McKinley, the first justice assigned to the Old Southwest, circuit riding would exact a particularly harsh toll. The first and most obvious cost of riding circuit was financial. At the time of his appointment, each of the associate justices received a $4,500 salary, while the chief justice received $5,000. Congress set that pay scale in 1819 and did not adjust it again until 1856, despite the huge increase in the justices' workload during the intervening four decades.[90]

As mentioned above, and unlike the benefit it provided to its own members, Congress had yet to authorize a travel allowance for the members of the Supreme Court. Such costs were far from negligible for any of the justices, including Chief Justice Taney, whose circuit encompassed only Delaware and Maryland, but they clearly weighed more heavily on those assigned to the larger circuits or those who had longer distances to travel to reach Washington for the Court's term there. Residing in Alabama and assigned to the Ninth Circuit meant that McKinley would pay a far larger proportion of out-of-pocket expenses to carry out his judicial duties than any other member of the Court. Before he was even confirmed, McKinley estimated that travel costs alone would require at least a third of his salary.[91]

The second major challenge that McKinley faced at circuit was the tremendous cultural, commercial, and economic diversity within the newly created Ninth Circuit. No other circuit could come close to matching the assortment of interests or lay claim to the unique legal problems therein. For example, in 1840, New Orleans was over 120 years old, was the cultural and commercial center of the South, and, with 100,000 residents, was one of the nation's largest and wealthiest cities. Little Rock, Arkansas, on the other hand, was home to less than 2,000 people and would not even have a true hotel in the city for another year. On the edge of the frontier, Jackson, Mississippi, was a young town awash with land speculators, settlers, and squatters. Mobile, the oldest city in Alabama, was a major seaport and the nation's second largest exporter of cotton. Such differences within the Ninth Circuit led to a vast spectrum of legal disputes that would have challenged the abilities of any Supreme Court justice.

The inclusion of Louisiana in this circuit was itself problematic because of the unique status of Spanish and French civil law there. As Louisiana senator Alexander Porter explained during an 1835 congressional debate on circuit expansion, "In Louisiana, the whole of our jurisprudence is based upon the civil law; but what is her situation? When her cases are tried and brought to the Supreme Court there is not a judge on the bench who has any knowledge of it."[92]

Like nearly every lawyer schooled outside that state (including all of the members of the Supreme Court), McKinley had trained in the English common law tradition and thus was initially ill prepared to consider disputes arising out of Louisiana's civil law heritage. And, if that were not enough, judicial proceedings at New Orleans were further complicated and protracted by the ongoing use of the French language by many citizens, which required additional time for translation.[93]

The third and perhaps most difficult obstacle McKinley faced at circuit was the arduous travel. The justices were not young, and each of their circuits undoubtedly had its own travel challenges, but McKinley's Ninth was arguably the most grueling because, with the exception of New Orleans, there simply was no convenient way to get to the courts in his circuit. Encompassing Alabama, Arkansas, the eastern portion of Louisiana, and Mississippi (all of which were among the top ten largest states at the time), Congress appeared to have organized the Ninth Circuit with little regard for the actual means of reaching the population centers in the Old Southwest. As a result, transportation difficulties in the largely unsettled area together with the congressionally mandated court schedule requiring him to zigzag his way across the circuit took a terrible toll on McKinley's health.

Contemporary judicial scholars have often noted that McKinley's lasting fame, such as it is, lies mostly in his frequent complaints regarding the difficulties of his circuit. Such characterizations are unfair for two reasons. First, they ignore the fact that McKinley was from the Old Southwest himself and given his business interests and the national political offices he held frequently traveled to, from, and throughout the area. His were not the concerns of an East Coast urban dweller unacquainted with life and travel on the American frontier. He was very familiar with the transportation challenges of his region long before he was appointed to the Court, and thus his concerns and complaints should not be casually dismissed.

When Justice Daniel of Virginia was assigned to Arkansas and Mississippi after Congress redrew the circuit boundaries in 1842, he, too, complained vociferously about the rigors of travel in that part of the country although he covered only half of the territory over which McKinley had previously presided. For McKinley, Daniel, and every other traveler passing through the area, it was just simply a very difficult region to traverse.

Second, many contemporary critics have failed to appreciate the court schedule imposed upon the Ninth Circuit by Congress, which required McKinley to crisscross his way across the Old Southwest in a ridiculously short time frame. The schedule, coupled with the difficulties of travel, as he mentioned in an 1842 petition to Congress, left him with little time to spend at home with his family. Other justices assigned to the newer and more rural parts of the country had similar complaints.[94] A brief review of what McKinley faced with respect to both transportation and the congressionally mandated dates for holding circuit court makes his concerns much easier to understand and appreciate.

The older states in the North and East, where the bulk of America's population resided, had a network of canals, bridges, turnpikes, and improved roads to facilitate travel within their borders. By 1830 these states were also encouraging the spread of the newest transportation marvel: the American railway system. At the time of McKinley's appointment to the Supreme Court in 1837, however, there were just 163 miles of railway scattered across the more than 200,000 square miles embraced by his Ninth Circuit.[95] By 1850, just two years before his death, only 120 additional miles of track had been completed. This paled in comparison to the 935 miles of rail line that existed in the Seventh Circuit of the upper Midwest (Illinois, Indiana, Michigan, and Ohio) or the 1,180 miles in operation within the states of the Sixth Circuit—the Carolinas and Georgia—that were also some distance away from Washington, D.C.[96]

The First through Sixth circuits covered all the states along the Atlantic seaboard and could thus be reached by sailing ship. The Eighth Circuit (encompassing Kentucky, Missouri, and Tennessee) lacked a coastline but travel to and throughout those states was facilitated by steamboats plying the Mississippi, Missouri, Ohio, and Tennessee rivers.

With limited water routes and even fewer railway lines, McKinley's circuit required a combination of rail, steamboat, canal, stagecoach, and even horseback to get to the cities where circuit court was held and back to Washington. He left just one description of the transportation problems he faced (an official report to Congress, which is discussed in chapter 7), but accounts from contemporaries passing over the same southwestern routes illustrate the challenges faced by McKinley and other travelers of his era.[97] Of course, modes of transportation that might be unacceptable to modern travelers were considered routine in McKinley's day, but even "routine" travel had its perils.

Traveling by railway or stagecoach from Washington to the Ohio River and from thence by steamboat to the Mississippi was the most convenient way for McKinley to get to New Orleans and Mobile. Some steamships were known as "great floating hotels" with all manner of entertainment and amenities for passengers, but most were merely serviceable, offering little more than room, board, and passage. However, all steamships on the great American rivers had to contend with varying weather conditions, above-water debris, snags, sandbars, and other underwater hazards, as well as rapid changes in the river itself, all of which literally made each journey on the same river a new and potentially dangerous enterprise.[98]

For their part, steamboat passengers had to deal with constant noise and shaking throughout the entire vessel, which were caused by the high-pressure steam engines—discomforts that could become maddening after a several-hundred-mile trip. Low water posed special problems, and even the briefest collision with a sandbar would send passengers tumbling. The food aboard ship was sometimes of questionable quality and cabin conditions frequently matched those outside: drafty and cold in the winter months and unbearably hot during the summer. To these were added the challenges of sharing dining rooms, restroom facilities, and cabin space with strangers. Of the latter, one historian has written, "[L]ate comers were often . . . obliged to sleep on cots or tables arranged in saloon or social rooms; many times they had to be content with a place on the carpeted floor. . . . At times the cabin passengers even had to shift for themselves as best as they could on deck."[99] Not surprisingly, the sum of these conditions aboard ship, particularly over long distances, "wore down the patience and endurance of travelers and magnified minor causes of [physical and emotional] irritation."[100]

Insects were a separate peril in themselves as water travel was often accompanied by swarms of flies and mosquitoes. Aboard a Mississippi River steamer just outside New Orleans, an 1845 traveler voiced a common complaint: "[S]warms of mosquitos [*sic*] came on board, and attacked us with the most bitter virulence. I have never seen so many, or such large ones. . . . I had gone to bed, but they did not respect my repose, and buzzed and bit, and stung again, with such vigour that to remain under their fire was impossible."[101]

McKinley's circuit route required him to pass between New Orleans and Mobile via steamship by way of the Gulf of Mexico. This passage was accompanied by its own hazards given the unpredictable conditions of the gulf as described by an 1835 passenger: "The sea was very high in the Gulf of Mexico, and as cross and troublesome as I have ever seen it. . . . [W]e shipped a great deal of water, and some of the passengers began to entertain apprehensions that the steamer would founder."[102]

Despite all of these challenges, steamships provided one of the most convenient modes of transportation for nineteenth-century Americans. Their major disadvantage, however, and one that was particularly acute in McKinley's case given the schedule he was expected to maintain, was the additional time required for water passage. An 1830 traveler lamented that a steamship traveling from Montgomery to Mobile, in following every twist and bend of the Alabama River, covered nearly twice as many miles as the overland stage route between the two cities.[103]

Passengers could be subjected to further delays when the business of business unexpectedly interfered with their travel schedule. After the circuits were reordered in 1842, Justice Peter Daniel began taking the same river route used by McKinley for five years. Daniel vehemently denounced those who put their own commercial interests ahead of their passengers. "[N]othing can surpass," he complained to his family, "if indeed it can equal the falsehood of the Steam Boat Captains, they lie without hesitation and without remorse."[104] They would "promise you the greatest expedition and diligence, and then put in at every point where holds the least promise of freight, and remain as long as there is the smallest hope of success."[105] To the extent that water travel was necessary to access the far reaches of their circuits, such delays directly impacted McKinley's and Daniel's ability to tend to their judicial duties.

The alternative to travel by steamboat was overland passage, which was much more direct than river travel but not without its own drawbacks, particularly in the South where the few stage roads that did exist were not well maintained. Justice McKinley would have shared a stagecoach with seven or eight people (and possibly with as many as eleven if the passengers squeezed together and some rode on top), all of whom were limited to ten pounds of baggage. Together they "shared the interior with bulky merchandise and bumped and jolted against each other, as the wagon creaked on its way at the rate of three or four miles an hour."[106]

Travelers felt every bump and depression in the hard-packed earthen road and were often bounced from their seats when the wheels passed over large holes. Notwithstanding the jostling they took on hard roads, passengers were even more wary of low-lying swampy areas. Passing through shallow depths, the wheels of the stage flung mud and water all over the vehicle with the passengers only imperfectly protected by lowered leather curtains. Longer stretches of marsh were traversed over "corduroy roads," which consisted of logs placed side by side, sometimes for hundreds of yards, through the low area to form an especially bumpy passage. An Irish traveler through Alabama in 1834 wryly described the feeling of such a ride: "Crack went the whip. 'Hold on with your claws and teeth!' cried the driver; the latter, we found, were only to be kept in the jaws by compression."[107]

Stage schedules were irregular at best since passage could be delayed by deep mud up to the hubs, lame horses, and the fording of rivers. Well-worn ruts, sandy soil, and obstacles in the road all tested the skills of the driver—and the nerves of passengers. There are accounts of scheduled stage lines that, because of problems with the stages running the mail, simply dropped their passenger service altogether in the middle of a route and sometimes far from the passengers' intended destination in order to assist the mail runs.

At the driver's command, passengers might be asked to "sway . . . left or right, or even [lean] out like small-craft sailors to keep the coach from tipping over."[108] They could also be expected to disembark and walk, sometimes with luggage in hand, if a muddy stretch proved too difficult for the horses to pull the stage completely loaded. In an 1839 report to Congress, Justice John McLean related that while on circuit in Indiana the previous year the mud was so deep "as to be almost impassable to a carriage of any description. The mails and passengers [including McLean] had to be conveyed in common wagons."[109]

The overland stage was a common mode of transportation, but for those, like Justice McKinley, who needed to take it over great distances, the stage could prove to be a real trial as captured by this detailed contemporary account:

> What a contrast is presented between the arrival and departure of a stage! On one occasion, you see a handsome vehicle in complete order, the horses slick and shiny, the harness clean, the passengers decently clad, bustling full of excitement and all in high glee. The driver cracks his whip and off they dash at a canter.
>
> On the other [end], the same vehicle comes rolling heavily into town, weighted down by its cumbrous load and spattered with mud. The horses are covered with foam and dirt, wearied, panting, and with heads drooped. The passengers are all of one color and a monotonous gloom is seen on their visages; they are the saddest, sorriest, vilest-looking set that can be imagined. They are alike tumbled, angry, dirty, and silent. The gentlemen have not shaved lately and the ladies have had their dresses crushed out of shape. They are hungry, thirsty, sleepy, and covered with dust. They started a genteel, well dressed, affable company; but now they have arrived a silent, haggard, unhappy-looking set of creatures. One has lost his trunk—another his temper. One has forgotten her traveling basket and they all have forgotten their good manners. . . . A painter might study their faces as they crawl out of the vehicle, and would find depicted upon them all the varieties of impatience, peevishness, and discontent.[110]

Between road conditions and sometimes reckless drivers, mishaps were frequent, and everyone who rode the stage risked injury. When Henry Clay's stage overset and he was dumped unceremoniously but unhurt on the streets of Uniontown, Pennsylvania, he famously quipped, "This is mixing the Clay of Kentucky with the limestone of Pennsylvania."[111] Chief Justice John Marshall, on the other hand, was seriously injured when his stage overturned in the spring of 1835. Nearly eighty and in declining health at the time of the accident, he never fully recovered and died the following July. That same year, as mentioned earlier, McKinley himself was injured in a stage accident just outside Nashville.

Overland travelers within the Ninth Circuit found lodging in hotels set up in the larger towns or inns along the route, and while some provided high-quality accommodations for travelers, most left much to be desired. The *best* hotel in Montgomery, according to an 1835 traveler, "seemed to breathe of whiskey and tobacco, and the walls of the bedroom to which I was shown were . . . incommunicably squirted over with a black-coloured tobacco-juice, and with more disgusting things."[112] Justice Peter Daniel, who succeeded to McKinley's route, angrily complained about his accommodations in Napoleon, Arkansas, which consisted of a six-by-four room within a dilapidated former steamboat that had been dragged ashore to function as a hotel.[113]

Separate sleeping arrangements could be had in some of these establishments, but they were not widely available. Hotels typically offered "sleeping rooms" where several people would spend the night. Describing a sleeping room from McKinley's era, a contemporary wrote: "The sleeping room commonly contains from four to eight bedsteads, having mattresses, but frequently not feather beds; sheets of calico, two blankets, a quilt. The bedsteads have no curtains, and the rooms are greatly unprovided with any conveniences."[114]

While these and other accounts offer a window into the world of American travel during the early and mid-nineteenth century, it is important to remember that Americans were far less mobile then and thus few people, comparatively speaking, used these modes to travel any great distance. The nature of Justice McKinley's responsibilities, however, as well as the size of his circuit, demanded that he spend a considerable amount of time each year traveling. These demands became so great that he eventually moved back to Kentucky where he had better access to water routes to carry him north for the Supreme Court's term in Washington and south to preside over circuit court.

An additional consideration to be noted with respect to McKinley's ability to carry out his Ninth Circuit duties was yellow fever. Although the disease had previously broken out in the North, by the early to mid-nineteenth century most yellow fever epidemics were occurring in southern cities. Among the hardest hit were the two Ninth Circuit court sites of Mobile and New Orleans. Goods offloaded there came from around the world, including areas in South America and Africa where yellow fever was endemic, and the watery surroundings of these port cities provided the perfect environment for the mosquitoes that transmitted the disease. Because of yellow fever's truly gruesome symptoms, the rapidity with which it spread, and the high mortality rate that often accompanied the disease, it was greatly feared and caused large numbers of citizens to flee their homes at the first sign of outbreak.

Yellow fever was an annual and dreaded visitor to New Orleans every year of John McKinley's tenure on the Supreme Court. Typically beginning in the early summer, the outbreak of the disease often lasted just a month or two but sometimes persisted into October and even as late as December. Several hundred people died from yellow fever each year in New Orleans; more than two thousand perished during the yellow fever epidemic of 1847, a mortality record that stood until the summer of 1853 when the Crescent City lost nearly eight thousand citizens to the disease.[115]

As if the modes of travel available to McKinley throughout his far-flung circuit and the annual prospect of contracting yellow fever were not challenging enough, he also had to deal with a congressionally mandated court schedule that was impossible to meet. McKinley and the other justices were expected to be in Washington when the Supreme Court's term began on the second Monday in January (later to be moved to the first Monday in December). Upon adjourning, typically in March, the justices would then embark upon their circuit duties.

Because there was no set date for ending the Supreme Court's Washington term, sessions that lasted longer than usual forced the justices to choose between leaving the Court early in order to attend to their circuit duties or remaining in D.C. until the Court finished its business at the risk of missing the early round of circuit courts. This was a problem for not only John McKinley and the other justices who oversaw far-off circuits but even occasionally for Chief Justice Taney who, despite a small circuit comprised of only nearby Delaware and Maryland, was occasionally forced to miss circuit court due to a protracted term in Washington.[116]

Congress set the beginning of the annual session of circuit court in Little Rock for the fourth Monday in March. McKinley was expected to conclude his business there in time to arrive at the southern Alabama city of Mobile by the second Monday in April. He then returned north to attend court in Jackson, Mississippi, on the first Monday in May and, two weeks later, journeyed back south to New Orleans where circuit court opened on the third Monday in May. His route would conclude with a trip to northern Alabama for Huntsville's circuit court on the second Monday in June.

The legislation creating the Eighth and Ninth circuits stipulated that circuit court be convened twice a year in some locations and annually in

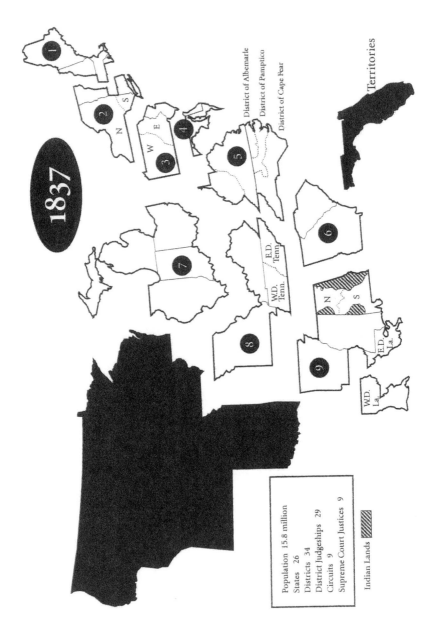

1837

District of Albemarle
District of Pamplico
District of Cape Fear

Territories

W.D. Tenn.
E.D. Tenn.

N
S

E.D. La.
W.D. La.

Population 15.8 million
States 26
Districts 34
District Judgeships 29
Circuits 9
Supreme Court Justices 9

Indian Lands

8. Boundaries of the federal circuits in 1837. Courtesy of the Federal Judicial Center.

others. This required McKinley to return to Mobile by the second Monday in October for its fall session. He would then head north to Jackson by the first Monday in November and back south to New Orleans two weeks later. From there, he would return to Washington, D.C., to await the beginning of the Supreme Court's term.[117] A more grueling route than this congressionally mandated zigzagged path is difficult to imagine. Not only did it make no sense in terms of efficiency, it also appeared that no one in Congress had actually traversed the route laid out for McKinley within the required time frame. In the words of two eminent judicial scholars, the Ninth Circuit's route was not only "unworkable, [but] bizarre."[118]

While Congress had mandated only the *start* dates for circuit court, the justices were left to decide on their own whether to leave some matters unfinished in order to make their next appointed circuit or devote as much time as possible to clearing their docket, knowing that in so doing they would be late to their next assignment. Between his large dockets, travel difficulties within the circuit, and the large area he was forced to traverse, McKinley was routinely late to his circuit court sessions.

Once the justices arrived at their circuit court sites, they confronted a whole new set of problems. While Justice Story greatly enjoyed his circuit and routinely praised the caliber of attorneys who argued their cases before him, such could not always be said of the newer states and/or the more rural circuit court sites where lawyering was in its infancy. With more than a hint of sarcasm, Justice John Catron, who served on the Tennessee Supreme Court for twelve years, recalled his first circuit court session in Kentucky in a letter to James K. Polk: "Met with a cool reception, under a belief brought home from Washington that [I] wanted legal skill—wanted lawyership in Kentucky! where the most important causes are heard and decided without reference to a single book, and any knowledge where the law is to be found."[119] As detailed in chapter 7, McKinley had a particularly difficult time with the lawyers in Mississippi who chafed at his brusque personality in the courtroom.

In addition to their relationship with the bar, the justices also had to contend with the federal district judges with whom they served at circuit. There was generally a respectful and professional relationship between the two, but several of the justices, including Catron, McLean, and McKinley, experienced some difficulty.[120] District judges were appointed from and lived full-time within the area they served. They were generally well educated and well regarded and were not always inclined to be deferential to the justices who slipped in and out of town for circuit court.

A final observation regarding the circuit activities of McKinley and other antebellum justices concerns the opinions they delivered there. As previously mentioned, the greatest proportion of a Supreme Court justice's work was at circuit and his rulings consequently had a broad impact on the people who lived and conducted business throughout that region. The great Justice Story openly acknowledged the significance of circuit court rulings when he remarked, "[I]f my fame shall happen to go down to posterity, my character as a Judge will be more fully and accurately seen in the opinions of the circuit [c]ourt than in the Supreme Court."[121] That statement applied to all of the antebellum justices, who were generally much more active and much better known at circuit than in Washington, but especially to those who took care to preserve their rulings as Story did.

Congress would not provide for federal court reporters until the early twentieth century and so disseminating circuit rulings, particularly during this early era, was up to the individual justices. Several of those with whom McKinley served published their own circuit opinions including, most notably, Justice Story, who edited, compiled, and published thirteen volumes of his circuit rulings. Other justices, like McKinley, who were far less intent than Story on preserving a written record of their decisions published only selected opinions that hardly reflected the breadth of their total work.[122]

Legal historian Carl B. Swisher, whose landmark work on the Taney Court is critical of Justice McKinley, observes that there were several reasons why antebellum justices refrained from publishing their opinions. These included the fact that "preparing written opinions for the scrutiny of the bench and bar added to the already heavy burden of the circuit work. There were [also] times when it was more comfortable to avoid publication of opinions on critical issues." He added, "In some instances refraining from writing opinions may have been a convenient means of avoiding display of sheer lack of ability—with Justice McKinley as an example."[123]

Regardless of whether Swisher is correct with respect to Justice McKinley's legal talents, he ignores entirely the circuit scheduling issues that seriously restricted McKinley's ability to write out and publish his circuit opinions. As mentioned earlier, the distances he was required to travel, particularly during the first half of his career on the bench, made it difficult for McKinley to arrive by the congressionally mandated date for holding circuit court. The heavy docket that confronted him there practically compelled him to dispense with cases as quickly as possible—something he simply could not have done had he resorted to written opinions. To write out such opinions after circuit court had adjourned was unfeasible as he needed to leave quickly for the next scheduled circuit.

McKinley's health also impacted his ability to publish his circuit opinions. There is no record of the extent of physical impairment he suffered during a November 1842 "paralytic stroke," but he was reported to be near death and later missed the entire 1843 session of the Court's term in Washington.[124] A few years later, the circuit court in New Orleans issued a formal order stating that all judgments and decrees would thenceforth be signed by the clerk of the court because disease prevented McKinley from even being able to sign his name.[125]

Swisher's sweepingly negative generalization of McKinley also fails to acknowledge one final rationale adopted by antebellum justices for not publishing their circuit rulings. Swisher himself invoked this reason when quoting from an 1866 memorial to Justice Catron: "[Catron] was opposed to the publication of circuit opinions because he thought the Justices of the Supreme Court should meet, *in banc* [*sic*], with minds perfectly open to conviction." The memorial went on to explain that Catron "was apprehensive that the natural desire to vindicate one's published views on circuit, or in the more imposing shape of text-books, would induce pride of opinion or of consistency to sway the final judgment."[126] While it is unknown if McKinley felt the same way, Catron was surely not the only justice from this era who held such reservations about the publication of his circuit opinions.

For John McKinley and the other antebellum justices with whom he served, the Taney Court was a unique fraternity that, at least in Washington, provided its members with opportunities for camaraderie, intellectual stimulation, and prestige. The circuit, however, was an entirely different matter. For nearly fifteen years, McKinley would struggle to fulfill his circuit-riding duties and his efforts were noted by the national press, both his friends and enemies in Congress, and other observers.

His duties combined with the size of his circuit, the long stretches of undeveloped land between the population centers there, and the circuit court schedule mandated by Congress would have challenged any of the justices. He was also no longer a young man. Of the twenty-six men who had served on the Supreme Court previously, only three had been older than McKinley at the time of their appointment. In fact, at fifty-seven years of age, he was already older than four of his Supreme Court colleagues when he joined them on the bench.

In 1842 the Ninth Circuit was divided and Justice Peter Daniel was assigned to Mississippi and Arkansas, while McKinley retained Alabama and Louisiana. Daniel found his duties virtually impossible to fulfill even though the circuit was now half the size that it was when McKinley had presided over it. As Daniel's biographer observed, and in words that could clearly apply to McKinley, "He . . . spent more time traveling than judging, and returned home not only exhausted from the constant strain of his movement but nervously tense from his everlasting rush from one means of transportation to another."[127] Given McKinley's age at the time of his appointment and his increasingly delicate health, it is no exaggeration to suggest that the rigors of the original Ninth Circuit truncated both his life and influence on the Court.[128]

The unique demands of his circuit challenged McKinley almost from the beginning and have served as the basis for much of the criticism that has been leveled against him by modern legal historians. In reality, however, those same challenges also brought out some of McKinley's finest attributes, a fact for which he was recognized not only by the circuits he served but also by his peers.

7

The Supreme Court and the
Original Ninth Circuit, 1837–1842

[I] would do [McKinley] justice . . . [and not] join in denunciations . . .
for not doing what it was physically impossible for him to do. Notwithstanding the complaints against him, he performed more labor than
any of the judges on the bench. The remedy for the evils complained of
should be cured by the legislation of Congress, and not by requiring an
impossibility of the judges of the Supreme Court.

—Congressman William Gwin, 1842

McKinley received notice of his September confirmation several weeks
after the fact, making it impossible for him to attend the fall 1837 session
of circuit court in Mobile, which began on the second Monday in October. However, he did arrive on schedule in Jackson, Mississippi, to convene court on the first Monday in November. The enormous docket awaiting him there coupled with the fact that New Orleans, the next scheduled
circuit site, was still recovering from a yellow fever epidemic caused him
to remain in Jackson far longer than he normally would have.

The extra time and effort McKinley devoted to his first circuit court
assignment did not go unnoticed. To show their appreciation, members
of the Mississippi Bar adopted the following resolution and had it published in Jackson area newspapers during the first week of December: "*Resolved*, That the thanks of this meeting be presented to the Honorable John
McKinley, for the able, dignified and impartial manner, and the unwea-
ried patience and industry with which he has discharged his duties during the present Term of this court." It went on to extend to him "the kind-
est wishes of the Mississippi Bar" and a prayer "for his safe return to his
family, and his health and prosperity through life."[1]

McKinley surely appreciated the commendation, especially coming so
early in his Supreme Court career, but it could not mask the harsh realities of his new circuit. The overland journey to Jackson from Florence
was 280 bone-jarring miles. After just one session of circuit court, it was
readily apparent to McKinley that dispensing justice throughout the far-

flung Ninth Circuit in the locations and according to the scheduled prescribed by Congress would be impossible.

When he arrived in Washington in mid-December to prepare for the
Court's upcoming term, McKinley raised the issue personally with President Van Buren. In a subsequent letter to Van Buren, McKinley reminded
him of their meeting and of the president's apparent sympathy for his concerns. He wrote, "At the time of the Supreme Court of 1838 I had the honor
to bring to your attention, by a conversation I then held with you, the great
inequality of the labors and duties of the several Judges of the supreme
court, while performing circuit court duties." McKinley hoped that Van
Buren would take up his cause with Congress, reminding the president
that he, too, "appeared to think it a proper subject to communicate in [his]
annual message."[2] However, Van Buren failed to mention the equalization
of the justices' circuit duties in his State of the Union address that year.

Aware that congressional authorization was necessary for any circuit
changes, McKinley turned to his friends and former colleagues in both
the House and Senate for assistance. Indeed, just three days into the congressional session, Clement C. Clay (in his first official act as Alabama's
newest senator, having filled the seat McKinley vacated) motioned that
the Senate's Judiciary Committee inquire into the possibility of altering
the Ninth Circuit's court schedule.[3] Two months later, Felix Grundy of
Tennessee reported a bill from that committee that offered the first pragmatic solution to the challenges of the Ninth Circuit. That proposal would
have directed McKinley to arrive first in Little Rock, followed by Jackson,
New Orleans, and Mobile. It was a far more rational circuit path, without
the crisscrossing and doubling back of the current route. It also allocated
additional time between the circuit court dates to allow for heavy dockets
and travel. The bill prompted spirited debate on both sides of the Capitol
at the very time that McKinley and his brethren were in session in their
basement chamber below.

McKinley's first Supreme Court term in Washington officially opened
on January 8, 1838, when the justices met briefly to discuss several administrative matters before adjourning to prepare for oral arguments the following day in the case of *McKinney v. Carroll*. McKinley would render a
decision in that case, his first for the Court, a month later. It was a short
ruling for a unanimous Court stating simply that the Court lacked jurisdiction in the matter because all of the pertinent questions had been resolved under the state law of Kentucky, where the dispute had originated.[4]

Given the socially charged issues that routinely confront the modern

Supreme Court, jurisdiction might appear to be a rather lackluster topic, but during the antebellum era it was critically important. As one of McKinley's colleagues, Justice Benjamin Curtis, later recalled, "questions of jurisdiction were questions of power as between the United States and the several states."[5] McKinley would address these questions of power in several subsequent cases.

Chief Justice Taney assigned McKinley to write the opinion of the Court in two other cases during his first term: *White v. Turk* and *Beaston v. Farmers' Bank of Delaware*.[6] The former was another jurisdiction case while the latter dealt with corporate rights. In *Beaston*, the Court considered the question of whether a federal bankruptcy statute giving priority for debts due to the United States applied to corporations.

The case arose out of a $500 debt George Beaston owed to an insolvent Maryland bank that was claimed by the United States and the Farmers' Bank in Delaware, both of which had won legal judgments against the bank. Although the Farmers' Bank was the first to obtain a court order of garnishment against Beaston, he paid the money to the United States instead, citing a 1797 federal law that gave government-owed debts priority over debts to other creditors. Attorneys for the Farmers' Bank responded that Beaston's debt was to the insolvent bank and as such could not possibly be governed by the priority statute because the bank was not a person. The priority statute law specifically stated that "[a] claim of the United States Government shall be paid first when . . . a *person* indebted to the government is insolvent."[7] It thus fell to the Court to decide "whether the bank is a person, within the meaning of the act."[8]

Writing for a narrow majority, McKinley upheld the government debt priority by declaring, "All debtors to the United States, whatever their character, and by whatever mode bound, may be fairly included within the language [of the legislation]. And it is manifest, that Congress intended to give priority of payment to the United States over all other creditors, in the cases stated therein."[9] In an oft-quoted passage, he went on to further delineate the theory of corporate personhood, which was still in its infancy: "No authority has been adduced to show, that a corporation may not, in the construction of statutes, be regarded as a natural person . . . , when the circumstances in which they are placed, are identical with those of natural persons."[10]

Justice Story vigorously disagreed with McKinley's ruling. While he, too, believed corporations could be viewed as persons, he thought the special provisions of the priority statute were meant to apply only to natural persons. More important, he saw the Court's ruling as "wholly extrajudicial and unauthorized by law" and "in no just sense, obligatory upon us, or upon our successors."[11]

McKinley participated in two other important rulings that term that demonstrate the significant role of the antebellum Court and its members during this formative era in American history. In the first of these, *Rhode Island v. Massachusetts*, the justices considered a long-running boundary dispute between the two states and, in the process, reaffirmed the Court's importance in the federal system.[12]

Attorneys for Massachusetts challenged the power of the Court by arguing that the determination of state boundaries was a political rather than a judicial question and thus the Court had no jurisdiction over the matter. During oral arguments, they also questioned the Court's authority to fully resolve the dispute, openly wondering how it would enforce its decision.

In a 7–1 decision (which McKinley joined), Justice Baldwin established that the Court did indeed have the jurisdiction to resolve state boundary disputes, if for no other reason than because there were few alternatives. Even if they wanted to, the Court noted, quarreling states were unlikely to fully settle the matter themselves because "[b]ound hand and foot by the prohibitions of the Constitution, a complaining state can neither treat, agree, or fight with its adversary without the consent of Congress." Thus, Baldwin wrote, "a resort to the judicial power is the only means left for legally adjusting or persuading a state which has possession of disputed territory to enter into an agreement or compact relating to a controverted boundary."[13] In announcing its jurisdiction over state boundary disputes, the Court also embraced a correspondingly important, if subtle, increase in its own power.

As far as the Court's authority to enforce its own rulings was concerned, the justices declared that the Constitution itself served as a persuasive force to conform. Baldwin gravely warned that should a state ignore the Court's decision, then "the Constitution becomes a solemn mockery, and the Nation is deprived of the means of enforcing its laws, by its own tribunal. So fatal a result must be deprecated by all."[14]

The second important case to emerge that term, *Kendall v. United States ex rel. Stokes*, saw eight days of oral arguments devoted to the question of presidential power.[15] At issue was whether Jackson's postmaster general, Amos Kendall, had (at Jackson's urging) properly ignored both congressional action and a circuit court order requiring him to pay a mail delivery contractor for services rendered. In a seminal decision for the Court, which McKinley joined, Justice Thompson sharply limited the scope of Jackson and Kendall's claim of executive branch power while upholding the authority of the lower federal courts. The justices rejected the contention that the postmaster general answered only to the president in assisting the latter to fulfill his constitutional responsibility to faithfully execute the laws. To recognize such a doctrine, Justice Thompson wrote, would be to vest "in the President a dispensing power which has no countenance for its support in any part of the Constitution."[16] Further, applying the same argument to every presidential appointee "would be clothing the President with a power entirely to control the legislation of Congress and paralyze the administration of justice," which the Court simply refused to do.[17]

As McKinley sided with the majority in both *Rhode Island* and *Kendall*, the faint outlines of his judicial philosophy begin to emerge: in the latter case, that the powers of the executive branch are constitutionally limited and its actions may be reviewed by the federal courts; in the former, and of perhaps even greater importance given the modern caricature of McKinley as a states' rights absolutist, it is clear that states are not free of federal judicial scrutiny even in areas that might have previously been considered strictly state matters. In short, the newest member of the Court possessed a healthy appreciation for the power of that body and its authority with respect to both the states and the other branches of the federal government.

Just a few weeks before the conclusion of the 1838 term, the Court declined to fulfill one of its unique ceremonial functions when Representative Jonathan Cilley of Maine was killed in a duel with a fellow member of Congress. Whenever a senator or representative died while Congress was in session, the entire city of Washington during that era, including the president and his cabinet, the vice president, and the Supreme Court, would turn out for the funeral services, which were typically held in the House of Representatives' chamber.[18] However, the Supreme Court as a body refused to attend Cilley's funeral, believing it inappropriate for the guardians of the law to honor one who had perished while engaging in a practice that was illegal in most states.[19]

The opportunity to participate in the dignified ceremonial role of a Supreme Court justice at a public event such as Cilley's funeral would have been a welcome diversion for McKinley. Just weeks into his first full term, as the *New York Spectator* recorded, McKinley was already the subject of "a great deal of complaint . . . by some of the representatives [from states in the Ninth Circuit] . . . that [he had] been remiss in the performance of his duties."[20] Their comments presaged the criticism that McKinley would receive during the next several years as he became the target of tremendous abuse both on and off Capitol Hill.

In mid-February, Representative Francis Thomas of Maryland reported the following resolution out of the House Judiciary Committee, which he chaired: "*Resolved,* That the Committee on the Judiciary be instructed to inquire whether any, and, if any, what, further legislation is required to ensure a steady administration of justice in the Circuit Court of Louisiana."[21] If there had been any doubt as to what prompted this resolution, there certainly was none after Representative Rice Garland of Louisiana arose to speak on the matter, complaining "of neglect on the part of the district judge [McKinley], whose face . . . had not been seen in New Orleans since his appointment."[22] McKinley's friend Representative Joshua Martin of Alabama responded, according to a Washington newspaper that covered the debate, by "admitt[ing] the present system to be defective, and hoped it would be improved, but defended the character and conduct of the judge referred to; repelling the imputation of willful neglect or incompetency."[23]

At virtually the same time on the other side of the Capitol, Senator Clement C. Clay was hoping to demonstrate just how "defective" the current circuit arrangements were. He moved that the Senate Judiciary Committee "be instructed to inquire into the expediency of making allowance for mileage to the judges of the circuit courts of the United States, in such manner as to equalize their compensation."[24] As mentioned earlier, each of the associate justices received the same salary (the chief justice received just $500 more), but their expenses, to and from Washington and at circuit, varied greatly. Since each member of the Court paid his own expenses, Clay, McKinley, and presumably several other justices hoped that the requested report would prompt the Senate to equalize the financial costs of serving on the Court. The motion was adopted and the Judiciary Committee instructed Secretary of State John Forsyth to prepare a detailed report on the distances traveled by the justices and their docket caseload at circuit.

In addition, under Clay's leadership, the bill to alter the schedule and starting dates of the courts within the Ninth Circuit successfully passed the Senate. It appeared poised to pass the House when Representative Joshua Martin, sensitive to both the charges against his friend McKinley and the practical difficulties of the large and unwieldy Ninth Circuit, offered an amendment to move Alabama into Justice James M. Wayne's Sixth Circuit, which then contained only Georgia and South Carolina. Not surprisingly, McKinley's allies in Congress encountered their greatest opposition when they advanced beyond merely simplifying the Ninth Circuit's schedule to the equalization of the justices' circuit duties. The former affected McKinley alone; the latter, by definition, meant that some justices could expect to do more as court sites and even whole states were added to their circuits. And just as McKinley had members of Congress looking out for his interests, so too did the other justices. Representative Charles Haynes of Georgia, for example, adamantly opposed Martin's proposal, arguing that "it would greatly increase the official labor of [Justice Wayne] by sending him into Alabama, where there was already a judge of the United States residing there."[25]

The Martin amendment refocused the House debate away from McKinley's alleged "neglect" of his circuit to the utter impossibility of any single justice to oversee the vast region encompassed by the Ninth Circuit. Sympathetic representatives from other parts of the country saw the amendment as a way to ensure timely access to the federal courts for litigants in the Ninth. As for any possible detriment to Justice Wayne, Representative Francis Thomas of Maryland bluntly noted that "even with the increased duty occasioned by the amendment, Judge Wayne would still have less to do than any of his brethren, Judge Barbour only excepted; while Judge McKinley would be relieved from a task too onerous to be performed by any judge."[26] Against the further protests from Representative Haynes on behalf of his fellow Georgian, Justice Wayne, the amendment passed.

When the amended bill returned to the Senate for final passage, however, both McKinley's critics and Justice Wayne's allies refused to yield. Without directly referring to McKinley, Senator Ambrose Sevier of Arkansas submitted an amendment that made the failure to attend circuit court an impeachable offense. He followed with a terse speech about how his constituents had suffered in the absence of a judge, concluding, "[I]f the judges do not hold their courts, and discharge the duties of their high offices, I shall, for one, endeavor to make them."[27] He was followed by William Preston of South Carolina, who agreed that impeachment was the proper penalty for both malfeasance and nonfeasance in office, suggesting that "an impeachment here [in McKinley's case] would do more towards securing fidelity in the public officers, than any affirmation in the statute book."[28]

Alabama senator Clement C. Clay immediately arose, questioning whether Sevier's actions were directed "to the present judge of the [N]inth [C]ircuit" and proceeded to defend McKinley against the allegations about his absence from circuit court. He began by gently ridiculing Sevier for overlooking the small fact that McKinley received his recess appointment at the end of May, which was *eight weeks after* the scheduled circuit court date in Little Rock. As to similar complaints from other senators, Clay reminded them, "[A]t the times appointed for holding the courts in New Orleans and Mobile last fall, it was well known the yellow fever was prevailing in both those places, and it would have been madness for the judge to have gone there."[29] McKinley could have convened circuit court there anyway, Clay posited, but if he had "he could have done nothing, for the parties, witnesses, and jurors, could not have been induced to attend."[30] In short, failure to preside at circuit before he was even on the Court or to sit in judgment in a diseased and largely abandoned city hardly constituted "neglect of duty on the part of the judge."[31]

Clay's passionate argument persuaded Sevier to withdraw his amendment, but it also had the unintended effect of undermining McKinley's plea for help when the amended House bill was taken up for consideration the next day. Senator Preston strongly objected to any measure that would "diminish the duties of the [Ninth Circuit], and increase those of the judge of South Carolina and Georgia."[32] His friend, Justice Wayne, had performed exemplary service at circuit, he argued, and adding anything to the justice's present duties would compromise his ability to serve effectively. Besides, he carefully noted, "[I]t was made ground of complaint the other day . . . that the judge [McKinley] had not yet performed the duties of his office; and yet here was a proposition . . . to make a change before we could tell how the system would be likely to work."[33]

Clay responded that the "system" would never work. He estimated that Justice Wayne traveled approximately 3,600 miles in his circuit while McKinley would log almost twice that amount. Equalizing their duties was the best way to ensure that the needs of the people were met. "It was utterly impracticable," he concluded, "for the judge of the [N]inth [Circuit] to get through the labors of the office."[34] Other senators, however, were persuaded that the year-old circuit arrangement needed to be maintained for a bit longer. The Senate ultimately rejected the amended House bill and thus, in no small part due to the interests of his colleague Justice Wayne, did John McKinley's hope to receive *any* relief at circuit that term die.

McKinley left no record of his feelings about either the failed congressional efforts on his behalf or his first Washington term in general.[35] After the Court adjourned in March, he had to leave immediately for circuit where some 4,700 cases awaited him, out of a total of 6,000 on the justices' cumulative circuit dockets.[36] Given the negative way he had already been characterized, he was probably eager to prove to his detractors in Congress that he was capable of performing his circuit duties. But what had been a trickle of criticism on Capitol Hill soon became a torrent nationwide when McKinley issued three controversial decisions while on circuit in Mobile that would later be consolidated before the U.S. Supreme Court as the *Bank of Augusta v. Earle.*[37]

Each of the cases addressed the right of corporations to do business in states in which they were not incorporated. Central to each was the use of bills of exchange as instruments of credit. Bills of exchange guaranteed that a seller (or drawer of the bill) would receive the full amount promised by a buyer (or drawee) at a certain point in the future. Rather than wait for the maturity date in order to collect on the bill, a drawer would typically transfer the bill of exchange to a bank that would, for a smaller amount of money to the drawer, take possession of the bill of exchange. Known as "discounting," this process allowed the drawer to receive money sooner than he would have otherwise and the bank, as the holder of the bill, to collect the full amount of the bill when it matured. With the onset of the Panic of 1837, gold and silver coin became increasingly difficult to find, especially after the suspension of specie payments by the nation's banks. Bills of exchange thus took on an even greater role in the national economy than they had prior to this time.

Each of the disputes that came before McKinley in these cases involved the refusal to honor the terms of bills of exchange that had since matured and were held by banks (or their agents). These simple facts obscured a larger confluence of forces that included desperate men who had overextended on their financial commitments, banking interests struggling to stay afloat in a stagnant economy, and the protectionist laws of Alabama and other states.

Unable to make good on their promise to pay, Joseph Earle and others in Alabama argued that the out-of-state banks that held their bills of exchange had no legal right to operate within the state. Alabama law at the time did indeed favor state-owned and state-chartered banks and prohibited out-of-state banks from engaging in banking activities within Alabama. But the law did not specify whether the buying or selling of bills of exchange constituted a "banking activity" since such transactions did not lie solely within the purview of financial institutions.

In his circuit opinion of April 18, 1838, McKinley ruled against the banks, contending that out-of-state corporations could not operate within a state without that state's specific blessing. As a result, such businesses could not enforce contracts that they had made or purchased in that state. The *Mobile Commercial Register* quickly pronounced its approval of McKinley's decision, declaring in addition that "the new Judge by his promptness, ability and urbanity has received an abiding popularity with the Bar and the suitors in the Court."[38]

Praise for the ruling was by far the exception, however, as McKinley's decision was roundly and often harshly condemned. It is important to note, however, that McKinley's opinion in *Bank of Augusta* was not inconsistent with the sentiment guiding a great deal of legislation throughout the country that sought to protect in-state commercial and financial interests. Two decades earlier, for example, legislatures in Indiana, Kentucky, Ohio, Maryland, Massachusetts, New York, and North Carolina enacted a variety of laws that creatively protected in-state debtors against their nonresident creditors.[39]

News of McKinley's circuit decision quickly spread throughout the nation where it was "the subject of general conversation and alarm."[40] The *Daily National Intelligencer* in Washington noted that "this startling decision of a Judge of the Supreme Court . . . amazed the men of business about here."[41] A Florida newspaper proclaimed, "[the] ruinous consequences [of the decision] if it be sustained, can scarce be imagined."[42] In North Carolina, the *Fayetteville Observer* declared the decision "highly immoral and alarming."[43] Newspapers readers in Philadelphia were told that "the case will go up . . . to the Supreme Court of the United States, where the question will be settled."[44] And New York residents were cautioned to prepare for the "utter demoralization which must follow this decision, if sustained [by the Supreme Court]."[45]

McKinley's fellow justices could not help noticing the national reaction to his circuit court decision as well. In a letter to Massachusetts senator Charles Sumner, Justice Joseph Story quipped, "My brother, McKinley, has recently made a most sweeping decision in the Circuit Court in Alabama which has frightened half the lawyers and all the corporations of the country out of their proprieties." He went on to explain the more serious consequences of the ruling: "[If a] corporation created in one State has no power to contract (or, it would seem, even to act) in any other State, . . . [the] banks, insurance companies, manufacturing companies, etc., have no capacity to take or discount notes in another State, or to underwrite policies or to buy or sell goods."[46]

The scope of these potential consequences led northern banking interests to immediately solicit the help of Chancellor James Kent of New York to undercut McKinley's decision in the court of public opinion. Kent was one of the nation's great jurists, the author of the enormously influential *Commentaries on American Law*, and more than happy to assist. A staunch Federalist, Kent was disgusted by the Jacksonian transformation of the Supreme Court. Upon learning of the appointment of Catron and McKinley, for example, he sullenly declared to Justice Story, "It absolutely overwhelms me in despair, and I have no hopes left especially when I consider that we have two new Judges [Catron and McKinley]—very feeble lights added to your bench. . . . I respect it no longer."[47]

With each additional personnel change on the bench, Kent's antagonism toward the Court became even more pronounced. Writing to Story in 1845 he proclaimed, "I do not regard their decisions (yours always excepted) with much reverence; and for a number of Associates I feel habitual scorn and contempt."[48] Indeed, when publicly criticizing the justices and their rulings, Kent was capable of marshaling arguments that were at once models of intellectual rigor and scathing personal denunciation.

He authored a full treatise on the Mobile decisions that was published in a prominent law review of his day, with selections reprinted in newspapers across the country, "at great length," as one put it at the time, "[and] in direct opposition to that of Judge McKinley."[49] Kent thought it preposterous that a contract entered into by a New York corporation to do business in the Deep South was somehow invalid but would have been "valid and cheerfully enforced" if entered into with another New York partner. "The distinction," he wrote, "is illusory, and has no foundation in law, and as [*sic*] little color for it in justice, or comity, or policy, or common sense."[50] National and international law supported the notion that both natural and corporate citizens had rights. To Kent, this meant that both stand "on an equal footing. The courts are bound to act, in the administration of justice, without being respecters of persons. The simple and most valuable principle of our law is . . . that all persons are at liberty to contract, deal and trade throughout the land as they please."[51]

In addition to recruiting both legal giants and the print media to their cause, business interests also successfully pushed to have the decision quickly appealed to the Supreme Court, where it was placed on the Court's docket for argument the following January.

McKinley's supporters did their best to counter the wave of negative press. In the same legal publication in which Kent had criticized the *Bank of Augusta* ruling, for example, an anonymous author responded, "It is against the policy of all the states by the rules of the common law, to deal

in a corporate name without legislative authority. It is a fundamental error to say, that the right exists *until it is prohibited.* Until the right is created by the laws of any particular state, it need not be prohibited, for it does
not exist."[52] Such efforts, however, yielded little protection for McKinley.
Against the backdrop of continued bitter partisanship between the Whigs
and Jacksonian Democrats, he was savaged in the media. As a sympathetic
correspondent from Mobile recorded, "*For this judgment* [*Bank of Augusta*],
so STRIKINGLY JUST AND PROPER, the bank press opened its bat-
teries of abuse not only against the judgment, but the character and purity
of the judge who gave it."[53]

It was during this period that the caricature of McKinley's life and abilities that modern scholars have perpetuated without careful study began to
emerge. A journalist in Boston, for example, portrayed McKinley as inept,
claiming to have witnessed the same negative characteristic in the justice
a decade earlier. "We saw a good deal of this Mr. McKinley during the
winter of 1827–8," he wrote. "He was then a member of the House of Representatives. He was seldom in his seat, but might generally be seen loung-
ing on the platform in the rear of the Speaker's chair." There, the writer
added, McKinley could be found "electioneering for Gen. Jackson, when
he was not asleep on one of the sofas, where he was probably dreaming of
the judgeship that was in store for him."[54] McKinley, of course, was serving in the Senate and not the House in 1827, but the facts were often the
first casualty in the battles fought by the partisan presses of the time.

Newspapers in Boston, New York, Washington, and other major cities
reprinted the impressions of an unidentified writer who claimed to have
known McKinley for thirty years. He described in detail McKinley's infamous Fourth of July toast in Kentucky insulting Thomas Jefferson. Of
McKinley's years as an attorney in Kentucky, the anonymous correspondent wrote, "He met with rather indifferent success in the practice for several years—being by no means a clear or attractive speaker. Yet he was even
then, I think, looked on as rather an ingenious (or more properly a '*cute*'
[cunning] lawyer)."[55]

After repeating the now twelve-year-old account of his political conversion to Jackson ("he was everywhere known as a Federalist in his politics,
. . . and respected as a consistent one"), the author offered a scathing denunciation of McKinley's abilities: "He is not without ingenuity, but he is
muddy and obscure. He is but an indifferent scholar. His general reading
is very limited, as well as his legal attainments. His vanity unbounded. . . .
To this end he will espouse any opinion that looks gratifying to him." He

added a final caustic note relative to the *Bank of Augusta* cases: "The late opinion he has given at Mobile . . . does not surprise me in the least. It is just like him. If such a folly can be sustained by the Supreme Court of the United States, he would be exalted, in his own opinion, above all judicial rivalry."[56]

Horace Greeley's *New-Yorker* magazine, a staunch supporter of Whig policies, sarcastically informed its readers that the Jacksonian justice responsible for the decision was "Mr. Justice McKinley, who favors the world with this specimen of his acumen and legal attainments."[57] After briefly recounting McKinley's studying law under Kentucky senator John Rowan, the magazine added in derision, "Neither master nor pupil was ever remarkable for mental perspicuity; and if the latter ever attained distinction as a counsellor or at the bar, it must have been very recently."[58]

Observing the national and primarily negative focus on the justice's intelligence, legal training, party affiliation, and work ethic, the *Washington Globe*, slanted as it was as the mouthpiece of the Democratic establishment in Washington, accurately summarized the general press treatment of McKinley in response to his *Bank of Augusta* decision: "Judge McKinley was abused like a pickpocket," it somberly noted, "not only by the . . . presses, but sneered at and trampled upon, in the opinion of the old Federal lawyer [James Kent], which was most improperly published and industriously propagated by those presses to influence and absolutely coerce the final judgments of the Supreme Court."[59]

McKinley's ongoing circuit responsibilities helped him flee the torrent of national abuse aimed at him, but only to a point. In early June he arrived at a special session of circuit court in Natchez, Mississippi (rather than Jackson), to find that U.S. District judge George Adams had dismissed the entire first panel of jurors because of improprieties and ordered a second one to be summoned. This caused an initial delay in the circuit court's business, but the judges quickly caught up—something a local paper, the *Mississippian*, noted approvingly: "Judge Adams, as well as Judge McKinley, have shown every disposition to be governed by a high sense of public duty, and to yield nothing, in these times, to mistaken views of delay."[60] Then, with perhaps a brief nod to McKinley's *Bank of Augusta* decision, the paper continued, "It is but just, also, to remark, that public opinion in Mississippi is sound on the subject of a due observance of the integrity of contracts."[61]

Continuing on to New Orleans, McKinley stumbled upon a new difficulty (arising out of purely local political patronage) that would greatly impact his role at circuit court that term. Nearly a year earlier, the incumbent federal judge for the eastern district of Louisiana, Samuel H. Harper, had died. His successor, Philip K. Lawrence, promptly dismissed the sitting clerk of the federal court upon taking office. In doing so, Lawrence made it clear that Duncan Hennen's service during his previous four years as clerk had been admirable and that he was only being terminated so that he (Lawrence) might reward a close friend with the position. District court judges were indeed empowered to appoint clerks, but it was not clear whether they could remove them. Hennen, accordingly, refused to give up his office and challenged his removal in the very federal court where he had clerked and where McKinley and Lawrence now sat together as circuit judges.

Upon consideration of the matter, McKinley sided with Hennen, while Judge Lawrence maintained that his friend, John Winthrop, was the duly authorized federal clerk. However the judges may have personally viewed the issue, their divided opinion had a far greater impact on the business of the Court as there was now no one responsible for the forms, filings, and procedures of the courtroom.[62] The result, as a Washington, D.C., newspaper reported, was that "no business could be transacted by the Court, and so far as concerns the District of Louisiana, the United States judicial authority is suspended."[63]

Thomas Slidell, the U.S. district attorney, pleaded with McKinley and Lawrence to appoint an interim clerk so that the court could attend to its business, but he was unable to break the impasse.[64] Instead, the case was quickly certified to the Supreme Court and slated for oral arguments during its January 1839 term. In the meantime, no federal court business at either the district or circuit court level was conducted until after the Supreme Court resolved the case the following spring. In its coverage of the dispute, the national press was just as divided as McKinley and Lawrence.

The *New Orleans Commercial Herald* opined, "[T]the Judge of the District Court has the power of appointing and removing the clerk. . . . That the Circuit Court has not the shadow of jurisdiction over the matter, we believe (with due deference to the ideas of Judge McKinley), will be the opinion of the Supreme Court."[65] The *Daily National Intelligencer* in Washington countered that "such an abuse of power by a Judge as removal of the Clerk, avowedly only to gratify a personal interest, would seem to be a clear case for the High Court of Impeachment."[66]

Even as Lawrence's power as a federal judge was being questioned, reports were circulating that Congress would expand his authority and that

A statement showing the number of miles which each Judge of the Supreme Court has to travel, in attending the courts of the circuit allotted to him, and in attending the Supreme Court of the United States.

Names of the Judges.	No. of miles.
Roger B. Taney	458
Henry Baldwin	2,000
James M. Wayne	2,370
Philip P. Barbour	1,498
Joseph Story	1,896
Smith Thompson	2,590
John McLean	2,500
John Catron	3,464
John McKinley	10,000

9. Secretary of State Forsyth's report to the Senate (1839).

of every other district judge within the Ninth by giving them full circuit court power. The rumored proposal was designed to help address the demands of large caseloads in Louisiana and Mississippi, but the *Arkansas Gazette* encouraged the extension of the measure to Arkansas as well. McKinley would never visit that state on circuit, a fact the *Gazette* sympathetically acknowledged: "[O]wing to the great extent of his circuit, and his conflicting duties, according to the present arrangement of the terms, we cannot expect the regular attendance of Judge McKinley."[67]

McKinley's first spring term at circuit ended to mixed reviews. In the national press, the furor caused by the *Bank of Augusta* ruling and his dispute with Judge Lawrence overshadowed virtually everything else that he accomplished that term. McKinley would be subjected to another round of mostly disparaging comments in the national press when these same controversial actions came before his brethren during the Court's 1839 term.

Just prior to the beginning of that session and in accordance with the directive given him by the Senate Judiciary Committee the previous year, Secretary of State Forsyth submitted his findings regarding the miles traveled by the justices while on circuit as well as their caseloads. The justices' self-reported traveling distances ranged from 458 miles (Taney's small Fourth Circuit) to a few thousand miles for seven of the remaining eight justices. John McKinley reported ten thousand.

This figure, which is almost three times greater than the next highest claim (John Catron's 3,464 miles), continues to raise eyebrows among modern legal historians who suggest that McKinley vastly exaggerated the distance required to cover the Ninth. However, McKinley himself acknowledged that his figure was an estimate as no precise measurement of the miles required by his circuit travel could be obtained.

In a letter to Forsyth that was included in the secretary's report, McKinley noted that taking the shortest routes available to and from his circuit sites, twice a year, as well as to Washington for the Court's term there would result in approximately 6,500 miles in annual travel. Though shorter, these direct overland routes were not necessarily proper roads. McKinley suggested that the condition of some of them did not permit "public conveyances, and the time allowed for holding the courts . . . render[ed] it impossible to perform the travelling by any private mode."[68] He was obligated, therefore, to rely on routes utilized by stagecoaches and steamboats even though they might add hundreds of miles to his travel.

Seasonal conditions also affected the routes available to him. He admitted he had yet to hold circuit court in Little Rock because it could only be reached by water routes in the spring. To travel there by steamboat would not only greatly increase the total number of miles covered but also make him late for all of his subsequent circuits at Mobile, Jackson, and New Orleans.

The main reason for McKinley's huge estimate was the Ninth Circuit's court schedule. With a nod to the failed congressional action of the previous year, the justice gently reminded both Forsyth and the members of the Senate who would be reading the secretary's report that "if the courts of this circuit were properly arranged the traveling would be greatly diminished."[69] As it stood, the route was so poorly designed, as McKinley informed Forsyth, that he was required to follow a zigzag path that took him through New Orleans three times. The same route (with the exception of Little Rock, which was excluded from the fall circuit) was to be followed in both the spring and fall of each year. McKinley combined the figures for this travel with the mileage to and from D.C. from his home in Florence to reach his loose estimate of ten thousand miles.

McKinley may have indeed exaggerated the total number of miles he traveled, but not by much. Water routes could entail twice as many miles as overland routes between the same two destinations. And when one factors the distance people traveled in order to access the roads used by "public conveyances" and the relatively few such routes that existed in the Old Southwest at that time, additional miles add up very quickly. Even today, retracing McKinley's mandated circuit route using the vast network of modern highways and interstate roads that directly link his circuit sites still requires nearly five thousand miles.[70]

As ordered by the Senate, Secretary Forsyth also included the number of cases on the circuit court dockets for the two previous years. U.S. attorneys from around the country provided the information, with those in the Ninth Circuit reporting over 7,300 cases, which comprised nearly two-thirds of the total number of cases on the circuit dockets.[71]

Forsyth's report was merely that—a report. The secretary of state fulfilled the mandate he was given but made no recommendations to the Senate. Despite conclusive evidence of an egregious imbalance in both the travel and workload demands of the justices, the Senate took no further action on Forsyth's report. The House did approve a resolution from Alabama representative Francis Lyon instructing the Judiciary Committee to study the possibility of changing the circuit court date in Mobile "to a later and more healthy season of the year," but nothing came of it.[72]

McKinley was not present when the Court convened for its January 1839 term, having delayed his travel to Washington to recuperate from an illness at home. He arrived two weeks later to find the Court had scheduled his two Ninth Circuit cases of *Bank of Augusta v. Earle* and *Ex Parte Hennen* back-to-back.

Duncan Hennen, of the latter case, had no intention of waiting for the Court to resolve his claim of having been improperly removed as the Ninth Circuit court clerk and had already sought assistance from friends in Congress. In early February 1839, just days before the Court issued its opinion in his case, a select House committee submitted a report on the Hennen incident and the subsequent dispute between McKinley and Judge Lawrence to the full House of Representatives.[73] The committee had questioned McKinley about the affair and included his response to several interrogatories in its report. On the strength of the testimony provided by McKinley and others, the select committee recommended that Judge Lawrence "be impeached for high misdemeanors in office."[74]

The justices, however, saw things very differently when the Court handed down its decision a few days later in the case of *Ex Parte Hennen*.[75] Writing for the Court, Justice Smith Thompson stated that unlike the federal judges whom they served, neither the Constitution nor Congress granted lifetime appointments to district court clerks. And, in spite of the fact that such clerks also often assumed circuit court responsibilities when those courts were in session, they still continued to serve at the pleasure of the district judge who, by federal law, was authorized to appoint them.[76]

McKinley, who had since arrived in Washington, declined to dissent in the case. However, his position at circuit received a more important endorsement when, immediately after and in response to the Supreme Court's decision in *Hennen*, Congress passed special legislation pertaining to the appointment of circuit court clerks. Such appointments were to be made jointly by the district court judge and Supreme Court justice at circuit, but in the event of a disagreement, the legislation authorized the latter to make the final decision.[77] McKinley took full advantage of this law to quickly return Hennen to his position as clerk of the Ninth Circuit court in New Orleans.[78]

Although the Hennen dispute was significant enough to prompt congressional action, the single most important case on the Court's docket that term was *Bank of Augusta v. Earle*. Commercial interests were still clearly worried that a Supreme Court dominated by Jacksonians might indeed uphold McKinley's lower court decision even though it had been roundly denounced throughout the country. To offset this possibility, they enlisted the services of well-known New York attorney David B. Ogden. They also secured John Sergeant and Daniel Webster, who were two of the three most prominent advocates to argue before the Supreme Court during that era. The third, Henry Clay, was also in the courtroom to assist as needed.[79]

For three days before a courtroom "crowded with a brilliant audience of both sexes, and from all parts," the three primary attorneys offered spirited denunciations of McKinley's circuit court ruling.[80] Webster prominently characterized it as "anti-commercial, anti-social, new and unheard of in our system, and calculated to break up the harmony which has so long prevailed among the states and people of this Union."[81] He argued that corporations should enjoy the full privileges and immunities guaranteed to citizens conducting business throughout the country. He concluded his oral argument in typically dramatic fashion by turning to the Court and declaring, "The guardianship of [America's] commercial interests; the preservation of the harmonious intercourse of all her citizens; the fulfilling, in this respect, of the great object of the [C]onstitution, are in your hands." He added solemnly, "I am not to doubt, that the trust will be so performed as to sustain at once high national objects and the character of this tribunal."[82]

McKinley's delay in reaching Washington caused him to miss the banks' entire argument. But, according to a local newspaper, he took his place on the bench "just in time to hear a complete vindication of his position" by opposing attorney Charles J. Ingersoll.[83] It was not so much the rights of corporations at stake, Ingersoll argued, but the authority of Alabama and every other state to regulate commercial activities within their borders. Corporations could not even exist, he claimed, much less operate, without the sanction of some governmental authority. To acknowledge otherwise would essentially permit them to be a law unto themselves. "Corporations are creations of municipal law," Ingersoll declared, "having no existence or power to contract whatever, until enabled so to do by a law."[84] He went on to add, "It is confidently submitted to the Court that it will best fulfill its duties by holding the States united by sovereign ties; by the State remaining sovereign and the corporations subject; not by sovereign corporations and subject States."[85]

On March 9, 1839, just two days before the end of its term, the Court announced its long-awaited decision in the *Bank of Augusta* cases. By an 8–1 margin, the Court overturned McKinley's lower court ruling. Some newspapers saw the decision as a blow against both McKinley and the radical wing of the Democratic Party (often referred to as locofocos), which generally supported state banks. Ohio's *Newark Advocate,* for example, stated, "Thus has the highest tribunal in our land rebuked the insane Loco Focoism which would in fact make our Union a rope of sand."[86]

There were others, however, who saw in the Court's opinion a devil's bargain between America's legal and corporate interests. The *Pennsylvania Reporter* decried the relationship between the business and financial sectors and the law that was only further strengthened by the Court's ruling. It bitterly proclaimed that lawyers were "the friends and advocates of these scrip aristocracies. They are fed and nurtured by them. Out of these lawyers, judges are made. . . . Friends thus made, are friends for life . . . and are even friends beyond the grave, for their decisions live after them."[87]

Such divergent views reflect what one of Chief Justice Taney's principal biographers acknowledged in 1935: that the decision was "widely misunderstood, both by the friends and by the foes of the banks involved."[88] Those who cite this decision to disparage McKinley's legal ability (including modern legal commentators) fail to recognize that the Court's decision actually upheld the underlying argument of McKinley's lower court ruling: corporations do not have the right to operate free of governmental regulation. As historian Arthur M. Schlesinger, Jr., wrote, Taney "steered

brilliantly between the alternatives. Recognizing the usefulness of corporations, he declined to destroy them; recognizing their danger, he declined
to sanctify them."[89]

The chief justice rejected Webster's argument that out-of-state corporations were citizens and thus constitutionally entitled to conduct business in other states as individual citizens were permitted to do. And he
agreed with McKinley that a corporation, organized under the laws of a
given state, could not exist independent of such laws. However, guided by
the rule of comity, the Court acknowledged that properly chartered corporations were permitted to do business in other states as long as there
was no state law forbidding such operations. Indeed, Taney wrote, "[W]e
can perceive no sufficient reason for excluding them, when they are not
contrary to the known policy of the state, or injurious to its interests." He
went on to add, "It is nothing more than the admission of the existence of
an artificial person created by the law of another state, and clothed with
the power of making certain contracts. It is but the usual comity of recognizing the law of another state."[90]

The majority clearly stated that corporations have the power to make
contracts in other states. However, states also retain the right to regulate
corporations or even prohibit them outright subject to clear and express
action. In short, because Alabama had yet to enact any prohibitory legislation against the out-of-state corporations involved in the *Bank of Augusta*
dispute, those companies were free to transact business, make contracts,
and deal in bills of exchange until the time such legislation was enacted.

Given the tremendous abuse he had received during the course of the
previous year, it would have been understandable had McKinley simply
dissented from the majority opinion without comment. Instead, in a solo
dissent, he asserted that the majority ruling had "imposed on me the un-
pleasant necessity of maintaining, single handed, my opinion, against the
opinion of all the other members of the Court."[91] Holding strongly to his
position at circuit, he again argued, "Alabama, as an independent foreign
state, owing no duty, nor being under any obligation to either of the states
by whose corporations she was invaded, was the sole and exclusive judge
of what was proper or improper to be done."[92]

He questioned the Court's reliance on the doctrine of comity in its decision. While comity was certainly appropriate to international law, he
believed the power to regulate commerce in the United States could only
come from two sources: the states or the national government. During oral
arguments, attorneys for the banks had argued "that the purchase and sale

of exchange related in an important way to interstate commerce and that Alabama's policy conflicted with the constitutional grant of the commerce power to Congress."[93] McKinley questioned this claim in his dissent:

> [T]he power of Congress to regulate commerce deprives Alabama of the power to pass any law restraining the sale and purchase of a bill of exchange; and by consequence, the whole power belongs to Congress. The Court, by the opinion of the majority, does not recognize this doctrine, in terms. But if the power which the Court exercised is not derived from that provision of the Constitution, in my opinion it does not exist.
>
> If ever Congress shall exercise this power, to the broad extent contended for, the powers of the States over commerce, and contracts relating to commerce, will be reduced to very narrow limits.[94]

McKinley's views in both his circuit ruling and dissent are often mischaracterized as adopting a stridently states rights' position on banking and commerce, but his jurisprudence in this and other cases was hardly that simple. As legal historian Earl M. Maltz has written, McKinley's "conclusion in *Earle* was state centered . . . [but] his analysis has implications that were nationalist."[95] Justice McKinley obviously believed that the states possessed the power to regulate their own commercial affairs because Congress, at that point, did not. It was an area that did not permit concurrent authority. As McKinley went on to stress, "If Congress have [*sic*] the power to pass laws on this subject, it is an exclusive power . . . it paralyzes all state power on the same subject."[96] This observation was not so much a complaint as an acknowledgment that the power to regulate commerce simply cannot be shared.

Subsequent Court rulings, particularly during the New Deal era, clearly underscored this point as they expanded congressional power under the commerce clause. These rulings have done exactly what McKinley predicted with regard to state authority over commerce, reducing it "to very narrow limits." For all the criticism generated by his circuit opinion in *Bank of Augusta*, it would serve as the first of several examples during his career on the Supreme Court where he reaffirmed his belief that where it was constitutionally justified, the power of the national government was indeed "exclusive within its sphere of authority."[97]

Upon the conclusion of the Court's Washington term, McKinley dutifully set off for circuit, no doubt hoping to avoid the negative attention he had attracted the previous year. When he arrived in Jackson, McKinley found 2,500 cases awaiting him. A month earlier, a Virginia newspaper had reported on the circumstances that created the overwhelming caseload there: "Our neighbors in Mississippi, from every account, appear to be in a bad way. . . . The simple fact appears to be, that the majority of the community are in debt over their means of extricating themselves, except by sale of their property." Their reluctance to pursue that course ("a ruinous alternative," the paper conceded) "and unable to obtain discounts from their banks, the law is resorted to."[98]

McKinley immediately set to work to clear the docket of frivolous claims and dilatory actions so that his time might be better spent on legitimate disputes. Newspapers took note of his efforts: "Judge McKinley did most perseveringly devote himself to the business of the Court . . . and performed the business more rapidly than is usually done by the State Judges."[99] "From a sense of duty," it continued, "he overruled all defences which were interposed by the counsel for the defendants for mere delay, and as far as he could, prevented lawyers from making long speeches upon plain and settled questions."[100]

In the midst of this progress and praise, Justice McKinley experienced a humiliating slight that profoundly embarrassed him as it was later recounted in newspapers across the country. The incident also served as the basis for a subsequent effort to impeach him. The entire episode had originated several months earlier in a January 1839 message from Governor Alexander G. McNutt to the Mississippi state legislature. In his comments, the governor accused the recently deceased state treasurer, James Phillips, of accepting payment for treasury drafts in depreciated paper money rather than in gold and silver as directed by law. Phillips's son-in-law, Richard L. Dixon, was outraged by the public slur and took every opportunity to express his disgust with the governor.

On April 25, 1839, the governor happened to walk by Dixon and a group of his associates on his way to the state capitol building. After the governor passed by, Dixon apparently commented to his friends that "he had spit on the damned rascal, and that he intended to insult him whenever he should meet him."[101] The remark was relayed to a friend of the governor's, an A. J. Paxton, who inserted Dixon's words into a local paper along with this commentary: "[I]f Dixon has told this story, without the indignity having been offered, as is manifest, he is an infamous liar and puppy. If he did, in fact, perpetuate this disgusting obscenity, he is a filthy blackguard and cowardly poltroon."[102]

Dixon was understandably upset by this characterization, especially in print, and set out to confront Paxton. He found him in the rotunda of the state capitol building and proceeded to beat him with a walking cane. Unfortunately for Justice McKinley, the fight spilled over into a side room in the capitol where he was holding circuit court. McKinley ordered the two men to be separated and brought before him on charges of contempt. However, both men were apparently armed and the federal marshal and deputies normally assigned to the courtroom were not present at the time. Three contemporary accounts provide contrasting views on the events that followed. The *Boston Courier* reported, "Amidst great excitement and confusion, the Court directed the Crier [James Boyd] to send for the Marshall. He returned perhaps twice with a confused and unsatisfactory excuse to the Court." Amid the tumult, the paper continued, "the presiding Judge [McKinley], who appeared to be a good deal excited by the scene, said, 'Why, sir, you appear to be as stupid as a jack; go yourself, and request the Marshall to come into Court.'"[103]

A correspondent for a Philadelphia newspaper recounted what happened next under the headline teaser: "An Affair at Jackson, Spitting on the Governor—A Street Fight—Contempt of Court—Judge McKinley's Nose Pulled."[104] Order was apparently restored to the courtroom, but after adjourning for the day, McKinley, "whilst on his way to his room, had his nose pulled severely, by a Mr. James H. Boyd, a young man who had been acting as an officer of the court . . . , and for not interfering was called 'a stupid jackass' by Judge McKinley, for which he had his smeller pulled."[105] The *Daily National Intelligencer* in D.C. offered a slightly different version, stating that Boyd "barely thrust his hand into the Judge's face, and may have touched his nose, but it was so slight as scarcely to be felt."[106]

The significance of this assault, such as it was, lay in what it represented, according to the mores of antebellum southern honor, rather than for any physical damage it caused. As Kenneth S. Greenberg has observed, "One of the greatest insults for a man of honor [in the South] . . . was to have his nose pulled or tweaked. . . . It was the ultimate expression of contempt toward the most public part of a man's face."[107] That disrespect more than violence was the intent behind the nose-pulling incident was suggested by the *Daily National Intelligencer*, which in its coverage of the incident opined, "Mr. Boyd seemed to be an inoffensive man, and wholly incompetent to the duties of his office; and no one that knows him will believe that he was any thing [*sic*] more than the tool of others in committing this outrage."[108]

The paper went on to suggest that the assault could be traced to McKinley's actions earlier in the session. He had refused several motions to set aside forthcoming bonds "amounting to a great number, and a very large sum of money," as part of his docket-clearing efforts. Although praised in some quarters, these efforts, the newspaper concluded, had also "rendered Judge McKinley unpopular with the debtor class and their counsel, which makes a large majority of the population in the district . . . where the Court is holden."[109]

Whatever the motivations for Boyd's actions, the *Boston Courier* was disgusted by the entire affair, declaring, "Judge McKinley ha[s] been assaulted by a mob in Mississippi. The atrocious proceeding is to be reprehended by every citizen, and should receive the decided censure of everybody, except, perhaps, Judge McKinley himself."[110] The last reference to McKinley was a political swipe the *Courier,* as a Whig newspaper, could not resist taking. McKinley, it continued, "should be the last to complain of the practical illustration of the principles of Jacksonianism, by the advocacy of which, he is what he is."[111]

It was widely reported that as McKinley left Jackson to return to circuit he swore to never return. Although only a rumor, the *New Orleans Bulletin* thought McKinley's vow perfectly justified. "After such treatment," it informed its readers, "it is not to be expected that Judge McKinley will ever revisit the *inhospitable* jurisdiction. Thus has Mississippi repudiated the salutary restraints and supervision of a Federal Court."[112]

Arriving in New Orleans a few weeks after the incident at Jackson, McKinley found a rather innocuous case on his docket involving maritime safety. In *U.S. v. Price and Company*, the owners of a steamboat plying the Mississippi and Ohio rivers between New Orleans and Louisville were fined three hundred dollars for navigating with customary wheel and tiller ropes instead of iron rods or chains as required by a federal law enacted the previous year. Congressional intervention was prompted by repeated accidents aboard steamboats that caused both property damage and loss of life. Such losses were often greatly aggravated by the vessel's inability to get to safety after its hempen steering ropes had been destroyed by fire. There was thus little debate about the need for the iron steering equipment, at least on large bodies of water, but steamboat operators on the nation's rivers argued that such devises were impractical and even dangerous on interior waterways.

In his circuit opinion, Justice McKinley argued that the legislation itself "must be subjected to a strict construction" if the three-hundred-dollar penalty were to stand.[113] Accordingly, he scrutinized the language of the act (which also called for licensing ships and annual safety inspections of steam boilers, among other things), noting several references to steamships operating "upon the bays, lakes, rivers, or other navigable waters of the United States." However, upon reaching the challenged section of the law, Section Nine, McKinley found explicit references only to "steam vessels employed on either the [Great] lakes . . . or on the sea." That clause was followed by the requirement "that iron rods or chains shall be employed and used in the navigating of all steamships instead of wheel or tiller ropes."[114]

McKinley interpreted "all steamships" in the latter part of Section Nine to apply to steam vessels on the lakes and seas to which the first part of that section had referred. He went on to state that Congress must clearly have known "that it would be very difficult if not impracticable to navigate boats on narrow rivers and on any river, so as to avoid collision with other boats, by using iron rods or chains instead of tiller ropes; and that therefore, they [sic] confined the use of these rods or chains to boats having greater sea room."[115] Thus, according to McKinley's strict interpretation of the statute, the requirement that iron rods and chains be used (and the penalty for noncompliance) could not be applied against steamboats upon the nation's rivers.

Newspapers along the Mississippi hailed the ruling, underscoring the impracticality of replacing the tiller ropes of every steamship on every American river. However, McKinley quickly came under attack from other quarters. With a brief nod to his previous circuit decision in *Bank of Augusta*, the *Cincinnati Gazette* excoriated the decision: "Judge McKinley has been again nullifying the laws of the land. . . . He produces this absurd result, a result directly contrary to the manifest intention of Congress, by a mere verbal criticism in which there is no perceptible force."[116]

Further north, the *Pennsylvania Inquirer* attributed a purported decrease in river safety to McKinley. "Since Judge McKinley's late extraordinary decision," it bemoaned, "that the Act of Congress has no application to steamboats navigating the Mississippi, some of the captains of steamboats have begun to indulge in the dangerous and most reprehensible practice of racing—the prolific source of the awful disasters which have so frequently occurred on the Western waters."[117] Steamboat racing, incidentally, was a common practice during the antebellum era (engaged in long before McKinley's circuit opinion), and both passengers and crew saw it as a welcome diversion from the monotony of water travel.[118] Greater speed, however, required greater steam, and the consequences of a boiler exploding (which happened with alarming frequency) and the attendant fire aboard ship could be devastating. Were McKinley aboard such a vessel, the *Inquirer* mused, crippled mid-river because its hempen tiller ropes had been burned, then perhaps the judge "would not have been skeptical either as to the necessity or applicability of the [S]teamboat Act" and its iron rod and chain requirement.[119]

Just a week after McKinley announced his ruling, a federal judge in New York reached the opposite conclusion in a virtually identical case. That ruling, proclaimed the *Daily National Intelligencer,* "came most opportunely . . . to arrest the ill effects which might otherwise have arisen from the decision . . . by Judge McKinley."[120] Four years later, Congress would sustain both judicial decisions by requiring all steamboats then equipped with the less expensive and more maneuverable hempen tiller ropes to install chains running the entire length of the ropes that would "take immediate effect, and work the rudder in case the ropes are burnt or otherwise rendered useless."[121]

In November 1839, with two full years of circuit-riding experience behind him, McKinley again turned to President Martin Van Buren for assistance. In a lengthy letter to the president, McKinley gave an unusually blunt assessment of the challenges facing him and the people of the Ninth Circuit. He began by reiterating what "must be obvious to everyone at all acquainted with judicial proceedings, that it would be impossible for any Judge to perform the duties of the [N]inth [C]ircuit with that deliberation which is due to the proper discharge of the judicial function, even if he were to sit the whole year."[122]

He reminded Van Buren of the annual yellow fever outbreaks in Mobile and New Orleans and the combination of the French language and civil law system in the latter city, which required "double the time to try a case than it would to try one, of like character," in the other circuits. The focus of his letter, however, was on those who looked to the federal courts to resolve their legal disputes. "To do anything like justice, to the parties," he told Van Buren, "in the short time allowed for the holding of the court, we are compelled to hurry over the docket as rapidly as possible, and to refuse to hear arguments upon plain and well settled questions."[123]

He then informed the president that having to rush through the docket "gave great offense to the host of debtors who thronged the court and who had employed counsel." It was this combination of circumstances, he acknowledged, nearly all of which were beyond his control, that "finally led to a gross personal indignity being offered to one of the members of the court, the history of which I need not here detail."[124]

McKinley's understated reference to the nose-pulling incident was not designed to garner sympathy from Van Buren but to demonstrate to the president the level of frustration that existed in Jackson and other areas where the docket was so large, the resources of the circuit court so few, and the circuit schedule so inflexible that he could only make but the barest progress before having to depart for his next assignment. It made a mockery of justice—and thus the Court itself and to a large extent Congress as well (because of its unwillingness to help) were both partially to blame for the frustration experienced by litigants in the Ninth Circuit.

Assessing both the people of Jackson and his own role as the presiding circuit judge under these difficult circumstances, McKinley questioned the wisdom of continuing to hold court there:

> A great majority of the people in this new settled country which surrounds Jackson—the place where the court is now holden—are greatly in debt. Many of these are desperate men, who, are determined to keep possession of their property by any and all means in their power. Under such circumstances and among such people it is easy to conceive how unpleasant and how unsafe the condition of a Judge must be, who is determined to do his duty. I am perfectly satisfied that justice cannot be fairly administered at that place and that public policy requires that the court be removed to Natchez where there is an old and respectable population, comparatively free from debt, and where impartial juries might be obtained. Natchez can, by means of steamboats, be more easily approached by a majority of the suitors, witnesses, and lawyers than Jackson can.[125]

McKinley was unable to personally follow up on the matter with Van Buren as he missed the Court's entire 1840 term because of illness. However, the president briefly mentioned the circuit inequities during his State of the Union address of December 1839. Citing the findings of Secretary Forsyth's report, he told Congress that "a great inequality appears in the amount of labor assigned to each judge." After briefly recounting the well-known difficulties of the Ninth, Van Buren then offered this rather tepid suggestion: "A revision, therefore, of the present arrangement of the circuit seems to be called for and is recommended for your notice."[126] It was hardly a rousing call to action, but McKinley's friends in Congress did the best they could to act on the president's recommendation. Committees in both the House and Senate reported bills to remove Mississippi from the Ninth Circuit. In reducing the size of that circuit, however, Congress also necessarily considered proposals to rearrange several other circuits to equalize the justices' workload. Opposition to such changes predictably ensued. When Chief Justice Taney learned that his tiny Fourth Circuit, consisting of only Maryland and Delaware, was to be enlarged by adding Pennsylvania and a portion of New Jersey he protested, "[M]y duties are more than doubled. . . . No man can perform the duties of the circuit intended to be assigned to me, in the manner in which they ought to be performed."[127] His complaints garnered little sympathy from those who were acquainted with McKinley's circuit, but with the help of key allies in Congress, the plan to alter Taney's as well as the other justices' circuits quickly died.

As mentioned earlier, McKinley was unable to witness the congressional efforts on his behalf because he was home in Florence recuperating from an illness. The 1840 term would be the first of five full terms that McKinley would miss during his tenure on the Court, and he would be absent from portions of several others. Court observers have long disparaged McKinley for his less than regular attendance at the Court's term in Washington. While such criticism is understandable, two other observations are in order.

First, contrary to the critics who claim McKinley had a poor work ethic, there were justifiable reasons for his absences. Among the most prominent of these were his health problems, which were exacerbated by both the rigors of circuit travel and old age. Matters at circuit court, too, such as large dockets or important cases, were responsible for delays in his returning to Washington. As detailed in chapter 8, the sensational case of the mysterious Myra Gaines in New Orleans was responsible for his missing the Supreme Court's entire 1850 term.

Second, while McKinley has somehow become the exemplar of absenteeism on the Supreme Court bench, he was by no means the only justice who was unable to attend part or all of the term in Washington. The Court began its 1843 session with only seven justices because both McKinley and Justice Story were absent the entire time, and only five justices were present when the Court adjourned.[128] The following year, illness prevented Chief Justice Taney from attending the Court's term, and in December 1849, just three justices attended the first day of the Court's term. There are many other examples of Taney Court justices frequently missing all or portions of the Washington term.

Such absences from Washington were to be expected given the conscientious manner in which the justices sought to fulfill their circuit duties (sometimes at the expense of the Washington term), the rigors of their circuit travel, and the fact that none of them was young. Indeed, the first justice born in the nineteenth century would not be appointed until 1850.[129] In short, it simply was not uncommon for a justice to be absent from all or part of the Washington term. The fact that these absences occurred regularly, however, did not minimize the serious consequences that they often generated.

As mentioned earlier, Chief Justice Taney frequently rescheduled oral arguments (in some instances across several terms) or delayed the final resolution of significant cases to ensure that all of the justices had a chance to participate.[130] Holding cases over from one term to another, however, only aggravated the Court's struggle to meet the demands of its ever-increasing docket. The absence of a single justice, be it McKinley or anyone else, thus had a very real impact on the business of the Court.

By the spring of 1840, McKinley had sufficiently recovered from his illness to report to circuit court in Mobile and New Orleans. He was spared the difficulties that had accompanied his public duties the previous year at circuit, but his personal affairs were becoming increasingly problematic. The economic depression that began shortly before McKinley's appointment to the Court still gripped the nation in 1840 and the justices were not spared. Writing from circuit court in Mobile, McKinley told William Pope in Louisville, "I have just received a letter from the Secretary of the Treasury informing me that unless the appropriations bill for the civil service of this year pass[es] before the first of next month—of which he says there is no hope—the draft which I drew in your favor cannot be paid." He profusely apologized to Pope and then directed him to look for a letter from the treasurer arriving at his (McKinley's) Louisville address. This, he instructed Pope, "you are hereby authorized to open . . . and demand and receive payment from the person or Bank required to pay the draft [e]nclosed in it."[131]

This letter is telling for two reasons. First, while it is not known how much McKinley owed Pope, the fact that he was forced to rely upon his Supreme Court salary to meet his obligations (despite extensive property holdings) indicates the precarious nature of McKinley's finances at the time. Second, this letter provides the first indication that after repeatedly failing to secure any assistance from either Congress or his brethren on the bench with the rigors of his circuit, McKinley had taken matters into his own hands. He had, in fact, moved back to Kentucky. Removing to Louisville on the Ohio River did not change the demands of his circuit, but it did give him ready access to a water route that would take him more comfortably to his primary circuit sites of New Orleans and Mobile and more rapidly back to Washington than the modes of travel he relied upon to get to and from Florence.

Leaving behind his Alabama home, property, and associates, the resting place of his beloved first wife, Julia, and the thriving community he helped found more than two decades earlier demonstrates the seriousness with which McKinley took his circuit responsibilities. But even this admittedly impressive attempt to better fulfill his Supreme Court duties was not spared congressional criticism the following year.

Although there were no residency requirements for justices, they typically lived in the circuits to which they were assigned. Some members of Congress, however, questioned the appropriateness of McKinley's move to Kentucky, which flouted this tradition. Just days before the Court convened its 1841 term, the House of Representatives approved the motion of Congressman George W. Crabb, a Whig from Alabama, charging the Judiciary Committee "to inquire and report whether it be legal for justices of the Supreme Court . . . to reside out of the limits of their circuits." Crabb's resolution went on to further task the Judiciary Committee with determining "the expediency of prohibiting, by statute, such a residence."[132]

McKinley also received censure that winter for again not completing his circuit duties. Infuriated that he had not attended circuit court in Jackson in 1840 (his illness permitted him to complete only a portion of his circuit duties that year), members of the Mississippi legislature retaliated. In Washington, the *Madisonian* reported, "Judge McKinley, of the United States Supreme Court, having refused, as in duty bound, to hold a session of the Circuit Court in Mississippi, the Legislature of that State have [*sic*] passed resolutions requesting their representatives in Congress to prepare a bill of impeachment against him. The resolutions have been approved by the Governor."[133]

At the same time as this personal controversy was unfolding, McKinley arrived in Washington for the start of the 1841 term to find his fellow justices preparing to guide the Court ever deeper into the issue of slavery. The Court had heard slavery-related cases before, but it was during this term that the Court discovered that "slavery as a constitutional issue could no longer be suppressed."[134] Perhaps the most prominent case of the term in which McKinley did *not* directly participate was that of the *Amistad,* which the Court considered during the last week of February.[135] One of the most celebrated cases of its time, "no slave case before *Dred Scott,*" according to Justice Story's biographer, "attracted so much national attention as *U.S. v. Amistad.*"[136]

McKinley was ill during the entire oral argument, but for four days the other justices listened to Attorney General Henry D. Gilpen, former president John Quincy Adams, and Roger S. Baldwin debate the status of forty-nine Africans who had rebelled and gained control of the Spanish ship *Amistad,* which was transporting them off the coast of Cuba in 1839. Gilpen maintained that when the crew members that had been spared by the Africans navigated the ship into U.S. territorial waters (instead of back to Africa as they had promised), international law required that the United States restore the ship and its cargo to its Spanish owners.

Baldwin and Adams, however, argued that Africans were not property but people who had been unlawfully kidnapped and forced aboard ship. Further, the United States was under no obligation to return the Africans to either Cuba or any other Spanish-owned territory, particularly since American participation in the foreign slave trade had been forbidden thirty years earlier and even Spanish law on the subject was far from settled.

The night before oral arguments in *U.S. v. Amistad* were to have concluded, Justice Philip Barbour died unexpectedly, and all remaining business in the Court was postponed for several days. When the Court finally adjourned after hearing final arguments in the case, John Quincy Adams noted in his journal that just seven justices were present, "Barbour having been taken away by death in the midst of the trial, and McKinley having been throughout the trial absent."[137] McKinley had evidently recovered by March 9 when the Court rendered its decision. Writing for eight justices, including McKinley, Justice Story affirmed the lower court ruling that declared the Africans to be free. Justice Baldwin alone dissented in the case but without opinion.

The other significant slavery-related case that term was *Groves v. Slaughter,* which originated in McKinley's own circuit.[138] The precise issue at hand was the validity of promissory notes accepted as partial payment for purchased slaves. The larger question, however, was whether state laws affecting slavery infringed upon the commerce power of the federal government. Given the issue involved and the fact that both Daniel Webster and Henry Clay were participating, it was not surprising to learn that on the first day of oral arguments in the Court's chambers, as a period newspaper put it, "[t]he solemn temple of justice was filled with an admiring auditory."[139]

The case turned on the claim of Robert Slaughter, who, in 1836, had imported slaves into the state of Mississippi for sale, accepting several thousand dollars in credit for their purchase. When Slaughter later went to collect on the notes, he was told they were invalid and thus uncollectible because the Mississippi Constitution of 1832 expressly barred the importation for sale of slaves after May 1, 1833. That ban, incidentally, was not imposed as an anti-slavery measure but as a way to stabilize the price of slaves already in the state. Slaughter contended that since the legislation actually implementing the constitutional ban was not enacted until 1837, his notes were valid.

When the Court announced its decision on the last day of the 1841 term, Justice Thompson's majority opinion ignored entirely the constitutional argument of whether the state ban infringed upon national commerce power, agreeing with Slaughter's attorneys that the provisions banning the importation and sale of slaves were inoperable absent implementation legislation. In so doing, as legal historian R. Kent Newmyer has observed, the Court essentially "validated several million dollars' worth of notes held by slave traders. By unavoidable implication, the Court sanctioned the slave trade itself."[140]

In separate concurring opinions, Chief Justice Taney and Justices McLean and Baldwin each voiced their views as to the constitutional question (state regulation of slavery versus the commerce power of Congress) that the majority decision avoided. McKinley, joined by Justice Story, dissented from Thompson's opinion in *Slaughter*. The official court reporter noted only that the two dissenters "consider[ed] the notes sued upon void."[141] There was apparently a longer statement on the matter for, as John Quincy Adams noted, McKinley read his dissent from the bench.[142] The content of that opinion has been lost, but, in a letter to one of the attorneys in the case, Justice Story provided some insight into both his and McKinley's dissents. "I was not present at the delivery of the opinion of the Court in your Mississippi case," he wrote. "Mr. Justice McKinley has, however, truly expressed my opinion, and as far as my present recollection goes, I believe that we entirely agreed in our views of the questions argued."[143] Those views were that the Mississippi Constitution "contained in itself a positive, present, operative prohibition of slaves and without any legislative act to aid it[;]

[t]hat such a prohibition was not in violation of the Constitution of the United States . . . [; and] [t]hat the notes given upon the sales in violation of the constitution of Mississippi were utterly void."[144]

Because Story was the leading opponent of slavery on the Taney Court, his concurrence with McKinley surely does not reflect the strong states' rights/pro-slavery sentiment so often attributed to the latter. For both Story and McKinley, the provisions of the Mississippi Constitution were simply self-executing and did not require additional implementation legislation. Although it might ultimately cost slave traders millions of dollars in promissory notes, they believed the ban took legal effect as soon as the constitution was ratified.

More important, the state's ban on slave importation did not infringe upon federal commerce power because these justices viewed slaves as persons and not as articles of commerce. This interpretation is not a modern attempt to cast a southern slaveholder like McKinley in a more positive light. Rather it draws support from both a comment made by the court reporter and Justice Baldwin's lengthy dissent in *Slaughter.* The former noted that McKinley, Story, Thompson, and Wayne all agreed that commerce power of Congress did not "interfere with the provision of the Constitution of the State of Mississippi which relates to the introduction of slaves *as merchandise* or for sale."[145]

Baldwin clarified that he alone among the justices saw slaves as merchandise: "Other judges consider the Constitution as referring to slaves only as persons, and as property, in no other sense than as persons escaping from service; they do not consider them to be recognized as subjects of commerce, either 'with foreign nations,' or 'among the several states.'" "[B]ut I cannot acquiesce in this position," he declared. "That I may stand alone among the members of this Court does not deter me from declaring that I feel bound to consider slaves as property by the law of the states."[146]

Whether viewed as persons or property, the Africans were still enslaved in Mississippi; McKinley and Story's dissent did nothing to change that. But McKinley's view of the supremacy of congressional authority to regulate under the commerce clause, although not implicated in the majority opinion, again runs counter to his modern-day reputation as a states' rights absolutist.

As these slavery questions were being decided in the Court's chambers, the Senate abruptly began debate on another plan to alter the justices' circuit duties. The cause of this sudden action was the death of Justice Barbour. He was loved by all of his brethren on the Court and they deeply mourned his passing. However, his death provided the unlikely opportunity for Congress to again address the equalization of the justices' circuit responsibilities. On February 27 (just two days after Barbour's death), Senator Oliver Smith of Indiana broached the topic by bluntly declaring, "That distinguished judge [Barbour] having been removed by Providence, the way [is] now clear to do that which would long since have been done, but for the locality of the judges." He reiterated what everyone in Congress already knew: "there was a most unequal and unjust imposition of duties" upon not just McKinley but other justices whose circuits did not lie along the Atlantic seaboard.[147]

As Supreme Court historian Charles Warren has written, there was a general appreciation for the fact that all of the justices assigned to the western and southwestern states had a greater workload than the others because "the traveling distances . . . were immense, and the amount of litigation, due to complicated land titles, the deranged state of the currency, and the rage for speculation, was unbearably heavy."[148]

Senator Smith reported that the members of the Court had already agreed to an arrangement (should Congress oblige by reordering the circuits) that would assign a third justice to the areas currently served by Justices Catron and McKinley. He then yielded the floor to Clement C. Clay of Alabama, who provided additional details of the proposed reorganization that would ultimately alter six of the circuits. Among other things, the plan called for Alabama and Louisiana to be paired together in one new circuit, Mississippi and Tennessee in another, and Arkansas, Missouri, and Kentucky in a third. Strong opposition immediately ensued but from an unexpected quarter. Unlike previous debates over equalization, none of the justices' friends in Congress arose to defend their interests against the proposed changes. In fact, if Smith was correct, there should be no reason for the senators to object as the justices themselves had already agreed to the circuit alterations.[149]

It was Senator William Roane of Virginia, however, who arose to defend not a justice but *a circuit* affected by the reorganization. He was stunned to learn that Clay's plan called for the dissolution of the Fifth Circuit and its historic pairing of Virginia and North Carolina. For more than forty years the two states had been paired in the same judicial circuit and now, as Roane put it rather melodramatically, they were to be "cut in twain, merged into two other circuits, and thus blotted out from [their] old position on the judicial map of the Union."[150]

To Roane's lengthy argument against the proposal, Senator James Buchanan from Pennsylvania responded that the issue before the Senate had little to do with Roane's beloved Virginia but rather the creation of a new circuit for the Old Southwest "where it is so much wanted that it is now physically impossible for the circuit Judge there to transact one-half the business, or even personally to attend all the courts appointed by law to be held."[151] He meant no disrespect to Virginia, he told Roane, but given the small amount of work in the Fifth Circuit, surely the time and efforts of the justices could be put to better use by adding another to the massive territory embraced by the Ninth.

Buchanan went on to remark that such a change was long overdue, but because a Virginian had sat on the bench for practically all of the previous four decades, it had been impossible to effect any circuit changes involving the Commonwealth.[152] Thus it was not Barbour's death per se that had created the opportunity to finally reorganize the circuits but the fact that there was no longer a Virginian on the Court to oppose such efforts.

With most members of Congress clearly aware of the utter impossibility of fulfilling all of the demands of the vast Ninth Circuit, Buchanan was convinced that there was no better time to adopt the much-needed changes and, when it came to a vote, three-quarters of the Senate agreed with the proposed circuit reorganization. However, the impact of the successful vote was tempered by the fact, as Buchanan publicly lamented, that it was very late in the session and the matter had yet to be introduced into the House.

Despite the most successful congressional efforts on his behalf to date, when the Court's term ended a few weeks later McKinley's Ninth Circuit route again remained unchanged. Proponents of circuit reorganization in the House had simply waited too long to take up the issue, which prevented the matter from even being considered before Congress adjourned for the year. For McKinley, the continually unfulfilled promise of relief at circuit had to be frustrating, particularly since the lack of substantive change this time was not due to congressional intervention by the justices' friends or staunch regional considerations but to poor planning on the part of advocates in the House.

Returning to New Orleans for circuit court, McKinley found himself taking the brunt of criticism that was more properly directed at the Court as a whole. He had always been faithful in discharging his duties in New Orleans and there were few public complaints, but in a letter to Justice Story, B. W. Godfrey privately grumbled about Justice McKinley's personality and lack of familiarity with the civil law that still domi-

nated Louisiana. "[I]t seems hard for us," he told Story, "that a man, totally ignorant of our laws, and at war with the whole system by which we
are governed and directed, should be sent to traduce our institutions, and
vilify the members of our bar, instead of fulfilling the objects of his mission, and adding a greater dignity to the bench."[153]

McKinley apparently vocalized his feelings about the civil law system
in Louisiana more than once during his early days on circuit, which offended local lawyers. A year after McKinley's death in 1852, Thomas Du-
rant, a former U.S. district attorney for Louisiana, recalled for Jefferson
Davis: "Judge McKinley told me from the Bench that he did know Louisiana law and did not want to know it, yet this was the law it was his official duty to administer; the uncourteous [sic] expression showed the condition of this mind, it was filled with contempt for our local system."[154]

It is clear that the frustration directed at McKinley probably would have
greeted any of the justices first called to preside over Louisiana's complex
legal heritage, as none of the members of the Court at that time was trained
in the civil law tradition. Indeed, the great Justice Story himself was not
spared criticism. "It is greatly to be regretted," Godfrey went on to complain, "as the annotator of our Code remarks that the other members of
the Supreme bench, as well as yourself, will not give to the civil law the
attention it deserves." He hoped to see the day when a bench trained in
common law and a bar of civil law attorneys would cease to be "at war and
justice suffering in the unnatural contest and struggle between the two."[155]

Louisiana's civil law background certainly added to the challenges of
the Ninth, but there are several reasons why, unlike some of the other elements of McKinley's circuit duties, it was not overwhelming. First, although Spanish and French civil law still predominated in the area, not
all of its principles were incompatible with English common law. Thus
McKinley was not wholly unfamiliar with the issues and procedures that
came before him.

Second, few of the state and federal judges in Louisiana at the time were
natives of the state, and nearly all of them had been trained in the common law tradition. Once in Louisiana, of course, they became versed in
the civil law because they needed to, but their earlier common law training and experience continued to influence them and their decisions.[156] This
contributed to an "admixture of common-law principles and methods of
decisions" particularly in areas upon which the civil law was silent.[157]

Third, the Judiciary Act of 1789 explicitly required that federal courts
follow state law where applicable.[158] That implies, of course, that there

would be some areas where local law would not apply, freeing federal judges to consult other sources. Fourth, and perhaps most important, it was not critical that justices of the Supreme Court have intimate knowledge of state law since they sat at circuit with a local U.S. district court judge who was familiar with local law and custom.

In short, while circuit court in Louisiana certainly held special challenges for judges trained in the common law, such obstacles were not insurmountable. The fact that McKinley attended court there more consistently than any of the other sites within the circuit during his career on the Supreme Court also suggests that he became comfortable with the unique legal environment in New Orleans. Indeed, forty years after his death, McKinley was remembered by his colleagues on the bench as someone "who was peculiarly familiar with the law of Louisiana."[159]

When McKinley returned to Washington for the Court's 1842 term, he learned that legislation to equalize the circuit duties of the justices was again before Congress. For five years McKinley had watched with disappointment as every attempt to balance the demands of the circuits had failed. Adding to his frustration was the fact that Congress seemed to clearly understand (and had for some time) that the huge Ninth Circuit it had created served no one's purposes and that it was physically impossible for McKinley or any other person to fulfill the duties of that circuit at the times and in the places mandated. Congress would finally provide some relief later in the year but not before the Court issued some momentous opinions of its own that were of far greater consequence.

In late January 1842, New York City's *Weekly Herald* ran an article about a visit to the Supreme Court by its Washington correspondent. The writer made generally favorable observations about all of the justices, commenting on both their physical and intellectual attributes. Of McKinley, the correspondent wrote, "Judge McKinley, of Alabama, [is] a plain unpretending gentleman, who says little, but thinks a great deal" and categorized him among the justices who "had acquired [a] national reputation" prior to their elevation to the Court.[160] The article appeared in the newspaper just a few days after the Court rendered its first decision of the 1842 term in the case of *Swift v. Tyson*.[161]

The dispute behind this important case originated in 1836 when George Tyson of New York used a bill of exchange to purchase $1,800 worth of land in Maine. Before the bill came due, however, the creditor whom Tyson had agreed to pay endorsed the bill of exchange to a John Swift to satisfy debts that he owed to the latter. When Swift attempted to collect on Tyson's bill of exchange, they both learned that Tyson had been defrauded—there was no land in Maine to which he would take title. And yet, because Swift had taken the bill of exchange to settle the debt with Tyson's creditor, he demanded that the latter fulfill his legal obligation to pay the debt. Tyson refused, contending that New York state law did not recognize the transaction because of the original fraud. More important, Tyson argued that the federal courts were obligated to follow state court decisions on the matter.

The case initially came to the Supreme Court during its 1840 term, but in McKinley's absence the justices divided evenly over the case and re-calendared it for a later date. When it came before the Court again in 1842, no such divisions were apparent as the justices unanimously followed Justice Story's lead in declaring that the federal courts were not bound by state court decisions. In doing so, the justices, including McKinley, laid the foundation "for a massive assertion of federal judicial authority."[162]

Section 34 of the Judiciary Act of 1789 explicitly required the federal courts to follow the "laws of the several states, except where the constitution, treaties, or statutes of the United States shall otherwise require or provide."[163] In its decision, the Court acknowledged the importance of state and local laws in a wide array of other areas. Commercial matters, however, were different. Justice Story, among others, had long been a proponent of a uniform commercial law, believing that the hodgepodge of state laws, regulations, and judicial decisions on the matter hampered the country's economic growth. That was especially pertinent at the time *Swift* was decided because the country had yet to emerge from the economic depression that began in 1837.

With regard to both commercial matters and Section 34, Story's decision for the Court proclaimed, "[W]e have not now the slightest difficulty in holding, that this section, upon its true intendment and construction, is strictly limited to local statutes and local usages of the character before stated, and does not extend to contracts and other instruments of a commercial nature."[164]

He held further that in the absence of applicable state statutes, the federal courts were free to apply generally accepted principles of commercial law. In fact, state court decisions in the area need not be respected because they simply were not embraced by Section 34's "laws of the several states." As Story put it bluntly, "Undoubtedly, the decisions of the local tribunals upon such subjects are entitled to, and will receive, the most deliberate attention and respect of this Court; but they cannot furnish positive rules, or conclusive authority, by which our own judgments are to be bound up and governed."[165]

Because of the struggling economic environment in which it was rendered, *Swift* was not particularly controversial in its day although it resulted in a huge expansion of federal court authority as the bounds of commercial law were stretched to include insurance, municipal bonds, torts, and other areas of law traditionally reserved to the states.[166] As Tony Freyer has written, it "gave the Court a unique opportunity to aid the national economy and to enhance federal power at the same time."[167] Justice McKinley, in contrast to his modern stereotype, endorsed that expansion and would do so again in another controversial case waiting on the Court's docket.

Prigg v. Pennsylvania was the Supreme Court's most significant slavery-related decision until *Dred Scott* in 1857.[168] It turned on an 1826 Pennsylvania law that made it much more difficult for escaped slaves to be returned to their out-of-state owners. A professional slave catcher named Edward Prigg was found guilty of violating the Pennsylvania law after he kidnapped Margaret Morgan and her children and brought them back to the Maryland plantation from which Morgan had escaped several years earlier. Attorneys for Prigg argued that the Pennsylvania law was unconstitutional because it violated the federal Fugitive Slave Law of 1793. The latter, they claimed, gave the national government exclusive authority over the issue of fugitive slaves.

The case promised to exacerbate existing sectional tensions because it called into question not only the right of slaveholders to recover their property but also the right of states to pass legislation within their borders free of interference by other states and even Congress in areas where federal authority was neither expressly granted nor necessary.

By an 8–1 margin, the Court struck down the Pennsylvania law. Justice Story again wrote for the majority, grounding his decision in the sections of Article IV of the Constitution that provided for the recovery of fugitives. He argued that the framers had intended that fugitives, enslaved or otherwise, should be returned to the state from which they had escaped. Between that constitutional provision and the Fugitive Slave Law, Story believed it was clear that "the power of legislation upon this subject [was] exclusive [to] the national government," thus striking down the Pennsylvania law as unconstitutional.[169] The Court's recognition of federal exclusivity in this area also meant that similar laws in other states were essentially nullified.

Because Story was an avowed opponent of slavery, his majority opinion upholding the Fugitive Slave Law attracted tremendous controversy. Yet in discussing the case with family and friends, he pronounced the Court's ruling a "triumph of freedom."[170] He justified this characterization by arguing that since fugitive slaves fell exclusively within the purview of federal powers, states could neither hinder nor assist that power. Story declared in Prigg, "By the general law of nations, no nation is bound to recognize the state of slavery, as to foreign slaves found within its territorial dominions, when it is in opposition to its own policy and institutions. . . . If it does it, it is as a matter of comity, and not as a matter of international right." For Story, then, "The state of slavery is deemed to be a mere municipal regulation, founded upon and limited to the range of territorial laws."[171]

Applying the same principles of international law to domestic affairs, Story reasoned that slavery, where it was permitted, was a local issue. And should slaves escape from those locales where it was sanctioned, neither state law nor state resources could be used to hinder the enforcement of the federal fugitive slave law. More important from Story's perspective, state resources also could not be used to assist the federal government in implementing the law.

To Story's astonishment, his majority opinion was castigated by northern abolitionists, who soon conferred a new title on the distinguished jurist: "Slave-Catcher-in-Chief for the New England States."[172] He was mortified by the label not only because of his own antipathy toward slavery but also because of the not-so-subtle anti-slavery strategy he had included in Prigg. Story had made it clear that just as states could not interfere with national law governing fugitive slaves, they also were under no obligation to help the national government execute its laws in this area. Several justices noted their strong disagreement with this portion of the opinion, arguing that states were not forbidden from assisting the federal government in the rendition of slaves. McKinley was not one of them.

McKinley was present but did not write one of the six additional opinions filed in the case. His majority vote with Story, however, has been the source of some scholarly inquiry and is another of several actions taken by McKinley that strikes at the oft-repeated caricature of the justice as an uncompromising states' rights presence on the bench.

Of all the members of the Taney Court, Justice Story was the most prominent and consistent advocate for the power of the national government. For him, Prigg was arguably less about kidnapping and slavery than about the right of states to pass legislation squarely at odds with both constitutional provisions and national statutes. Of such a situation, and in an oft-quoted excerpt from an 1843 lecture at Harvard Law School, Story declared, "If one part of the country may disregard one part of the Constitution, another section may refuse to obey that part which seems to bear hard upon its interests, and thus the Union will become a 'mere rope of sand.'"[173]

While McKinley could hardly be characterized as a similar sort of nationalist, his majority vote in *Prigg*, particularly his tacit support of Story's views, clearly acknowledges the primacy of national authority over state law regardless of whether those laws be pro- or anti-slavery in nature. As one scholar put it, "like a number of other justices in *Prigg*, McKinley seems to have viewed the case predominantly through the lens of federal-state relations."[174]

Because it offered support to both the abolitionist and the slaveholder as well as recognizing the federal government's exclusive responsibility for fugitive slaves, *Prigg* fundamentally changed the tenor of the slavery debate in America. Northern abolitionists invoked the ruling to protest any state or local measure that might assist the return of fugitive slaves. For their part, southerners demanded, and in 1850 won, a new and even more severe federal fugitive slave law that bypassed both state laws and state officials by establishing federal commissioners in each state to facilitate the rendition of slaves. Instead of being hailed as "a triumph of freedom," as Story hoped, the *Prigg* ruling led, instead, to a nationalization of slavery, the Court's infamous 1857 *Dred Scott* decision, and even the Civil War itself.

Just days after the oral argument in *Prigg*, McKinley submitted a formal petition to Congress again seeking fundamental changes in the circuit court responsibilities of the justices. Senator William R. King of Alabama introduced the petition to his colleagues, acknowledging what everyone there already knew: that "[g]reat complaince [*sic*] existed against the judge in consequence of the non-performance of his duties which it is physically impossible for one man to perform." "No physical strength," King declared, "could enable one individual to perform the extensive travel in the circuit and attend to the duties of the court." He suggested that McKinley's petition be printed and sent "to the lawyers and judges [in the Ninth Circuit] to enable them to know the cause of the interruptions to the business of the courts."[175] The Senate Judiciary Committee agreed and ordered the appeal to be published.[176]

McKinley's 1842 petition represents the single most detailed statement

PETITION

OF

JOHN McKINLEY,

Praying an alteration in the Judicial circuits of the United States.

FEBRUARY 7, 1842.

Referred to the Committee on the Judiciary, and motion to print referred to the Committee on Printing.

FEBRUARY 8, 1842.

Ordered to be printed.

To the Senate and House of Representatives of the United States in Congress assembled:

Your petitioner, John McKinley, one of the associate justices of the Supreme Court of the United States,

RESPECTFULLY REPRESENTS:

That the ninth judicial circuit, consisting of the southern district of Alabama, the eastern district of Louisiana, the southern district of Mississippi, and the district of Arkansas, has been allotted to him. On entering upon the duties of his office, he found the business of the circuit greatly beyond the physical capacity of any one man to perform; and so far exceeding his fair proportion of circuit court duties, as to justify the expectation, that when this great inequality should be made known to the other judges, and to Congress, that by amicable arrangement among the judges, and legislation by Congress, a more equal division of the labors and expenses of the judges, would, at once, be made.

The subject has been brought to the consideration of the judges, and to the consideration of Congress, directly or indirectly, every year since the appointment of your petitioner; and after nearly five years have elapsed, he finds himself in no better condition than at first. All hope of an amicable arrangement, by agreement among the judges, he believes to be now at an end; he is, therefore, reduced to the necessity of appealing directly to Congress for their interposition. And he cannot bring the subject to their consideration more appropriately, than by referring to the report of the Secretary of State, made in obedience to a resolution of the Senate, of the 13th of March, 1838; which will be found in the second volume of Senate documents, No. 50, for the years 1838–'39. The object of the resolution was to ascertain the number of suits in each circuit, in the two years next preceding the date of the information sought, and the number of miles which each judge of the Supreme court had to travel in the performance of his duties. The following synopsis of the report will exhibit, at one view, the whole information obtained:

Thomas Allen, print.

he ever made regarding the practical difficulties of the Ninth Circuit. It is notable for what it says about both McKinley and the Court itself. As to the latter point, McKinley reminded Congress that he had sought relief directly from the Court (where circuit assignments were made) nearly every year since his appointment because, as he put it, he "found the business of the circuit greatly beyond the physical capacity of any one man to perform."[177] Early in his career he had suggested that circuit assignments simply be rotated between the justices. The lack of support among his brethren for such an idea is perhaps a tacit acknowledgment of the genuine rigors of his circuit since none of his colleagues could be convinced to take their turn presiding over the Ninth. Finding that "all hope of an amicable arrangement, by agreement among the [justices], . . . to be now at an end," he again turned to his former colleagues in Congress for their direct intervention.[178]

After reiterating Secretary of State Forsyth's 1839 report detailing the huge differences in miles traveled by the justices and the case dockets they encountered on circuit, McKinley acknowledged the financial impact of riding circuit as well. He reminded Congress that the justices still paid their own expenses, and "those of the [N]inth [C]ircuit," he added, "amount to a very considerable sum every year."[179] McKinley admitted that in order to better fulfill his duties he had, in fact, relocated to Louisville. The move from Alabama was necessitated, he argued (in the third person), because of the "celerity with he was obliged to travel, to reach the places of holding the several courts at the times fixed by law, and the difficulty and infrequency of steamboat conveyances to and from [Florence]."[180]

In response to the criticism he had already received for moving out of his circuit and thereby violating an unwritten norm for Supreme Court justices, McKinley acknowledged that relocating to cities already in the Ninth such as New Orleans or Mobile appeared to make more sense than going back to Kentucky. On closer examination, he informed Congress, there were two serious obstacles to such a move: "First, the salary of your petitioner would not pay the expenses of his family in either place. Secondly, the only leisure he would have in the year would be at the time those places are very sickly; and generally from yellow fever." Thus, he told Congress, "on the score of health, convenience, and cheapness of living," he was "induced to fix his temporary residence at Louisville."[181]

More so than in his previous appeals, family and other personal considerations factored prominently in McKinley's 1842 petition. When their session was over, members of Congress returned to their homes, families, and full-time professions. Members of the Court left Washington immediately after their term ended as well, but their ability to manage their own personal or business affairs depended greatly upon where they lived and the time required to complete their circuit duties. Residing in Baltimore, with only Maryland and Delaware in his circuit at the time McKinley joined the Court, Chief Justice Taney had considerably more time than the other justices to devote to his well-documented twin passions of family and flowers.[182]

Justice Story would have undoubtedly put his legendary work ethic and prodigious intellect to use anywhere he was assigned, but his responsibility for the First Circuit in New England, where his judicial duties took a little less than two months to complete, gave him ample time to pursue other interests. In 1829, as a sitting member of the Court, Harvard appointed Story as its first Dane Professor of Law and tasked him with the salvage and improvement of its faltering law school. Story not only had teaching and administrative duties at Harvard during that time, he was also required to publish his lectures. Between 1829 and his death in 1845, Story published eleven major works on nine separate areas of law, including his landmark three-volume *Commentaries on the Constitution of the United States*.[183]

The other justices had varying amounts of time to spend with their families and on personal business, but the Court's scheduled term in Washington coupled with the size of the Ninth Circuit gave McKinley very little time for either. Now, with several years of experience riding circuit behind him, McKinley set forth in practical terms what the congressionally mandated court schedule, transportation challenges, and huge circuit meant to him personally. As he told Congress, "The Court at Mobile, which is the last that can be held without interfering with the Supreme Court, generally adjourns about the middle of December, leaving very little more than sufficient time to reach Washington, so as to avoid the ice in the Ohio [R]iver, and before the commencement of the Supreme Court." The result, he said, was that he was "deprived of the privilege of visiting his family, or of attending in person to any private affairs, at home, from about the twentieth of October till the last of July or first of August of the next year." By removing to Louisville, he could now spend some "eight or ten days at his home, in going to and returning from his circuit to Washington."[184]

He went on to state bluntly that regardless of whether he lived in Florence, Louisville, Mobile, or New Orleans, his circuit was simply too big and that he alone of all the justices was "employed ten months of the year in holding courts, and a great portion of the time in the most southern and most sickly portion of the Union." He asked Congress to consider whether it was "proper that a judge should have no time allowing him for attending to his private concerns? [N]o time for relaxation? [N]o time for reading and study?" Just as important, he questioned whether it was "just to the suitors in the [N]inth [C]ircuit to deprive them of the services of the judge, requiring more of him than he can possibly perform?"[185]

Purporting to speak for all of the justices, McKinley then proffered that Congress could provide a great service to the Supreme Court by simply removing the requirement that the justices attend both sessions of circuit court. He also suggested that Congress seriously consider dividing his circuit as "no more than two of those southern districts [Jackson, Mobile, and New Orleans] could, . . . with propriety, be put into one circuit."[186]

Some members of Congress were indeed sensitive to McKinley's concerns, and his petition received a sympathetic hearing together with still another circuit rearrangement proposal then under consideration. At the same time, there were other members of Congress who were just simply fed up with him. On April 6, 1842, in the course of debating a general appropriations bill that would have increased the salary of Supreme Court justices, Representative Edward Cross of Arkansas offered an amendment to withhold $500 from any justice who did not complete his circuit-riding responsibilities unless he was ill. This was in clear reference to McKinley, who had yet to hold circuit court in Arkansas. According to former president John Quincy Adams (then serving as a representative from Massachusetts), this amendment "started a debate of nearly two hours, in which Cross and Thompson, of Mississippi, vehemently denounced Judge McKinley."[187]

Representative John Pope of Kentucky was the first to rise in defense of McKinley.[188] Pope pleaded with his colleagues to understand that it was virtually impossible for McKinley or any other man to cover the Ninth Circuit in its entirety and make it back to Washington in time for the Court's term. But if the House was determined to punish him, he argued, it could not do so by withholding part of his salary. The only punishment for federal judges that the Constitution authorized was that of impeachment, which could only happen, he claimed, if the House found McKinley guilty of criminal negligence.[189]

Pope's argument may have been designed to dissuade his colleagues from levying either punishment against McKinley since withholding $500 was not authorized as a penalty and impeachment appeared too harsh. As to the latter punishment, Representative Jacob Thompson of Mississippi responded by noting the resolution from his state legislature the previous year instructing him to do just that because of the incident at Jackson. He then recounted the episode again for his colleagues including the rumor that "[w]hile the judge's wrath was up he swore that he would never return to Jackson again. Of course, our citizens supposed that he spoke in anger and that when his passions subsided he would return to the discharge of his duties. But not so; thus far he has obstinately staid [*sic*] away from that place." Thompson concluded by declaring, "[T]his conduct evinces, on the part of the judge, cowardice, a want of moral firmness, or else an unblushing effrontery and bare-faced impudence."[190]

A number of other representatives rushed to defend McKinley, whom they believed had been "unjustly assailed" and "maltreated most flagrantly."[191] One of these was William Gwin, who, as a representative from Mississippi and an unlikely source of sympathy, took the opportunity to have McKinley's recent petition read to the full House. As recounted by the *Congressional Globe,* Gwin declared that "the charges [against McKinley] were unjust, and had no proper foundation, for he knew of his own knowledge that this judge had discharged more duty than any judge on the Supreme Bench." He acknowledged that "Judge McKinley was unpopular among his constituents, [but] he would do him justice . . . [and] would not join in denunciations . . . for not doing what it was physically impossible for him to do."[192]

Gwin reminded the House that McKinley "was the first judge of the Supreme Court that ever presided in that circuit, which was created in the spring of 1837, and he could form no conception of the enormous amount of business he found in the circuit. In fact, since the creation of the circuit, the business had increased fourfold." In short, he concluded, "The remedy for the evils complained of should be cured by the legislation of Congress, and not by requiring an impossibility of the judges of the Supreme Court."[193]

Representative Samson Mason of Ohio agreed, stating, "This judge had a very hard task to perform; he had been insulted and repudiated in one portion of his circuit, and had a mass of business to attend to which no man possessed the ability to do." The obvious answer, he argued, was for Congress to legislate "something like an equalization of labor of the judges."[194]

Ultimately, John Quincy Adams prevailed upon Representative Cross to withdraw his amendment, and the issue of how to penalize the justice died. However, rumors regarding McKinley continued to swirl. In

Washington there was continued discussion about the creation of two or three additional circuits to aid the justices who "have upon their hands more business than they can transact," referring to the thousands of cases that awaited McKinley on circuit.[195] In Mississippi the rumors were more negative. It was said that he was so cowardly that he refused to hold circuit court there unless the marshal of the Southern District Court could guarantee his safety, which he (McKinley) sincerely doubted. That this rumor continued to circulate, *at the very time McKinley was in Jackson presiding at circuit court,* says much about journalistic care and quality and the prejudice against him.[196]

The Jackson bar even held a public dinner in McKinley's honor on June 2, which the *Mississippian* newspaper cited approvingly as a means of alleviating some of the courtroom tension between McKinley and local attorneys. "It must be recollected that he [McKinley] is naturally somewhat irritable and impatient," the paper noted, "and perhaps sometimes seems rude when he does not intend it. It should also be remembered, that our bar is rather given to much talking, and have hitherto been a good deal indulged in that way, and are therefore restive under restraint."[197]

The rumor that McKinley feared to come to Jackson prompted the local U.S. marshal, Anderson Miller, to pen a public letter, much of it directed at Representative Thompson, which was later reprinted in several Washington newspapers. Anderson wrote the letter to both refute the rumor and respond to the manner in which McKinley "was very roughly handled" by members of the House during their recent debate. Anderson declared,

> [T]he last charge I expected to be made against Judge McKinley was cowardice; . . . I had known him for upwards of thirty years intimately, and had always considered him as brave as any man; and further I was acquainted with the district he had to attend courts in, from the first settlement of the country, and . . . I was satisfied that no man had the physical ability to discharge the duties assigned to him. And I can further state that he has been holding courts here for five weeks, to the entire satisfaction of the whole bar, and indeed every other person, so far as I knew. . . . I have thought it due to Judge McKinley, so far as I was concerned, to contradict the abuse that has been so lavishly heaped upon him.[198]

At the same time, McKinley's allies in Congress continued to press the issue of circuit reorganization. In May, Senator William King of Alabama queried whether the Judiciary Committee to which McKinley's petition had been forwarded had taken any action. Given the tenor of the recent debate, he pleaded with his colleagues to again consider that "Judge McKinley . . . has been mostly unjustly censured. He could not perform all the duties assigned him." He reminded them of the circuit schedule that McKinley faced upon the Supreme Court's adjournment in mid-March: "The Alabama term of his Court was held on the second Tuesday of the same month. The Arkansas term commenced on the fourth Tuesday of the same month. He is now at Jackson, Mississippi, holding a term of his Court, and there are eleven hundred cases upon the docket."[199] He stressed to the committee that "[t]here was not a member of Congress from the Western and Southern States who did not know that serious inconvenience was hourly experienced both by the suitors and the officers of the court themselves" because of the impossibly large Ninth Circuit.[200]

The efforts of King and other senators finally bore fruit in July when the Judiciary Committee reported a circuit reorganization bill that took into account the vast territory of the Old Southwest. Several circuits were affected, but as McKinley had requested, the Ninth Circuit was divided in half: Mississippi and Arkansas remained in the Ninth while Alabama and Louisiana occupied a newly reconstituted Fifth Circuit. There was little debate on the matter in the Senate, and the bill easily passed.

Coming before the House, however, and again in the waning days of the session, there was considerable outcry from Virginia's representatives. They opposed the reorganization, as they had before, not only because it would separate Virginia from its historic judicial connection with North Carolina but also because the proposal would combine Virginia with Delaware and Maryland. Since the latter was the home of Chief Justice Taney, it was clear to these representatives that the newest member of the Court, Justice Peter Daniel of Virginia, would complete his circuit duties far from home.

The same members of Congress who had previously waved off McKinley's complaints were suddenly very concerned about the travel conditions and climate in the Deep South where Daniel would inevitably be assigned. Representative John W. Jones, for example, protested that Daniel would be leaving "at the sacrifice of all the social ties which bind him, and which have been going on through life—and a transfer from a climate which [was known] to be salubrious, to the pestilential atmosphere of New Orleans and Mobile."[201] On August 11, 1842, the House rejected the Virginians' arguments and by a vote of 115–68 approved the new circuits. President John Tyler signed the legislation into law five days later

Upon the law's passage and for the first time since his appointment to the Court, John McKinley must have looked forward to circuit. He would now have a smaller route, and the courts over which he would preside were easily accessible by steamboat. He would be able to spend far less time traveling and more on resolving the substantive legal issues of his circuit. A reduced circuit also meant he could focus on personal interests away from the courtroom, such as his family and business pursuits.

As the first and only justice to oversee the original Ninth Circuit, McKinley had grappled with the unique transportation challenges, cultural diversity, and vast territory of the Old Southwest. He also experienced the frustration of desperate litigants, the embarrassment of personal humiliation, and the sting of national denunciation. For five years, the same Congress that ultimately provided McKinley with relief had also ridiculed and belittled him, letting regional loyalties smother any attempt to reorganize the federal judiciary. Even the justices with whom he had lived and worked were not exempt from considerations of self-interest that had hindered congressional attempts to help him. With the passage of the circuit reorganization law, however, this was all in the past. The only question that remained to be resolved was which justices would be assigned to these newly configured circuits. New circuit assignments would not be made until the next Washington term of the Supreme Court, so McKinley made plans to return to the second session of the circuit court in Jackson, Mississippi, in order to get ahead of his docket. This would presumably be his last circuit court in Mississippi, as he expected to be assigned to the new Fifth Circuit, which encompassed Alabama and Louisiana.

Prior to his arrival, however, he suddenly took ill. In early November, Mississippi newspapers were the first to report that McKinley would not be attending circuit court because he had been "stricken with paralysis whilst on his way" to Jackson.[202] The once robust McKinley was now sixty-two years old, and while he had long complained of a variety of maladies, some of which were certainly aggravated by his circuit travel, the paralytic stroke was by far the most serious. By the end of the month, the *Vermont Gazette* in Bennington would announce: "[The] Hon. John McKinley . . . has been stricken with paralysis, and lies dangerously ill at his residence [in] Alabama. He is not expected to recover."[203]

8
Circuit Relief and Declining Health, 1843–1852

[McKinley] was a conscientious, hard-working judge, and even in his last years when he was ill and increasingly feeble he forced himself to attend to the duties of his office.

       —American historian Dumas Malone, 1931

Contrary to reports, McKinley survived the stroke and eventually resumed his judicial duties. However, he never regained his full health. The extent of the damage caused by the stroke is unknown, but it was severe enough to induce the justice's son, Andrew, to relocate his own family from St. Louis to the McKinley property in Louisville (named "Lauderdale" in a nod to their Alabama heritage), where they remained until after his father's death in 1852. Andrew McKinley was an able attorney who had practiced for several years in St. Louis but, according to one account, became a better one by "assisting his father, who was many years an invalid."[1]

Observers predicted that the convalescing McKinley would be the only justice absent from the Court's upcoming session. When the Court convened its January 1843 term, however, just five justices were there. Chief Justice Taney wryly noted in a letter to his wife that "We are likely to have a crippled Court this term."[2] Two more justices would arrive later, but McKinley and Story, who was also in poor health, missed the entire session.

The absence of these two justices factored into a pair of important and controversial internal decisions made by the Court on January 25, 1843. The first of these was the selection of Benjamin Howard as Supreme Court Reporter, replacing Richard Peters, who had served in that capacity since 1828. For several years Peters had clashed with a handful of justices who disagreed with the manner in which he edited and compiled the Court's decisions for publication. In addition, he apparently committed an unforgivable mistake when Justice Peter Daniel joined the Court in 1841 by misspelling his name in the Supreme Court reports of that year (he had appended an "s" to his last name). With McKinley and Story absent, the remaining seven justices, dividing 4–3, voted to remove Peters.

Peters angrily and publicly complained about the incident, arguing that the Court had timed his removal to take advantage of the delicate health of two of its members who would have supported him. Story was embarrassed by the Court's action. He was particularly distressed that the justices had done such a thing in his absence, since Peters was a good friend whom he had known longer than any of the other justices.[3] McKinley wrote to Peters to express his own regret and surprise at the Court's decision, claiming not only that he had never heard any of the justices speak poorly of him but also that the question of replacing Peters had never even been discussed in his presence.[4] In the same letter, McKinley also noted his surprise at the Court's allocation of the newly configured circuits. This was the second important decision made by the seven-member Court in January 1843.

Consistent with the congressional action of the previous year, four justices received new circuit routes. Chief Justice Taney took Delaware, Maryland, and Virginia into a new Fourth Circuit, Justice Wayne added both Carolinas to Georgia in his Sixth Circuit, and Justice Daniel grudgingly accepted the new Ninth Circuit of Arkansas and Mississippi. The Court assigned Justice McKinley to the reconfigured Fifth Circuit, which covered Alabama and Louisiana, the only time before the admission of Hawaii and Alaska to the Union that noncontiguous states were placed in the same circuit.

McKinley informed Peters that he was fine with the new assignment. "I did, to be sure, express to be allotted to the [N]inth [C]ircuit," he wrote, "and would, for some reasons, have preferred it; but do not consider myself at all injured or seriously aggrieved by the arrangement." He added, "I hope most seriously that the allotment was made more with a view to the public good, than to promote any private end."[5]

McKinley's allusion to dubious motives behind the circuit allotments was probably made in reference to the political intrigue that took place both on and off the bench in the wake of the 1842 circuit reorganization. The justices collectively made the assignments, but not before being heavily lobbied by members of Congress who sought to influence the circuit allotment process.

Justice Catron, for example, spoke bluntly about his fellow justices in responding to inquiries from the congressional delegations of Arkansas

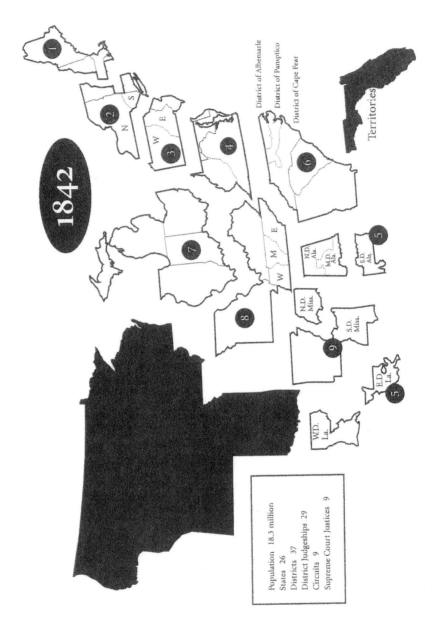

1842

District of Albemarle
District of Pamptico
District of Cape Fear

Territories

N
S
W
E

W
E

3

W
M
E

N.D.
Ala.
M.D.
Ala.

S.D.
Ala.

5

N.D.
Miss.

S.D.
Miss.

9

E.D.
La.

5

W.D.
La.

Population 18.3 million
States 26
Districts 37
District Judgeships 29
Circuits 9
Supreme Court Justices 9

11. Boundaries of the federal circuits in 1842. Courtesy of the Federal Judicial Center.

and Mississippi. He told them not to worry about the justice assigned to their circuit because whoever it was would probably not be there for long. Catron predicted that personnel changes on the bench would necessitate additional circuit assignments relatively soon. "The Chief Justice is exceedingly frail," he informed those members of Congress, "indeed he will hardly outlast the next three years, I think clearly not. If he dies, then Judge Daniel will of course be retained in the Virginia circuit." On the other hand, he noted, "Daniel is a feebler man than McKinley, and not likely to last as long. [Either way] . . . we get another Western judge."[6]

By a narrow majority vote, the seven-member Supreme Court allotted the new Ninth Circuit to Justice Daniel, who attributed his assignment to the efforts of his political enemies in Congress who were determined to drive him from the bench.[7] He detested his circuit and was much more vocal about his unhappiness than McKinley had been when the latter oversaw the entire old Ninth Circuit rather than just the half of it as Daniels did. Far from his beloved Virginia, Daniel left several letters complaining about his travel to and from the Old Southwest. He described riding a canal boat for 104 miles with vulgar men and filthy women, arriving in Arkansas only to find that the steamboats from Napoleon to Little Rock ran on no fixed schedule, running atop a huge tree snag on the Mississippi, surviving a cholera outbreak aboard ship, and holding court in Jackson where, as his biographer put it, "there were more dogs than people and his quarters he could only compare to a hog sty."[8] Catron's letters are instructive in the way they characterize the difficulties McKinley had also faced in traveling much of the same route the previous five years.

McKinley's absence from the 1843 term not only impacted the Court's decisions regarding circuit assignments and Richard Peters, it also played an important role in *Strout v. Foster*, one of the first cases the Court heard that session, which involved an admiralty decision rendered by McKinley at circuit.[9] The case turned on an incident that had occurred seven years earlier when the ship *Harriet*, outbound from New Orleans on its way to London in May 1836, came to anchor in one of the outlets of the Mississippi River, partially blocking the thoroughfare for other ships. As the ship *Louisville* was passing through the same outlet near the *Harriet*, the wind suddenly and almost completely ceased. Without the use of its sails, the *Louisville* was carried by strong currents into the *Harriet* before the former could cast its own anchor. Owners of the *Harriet* brought suit in U.S. District Court and won $2,700 in damages against the *Louisville*.

The owners of the *Louisville* appealed and McKinley heard the case at circuit in New Orleans. There, relying on an 1815 British admiralty law decision, he reversed the lower court ruling.[10] It was true, he noted, that a ship under sail would typically be liable for a collision with an anchored vessel. However, "the place where the *Harriet* anchored was an improper place, and therefore the [owners of the ship] must abide the consequences of the misconduct of the master."[11] McKinley's decision was favorably noted and quoted in maritime and commercial law journals for the next several decades. In 1848 the editors of the *Merchants Magazine and Commercial Review* wrote that the ruling "is one of those quiet and sensible opinions for which Judge McKinley is eminently distinguished."[12]

The owners of the *Harriet*, however, appealed McKinley's ruling to the U.S. Supreme Court. Their attorneys at oral argument invoked a host of maritime law precedents holding the vessel in motion liable for colliding with a ship at anchor. By the time the Court rendered its decision in *Strout*, just six justices were present as Justice Smith Thompson had left Washington. Three of the justices ultimately sided with the *Harriet*, but the other three believed the *Louisville* to be free of any liability. Rather than recalendar the case for future argument, the Court announced its divided opinion and, lacking a tie-breaking vote, McKinley's lower court ruling was affirmed.

Having recovered enough of his health to travel by the spring of 1843, McKinley set out to attend the courts in his new Fifth Circuit. He arrived in New Orleans to find himself involved in another, albeit minor, public controversy. At the commencement of the circuit court session, a young man named Joseph Clark was summoned as a federal juror. Clark, however, had also been summoned by the parish court, which was meeting at the same time, and had, in fact, already been sworn in as a juror there. When he subsequently failed to appear at federal court, circuit court officials confronted him, chastised him for not attending to his duty, and brought him back to the circuit proceedings. Shortly thereafter, the parish court ordered the local sheriff to bring Clark back. McKinley confronted the sheriff and told him not to interfere again with the business of the federal court.

Area newspapers reported the story with the *Pensacola Gazette* offering this biting assessment of McKinley's action: "We will make an even bet, of the stump of gray goose quill with which we are writing, against that Judge's stock of legal learning, that he is wrong in the matter—we never heard of his being right in any thing [*sic*], and bearing accidents, he never will be."[13]

Of far greater significance was McKinley's ruling in New Orleans regarding the constitutionality of the nation's second federal bankruptcy law. One of the prominent campaign themes of the 1840 presidential election was relief for the millions of Americans who had been plunged into debt by the Panic of 1837. When William Henry Harrison and the Whig Party captured both the White House and Congress, they quickly set to work on a bankruptcy law that, unlike previous legislation, permitted individual debtors to declare voluntary bankruptcy.

The Bankruptcy Act of 1841 was very unpopular among those who feared the law would allow a massive discharge of debt, and legal challenges to the constitutionality of the law were immediately brought in federal courts around the country. Congress repealed the Bankruptcy Act just eighteen months after its passage, but disputes under the law that were still unresolved in court after its repeal continued to be adjudicated in the federal courts, including in New Orleans where McKinley presided over one such case.

As mentioned earlier, McKinley devoted much attention to the issue of debt relief during his political career. His circuit ruling thus underscored both his view of congressional authority and the necessity of assistance for individual debt relief. He ruled the "act of Congress to establish a uniform system of bankruptcy throughout the United States . . . as a valid and binding law according to the Constitution."[14] Newspapers nationwide reported the significance of McKinley's holding as well as that of the other circuits where litigation under the law continued. As one Boston paper noted to its readers in explaining McKinley's ruling, "This decision is of the more importance, inasmuch as it is final. The Supreme Court . . . decided expressly that the provisions of the General Bankrupt law gave that court no jurisdiction in cases of bankruptcy; in consequence, the decisions of the United States Circuit Courts will be final, each in its respective district."[15] The *Daily National Intelligencer* in Washington offered an additional personal note in reporting on the New Orleans decision, expressing its great "pleasure to learn, from this notice . . . that [McKinley] has so far recovered from the severe illness which prevented his coming to Washington last winter."[16]

Throughout the remainder of 1843 and into the next year, the nation's attention increasingly focused on the presidential election of 1844, which would bring together three of the most important men from McKinley's past: Henry Clay, Martin Van Buren, and James K. Polk. The sitting president, John Tyler, had been expelled from the Whig Party just a few months after assuming the presidential office upon the sudden death of William Henry Harrison in 1841. With a heretic in the Oval Office, Whig Party leaders quickly turned to Henry Clay, in what would be his final attempt to win the presidency, to retain the White House while bringing ideological purity to the party.

It was presumed that Clay's Democratic opponent would be Martin Van Buren, who still enjoyed broad national support and who was eager for a rematch against the Whigs. However, when he announced his opposition to the annexation of Texas, which was under consideration at the time, Van Buren infuriated many members of his party and lost key southern support. At the subsequent Democratic National Convention in May 1844, Van Buren was unable to muster the necessary two-thirds votes necessary to win the nomination. Instead a dark-horse candidate, the first of its kind in the presidential nomination process, won his party's nod. James K. Polk had initially set his sights on the vice presidential slot, but when the convention deadlocked—giving Van Buren a majority of delegate votes (but still far shy of the required two-thirds)—he permitted his name to be put forward. On the ninth ballot, Polk secured the party's nomination.

Despite his personal and political relationship with all three men, McKinley—now living in Kentucky—apparently signaled his support of favorite son candidate Clay. Quoting a Louisville source, a Whig newspaper in Ohio reported that "Judge McKinley, formerly a Loco Foco U.S. Senator from Alabama, and now judge of the Supreme Court of the United States, and a resident of Louisville, is in favor of Mr. Clay. He thinks that Mr. Clay's election is demanded by the great interests of the country."[17] As the quote was from a secondhand source, it is difficult to test its veracity. McKinley may have indeed made the reported comment. It might also have been put forward by a Whig partisan hoping to win supporters by highlighting the old friendship between Clay and McKinley. Whether real or alleged, however, it would be incorrect to interpret McKinley's preference for Clay as an abandonment of his Jacksonian ideals, which his decisions on the Supreme Court would continue to affirm until his death. McKinley made no other public endorsement of Clay or any other candidate for the presidency that year.

In Washington, shortly after the commencement of the January 1844 term, Chief Justice Taney became seriously ill and missed the remainder of the session.[18] McKinley was also absent from several days of oral argument because of illness but did participate in the Court's most interesting case of that term.[19] In *Vidal et al. v. Philadelphia*, the Court considered the validity of Stephen Girard's will. Arguably the richest man in America when he died in 1831, Girard left several million dollars to the city of Philadelphia for the establishment of a male orphanage and boarding school. One of the few stipulations mentioned in his will was that "no ecclesiastic, missionary, or minister of any sect whatsoever shall ever hold or exercise any station or duty whatever in the said [boarding school], nor shall any such person ever be admitted for any purpose, or as a visitor, within the premises." Girard insisted that he held no animosity toward religion; he just wanted the boys to "be free from the excitement which clashing doctrines and sectarian controversy are so apt to produce" during their formative years."[20]

Girard's name, the huge sum involved, the implied censure of religion, and the fact that his own heirs had challenged the will for over a decade guaranteed its appeal to the American public long before it came before the Supreme Court in 1843. Because of absences on the bench that year, the Court rescheduled the case for the 1844 term where it consumed ten more days of oral arguments in February headlined by Daniel Webster and John Sergeant. The *New York Herald* described the scene in the Court's chambers:

> There is a tremendous squeeze. . . . Hundreds and hundreds went away, unable to obtain admittance. There never were so many persons in the Court-room since it was built. Over 200 ladies were there; crowded, squeezed and almost jammed in that little room; in front of the Judges and behind the Judges; in front of Mr. Webster and behind him and on each side of him were rows and rows of beautiful women dressed "to the highest." Senators, Members of the House, Whigs and Locos, foreign Ministers, Cabinet officers, old and young—all kinds of people were there. . . . The body of the room, the sides, the aisles, the entrances, all were blocked up with people. And it was curious to see on the bench a row of beautiful women, seated and filling up the spaces between the chairs of the Judges, so as to look like a second and a female Bench of beautiful Judges.[21]

On February 27 a unanimous Supreme Court affirmed the validity of Girard's will, holding that the provisions were not "derogatory and hostile to the Christian religion" and thus not "void, as being against the common law and public policy of Pennsylvania."[22]

McKinley left Washington the next week, five days before the Court

adjourned, to get an early start on his circuit travel. En route he unexpectedly ran into the Boston attorney Richard Henry Dana, whom he had
met a month earlier when Dana visited the boardinghouse where McKinley and several other justices lived. In his journal, Dana recorded, "Dined
and took the [railway] cars at 4 P.M. for Baltimore. Found Judge McKinley
among the passengers, with whom I had some pleasant conversation upon
the N[ew] Eng[land] and the [Southwest] states, he never having seen the
one, I never the other." Dana wrote that McKinley planned to "spend the
night at a small hotel, at the junction of this and the Western railroad,
to take the cars for Wheeling in the morning. He was on his way to hold
Court in N[ew] Orleans and said he should go 2500 miles by steam."[23]
Dana went on to marvel at the ability of someone McKinley's age to perform such demanding work. Others were paying attention to McKinley's
age and physical health as well.

John C. Calhoun, then serving as secretary of state in the Tyler administration, anticipated the opportunity to remake the Supreme Court
that awaited President Tyler in a May 1844 letter. With the recent passing
of Justice Henry Baldwin, the death of Justice Smith Thompson the previous December, and the continued poor health of Chief Justice Taney,
Calhoun declared, "The prospect is, that the majority of the places on [the
Supreme Court] will be vacant, including the two that now are, in a short
time." He added, "Judges Story and McKindly [sic] are both said to be in
infirm health."[24]

Several of the justices were indeed in poor health, which affected their
ability to do their jobs in Washington and at circuit. Congress noted the
problem and, uncharacteristically, was quick to help. In June 1844 it added
an additional month to the Supreme Court's term, which would now start
on the first Monday in December, beginning later that year. The rationale
behind this action was that if the Court started earlier, it could end earlier
and the justices could get to their circuits without being rushed.

Congress also stipulated that the justices could attend either the spring
or fall session of their circuit courts, something McKinley had specifically
requested in his 1842 petition, so that if their term in Washington made
them miss one circuit session, they could always attend the other. Neither
of these reforms did much to alleviate the demands faced by the justices
and, taken together, they may have exacerbated them. For example, since
Congress had not altered the dates for holding circuit (where the caseload
was also growing), justices choosing to attend the fall session might still

find themselves hard-pressed to make it back to Washington by the first week of December.

Similarly, the Court's lengthened term was quickly filled up by an ever-increasing docket such that the justices soon found themselves still in session in Washington until as late as May. Again, as before, some justices were forced to choose between staying until the end of the Washington term or leaving early to make it to the spring sessions of circuit. In short, as Swisher has written of the congressional reforms, "the problem of the Supreme Court was solved at the expense of work on circuit[,] . . . [s]ince circuit work was likewise expanding in quantity."[25]

The Court commenced its newly lengthened term on December 2, 1844, with newspapers reporting that "the high and dignified tribunal is now in session in Washington."[26] It was short-handed again, however, as only five justices, including McKinley, were present the first day. But even after the others arrived, the Court made painfully slow progress. The additional month mandated by Congress was of little help that term, according to an 1845 New Year's Day letter from Justice Story to his family. He lamented, "We have one hundred and fifty cases, all of which are for argument, and after one month we find ourselves just at No. 29. You may judge, therefore, that we are not likely to make a decisive impression upon the docket."[27]

The Court's docket that term contained several cases from McKinley's circuit. One of these, a rather minor case called *Ex Parte Christy*, again illustrates that McKinley not only respected federal power but used his office on the bench to sustain that authority. At issue in this case was whether a U.S. district court, under the Bankruptcy Act of 1841, possessed jurisdiction over bankruptcy and mortgage claims, which had traditionally been regulated by state law.

At circuit McKinley wrote, "[T]he said District Court has, under the statute of bankruptcy, full and ample jurisdiction of all questions arising under the petition . . . , and that said last-mentioned court has full power and authority to try and determine the validity of said mortgages."[28] That opinion did not sit well with Justices Catron and Daniel, who proclaimed that McKinley's circuit ruling had "annulled . . . the judgments of the state courts, and assumed to extinguish the title acquired under them; and has extinguished in form and fact . . . a title indisputable according to the laws of Louisiana standing alone."[29]

Writing for a majority of the Court, however, Justice Story affirmed McKinley's lower court opinion. "The obvious design of the Bankrupt Act of 1841," he wrote, "was to secure a prompt and effectual administration and settlement of the estate of all bankrupts within a limited period." In order to accomplish this, he added, "it was indispensable that an entire system adequate to that end should be provided by Congress, capable of being worked out through the instrumentality of its own courts, independently of all aid and assistance from any other tribunals over which it could exercise no effectual control."[30] Story wrote a letter to his family the following day in which he proudly declared, "Yesterday I delivered the opinion of the Court in a great Bankrupt [*sic*] case from New Orleans, embracing the question of the nature and extent of the jurisdiction of the District Court in matters of bankruptcy. . . . [W]e sustained the jurisdiction of the District Court over all matters whatsoever."[31]

In addition to considering several cases from his circuit, this term also saw McKinley assigned to write six separate majority opinions for the Court—the most in a single term that he would ever write. Four of these involved land-related issues, which had also characterized much of his congressional career. The most important of these land cases, and the majority opinion for which McKinley is best known, is *Lessee of Pollard v. Hagan.*[32]

This case, making its third appearance before the Court, arose from the claim of a private landowner in Mobile who argued that land patents granted by the U.S. government in 1824 and 1836 infringed upon a tract of swampy property he owned near the Mobile River. Specifically, he argued that the Spanish government, from whom he had received his grant several years before, recognized his claim to the land between the high- and low-water marks of the river. Whatever importance the case may have had for the landowners involved, its significance went far beyond the land abutting the Mobile River. Indeed, it questioned the very ownership rights of the United States to all the land that it acquired as the country continued to expand.

The difficulty for those who believed that the national government obviously took title to property as it came under its control was the fact that it had taken none from the original thirteen colonies. With the noted exception of the District of Columbia, which Maryland and Virginia ceded to the United States in 1791, all the property within the borders of the thirteen original states belonged to those states or the private landowners within them. Given that fact, citizens and policymakers in the newer states, including McKinley, wondered how the federal government even after a state had been admitted to the Union could constitutionally claim all the land within those borders that had not already been appropriated. What authority did Washington have to sell (or refuse to sell) that land, to permit or forbid internal improvements on it, and to dictate every other aspect relating to the public land that lay within the boundaries of the newer states? McKinley had asked these questions several times since his first election to the Senate in 1826; he would answer them now as he spoke for the Court in *Pollard*.

McKinley broadly declared that "the United States never held any municipal sovereignty, jurisdiction, or right of soil in and to the territory of which Alabama or any of the new States were formed, except for temporary purposes."[33] It did indeed accept new territory, but it did so only as a trustee, retaining "the municipal eminent domain for the new States" and turning it over to them upon their admission to the union.[34] Only by recognizing this doctrine, McKinley wrote, could the federal government place the newer states on equal footing with the original thirteen states.

It is not clear to what extent the other justices agreed with this dictum, but McKinley spared them from having to decide by focusing the remainder of his opinion on the specific facts of the case at hand. He coupled his interpretation of the equal footing doctrine with Chief Justice Taney's 1842 opinion in *Martin v. Lessee of Waddell*, which stated: "When the Revolution took place, the people of each State became themselves sovereign, and, in that character, hold the absolute right to all their navigable waters, and the soils under them for their own common use."[35] Without further comment on landownership generally, McKinley cleanly resolved the precise question in the *Pollard* case: just as the original states had the right to "the shores of [their] navigable waters, and the soils under them," so too did the newer states.

Justice Catron was the only member of the Court to dissent from McKinley's opinion. In doing so, he revealed two significant aspects of that ruling that are rarely noted by modern legal commentators. First, the issue of who held title—the states or the national government—to the land acquired as the United States rapidly expanded was of far greater significance than Pollard's tract of swampland. Not one for hyperbole, Catron wrote of the case, "[T]his is deemed the most important controversy ever brought before this Court, either as it respects the amount of property involved or the principles on which the present judgment proceeds—principles, in my judgment, as applicable to the high lands of the United States as to the low lands and shores."[36] On the merits of the case alone, as one legal scholar has written, Catron was not exaggerating the ramifications of *Pollard* for the "dispute over ownership of riverbeds when a territory became a state was far more politically interesting than the debates underlying the vast majority of antebellum federal cases."[37] The prospect of extending *Pollard* to other land coming under the control of the national government only underscored the magnitude of this ruling.

Second, for a decision that has been characterized as showing "just how far the Taney Court was willing to bow in the direction of states' rights," it also demonstrates an almost unanimous affirmation of federal court power.[38] Having struck down congressional legislation by way of judicial review in the case of *Marbury v. Madison* in 1803, the Court would not again explicitly use that power until its 1857 decision in *Dred Scott*.[39] Justice Catron's dissent, however, acknowledged that McKinley's decision both nullified congressional action and overturned several Supreme Court precedents.

> The front of the City of Mobile is claimed by the Act of 1824, sanctioned by this Court as a valid grant in the five cases of *Pollard v. Kibbe*, of *The City of Mobile v. Eslava*, of the *[The City of Mobile] v. Hallet*, of the *[The City of Mobile] v. Emanuel*. Except the grant to Pollard, the Act of 1824 confers the entire title (so far as is known to this Court) of a most valuable portion, and a very large portion, of the second city on the Gulf of Mexico in wealth and population. This act is declared void in the present cause; and the previous decisions of this Court are either directly or in effect overthrown.[40]

Mark Graber, one of the few legal scholars to recognize the Court's use of judicial review between 1803 and 1857, has written, "Justice McKinley's majority opinion did everything necessary to declare a federal law unconstitutional but explicitly utter the sentence 'the federal law is unconstitutional.' . . . His crucial conclusions were constitutional conclusions, highlighting the lack of federal power . . . to exercise constitutional powers in a particular circumstance."[41] In short, even in a decision that favored state interests, McKinley again demonstrated the authority of the national institutions of government.

At circuit that term, McKinley rendered a decision in New Orleans that again piqued some of his critics because of his strict construction of a federal customs law. The case turned on the actions of a U.S. customs inspector who, before retiring from his duties for the day, had sealed the hatches of the ship *William and Elizabeth* with tape and sealing wax to guard against the removal of cargo during the night.[42] When he returned the next day, he discovered that the seals had been broken and immediately penalized the master of the ship five hundred dollars as prescribed by law. The penalty was upheld by a U.S. district judge, but on appeal, both parties asked McKinley to determine if tape and wax, both of which were commonly used, were a proper means of fastening hatches under the federal revenue law of 1799.

McKinley reviewed Section 54 of the act, which permits customs officials to seal any "box, trunk, chest, cask, or other package" with tape or wax but requires that hatches be sealed with "locks or other proper fastenings."[43] Concluding that the customs inspector had not used the proper means for securing the hatches, McKinley reversed the lower court holding and threw out the penalty against the shipmaster. The *New York Herald* declared the decision to be of considerable "importance to persons engaged in commerce and to revenue officers."[44]

While returning to Louisville from New Orleans that term, McKinley was involved in an altercation with William Wood, a Scottish financier and educator who would later found the Normal College of New York City. McKinley's sometimes brusque temperament is well documented, but no other accounts substantiate or refute the version of this curious incident given in Wood's autobiography.

Apparently the Wood family was returning home to New York when low water prevented their large steamboat from proceeding beyond Paducah, Kentucky. There they were put aboard a smaller vessel where McKinley was already a passenger. When the travelers took their places for dinner, McKinley reportedly found the seat that he had used during his entire trip from New Orleans occupied by Wood's young daughter. According to Wood's autobiography, McKinley became very upset by this and proceeded to harangue Wood even after he moved his daughter to another seat. Wood recorded, "[McKinley] still kept asserting that the place was his, which I stoutly denied, whereupon he takes his tumbler and shies it at my head, but it fortunately missed me, and I, of course, struck at him, and hit him, I believe, under the left eye, as his face was cut a little, and his spectacle glass broken."[45]

McKinley returned to his cabin to fix his glasses and Wood followed, as the latter recalled, "for the purpose of explaining calmly to him that *he* was wrong," but McKinley refused to see him unless Wood apologized, which he refused to do. The sixty-five-year-old McKinley then said (according to Wood) that "he was on the bench and could do nothing, but if *not he would . . .* , as he would knock any man down who gave him the lie, as I had done."[46] The two separated, but later that night they both found themselves pacing past each other on the upper deck with, as Wood recorded, "I, and I daresay he, thinking every minute that the other might attempt to throw his adversary into the Ohio!"[47] They arrived the next day in Louisville where both disembarked, Wood and his family to a hotel and McKinley for home.

When the Court began its 1845 term on December 1, only four justices were present. Two new justices, Samuel Nelson and Levi Woodbury, had also joined the Court since the previous Washington term, the latter replacing Joseph Story, who had died in September. The fact that both men were in their mid-fifties did little to reduce the average age of the Court's members. The rigors of circuit riding coupled with the justices' health and advancing age contributed to the marked increase in absenteeism in Washington and at circuit over the next several years.

Such absences exacerbated the problem of the Court's growing docket. Between 1840 and 1845, the number of cases pending on the Court's docket increased from 92 to 173, but the Court continued to resolve only about sixty cases per term during that period even with the additional month it was in session.[48] Not surprisingly, the increasing inability of the Court to handle its business did not go unnoticed by Congress. Senator Henry Johnson of Louisiana proposed that the justices be entirely relieved of their circuit duties. This was necessary, he argued, because of the growing number of cases held over from term to term. "Such a postponement of the business of the court," he declared, "amounts almost to a denial of justice."[49] Ultimately, however, no action was taken that year on either Johnson's proposal or a similar measure in the House.

McKinley arrived a week late to the Court's December 1845 term and his presence at oral arguments was irregular—his frequent absences duly noted in the nation's papers.[50] He was present, however, along with the rest of the Court, to hear arguments in *Rhode Island v. Massachusetts*.[51] This was the same dispute the justices had considered during McKinley's first term in 1838. The earlier case, over Taney's dissenting vote, had established the Court's jurisdiction over state boundary disputes, but the resolution of the boundary itself had been delayed for a number of reasons until January 1846. After eight days of spirited oral arguments, the Supreme Court unanimously decided in favor of Massachusetts.[52] Just as in the earlier case, the Court's decision was of far greater significance than the 150 acres that were at stake in the case would indicate.

Article III of the Constitution authorizes the Court to settle controversies between states. Few of these were more important to the early states than boundary determination. Although boundary disputes had come before the Court prior to *Rhode Island v. Massachusetts*, none of these cases had been resolved on their merits. With this 1846 decision, the Supreme Court formally asserted, and the states recognized, its authority to resolve boundary claims of sovereign states. Indeed, three years later, after Missouri and Iowa called out their respective militias to defend land that both states claimed in the so-called Honey War, they took their dispute instead to the Supreme Court.[53]

Commenting on the Court's authority in these and several other such cases, Senator Lewis Cass of Michigan later declared, "[I]t is a great moral spectacle to see the decrees of the Judges of our Supreme Court on the most vital questions obeyed in such a country as this. They determine questions of boundaries between independent States, proud of their character and position, and tenacious of their rights, but who yet submit." How different this was, he maintained, from the way boundaries were determined in other parts of the world. "In Europe, armies run lines, and they run them with bayonets and cannon. They are marked with ruin and devastation. In our country they are run by an order of the Court."[54]

McKinley missed the last three weeks of the term, leaving Washington shortly after the oral arguments in the boundary case to return home. Continued poor health caused him to miss circuit that year, as well as the entire December 1846 term in Washington. He was one of several justices who missed all or portions of that term; just five members of the Court were present when it ended.[55] His health was apparently good enough for him to return to his circuit that spring, but he again missed the 1847 term in D.C.[56] McKinley's absence from the Washington term that year, however, had nothing to do with his health but rather his desire to get caught up on his circuit docket. On December 6, 1847, the first day of the Washington term, Chief Justice Taney wrote his wife, "I have a letter from Judge McKinley's son saying that he goes south this winter to hold his court in New Orleans and will not be here this season."[57]

Counsel who argued before the Supreme Court that term took note of McKinley's absence for strategic reasons since a tie vote among the eight participating justices was the least desirable outcome for their cases. Daniel Webster, for example, while awaiting the Court's decision in the pending *Lexington* case, informed a friend that "At this moment, the . . . Judges stand thus [4–3] . . . ; It is uncertain how Judge W[oodbury] will finally go."

He went on to explain, "If [Woodbury] continues to hang off, the cause will be continued, till the next Term, and then if all the members of the Court should be present, *we shall get judgment*, as Mr. McKinley, the absent Judge, is known to be on our side of the question."[58]

Rather than work around the ongoing absences of McKinley and other members of the Court, the Boston *Daily Atlas* argued that the justices themselves should take responsibility for the procedural delays that enlarged their docket. It suggested that a way be found to convince Taney to step down and have "a *progressive* Democrat . . . be appointed to the Bench [who] might be made Chief Justice" to more effectively manage the Court's docket. With only a trace of sarcasm, the newspaper also held out hope that "Judge McKinley would not insist on living so long, or would at least resign on account of ill health."[59]

As the 1847 term came to a close, Congress was again asked to consider relieving the Court of its circuit responsibilities. Similar proposals in the past had been motivated by the frequent absences of several of the justices (not just McKinley) and the impact that had on the final resolution of many of the cases before the Court. However, the plan then under consideration had apparently been suggested by the justices themselves.[60]

Pennsylvania representative Joseph Ingersoll brought the initial proposal to the House on February 27, 1848. He introduced an amendment to the 1844 legislation requiring the justices to attend just one session of circuit court annually that would temporarily suspend the justices' circuit responsibilities for two years so that they might fully dispense with their Supreme Court docket. Noting the increasing length of the Supreme Court's term (from fifty-five days in 1840 to ninety by 1846) and the growing docket (the 182 cases in 1846 nearly doubled the number docketed in 1840), Ingersoll correctly observed that the justices were only getting further behind.[61] As evidence, he noted that during the term in which the Court was then sitting, it had 190 cases on its docket. Yet with just two weeks remaining of their term, the justices had only considered 39. He believed his plan offered the justices a chance to catch up.

Representative James Bowlin of Missouri was quick to excoriate the plan. He questioned the motivation behind Ingersoll's proposal: "Who seeks this change? The people had not demanded it. There were no petitions from them asking for a dearer and less efficient administration of justice for the convenience of the judges. The press—the representatives of popular sentiment—had not clamored for the change." He then went on to answer his own question, "Who, then, wanted it? The judges, and the judges alone, to escape from the labors of their circuit duties."[62] Without referring to them by name, Bowlin castigated Justices McKinley and Daniel for their absences from circuit in previous years, arguing that the large dockets in New Orleans and Jackson would only increase should Congress temporarily relieve them of their duty there.

Although the two-year break was not approved in the House, a similar measure to remove circuit duty from the justices for one year appeared to have a chance in the Senate before it met with heavy opposition led by Senators Chester Ashley of Arkansas and William Allen of Ohio. Reviewing the Court's docket since 1842, Ashley concluded that the numbers simply did not support the claim that the justices were excessively overworked. Indeed, he argued, authorizing a single session of circuit court each year and expanding the term in D.C. by several weeks had resulted in just a handful of additional rulings on the part of the justices than before.

Senator Allen agreed, stating that the justices could easily handle their circuit and Washington dockets if they had the will to do so. The problem, he bluntly suggested, was not the caseload but the work ethic of the justices themselves. "It is by the agency of counsel that the materials for judgment are collected, digested, and arranged, and laid before the judge, so that nothing remains but to make up the decision," he argued. "And here sit nine full-grown men, in solemn deliberation, as if deciding matters of awful importance. Oh! What an amount of humbug there is in this world." Allen added that perhaps there was a strategic element to the justices' growing caseload as the only reason he could see for the large docket was that "they desired to see cases accumulate, until it would become necessary to dispense with their attendance on circuit duties altogether."[63]

Maryland senator Reverdy Johnson, himself a frequent advocate before the Supreme Court, immediately arose to defend the justices, finding his colleagues' comments to be "not only most unjust and unnecessarily harsh, but totally unfounded." To Allen's suggestion that the justices were lazy, Johnson retorted that the "Senator has not the most remote idea of the labors of the bench." He then provided the Senate with a detailed account of the justices' daily schedule, to which he added,

> The labors of these judges are herculean. Their physical labor breaks them down at the end of six or seven weeks. . . . We [members of Congress] go to our sleep, and sleep long, and come back here at twelve o'clock on the following day, having, comparatively, no morning labor for the body or the mind. The labors of a former day find us

nevertheless exhausted, and what have we done in comparison to the labors of the Supreme Bench? . . . [W]hat are our labors compared with those of the judges? They are nothing, literally nothing. [The judges] deserve to be honored and applauded instead of aspersed. They have not done more, because they cannot do more.[64]

The arguments offered by Johnson and several others senators, however, failed to persuade the Senate that the removal of the justices' circuit duties would only be a temporary measure. The bill ultimately failed to pass by a 23–17 margin.

Over the next few years, several other proposals to alter or curtail the justices' circuit responsibilities were introduced into Congress; none was successful. However, contrary to earlier efforts, these bills sought to address the problems of circuit riding to the Court as a whole rather than focusing on McKinley or any other individual member. Congress was increasingly cognizant of the fact that the rigors of the circuit and the expanding docket within both the circuits and Washington simply were not compatible with each other. As an exasperated Senator Andrew Butler of South Carolina would later demand of his colleagues, "Why, is not the fact before us that they [the justices] cannot do it . . . ? Judge Daniel is required to hold circuit courts in Arkansas. When was he in Arkansas or Mississippi? He cannot be there and here at the same time. . . . They cannot do it; and yet gentlemen talk about requiring these judges to go on circuit." His colleague Isaac Toucey of Connecticut added, "Is there a member of the Senate who can doubt the time is near at hand—if it has not already come—when it is an absolute impossibility for the Judges of the Supreme Court to go through the Union and adjudicate those cases [at circuit]?"[65]

With the onset of the Civil War, there was little further substantive discussion in Congress about the justices' circuit duties. It would take six more decades before Congress provided real relief, but in 1911, Congress finally and entirely removed the Court's circuit-riding responsibilities.

In early June 1848, Justice McKinley traveled to Arkansas where his arrival was reported in the Little Rock newspapers.[66] His presence was particularly noteworthy because he had never been to the state when it was part of his judicial circuit. His delicate health appears to have been the reason for his journey to Arkansas as he spent several days at Jacob Mitchell's hotel in Hot Springs. Mitchell bought the hotel in 1846 and opened a bathhouse. He later made a vast number of improvements to the property, enlarged the hotel to accommodate one hundred "invalids" (and their families) who sought out the therapeutic water, and established a stage line between Little Rock and Hot Springs for the benefit of his patrons. Mitchell widely advertised the curative properties of his thermal waters and attracted thousands, including Justice McKinley.

Just a few days after his arrival, McKinley's name again appeared in the Arkansas papers as one of several signatories to a public letter written in support of Jacob Mitchell. The statement itself noted that its publication was designed to counter "the circulation of various reports, injuriously affecting the reputation of [Mitchell's] establishment." McKinley and the other signees stressed that "the character of his establishment is, in every particular, above reproach, and that as a host, his table is beautifully supplied, and he is indefatigable in his endeavors to render his visitors pleased and comfortable."[67] The letter did not specify whether the criticism was directed solely at the services provided by Mitchell's hotel or at the man himself who, as a Jewish immigrant, had arrived in Arkansas from Spain in 1830.

Whatever salutary effect, if any, the hot springs had on McKinley's health, his well-being again became an issue as the Court approached its December 1848 term. As mentioned before, those who argued before the Court were well aware that if McKinley attended, he would provide the crucial swing vote in controversial cases where the justices' votes were expected to be close. Several months earlier, Daniel Webster publicly expressed his concerns about McKinley's health and even sought out Chief Justice Taney's thoughts as to the probability of McKinley's attendance for oral arguments in one of the most closely watched cases on the docket that term.

At issue in the *Passenger Cases* were state statutes levying a head tax on passengers aboard ships arriving at New York and Massachusetts ports.[68] The shipmaster was responsible for collecting the fees, which ranged from twenty-five cents to two dollars a person, and was required to do so before anyone could disembark. Critics of the laws, including Webster, claimed that such statutes infringed upon congressional authority over commerce. New York and Massachusetts, however, argued that Congress did not possess exclusive authority over commerce and that they were well within their rights to pass such laws. The states also viewed the head tax as an important source of revenue that could be used to care for the sick and poor immigrants who were about to become part of their citizenry. For his part, Daniel Webster saw the *Passenger Cases* as potentially the most "important to the country than any decision since that in the steamboat cause," referring to the Court's landmark 1824 ruling in *Gibbons v. Ogden* that upheld Congress's exclusive authority to regulate interstate commerce.[69]

Collectively the cases had been on the Court's docket since 1845 and had already been argued four times without the justices ever rendering a decision, largely because of absences on the bench involving McKinley and several others. The Court's seeming inability to resolve the issue coincided with the dramatic increase in the number of immigrants reaching America's shores during the late 1840s and contributed to strong public sentiment in the North that the cases be settled once and for all. An important subtheme to the case, however, as it was with so many other issues at the time, was slavery.

Even though the statutes dealt most directly with "white immigration," southern slaveholders feared that if the Court held that Congress possessed the exclusive right to regulate commerce under its Article I commerce clause powers, it would only be a matter of time before that authority would be used against the institution of slavery itself.[70] Given the significance of the regulatory authority in question, the inextricable link with slavery, and the Court's difficulty in resolving the issue, Webster's concerns about McKinley's absence from the bench were justified.

On October 11, 1848, Taney responded to Webster's query. "I am very sensible of the importance of having a full Bench in the New York and Boston passenger cases," he wrote, "[and] I have today written to Judge McKinley and hope he will be able to attend. Gentlemen who have seen him tell me that he is much better than he was when he was last at Washington."[71]

McKinley's health had indeed improved enough that not only was he present when the Court opened its December 1848 session but he attended nearly every day before leaving Washington just before the term ended to embark upon his circuit.[72] Concerns about his health lingered, however. In a letter written in early January 1849 and in apparent reference to McKinley, Daniel Webster expressed confidence that he would prevail in the *Passenger Cases* so long as "no Judge dies, or is obliged to leave the Bench."[73]

On February 7, 1849, the Court assembled to announce its decision. As Webster predicted, the Court decided the case by the narrowest of margins, with John McKinley providing the fifth vote striking down the state laws as an infringement upon the commerce clause powers of Congress. The *Boston Post* noted the critical role McKinley had played: "The New York case was once about to be decided on the opinion of four to three. It was then concluded to postpone judgment, until after another argument before a full Bench. Since then, the Judges have stood four to four, and upon the arrival of Judge McKinley, it was found that his opinion was adverse to the claims of the States."[74]

In an unusual departure from conventional practice, no single opinion represented the majority. Instead, Justices Wayne, McLean, Catron, McKinley, and Grier each wrote separately to explain their decision. Seven hours were required to read these seriatim opinions and Chief Justice Taney's dissent from the bench.[75] McKinley happened to be sick on the day the decision was rendered and was not able to deliver his opinion personally. He asked Justice Catron to read it for him instead.[76]

Perhaps because he was not there to deliver it personally or perhaps because it simply got forgotten or ignored because of the sheer volume of words generated by the collective opinions (which led one newspaper to complain that "[t]hese separate decisions are to be deprecated as a great nuisance"), McKinley's opinion has garnered little attention.[77] However, it again demonstrates his appreciation for national power that directly conflicts with the states' rights stereotype his critics (both historical and modern) have ascribed to him.

McKinley began his short concurrence by focusing on the literal meaning of the first clause of Article I, Section 9 in the Constitution. The fact that the framers included the word "or" in the phrase "the migration or importation of such persons" clearly demonstrated to McKinley that "there are two separate and distinct classes of persons intended to be provided for by this clause."[78] The fact that the remaining portion of that clause gave Congress the authority over the "whole subject of migration *and* importation" after 1808 basically left McKinley with just one question: On what grounds could states ever plausibly assert any authority over this issue?

McKinley argued that the national government's authority over immigrants began even before they set foot on American soil. When flying under the colors of the United States, for example, he wrote, "[t]he ship, the cargo, the master, the crew, and the passengers are all under the protection of the laws of the United States, to the final termination of the voyage; and the passengers have a right to be landed and go on shore, under the protection and subject to *these laws only*."[79]

He went on to emphasize that in this area, Congress and the national government had considerably more authority than the states and had received this power by way of both direct constitutional mandate and Supreme Court precedent. McKinley declared, "The [commerce] clause of the Constitution already referred to in this case, taken in connection with

the provision which confers on Congress the power to pass all laws necessary and proper for carrying into effect the enumerated and all other powers granted by the Constitution, seems necessarily to include the *whole
power over the subject*."[80] Simply put, from McKinley's perspective there
was no concurrent authority in this area for "the Constitution and laws of
the United States being the supreme law of the land, State power cannot
be extended over the same subject."[81]

Predictably, newspapers in Massachusetts and New York blasted the
decision while taking shots at the man whose swing vote had made it possible. A correspondent for the Boston *Daily Atlas* lamented, "These laws
have been adjudged to be constitutional by the unanimous opinion of
the highest Courts of Massachusetts and New York; and now they are to
be destroyed by the casting vote of Judge McKinley, of Alabama, whose
mind, it is said, has been long in a balanced and vacillating condition." The
paper went on to warn its readers, "If the laws of Northern States which
assume to regulate the introduction of aliens, whether white or black, are
to be destroyed by the judgments of Southern Judges, while the laws of
Southern States regulating the introduction of free blacks are to stand, it
will awaken reflections of no pleasant character."[82]

When it adjourned in mid-March 1849, the Court reportedly left one-
quarter of the cases on its docket to be decided the following term. Congress ignored the issue entirely, but there were public cries for reform from
across the country. In Mississippi, the *Natchez Semi-Weekly Courier* proclaimed, "Without a reorganization of this tribunal, vexatious and ruinous delays must continue to occur, to the manifest injustice of litigants,
and to the serious prejudice of the court itself." Without some type of re-
structuring of the Court's duties, it predicted that "appeals to the Supreme
Court will require the duration of a life, and recompense the contestants
with perseverance."[83]

Justice McKinley's health, already the subject of considerable speculation, was the focus of a particularly curious article that ran in newspapers
nationwide during the summer of 1849. The report, quoted below in its entirety, described a hydrotherapy remedy that apparently restored McKinley's poor eyesight.

> We are much gratified in being able to state that Judge McKinley,
> the distinguished jurist of the Supreme Court of the United States,
> after having his vision so seriously impaired for fifty-two years that
> he could not see without glasses, has recovered his sight so perfectly,

that he is now able to read without glasses. For half a century this faculty was so seriously impaired that without glasses he was almost blind, and the recovery of his constitutional health, by which the sight has been reinvigorated, Judge McKinley very properly ascribes to the daily use of cold water on the head and surface of the body. Of the importance of the use of cold water in maintaining and restoring health, no one who has ever tried it can entertain a doubt, and we refer to Judge McKinley's gratifying success in the restoration of his vision from its long sleep, for the purpose of encouraging other invalids to resort to this cheap and powerful mode of medication.[84]

McKinley's most significant action at circuit that year took place later that summer when he played a central role in a famous dispute involving Samuel F. B. Morse, the inventor of the telegraph. The legal dispute between Morse and a former business associate, Henry O'Reilly, was heralded nationwide as the "Telegraphic War in the West," the "Telegraph Controversy," and the "Great Telegraph Case."[85] McKinley's role was all the more unusual because he issued his decision from the Eighth Circuit, even though he was formally assigned to the Fifth.

In August 1848 Morse brought suit in federal court in Frankfort, Kentucky, against O'Reilly, who, Morse argued, in laying a telegraph line from Louisville to New Orleans, had utilized equipment that infringed upon Morse's patent. District judge Thomas B. Monroe agreed with Morse's claims and issued a broad injunction against the further operation of O'Reilly's telegraph line in Kentucky.[86]

A year later, armed with the telegraphic device of the Scottish inventor Alexander Bain who had secured his own patent, O'Reilly asked Monroe to lift the injunction as it applied to the Bain device. The judge agreed but set aside several related questions to be answered at a later date. In the meantime, Morse sought a similar injunction against O'Reilly's operations in Tennessee, Alabama, and Louisiana, and attempted to do so before the same federal court in Frankfort. Judge Monroe, however, was not present at that time and neither was Justice Catron, who was assigned to the Eighth Circuit, which included Kentucky. Because Monroe lectured part-time at the University of Louisiana in New Orleans and Catron was not available, McKinley heard the case. Congress had anticipated this very situation and had previously authorized McKinley to convene circuit court in Kentucky where he now lived in the absence of the other two judges.[87]

McKinley's first official action was to adjourn the court in Frankfort and remove it to Louisville. The trial subsequently commenced on June 19 and lasted nearly two weeks. On July 2, 1849, Justice McKinley handed down his decision. As reported in the *Natchez Semi-Weekly Courier* of that week, McKinley began by citing the jurisdictional latitude granted to Supreme Court justices in dismissing the first and most obvious argument of O'Reilly's that he (McKinley) lacked the authority to render a decision outside his own circuit. He then rejected O'Reilly's claim that Morse's patent was not so much about a specific device as it was about scientific principles that could not be copyrighted. McKinley declared, "[T]he patent is not for a principle. It is not for electricity or electro-magnetism, or their use for *all* purposes, or even *all telegraphic purposes;* but it is for the application of this power to a specific purpose." "[Morse's] claims are not broader than his discovery and invention," he continued, "and therefore his patent is valid."[88]

Finding there to be a case for patent infringement, McKinley agreed to grant Morse's request for an injunction but did so only in part. He questioned whether, as the presiding judge sitting in the Eighth Circuit, he had the authority to shut down O'Reilly's operations in Alabama and Louisiana. Presumably that would require a separate action before the Fifth Circuit Court (where McKinley would sit a few months later). He also reminded both parties of the "great public inconvenience" that would result should O'Reilly's telegraph cease to operate from Memphis south to New Orleans, particularly since neither Morse nor anyone else had established a competing line along that route.[89] In short, he would grant the injunction, but only within the borders of Tennessee, which also fell within the jurisdiction of the Eighth Circuit.

Together with Judge Monroe's second ruling, newspapers viewed McKinley's decision as a boon for technology and communication. As one put it, "We regard this decision as the most important that has been rendered since that which, thirty years ago, abolished the monopoly of steamboat navigation." Permitting O'Reilly's line to continue its operations ensured that "the Magnetic Telegraph, which no man exclusively invented—*though Prof. Morse deserved* both fame and wealth for his labors therein . . . —will be a public benefit and not a blighting monopoly. Henceforth, competition in telegraphing will be general."[90]

When the December 1849 term in Washington began, McKinley was not there and his absence was initially attributed to illness in the first volume of published reports for the term. However, the Court reporter made a correction in the following volume to read, "Mr. Justice McKinley was prevented from attending the court during this term, being engaged that period in holding an important session of U.S. Circuit Court in New Orleans."[91] Reporting on McKinley's absence, a Philadelphia newspaper was piqued (given an important Pennsylvania case that was on the Court's docket) that he was still at circuit court in New Orleans. "The Judge's absence from Washington," it declared, "has been productive of serious inconvenience, in preventing the decision of a most important question, in which the Supreme Bench is equally divided."[92]

What compelled McKinley to again miss the Court's Washington term in favor of circuit business was the famous case of Mrs. Myra Clark Whitney Gaines. She was the celebrated protagonist of one of the longest legal disputes in U.S. history, consisting of over fifty years of litigation in the federal courts and sixteen separate decisions by the U.S. Supreme Court. Because most of the litigation originated in New Orleans, McKinley played a major role in the dispute, presiding over several *Gaines*-related cases for a least a decade before he died.[93] It is also believed that the case indirectly hastened his death when, already seriously ill, McKinley attempted to reach Washington to participate in another of its many oral arguments before the Supreme Court.

Myra Gaines claimed to be the daughter and heir of the deceased New Orleans merchant Daniel Clark, who, she insisted, had entered into a secret marriage with her mother. The fact that Clark had been one of the richest men in early nineteenth-century America naturally made Gaines's story appealing. She captivated the nation with her tale involving a massive fortune, an illicit romance, a long-lost heir, a missing will, murder, and other elements of a classic dime-store novel.[94]

The legal issues associated with her claims, however, were considerably more serious and complex. Clark had been dead for many years by the time Gaines emerged to claim his fortune, and his executors had long since disposed of the bulk of his estate. One of Gaines's primary claims was that a will listing her as heir had been drawn up by Clark subsequent to the one upon which his executors had acted. This explosive claim automatically created a clouded title on all land sales from Clark's estate, many of which lay within New Orleans' lucrative commercial district. While newspapers across the country stoked sympathy for Gaines's cause by supplying their eager readers with sensational details of the melodramatic story, she received a considerably different reception from residents and property owners in New Orleans.

In 1848, having already ruled on a number of procedural and jurisdictional aspects of the Gaines case, the U.S. Supreme Court, absent McKinley, ruled on the ultimate question of whether Daniel Clark had indeed married Gaines's mother.[95] In *Patterson v. Gaines* (a case brought by Gaines against the current holder of property that had once been part of the Clark estate), the Court unanimously concluded that a legal marriage had been contracted, thus making Gaines the legitimate heir to Clark's fortune. The Court accordingly ordered that "the property described [in this case] . . . [was] a part of the estate of Daniel Clark at the time of his death, that it was illegally sold by those who had no right or authority to make a sale of it, that the titles given by them to the purchaser and by the purchaser to the defendant . . . are null and void."[96]

Stung by the Court's decision that took the title from Mr. Patterson and the precedent it set with regard to all others who had purchased property from the Clark estate, the two men who executed Clark's will, Richard Relf and Beverly Chew, filed suit in federal court. On January 23, 1850, Justice John McKinley and U.S. district judge Theodore H. McCaleb sitting at circuit court in New Orleans commenced one of the most significant hearings in the legal history of the Gaines case. A newspaper covering the case suggested that McKinley's presence at circuit, at the very time the Supreme Court was holding its term in Washington, could only be explained by the "deep interest he feels in this case, and his desire to bring it to a close."[97]

Having already presided over several *Gaines*-related trials, McKinley was indeed frustrated by the commencement of another round of litigation and insisted that counsel for Relf and Chew demonstrate explicitly how their case was materially different from that which the Court had just dispensed with in *Patterson.*

A full four days were required to read twelve hundred pages of testimony into evidence. Attorneys for both sides then spent nearly two additional weeks presenting their arguments, much of which traversed familiar ground regarding Daniel Clark's disputed will and his alleged marriage to Gaines's mother. In seeking to satisfy McKinley's demand that they distinguish their case from *Patterson,* attorneys for Relf and Chew argued that the *Patterson* decision could not be considered conclusive for several reasons. First, none of the justices who had ruled on the case was familiar with Louisiana civil law. The lawyers noted that McKinley, the only Supreme Court justice now acquainted with Louisiana's unique legal system and who might have helped his brethren in that case, missed the entire 1848 term of the Court because of illness. Second, the justices had wrongly accepted the testimony of an impeached witness in the *Patterson* case. Third, and most significant, they charged that Gaines and Patterson had actually colluded to bring the earlier case to trial, thus the "whole proceedings in the case of *Patterson* were false and fraudulent."[98]

On the first point, counsel for Relf and Chew correctly noted that only five justices were present when the *Patterson* decision was handed down and that John McKinley was not one of them. This mattered, they argued, because none of the remaining justices, all products of the common law tradition, could possibly have understood the mixture of French and Spanish civil law that governed Louisiana at the time of Clark's purported marriage. In other words, what might have appeared to have been a legitimate, if unorthodox, marriage according to common law would have been null and void under civil law in Louisiana.

Counsel for Relf and Chew then proceeded to discredit the testimony of a Madame Despau (who claimed to have witnessed Clark's marriage), upon which the Court's decision in *Patterson* had relied heavily. Despau, they argued, could not be considered a credible witness because there was virtually no evidence to corroborate even the minor points of her testimony. Her "memory" of the marriage and subsequent testimony of such appeared to have been coached, and her integrity was forever in question owing to an adulterous affair in which she was involved.

At this, McKinley interrupted to strongly object to counsel's characterization, displaying his own wit in the process. "Will it be seriously insisted that this is a proper ground for rejecting this deposition?" he asked. "If it is, will it not apply as well to men as to women; and, if so, would we not be hard off sometimes for witnesses?" To demonstrate his point, McKinley then offered this hypothetical: "Suppose a murder was to take place in a brothel, would not the occupants be good witnesses? You must show what the reputation of the witness is for truth and veracity."[99]

Counsel then proceeded to their most explosive claim: that Gaines and Patterson had actually colluded in bringing the case. McKinley was deeply skeptical of the collusion theory and interrupted counsel to state unequivocally, "I will not consent to review and reverse a decision of the Supreme Court. I shall consider this Court bound by the decision of the Supreme Court in all points determined in the *Patterson* judgment." He reminded counsel, "I stated this before the argument commenced, and warned gentlemen to confine themselves to those points which did not arise in the *Patterson* case." At this, Judge McCaleb interjected that he *would* consider it his duty to determine whether the *Patterson* decision conflicted "with our own jurisprudence, by which the decision in the case ought to be controlled."[100]

With the two judges publicly at odds, counsel proceeded to inform the court that Gaines had isolated Patterson from a group of fifty people against whom she had brought suit who all held land from the former Clark estate. Gaines allegedly promised Patterson that he could keep his property in return for helping her establish her title to the Clark fortune by being party to a friendly suit. The result, counsel declared, was "the momento of disgraceful and outrageous fraud, perpetrated upon one of our highest judicial tribunals."[101]

On Thursday, February 21, 1850, before a packed courtroom, Justice McKinley and Judge McCaleb arrived to announce their decision. In a move that startled many observers, McKinley announced that he was stepping aside, allowing McCaleb to decide the case. His reasons for doing so were detailed in an account of the trial published later that same year. McKinley "was induced to do this, because he was a Judge of the Supreme Court, and would have to sit in this case when it came up before that tribunal; that he never knew a case in which the Supreme Court overruled its own decision." It was a small thing for McCaleb to issue a ruling contrary to a Supreme Court's decision in *Patterson*, but McKinley "consider[ed] it disrespectful to his brother Judges to undertake to review and reverse their judgment."[102]

In addition, McKinley thought it important to allow McCaleb to write the opinion as he "was better acquainted with the local or State laws of Louisiana than he was, and the case would go up to the Supreme Court with an opinion written by a Judge familiar with the peculiar jurisprudence of this State." McKinley stated that, taken together, these actions provided "the most satisfactory course, as it would lead to the early decision of this case" by the full Supreme Court.[103]

Judge McCaleb subsequently relied upon the "peculiar jurisprudence" of Louisiana in noting that the Spanish laws that were still in place at the time of Clark's reported wedding simply did not recognize clandestine marriages. In addition, while professing his utmost respect for the Supreme Court, McCaleb nevertheless ruled that collusion between the parties entirely undercut the legal authority of the Court's *Patterson* ruling. Attorneys for Gaines immediately appealed to the Supreme Court.

As usual with all things related to the Gaines story, newspapers closely observed the proceedings. In reporting the outcome of the case in New Orleans, newspapers across the country also hailed McKinley's action. A

Philadelphia paper declared, "Judge McKinley gave his opinion in favor of the plaintiff, but in order to facilitate the decision of the case by the Supreme Court, he withdrew from the bench. . . . This act of Judge McKinley's will make a difference of two or three years in the final decision of the case."[104]

By the time McKinley had reached New Orleans for the Gaines case, his health had become even more fragile. Just two days into the hearing, a formal rule was adopted by the circuit court and entered on the minutes that sheds additional light on McKinley's growing physical limitations. The rule stated, "Whereas the honorable John McKinley, judge of the court, is, in consequence of an infirmity resulting from disease, unable to sign his name, it is ordered, that all judgments and decrees rendered in appeal causes be signed by the clerk of this court in the name of said judge."[105]

He did the best he could under these health constraints, and some of the justices apparently entertained hope that McKinley would participate in the latter part of the Court's session in Washington. But nearly a month after the circuit court had rendered its decision in *Gaines,* Chief Justice Taney wrote to his wife, "I hear nothing from Judge McKinley, and do not know whether he will be here or not."[106] McKinley spent the better part of the rest of the year recuperating at home.

Even in broken health, he continued to be spotlighted in national newspapers. In the latter part of 1850, McKinley was again praised and vilified for decisions made earlier in his life. In November, for example, a Milwaukee paper flattered McKinley by listing him along with several other well-known political and military figures who had had arisen from humble circumstances to become "men of eminence."[107] McKinley's current position as a member of the U.S. Supreme Court after having started out working as a carpenter and joiner qualified him to stand alongside "Benjamin Franklin, Roger Sherman, General [Nathaniel] Greene, General [Israel] Putnam, and hundreds of others who have been elevated to stations of honor, are full of instruction, and worthy of emulation by the youth of the present generation."[108]

A month later, a Boston newspaper offered mostly unflattering descriptions of several of Henry Clay's early associates. The writer regurgitated quarter-century-old claims about McKinley's political allegiance, stating simply, "John McKinley trimmed his sail to the popular breeze; rendered himself useful to all parties, and, was elevated to the bench of the Supreme Court of the United States."[109]

Health concerns notwithstanding, McKinley was present on the first day of the Court's December 1850 term to hear Daniel Webster beg off arguing several cases that had been docketed because his duties as secretary of state had not allowed him proper time to prepare without the assistance of other counsel who were not yet in Washington. The Court graciously granted the postponement and then proceeded to call up ten additional cases for argument—"the counsel in none of them [being] ready," according to a reporter from the *New York Commercial Advertiser*.[110] The minutes of the Supreme Court indicate that McKinley missed just two days of oral arguments that session.

The most significant case on the Court's docket that term, although it was not viewed as such at the time, was *Strader v. Graham*.[111] That case involved a lawsuit by a Kentucky slaveholder against those who had enabled three of his slaves to escape to Canada from Ohio, where he had sent them for music training. Against the claim that the slaves had become free when they touched Ohio soil by virtue of the Northwest Ordinance of 1787, which forbade slavery, Chief Justice Taney—for a unanimous Court—countered that the ordinance was supplanted upon the ratification of the U.S. Constitution. The Court had no jurisdiction under the Constitution, he maintained, to interfere with the status of slaves. Taney wrote, "Every state has an undoubted right to determine the status, or domestic and social condition of the persons domiciled within its territory except insofar as the powers of the states in this respect are restrained, or duties and obligations imposed upon them, by the Constitution of the United States." He added, "There is nothing in the Constitution of the United States that can in any degree control the law of Kentucky upon this subject . . . , and we have no jurisdiction over it."[112]

Focusing on the jurisdictional question spared the Court from having to definitively determine the status of slaves on free soil. With the Compromise of 1850 already roiling the country, the Court's decision to allow state courts to continue to determine such issues according to their own state laws was viewed as doing little harm. It would not be so fortunate six years later when the precedent established by *Strader* and Taney's dicta became the foundation for the Court's opinion in *Dred Scott*.[113]

McKinley was not among the five justices who were present when the Court convened the following year on December 1, 1851, for his final term on the bench.[114] That session was highlighted by a particularly devastating event in the Capitol. Shortly after the Court began oral arguments on Christmas Eve morning, a fire broke out in the Library of Congress, which was then located in the Capitol's west-central section, destroying more than two-thirds of the fifty-five thousand books in the library's collection. Two stories below, as Justice Benjamin R. Curtis recalled, "The Court was not disturbed by the fire, and sat as usual while the building was burning." He went on to dryly remark, "[H]aving made all necessary arrangements to have the records, etc., removed in case of need, we saw no reason why the business of the day should not proceed."[115] McKinley had not yet arrived at the time, but the justices still expected him to join the Court sometime later during that term.

For more than a week during the last few days of January and into the next month, the Court held oral arguments on the *Gaines* case that had been expedited by McKinley's decision months earlier. A correspondent for the *New York Daily Times* recorded the scene on February 5, the last day of oral arguments: "The Supreme Court was again crowded today. Hundreds of persons listened to Mr. Duncan's argument in the case of Mrs. Gaines, with ears as greedy as if they were all to be recipients of the vast estate of Clark. . . . Mr. Webster [serving as counsel for Relf and Chew] will bring down the big guns, and perhaps demolish her cause."[116]

An increasingly enfeebled Daniel Webster was scarcely capable of "bring[ing] down the big guns" anymore, but he could still attract a crowd to his oral arguments. The *Gaines* case would be one of his last before the Supreme Court. The *Daily Times* reporter went on to note that just six members of the Supreme Court were present to hear the case. Chief Justice Taney and Justice McLean recused themselves (as they had in the earlier cases) because of their previous association with Myra Gaines and her attorneys. Justice McKinley was the third absent member of the Court, although he was not named.

At noon on March 1, 1852, again before a large number of spectators, the justices entered their chamber to announce the Court's decision in the *Gaines* case. Over the dissent of Justices Wayne and Daniel, Justice John Catron read aloud the plurality opinion upholding the lower court ruling.[117] After castigating Patterson for colluding with Gaines in the earlier case and rejecting the depositions of some of the more questionable witnesses, the Court announced that the mass of evidence demonstrated that Gaines's mother could not have been legally wedded to Clark. It then concluded tersely, "[C]omplainant is not the lawful heir of Daniel Clark, and can inherit nothing from him: And consequently . . . the complainant can take no interest under her mother, by the conveyance set forth in the amended bill, she not being the widow of Daniel Clark."[118]

The Court recessed later that week, and when it resumed its session a month later newspapers reported that McKinley was finally making his way to Washington. With the *Gaines* decision still in the headlines, newspapers saw McKinley's expected presence as central to any hope Myra Gaines had at a future hearing before the Court. As one reported, "There are . . . several more cases, involving [Gaines], to come up from the Court below, as soon as they can be prepared; and therefore, Mrs. Gaines' case will be heard again, and possibly under more favorable circumstances, as Justice McKinley is supposed to be in her favor."[119] McKinley was indeed traveling to Washington at the time, but the arduous trip was taking a heavy toll on his already poor health, something that he apparently anticipated would happen, having made out his will just before he left Louisville.

On Monday, April 5, 1852, when the Court reconvened after its month-long recess, Justice John McKinley was listed in the Court's minutes as present.[120] Given the status of his health, his presence was noteworthy and was reported in the newspapers covering the Court.[121] He attended every oral argument until April 14, the same day another fire broke out in the Supreme Court clerk's office, causing minimal damage to the records that were stored there. According to the Court's records, McKinley was able to participate in just four more days of Court business over the next two weeks, with his last recorded attendance on April 30. He then returned to Louisville with nearly a full month remaining on the Court's calendar.

9
The Legacies of
Justice John McKinley

> No man could be more free from guile, or more honestly endeavor to
> fulfill the obligations which his office imposed on him.
> —Chief Justice Roger Taney, 1852

Although Justice McKinley endeavored to fulfill his responsibilities on the
Court to the end, his last months were filled with great pain, increasing
physical limitations, and an awareness that his own death was not far distant. In March 1852, just prior to his departure for Washington to attend
the remainder of the Court's term, he prepared his last will and testament. The ailing McKinley, "being unable from bodily infirmity to write
[his] own name," as his will put it, asked a witness, Kentucky jurist Henry
Pirtle, to sign his name for him.

McKinley left his home and several lots in Louisville to his wife,
Elizabeth, and directed his son, Andrew, as executor, to purchase real estate that would yield her an annual income of $300. She was also to have
"certain slaves, [McKinley's] carriage, and certain furnishings for life." To
his son, he gave another house in Louisville, plus "slaves and his law and
political books."[1] The will directed Andrew to sell McKinley's stock in
the Florence Bridge Company, as well as his other homes, lots, and acreage spread throughout Kentucky, Tennessee, and Alabama. Although the
elder McKinley had already disposed of a great deal of property himself,
he still possessed extensive landholdings. Two years before he died, he estimated the value of his real property at $85,000 on the 1850 federal census which, according to a conservative estimate, would equate to over two
million dollars today.[2] The will stipulated that the proceeds from the sale
of these properties were to be invested in "productive real estate" in or near
Louisville, the benefits of which were to be divided in half between his two
living children and their families. McKinley's daughter, Mary McKinley Churchill, was willed the "tea set, spoons, pitcher, tumblers, forks and

plated ware," and the justice's watch was to be given to his oldest living grandson when he turned twenty-one.[3]

After observing him in poor health for so many years, McKinley's family was undoubtedly prepared to see their long-suffering patriarch pass on. Regrettably, however, they were forced to deal with more than just his passing. McKinley's own death in the summer of 1852 was preceded by that of two grandsons, both namesakes, earlier the same year. John McKinley Churchill was the third of Mary's five children. His cousin John McKinley was Andrew's firstborn and the justice's eldest grandson. Both boys died just short of their eighth birthday when they passed away in February and May 1852, respectively.[4]

On July 19, 1852, "an enduring but exhausted" John McKinley died at the home of his son in Louisville.[5] He was buried beside his two grandsons on a small promontory in Louisville's newly created garden cemetery, Cave Hill.[6] His marble headstone is topped by a ten-foot column and reads simply: "Sacred to the memory of John McKinley, Associate Justice of the Supreme Court of the United States. Born May 1, 1780, Died July 19, 1852."

Remarkably, but consistent with the circumstances that had dogged much of his career on the Supreme Court, even his death was poorly timed. His old friend Henry Clay had passed away three weeks earlier and the newspapers were still so filled with memorials to his life and accounts of public mourning at his passing that McKinley's death, albeit in papers nationwide, was only briefly mentioned. However, even in these short notices, something of the respect and esteem in which he was held can still be observed. For example, a Baltimore newspaper declared that McKinley's "name and reputation for legal ability are well known to the country."[7] And the *Adams Sentinel* in Gettysburg noted simply that he "was esteemed an upright and conscientious magistrate."[8]

A more meaningful remembrance of his passing was offered the following December when the Court held a special memorial service to open its 1852 term.[9] The commencement of that session was marked by mourning for McKinley as well as for Henry Clay, Daniel Webster, and John Sergeant, who had also died a few months earlier. For thirty years, the latter three had together delivered some of the most memorable and significant oral arguments in the history of the Supreme Court.[10] That all three men and a fellow justice would pass away within a single year was a staggering blow to the Court, and it devoted its entire morning business that day to memorializing the four men.

Attorney General John J. Crittenden began the memorial by first eulogizing Justice McKinley. His public office dictated that he do so, but his comments were more personal than those offered for other departed justices because he had known McKinley for nearly forty years, dating back to their time as young lawyers in Kentucky.[11] Crittenden said,

I had the good fortune to be acquainted with Judge McKinley from my earliest manhood. In the relations of private life he was frank, hospitable, affectionate. In his manners he was simple and unaffected, and his character was uniformly marked with manliness, integrity and honor. Elevation to the Bench of the Supreme Court made no change in him. His honors were borne meekly, without ostentation or presumption.

He was a candid, impartial, and righteous Judge. Shrinking from no responsibility, he was fearless in the performance of his duty, seeking only to do right, and fearing nothing but to do wrong.

For many of the last years of his life, he was enfeebled and afflicted by disease, and his active usefulness interrupted and impaired; but his devotion to his official duties remained unabated, and his death was probably hastened by his last ineffectual attempt at their performance by attending the last term of this Court.

Death has now set her seal to his character, making it unchangeable forever; and, I think, it may be truly inscribed upon his monument that as a private gentleman, and as a public magistrate, he was without fear and without reproach.[12]

Crittenden then presented the following series of resolutions to the Court that had been prepared and approved unanimously by members of the Supreme Court Bar:[13]

Resolved, That among the afflictive dispensations with which it has pleased Almighty God to visit us, in common with the entire nation, during the last few months, we are especially called upon to deplore the death of the Honorable John McKinley, who, for the period of fifteen years, had filled an honorable position on the Bench of the Supreme Court, which he adorned by his simple purity of character, his learning, industry, and courtesy of manner.

Resolved, That this meeting deeply lament the death of Judge McKinley, and will cherish an affectionate remembrance of his many virtues and eminent worth as a judge, a patriot, and a man, and that we will wear the usual badge of mourning during the residue of the term.

Resolved, That the Chairman and Secretary of this meeting transmit a copy of these proceedings to the family of the deceased, and to assure them of our sincere condolence on account of the bereavement they have sustained.[14]

Chief Justice Roger Taney accepted the resolutions and directed that they be included in the official records of the Court. He then offered a memorial to McKinley on behalf of the entire Supreme Court. Taney's kind disposition and genuine concern for his brethren caused him to be well regarded by all who served with him.[15] He had been exceptionally patient with McKinley and his absences from the Court. Being three years older, in chronically poor health for several years, and the subject of intense public criticism himself (which would only increase after his 1857 decision in Dred Scott), Taney fully appreciated the toll that McKinley's Supreme Court duties had taken on him. From the bench, the chief justice read,

We cordially unite with the Bar in all that they have said of the character and worth of Judge McKinley. He was a member of this Court for fifteen years, and we knew him well. He was a sound lawyer, faithful and assiduous in the discharge of his duties while his health was sufficient to undergo the labor. And his life was probably shortened by the effort he made to attend this court at the last adjourned term, when his health had become too infirm to encounter the fatigue of a journey to Washington. He was frank and firm in his social intercourse, as well as in the discharge of his judicial duties. And no man could be more free from guile, or more honestly endeavor to fulfill the obligations which his office imposed on him. We truly deplore his death.[16]

No other business was scheduled for the remainder of the day, and the Court adjourned until the following morning.

Over the next one hundred and fifty years, only a handful of additional remembrances were accorded to Justice John McKinley.[17] His name and memory were again invoked before the Court when his property in Tennessee became the subject of a long-running legal battle that finally reached the Supreme Court in the 1878 case of Sherry v. McKinley. The case originated with an 1862 act of Congress authorizing the seizure of private land for nonpayment of taxes "in insurrectionary districts within the United States" as a means of both dissuading and punishing Confederate loyalists.[18] The confiscated land was then put up for sale at public auction. In June 1864, U.S. military authorities seized and auctioned off several parcels of land in and around Memphis, including several acres owned by McKinley.

Andrew McKinley, the justice's son and executor, did not learn that the property had been transferred until after the Civil War. He quickly filed suit claiming that the federal statute authorizing the seizure was unconstitutional, that the property in question had never been assessed for tax purposes since before the war, and that the public sale of the land was not properly advertised. He was particularly piqued at the fact that the federal government's military occupation of Tennessee during the war had rendered both communication and travel so difficult that it was virtually impossible for him to determine the status of his land there.[19] The younger McKinley's arguments echoed those of other landowners throughout the South affected by the law and ultimately prevailed when the Supreme Court of Tennessee considered the issue. However, on appeal, the U.S. Supreme Court bluntly rejected McKinley's claims, as it had in previous suits against the land forfeiture law.[20] In recounting the history of the disputed property, depositions taken in the case remembered Justice John McKinley as someone who "was always regarded as a high-minded, honorable, [and] good citizen."[21]

Nearly two decades later, newspapers around the country would again remark on the McKinley name and legacy in the weeks preceding the inauguration of President William McKinley. Lauding the "mental characteristics which distinguish [the] bearers" of the McKinley name, an Oregon newspaper traced Justice McKinley's life and judicial career, concluding with Alabama writer Willis Brewer's oft-quoted characterization of Justice McKinley: "His ability was very considerable, and his tenacity of purpose and great energy proved to be winning cards in the game of life."[22]

With the exception of his marble headstone, physical memorials to the justice were also scarce for the first century and a half after his death. The United States Maritime Commission honored him in 1943 with the *SS John McKinley*, one of 2,700 Liberty cargo ships built during World War II.[23] Fifty years later, the Alabama congressional delegation introduced legislation to change the name of the United States Post Office and Courthouse in Florence, Alabama, to the Justice John McKinley Federal Building.[24] Prior to this time, the only monument to McKinley in the entire state was a historic marker in Florence near the site where his three-story home once stood. President Bill Clinton approved the bill on November 2, 1998, and six months later the government building was officially rededicated.[25]

In 2008 the city of Florence created a "Walk of Honor" within its River Heritage Park to commemorate sixteen notable men and women from the area, including McKinley, who had "excelled at the national or international levels" and had brought attention to the town. Situated on the banks of the Tennessee River, the park memorializes the honorees with a large brick column and a bronze plaque on which is inscribed their likeness and a simple tribute to their achievements.[26]

Justice John McKinley's legacy, however, is greater than that suggested by the words of praise offered at his passing in 1852, the few physical memorials established more recently, and the dismissive comments of past and present Court observers. Although he is essentially unknown to the present generation, his influence is still felt throughout Alabama and the nation relative to four areas of institutional power and policy change. These areas are: ongoing debates over the use of public land within the United States; the power of the national government; the authority of the Court; and changes to the circuit court responsibilities of the justices. Each of these four public legacies is detailed in what follows, along with a fifth legacy, which is more personal in nature.

More than the Court, the law, his political offices, and his personal connections, John McKinley was tied to the land. It brought his uncle and father to Kentucky and brought him to Alabama. He seemed especially concerned with not just owning the land but making it productive. And even though Cypress and other land speculation companies made fortunes by taking advantage of other men's dreams of productive land, McKinley consistently argued that land had a purpose. Land that was cultivated, opened up to settlement, and improved with roads, canals, homes, and cities benefited the citizens who lived there. Idle land, on the other hand, benefited no one. That philosophy was the foundation of many of McKinley's efforts in the Senate and helps explain his important decision in *Pollard v. Hagan*.

As a land speculator, he clearly knew the value of holding onto land until it fetched a higher price. But no individual speculator had the resources to immediately take ownership of all the land in a newly opened territory as the national government could and did. No speculator had the authority, like the national government, to strip men of the land that they had cultivated and improved and then price it beyond their ability to repurchase because of those very improvements. No speculator could make decisions as to what was proper on someone else's land with such finality as the national government.

McKinley appreciated the role of government in land sales and land improvement, but he could not accept the presumption that the U.S. government automatically took and retained title to every square inch of new land, even after a sovereign state had been created, particularly when that practice only applied to the newer states in the Union. It was even harder for him to fathom why the national government, already in possession of millions of acres of land, would make that land harder to obtain or retain.

To McKinley, the national government utterly failed to appreciate the benefit of land to its citizens. Being closer to their people and as primary beneficiaries of their land improvement efforts, he argued, the states were best positioned to understand and to work with the needs of their citizens relative to the land. McKinley's positions certainly did not prevail, and they are just as ridiculed in some circles today as they were during his lifetime. But he was not the only one who held such views. As legal historian Frank Otto Gatell has observed, "Other southerners, both jurists and nonjurists, were saying the same things as McKinley, and saying them with more bite and with more eloquence, but no one was saying them with more consistency or conviction."[27]

In the modern era, many of McKinley's concerns have been revisited. The federal government now owns 650 million acres of land, nearly a third of the total land area in the United States. Federal landownership is concentrated in the western part of the country where the government owns or manages 30 percent of the land in *every* state west of Nebraska (more than 80 percent of Nevada), except for Hawaii. Much of the debate in the West focuses on whether the national government should impose further restrictions on public land for environmental purposes, for example, or embrace broader multiple-use policies. Underlying the entire discussion, however, is the question McKinley repeatedly asked throughout his public life: Should not the states, rather than the national government, have the ultimate decision-making authority over what happens to the land within their borders?

A second legacy of John McKinley's, although admittedly ironic given his concern about national government land policies, was his appreciation for national government power. McKinley's legacy in this area is obviously tied to that of the Taney Court, which means that popular misconceptions of that Court as a whole have been extended to him as well.

Without question, the Taney Court viewed state power differently from its predecessor. Chief Justice John Marshall was largely successful in establishing not only the Supreme Court's authority but also that of the national government during his thirty-five-year tenure on the bench.[28] State interests were not unimportant to Marshall, but according to Supreme Court scholar John R. Schmidhauser, "Little attention was given to commensurate safeguarding of state authority because, at least for Marshall and the more nationally-inclined of his colleagues, the overriding federal problem of their period was the protection of a weak national government from state interference."[29]

The "federal problem" for the Taney Court was not a weak national government pitted against strong states but rather balancing the considerable power of both. As Schmidhauser again points out, the Taney Court attempted to do this not by undermining the national government but by sustaining it (when appropriate) and the states as well. "Whenever state authorities threatened or interfered with legitimate federal powers," he wrote, "this Court, like its predecessor, was firm in its application of the constitutional principle of national supremacy." On the other hand, Schmidhauser noted, "[W]henever the absence of clear-cut interference with federal authority or constitutional limitations permitted it, this Court tended to sustain the freedom of state legislative authority." "The second attitude," he went on to say, "was not based upon suspicion or distrust of federal authority on the part of the Taney justices, but simply upon the concept, originating with the framers, that the states have vital roles to play in the operation of a truly federal system."[30]

McKinley adopted neither the enthusiastic nationalism nor the rabid states' rights philosophy of some of his brethren on the bench. Rather he held steadily to the view that the national government was supreme within its sphere of authority. *Prigg*, the *Passenger Cases*, and even *Bank of Augusta v. Earle* in its own way all recognize the exclusivity of federal power. Few politicians or jurists of his era could have predicted the subsequent and tremendous growth of federal authority that accompanied wars and economic depressions over the next century. It is likely that neither he nor most of his peers believed that *every* sphere of governmental regulation was the exclusive responsibility of the national government. Yet his votes, which sometimes decided the matter, clearly reflected his belief that even during the antebellum era some regulatory powers were enjoyed by the national government alone.

A third and related legacy of John McKinley was that his appreciation for national governmental power extended to his own judicial branch. For whatever other faults his critics ascribed to him, he did not avoid the opportunity to exert the authority of a federal judge when necessary. He did so by regularly looking to the plain wording of statutes and the Constitution. Where the meaning or intent of the wording was unclear or where sources were lacking, he turned to the Founders, reviewing the Constitutional Convention debates and even the *Federalist Papers* for guidance, as he did in his seriatim opinion in the *Passenger Cases.*

McKinley appreciated the role of the federal judiciary in the American republic. Whether rejecting executive authority in *Kendall v. Stokes,* rendering congressional laws inapplicable at circuit as he did in the steamboat steerage case of *U.S. v. Price and Company,* making the Court's decisions relevant and then final on the matter of state boundary disputes in *Rhode Island v. Massachusetts,* or in joining the Court's opinion in *Swift v. Tyson* to rule that the federal judiciary is not bound by the commercial laws of the states, McKinley knew that the federal judiciary possessed power unto itself. He was not afraid to use it.

McKinley's greatest legacy, however, may be the changes Congress finally authorized relative to the justices' circuit duties. Modern commentators who are quick to criticize McKinley for his complaints at circuit fail to remember that some of the changes he advocated were originally sought by the justices appointed by George Washington to sit on the first Supreme Court. For fifty years, due to legitimate concerns about changing the duties of the judiciary, irrational fear of the political consequences of tinkering with the circuits, and outright lack of political will, Congress did virtually nothing to provide significant relief for the justices who issued the same protests as McKinley but who did so from smaller circuits that were closer to Washington.

Only after Congress created a huge geographic circuit (that many members knew was unworkable before it was even officially formed) governed by a bizarre court schedule in a region with the worst transportation difficulties anywhere in the nation encumbered by an impossible amount of litigation arising out of the new states in that area and assigned a single justice to deal with it all did they finally realize the justices needed help. Even then, circuit reform was a matter of fits and starts. Ultimately, however, it accomplished exactly what McKinley had requested: smaller, more equitable circuits and attendance at only one circuit court session annually.

It is not inappropriate to suggest that much of the criticism, both historic and contemporary, leveled at Justice McKinley relative to his circuit duties has been misdirected. McKinley's brethren on the bench certainly shared some responsibility for the frustration he experienced when they refused to rotate circuit routes. As difficult and unorthodox as it might have been, for example, to have assigned Justice Story to the Old Southwest and McKinley to Chief Justice Taney's tiny Fourth Circuit and home state of Maryland, the Court could have done so. It was entirely within their power to relieve McKinley through a periodic rotation of circuit duties, but the justices utterly failed to assist in this manner.

Of course, the original Ninth Circuit would have overwhelmed any of the justices. Since the circuits were organized by Congress, any real changes to their boundaries had to be authorized by that body. Congress thus also shares responsibility for the aggravation, delays, and even violence that accompanied McKinley's circuit duties. It appears obvious that many members of Congress despite living and dining with the justices, attending the Court's oral arguments, and being generally aware of the Court's presence in Washington during its term there, simply did not fully understand what the justices did outside their basement chamber in the Capitol.

During the antebellum era, members of Congress left for home, family, and their regular jobs when their session ended. When the Court ended its term, however, its members headed for circuit where they encountered their real work. For John McKinley, that meant many more weeks of court, many more months of traveling, and, ultimately, many more years of poor health.

Congress's removal of the Supreme Court's circuit-riding duties in 1911 was more than just a recognition that such responsibilities were by then just too much for the justices. It was also a belated acknowledgment that the members of the first Supreme Court were correct when they complained to George Washington that the burdens of circuit riding far outweighed its benefits and that the justices themselves paid the greatest personal price during the continuance of this practice.

John McKinley's final contribution is more personal. He lived and worked during a time of tremendous political partisanship. His infamous Fourth of July toast in Kentucky demonstrates that he could give as well as he got as a politician, but a judge—both then and now—has little recourse against personal attacks. During his fifteen years on the Supreme Court, McKinley's education, intellect, politics, health, presence at circuit, absence from circuit, what he wrote as a justice (such as his dissent in *Bank of Augusta*), and what he failed to write as a justice were all publicly denigrated. Some of this criticism raised legitimate questions, but much of it was unfair and can be directly traced to the partisan spirit of the time. In addition, particularly after his 1842 stroke, the beginning of each new term in Washington saw McKinley become part of a parlor game for Court observers, Supreme Court attorneys, and, to an extent, his fellow justices, in which they wondered whether or not he would make it.

McKinley's final legacy may be that he *did* make it, as best as he could. Despite the repeated public denunciations, the very real difficulties of his circuit, and, later, his own physical health issues, he faithfully attended the Court's terms in Washington as well as the circuit sessions that permitted him to conduct the most business in the most efficient manner that he could given the circuit schedule. Twice he deliberately missed the Supreme Court's term in Washington so that he could continue his business at circuit. His attendance both there and in Washington was affected by chronically poor health, a stroke, and eventual partial paralysis. He might have followed the precedent of seven previous justices and simply resigned from the Court, but he did not.[31]

In March 1844, Richard Henry Dana, who was first introduced to McKinley a month earlier, unexpectedly met the justice again just as the latter was leaving Washington for circuit court. In his journal, Dana marveled, "Here was a man of sixty, who had a competent estate, and had been many years in public life, sleeping at small inns and traveling his 2000 and 3000 miles every half year, to discharge the duties of a judge. Verily it is no sinecure."[32]

Indeed, it was not. John McKinley understood the difficult responsibilities that accompanied his appointment as a justice of the antebellum Supreme Court and endeavored to perform them to the end. He was stubborn, prideful, and sickly in his later years, but he was also determined and dedicated. And in that respect, the life and legacy of "the most prominent man in Alabama" continues to be instructive today.

Appendix
Justice John McKinley's Supreme Court Opinions and Dissents

1. Majority Opinion, *M'Kinney v. Carroll,* 37 U.S. 66 (1838).
2. Majority Opinion, *Beaston v. Farmers' Bank,* 37 U.S. 102 (1838).
3. Majority Opinion, *White v. Turk,* 37 U.S. 238 (1838).
5. Joined Justice Wayne's dissent in *Strother v. Lucas,* 37 U.S. 410, at 462 (1838).
5. Majority Opinion, *Moncure v. Dermott,* 38 U.S. 345 (1839).
6. Majority Opinion, *Wilcox v. Hunt,* 38 U.S. 378 (1839).
7. Concurrence (no opinion), *Bagnell v. Broderick,* 38 U.S. 436 (1839).
8. Dissent, *Bank of Augusta v. Earle,* 38 U.S. 519, 547 (1839).
9. Majority Opinion, *Smith v. Clapp,* 40 U.S. 125 (1841).
10. Majority Opinion, *Levy v. Fitzpatrick,* 40 U.S. 167 (1841).
11. Majority Opinion, *United States v. Fitzgerald,* 40 U.S. 407 (1841).
12. Dissent (no opinion), *Groves v. Slaughter,* 40 U.S. 518 (1841).
13. Majority Opinion, *Nixdorff v. Smith,* 41 U.S. 132 (1842).
14. Majority Opinion, *Randolph v. Barrett,* 41 U.S. 138 (1842).
15. Majority Opinion, *Amis v. Smith,* 41 U.S. 303 (1842).
16. Majority Opinion, *Randel v. Brown,* 43 U.S. 406 (1844).
17. Dissent, *Barry v. Gamble,* 44 U.S. 32 (1845).
18. Majority Opinion, *Dickson v. Wilkinson,* 44 U.S. 57 (1844).
19. Joined Justice McLean's dissent in *United States v. Gear,* 44 U.S. 120 (1845).
20. Majority Opinion, *Lessee of Croghan v. Nelson,* 44 U.S. 187 (1845).
21. Majority Opinion, *Lessee of Pollard v. Hagan,* 44 U.S. 212 (1845).
22. Dissent, *Lane v. Vick,* 44 U.S. 464 (1845).
23. Majority Opinion, *Lessee of Brown v. Clements,* 44 U.S. 650 (1845).
24. Majority Opinion, *McFarland v. Gwin,* 44 U.S. 717 (1845).

25. Majority Opinion, *Lessee of Hickey v. Smith*, 44 U.S. 750 (1845).
26. Majority Opinion, *Musson v. Lake*, 45 U.S. 262 (1845).
27. Dissent (no opinion), *Harris v. Robinson*, 45 U.S. 336 (1845).
28. Dissent (no opinion), *McLaughlin v. Bank of Potomac*, 48 U.S. 220 (1849).
29. Seriatim majority opinion, *Passenger Cases*, 48 U.S. 283 (1849).
30. Dissent (no opinion), *United States v. King*, 48 U.S. 833 (1849) with Mclean, Wayne, and Grier.
31. Joined Justice Woodbury's dissent in *Henderson v. Tennessee*, 51 U.S. 311 (1851).
32. Dissent (no opinion), *United States v. Boisdore*, 52 U.S. 63 (1851), with McLean and Wayne.
33. Joined Justice Wayne's dissent in *United States v. Philadelphia*, 52 U.S. 609 (1851), with McLean, Wayne, and Grier.
34. Dissent (no opinion), *United States v. Turner*, 52 U.S. 663 (1851), with McLean, Wayne, and Grier.

Notes

Chapter 1

Epigraph. Henry S. Foote, *The Bench and Bar of the South and Southwest* (St. Louis: Soule, Thomas, and Wentworth, 1876), 7.

1. Marengo County Heritage Book Committee, *The Heritage of Marengo County, Alabama* (Clanton, AL: Heritage Publishing Consultants, 2000), 9. At least one source suggests that the name of McKinley was used to refer to the town of New Ruin nearly a decade earlier. In a June 1839 letter, James Moore King informed his son Henry King of Murfreesboro, Tennessee, that he was writing from "Moringo County—Mckinley." See James Moore King to Henry King June 13, 1839, Tennessee: A Documentary History, http://diglib.lib.utk.edu/cgi/t/text/text-idx?c=vvt;cc =vvt;rgn=main;view=text;idno=0039_000050_000253_0000&q1=james moore king &op2=&q2=&op3=&q3=&rgn=main (accessed April 13, 2009).

2. Ibid.

3. Anne Newport Royall, *Letters from Alabama: 1817–1822* (Tuscaloosa: The University of Alabama Press, 1969), 229.

4. *Literary Cadet and Saturday Evening Bulletin* (Providence, RI), November 18, 1826, vol. 1, no. 31, p. 2.

5. Andrew Jackson to John Coffee, February 17, 1823, *The Papers of Andrew Jackson,* ed. Harold D. Moser, David R. Hoth, and George H. Hoemann (Knoxville: University of Tennessee Press, 1996), 5:249.

6. William Smith, a former U.S. senator from South Carolina and a childhood friend of Andrew Jackson's, was the first Supreme Court nominee from Alabama. He moved to Alabama in 1833 and was serving in the Alabama state legislature when Jackson nominated him to the Supreme Court. Although confirmed by the Senate, Smith declined the honor, which left the seat open for Martin Van Buren to fill with McKinley. Upon McKinley's death in 1852, he was replaced by another Alabamian, John Archibald Campbell. One of the most prominent lawyers of his era, Campbell

resigned his seat when Alabama seceded from the Union in 1861 but went on to argue several important cases before his former colleagues in later years. Arguably, the best-known Alabamian on the Court is Hugo L. Black, who was appointed by Franklin D. Roosevelt in 1937. Black led a constitutional revolution that saw the Court extend most of the provisions of the Bill of Rights against state and local government action. Vilified in his home state during his lifetime, Black is generally regarded as one of the greatest justices ever to sit on the Court.

McKinley also became the first of just four persons ever to sit on the Supreme Court after having served in both houses of Congress. The others were Lucius Q. C. Lamar from Mississippi, who was appointed to the Court in 1888, George Sutherland, appointed in 1922 from Utah, and James F. Byrnes, who was appointed in 1941 from South Carolina. See Joan Biskupic and Elder Witt, *The Supreme Court and the Powers of the American Government* (Washington, DC: Congressional Quarterly, 1997), 157.

7. Henry J. Abraham, *The Judicial Process,* 7th ed. (New York: Oxford University Press, 1998), 376. McKinley's death in 1852 likewise spared him from what was inarguably the Court's nadir. During the early nineteenth century, the Court and every other institution in the country were affected by the increasingly strident debates over sectionalism, states' rights, and slavery, but none of the justices was prepared for the consequences of the Court's 1857 decision in *Dred Scott.* The ruling not only cast a permanent cloud over the name of its author, Chief Justice Roger Taney, it also caused a decline in the Court's reputation that was so precipitous and so profound that it would take nearly a century for it to recover. Most important, the Court's decision would contribute in no small way to the onset of the Civil War.

8. Hampton L. Carson, *The History of the Supreme Court of the United States* (Philadelphia: P. W. Zeigler and Company, 1902), 301. McKinley has received some brief attention recently. Kurt X. Metzmeier, associate director of the University of Louisville's Law Library, created a webpage that touched on McKinley's life and career. See his "John McKinley: Louisville's Lost Supreme Court Justice," posted March 31, 2008, http://www.law.louisville.edu/node/1656 (accessed November 10, 2008).

9. Tom Campbell, *Four Score Forgotten Men* (Little Rock, AR: Pioneer Publishing Company, 1950), 167. A recent and notable indignity occurred in March 2008 when the Supreme Court Historical Society, which is tasked with "the collection and preservation of the history of the Supreme Court of the United States," referred to Justice John McKinley in its own scholarly journal as "William" McKinley. See Artemus Ward, "The 'Good Old #3 Club' Gets a New Member," *Journal of Supreme Court History* 33 (March 2008): 113.

10. Gerhard Casper and Richard A. Posner, *The Workload of the Supreme Court* (Chicago: American Bar Association, 1976), 15.

11. See Alexandra K. Wigdor, *The Personal Papers of Supreme Court Justices* (New York: Garland, 1986), 31–32.

12. McKinley authored nineteen majority opinions for the Court, one seriatim

opinion, and three dissents. He concurred or dissented, without opinion, seven times, and joined in other justices' dissents four times. See appendix 1.

13. David N. Atkinson, *Leaving the Bench: Supreme Court Justices at the End* (Lawrence: University Press of Kansas, 1999), 36.

14. See David P. Currie, "The Most Insignificant Justice: A Preliminary Inquiry," *University of Chicago Law Review* 50 (1983): 466–80; and Frank H. Easterbrook, "The Most Insignificant Justice: Further Evidence," *University of Chicago Law Review* 50 (1983): 481–503.

15. Legal historians and scholars have characterized his record on the bench as "undistinguished" and "lacking any legal significance." See Kermit Hall, ed., *The Oxford Companion to the Supreme Court of the United States* (New York: Oxford University Press, 1992), 540. One described him "as one of the least effective Supreme Court justices in Supreme Court history" (Timothy S. Huebner, *The Taney Court: Justices, Rulings, and Legacy* [Santa Barbara, CA: ABC-CLIO, 2003], 10) while another noted his capacity for "ineptitude" (R. Kent Newmyer, review of *History of the Supreme Court of the United States: The Taney Period*, by Carl B. Swisher, *Stanford Law Review* 27 [May 1975]: 1377). Even the more charitable accounts portray him as only "[c]ompetent at best." See Timothy L. Hall, *Supreme Court Justices: A Biographical Dictionary* (New York: Facts on File, Inc., 2001), 106.

16. Carl Brent Swisher, *Roger B. Taney* (New York: Macmillan, 1935), 427.

17. Carl Brent Swisher, *The Taney Period, 1836–64*, vol. 5 of *History of the Supreme Court of the United States* (New York: Macmillan, 1974), 67.

18. Ibid.

19. Foote, *The Bench and Bar of the South and Southwest*, 7.

20. John M. Dollar's master's thesis is the longest treatment to date of John McKinley. See his "John McKinley: Enigmatic Trimmer" (master's thesis, Samford University, 1981). Dollar relies heavily upon shorter monographs, articles, and chapters within larger books on the Court such as Campbell, *Four Score Forgotten Men;* Herbert U. Feibelman, "John McKinley of Alabama—Legislator, US Congressman, Senator, Supreme Court Justice," *The Alabama Lawyer* 22 (October 1961): 422–26; Frank Otto Gatell, "John McKinley," in *The Justices of the United States Supreme Court, 1789–1969: Their Lives and Major Opinions*, ed. Leon Friedman and Fred L. Israel, vol. 1 (New York: Chelsea House, 1969), 769–92; Jimmie Hicks, "Associate Justice John McKinley: A Sketch," *Alabama Review* 28 (July 1965): 227–33; John M. Martin, "John McKinley: Jacksonian Phase," *Alabama Historical Quarterly* 28 (Spring 1966): 7–31; and George C. Whatley, "Justice John McKinley," *Journal of Muscle Shoals History* 12 (1988): 27–30. The amateur historian William L. McDonald has researched McKinley, using mostly anecdotal references about his founding of and subsequent life in Florence, Alabama (McDonald's hometown). See his *A Walk through the Past: People and Places of Florence and Lauderdale County, Alabama* (Killen, AL: Heart of Dixie Publishing, 1997).

21. Mark A. Graber, "The Jacksonian Makings of the Taney Court," available

at http://digitalcommons.law.umaryland.edu/cgi/viewcontent.cgi?article=1004& context=fac_pubs (accessed September 9, 2010).

22. John R. Schmidhauser, "Judicial Behavior and the Sectional Crisis of 1837–1860," *Journal of Politics* 23 (November 1961): 627.

23. Newmyer, review, 1375–76.

24. Ibid.

25. Henry J. Abraham, *The Judiciary: The Supreme Court in the Governmental Process,* 10th ed. (New York: New York University Press, 1996), 35. According to one study, of the 1,244 opinions issued by the Court during the Marshall era, 508 were authored by John Marshall himself. See Albert P. Blaustein and Roy M. Mersky, *The First One Hundred Justices* (Hamden, CT: Archon Books, 1978), 97. A later study counted 1,100 cases for the Court during that period, with Marshall writing 547. See G. Edward White, "The Internal Powers of the Chief Justice: The Nineteenth Century Legacy," *University of Pennsylvania Law Review* 154 (2006): 1476.

26. Earl M. Maltz, "Majority, Concurrence, and Dissent: *Prigg v. Pennsylvania* and the Structure of Supreme Court Decisionmaking," *Rutgers Law Journal* 31 (Winter 2000): 345–46.

27. Ibid.

28. Mark A. Graber, "The New Fiction: *Dred Scott* and the Language of Judicial Authority," *Chicago-Kent Law Review* 82, no. 1 (2007): 180.

29. Swisher, *The Taney Period,* 747.

30. Saul Brenner, "The Chief Justices' Self Assignment of Majority Opinions in Salient Cases," *Social Science Journal* 30 (1993): 148.

31. David P. Currie, "The Constitution in the Supreme Court: Article IV and Federal Powers, 1836–1864," *Duke Law Journal* 4 (September 1983): 746.

32. Foote, *The Bench and Bar of the South and Southwest,* 7.

Chapter 2

Epigraph. *Western World,* March 5, 1807, vol. 1, no. 36, p. 4.

1. Royall, *Letters from Alabama,* 229–30.

2. Willis Brewer, *Alabama: Her History, Resources, War Record, and Public Men from 1540 to 1872* (Montgomery, AL: Barrett and Brown, 1872; reprint, Tuscaloosa, AL: Willo Publishing Company, 1964), 298 (page references are to reprint edition).

3. H. Levin, ed., *The Lawyers and Lawmakers of Kentucky* (Chicago: Lewis Publishing Company, 1897), 150.

4. Thomas Marshall Green, *Historic Families of Kentucky* (Cincinnati: Robert Clarke and Company, 1889), 227.

5. E. F. Ellet, *The Court Circles of the Republic* (Hartford, CT: Hartford Publishing Company, 1869), 330.

6. *Weekly Herald,* January 29, 1842, vol. 6, no. 19, p. 150.

7. Richard Henry Dana, *The Journal,* ed. Robert F. Lucid (Cambridge, MA: Belknap Press of Harvard University Press, 1968), 257.

8. Levin, *The Lawyers and Lawmakers of Kentucky*, 150.

9. Quoted in Bernarr Cresap, "History of Lauderdale County, Historical Address," *Journal of Muscle Shoals History* 5 (1977): 77.

10. *Cherokee Phoenix and Indian's Advocate* (Georgia), May 15, 1830, vol. 3, no. 4, p. 2.

11. Brewer, *Alabama: Her History*, 298.

12. McKinley interview, fall 1846, Kentucky Papers of the Lyman C. Draper Collection (microfilm, 12CC47).

13. The 1846 interview identified McKinley's grandfather as "John." A recent genealogical study suggests that McKinley's great-grandfather was named Benjamin. See Charles G. Talbert, *Benjamin Logan: Kentucky Frontiersman* (Lexington: University of Kentucky Press, 1962), 3.

14. Jane reportedly lived until 1791. See Bessie Taul Conkwright, "A Sketch of the Life and Times of General Benjamin Logan," *Register of the Kentucky State Historical Society* 14 (January 1916): 21. See also Green, *Historic Families of Kentucky*, 118. The family intermarriages that were common during this era are observed in the relationship between the Logans and McKinleys. Not only were his parents first cousins, but in 1811 Justice McKinley's sister Betsy became the second wife of her cousin David Logan. See Green, *Historic Families of Kentucky*, 226.

15. Green, *Historic Families of Kentucky*, 226. There is some confusion as to the identity of McKinley's mother. Many modern sources list his mother as Sarah Logan, the younger sister of Benjamin, while the majority of earlier sources list his mother as Mary, the eldest sister in the Logan family. The confusion appears to stem from a 1792 Kentucky probate record in which Samuel Briggs's wife is identified as Mary. See Mrs. Harry Kennett McAdams, *Kentucky Pioneer and Court Records* (Lexington, KY, 1929; reprint, Baltimore: Genealogical Publishing, 1975), 49. Samuel Briggs did indeed marry a Logan, but again, earlier sources identify her as Sarah. Given the common practice during that era of passing down family names, it may be significant that Justice John McKinley named two of his children Andrew and Mary.

16. Lewis Collins, *Historical Sketches of Kentucky* (Cincinnati: J. A. and U. P. James, 1848; reprint, New York: Arno Press, 1971), 412.

17. Robert Morgan, *Boone: A Biography* (Chapel Hill: Algonquin Books, 2007), 173. Logan's Fort was also called Logan's Station and in subsequent years was given its current name of Stanford.

18. The significance of Logan's efforts are perhaps best illustrated in early historical accounts of the settling of Kentucky, which make almost worshipful reference to the man. For example, in his 1848 history, Lewis Collins reverently declared, "As the eye wanders along the serried ranks of those stern and iron men, who stand so firm and fearless amid the gloom of the overhanging forest, it is arrested by a commanding form which towers conspicuous among them all—tall, athletic, dignified—a face cast in the finest mould of manly beauty, dark, grave and contemplative, and which, while it evinces unyielding fortitude and impenetrable reserve, invited to a confidence which never betrays. Such was Benjamin Logan" (*Historical Sketches of Kentucky*, 411).

19. Logan had personally experienced the dangers of frontier living, losing his father-in-law, several brothers-in-law, and a young niece in a March 1781 Indian attack. See Green, *Historic Families of Kentucky*, 133–34.

20. Collins, *Historical Sketches of Kentucky*, 147–49.

21. McKinley interview, fall 1846.

22. See Patricia Watlington, *The Partisan Spirit* (New York: Atheneum, 1972), 59.

23. Talbert, *Benjamin Logan*, 140.

24. Collins, *Historical Sketches of Kentucky*, 146–49.

25. Green, *Historic Families of Kentucky*, 186. See also the Kentucky Department for Libraries and Archives at http://www.kdla.ky.gov/resources/KYOfficials_pg1.htm (accessed November 19, 2008). A third brother, Hugh, was elected to serve as a justice of the peace and sat on the Lincoln County court with his two brothers. See Green, *Historic Families of Kentucky*, 204.

26. Green, *Historic Families of Kentucky*, 145. William Logan was first elected Speaker of the Kentucky House of Representatives at age twenty-eight.

27. Justice McKinley himself provided the date of his move from Virginia. See McKinley interview, fall 1846. For the record of Andrew McKinley's appointment, see Lucien Beckner, "History of the County Court of Lincoln County, VA," *Register of the Kentucky State Historical Society* 20 (January 1922): 176; and Michael L. Cook, ed., *Lincoln County Kentucky Records*, vol. 2 (Evansville, IN: Cook Publications, 1988), 70.

28. He was also involved in a handful of lawsuits and was once ordered to pay some two hundred pounds of tobacco each to two witnesses who participated in a multiday trial to which he was party. See Cook, *Lincoln County Kentucky Records*, 2:354.

29. Ann Pennington MacKinnon, Peggy Selby Galloway, and Michael C. Watson, comps., *Lincoln County, Virginia/Kentucky Deed Abstracts, 1781–1795* (Harrodsburg, KY: MGW Publications, 1998), 49.

30. Green, *Historic Families of Kentucky*, 226. Hannah married Francis Slaughter Read on January 10, 1804, at Stanford, Kentucky, and bore him six children. Their youngest, Mary, was born on October 30, 1816. Although Hannah's death is not recorded, she presumably died shortly after Mary's birth. Kentucky court documents record that Read married his second wife, Ann Waggener, on August 8, 1819. See "Genealogical Queries," *William and Mary Quarterly*, 2nd ser., 10, no. 1 (January 1930): 93. Betsy became the second wife of her cousin David Logan (the son of John Logan). See Green, *Historic Families of Kentucky*, 226. Justice McKinley may have had had other siblings besides these two sisters, but they have not been identified.

31. Andrew McKinley's inventory is recorded in *Lincoln County Kentucky Will Inventories*, Book A, 1781–1806, p. 184, Filson Historical Society, Louisville, KY.

32. *Literary Cadet and Saturday Evening Bulletin*, September 8, 1827, vol. 2, no. 42, p. 2. In 1850 a Wisconsin newspaper, discussing eminent men who had risen from humble beginnings, described McKinley's first career as that of "a carpenter and joiner." See the *Milwaukee Daily Sentinel and Gazette*, November 14, 1850, issue 494, col. A.

33. Thomas P. Abernethy, *From Frontier to Plantation in Tennessee: A Study in Frontier Democracy* (Tuscaloosa: The University of Alabama Press, 1967), 286.

34. Levin, *The Lawyers and Lawmakers of Kentucky*, 150.

35. Charles Warren, *History of the Harvard Law School and of Early Legal Conditions in America* (Clark, NJ: Law Book Exchange, 2008), 132.

36. Green, *Historic Families of Kentucky*, 226.

37. By 1815 the Federalist Party had essentially collapsed, moving the country, as the historian Richard Hofstadter has written, "from the party-and-a-half system under which it had in fact been functioning to the one-party system which lasted until 1828." Hofstadter, *The Idea of a Party System: The Rise of Legitimate Opposition in the United States, 1780–1840* (Berkeley: University of California Press, 1969), 182.

38. Judge Charles Kerr, ed., *History of Kentucky*, vol. 1 (New York: American Historical Society, 1922), 472–73.

39. Ibid., 474.

40. Rowan's early Federalist leanings are discussed in Mary K. Bonsteel Tachau, *Federal Courts in the Early Republic: Kentucky, 1789–1816* (Princeton: Princeton University Press, 1978), 189.

41. Quoted in Robert Pettus Hay, "A Jubilee for Freemen: The Fourth of July in Frontier Kentucky, 1788–1816," *Register of the Kentucky Historical Society* 64 (July 1966): 183–84.

42. Quoted in Kerr, *History of Kentucky*, 473, emphasis in original.

43. See James F. Sutherland, comp., *Early Kentucky Landholders, 1787–1811* (Baltimore: Genealogical Publishing, 1986), 223. In 1805 McKinley would take title to one thousand additional acres within Fayette and Muhlenberg counties and one thousand more of prime land on the Ohio River in Logan County. See Michael L. Cook and Bettie A. Cook, eds., *Kentucky Court of Appeals Deed Books* (Evansville, IN: Cook Publications, 1985), 2:348.

44. Bettie Cummings Cook, comp., *Kentucky Federal Court Records, District and Sixth Circuit Order Books, 1804–1815*, vol. 2 (Evansville, IN: Cook Publications, 1995), 153.

45. Ibid., 157.

46. Buckner F. Melton Jr., *Aaron Burr: Conspiracy to Treason* (New York: John Wiley and Sons, 2002), 112–13. General James Wilkinson, one of the founders of Frankfort, was later charged as a co-conspirator with Burr.

47. Nathan Schachner, *Aaron Burr: A Biography* (New York: A. S. Barnes and Company, 1961), 345. In 1888 the partisan efforts of the *Western World* were remembered for having "inaugurated a bitter style in political discussion which did not entirely disappear from editorials until the 'era of good feeling' in Kentucky politics since the close of the late civil war." Quoted in William H. Perrin, *The Pioneer Press in Kentucky*, Filson Club Publications (Louisville, KY: John P. Morton and Company, 1888), 41.

48. Milton Lomask, *Aaron Burr: The Conspiracy and Years of Exile, 1805–1836* (New York: Farrar, Straus, and Giroux, 1982), 142–43.

49. Samuel M. Wilson, "The Court Proceedings of 1806 in Kentucky against Aaron Burr and John Adair," *Filson Club Historical Quarterly* 10, no. 1 (1936): 33.

50. Ibid., 35.

51. Albert J. Beveridge, *The Life of John Marshall* (Boston: Houghton Mifflin, 1919), 3:318.

52. Burr was also acquitted at his Richmond trial.

53. *Western World* (Frankfort, KY), March 5, 1807, vol. 1, no. 36, p. 4.

54. Ibid.

55. Cook and Cook, *Kentucky Court of Appeals Deed Books*, 4:285–88.

56. *Literary Cadet and Saturday Evening Bulletin,* September 8, 1827, vol. 2, no. 42, p. 2. Another indication of his rising fortune in Lexington is the fact that in October 1810 he, Paschal Hickman, John J. Marshall, and William Trigg signed a $10,000 bond to the Commonwealth of Kentucky "conditioned upon the said William Trigg faithfully discharging his duties as Clerk of the Circuit Court for Franklin County." See Cook and Cook, *Kentucky Court of Appeals Deed Books*, 2:348.

57. *1810 Census of the United States,* http://www.ancestry.com.

58. See Charles D. Hockensmith, *The Millstone Quarries of Powell County* (Jefferson, NC: McFarland and Company, 2009), 32.

59. Other notables on the petition included Robert Smith Todd (father of Mary Todd Lincoln) and Farmer Dewees, a prominent local banker. See "A Brief History of Second Presbyterian Church," http://www.2preslex.org/about/our-history.

60. See *Kentucky Gazette,* July 3, 1815, vol. 1, no. 27. See also George W. Ranck, *History of Lexington, Kentucky: Its Early Annuals and Recent Progress* (Cincinnati: Robert Clarke and Company, 1872; reprint, Bowie, MD: Heritage Books, 1989), 281 (page references are to reprint edition). Still in existence, the church is officially known as the Second Presbyterian Church of Lexington, although in McKinley's time it was known simply as Market Street Church.

61. See generally, James A. Ramage, *John Wesley Hunt: Pioneer Merchant, Manufacturer, and Financier* (Lexington: University Press of Kentucky, 1974).

62. *Boston Courier,* June 11, 1838, issue 1035, col B.

63. *Kentucky Gazette,* August 13, 1811, vol. 2, no. 33.

64. Johnson would later serve as a member of the U.S. House of Representatives from Kentucky.

65. Richard M. Johnson would serve in both houses of Congress before serving as vice president in the Van Buren administration.

66. "M'Kinley, the Poltroon and Assassin, in his True Colors," (Frankfort, KY), October 8, 1811, Kentucky Papers of the Lyman C. Draper Collection (microfilm, 5CC19).

67. Ibid.

68. Richard M. Johnson to John McKinley, October [?], 1811, Kentucky Papers of the Lyman C. Draper Collection (microfilm, 5CC21).

69. See Theodore Dwight Weld, *American Slavery as It Is: A Testimony of a Thousand Witnesses* (New York: American Anti-Slavery Society, 1839), 185.

70. *Boston Courier,* June 11, 1838, issue 1035, col B.

71. *Kentucky Gazette,* January 14, 1812, vol. 3, no. 3.

72. Ibid.

73. Ibid.

74. Ibid.

75. See *The Bench and Bar of St. Louis, Kansas City, Jefferson City, and Other Missouri Cities* (Chicago: American Biographical Publishing Company, 1884), 68, for the brief reference to Julia's family. It is possible that she was related to Guy Bryan, a prominent Philadelphia merchant who owned several hundred thousand acres in Kentucky at the time, but no definitive relationship has yet been established. The marriage date is mentioned in Dona Adams Wilson, comp., *Woodford County, Kentucky Marriage Bonds and Consents, 1789–1830* (Lexington, KY: Lynn Blue Print, 1998), 106, but it may not have been the actual day they were married. The Woodford County (Kentucky) Historical Society has the marriage bond that McKinley and a William Duncan signed on April 16, 1814. Marriages did indeed take place on the same day that the bond was secured, but not always. Marriage bonds essentially ensured that (1) there was no moral or legal reason why the marriage should not take place and (2) the groom would not back out. Because women of that era did not have the ability to contract, only McKinley's signature and that of his surety, Duncan, are on the bond.

Julia's name has been the source of some confusion. Thomas Marshall Green's 1889 history of Kentucky families identifies McKinley's wife as "Juliana," which has been repeated by later historians (*Historic Families of Kentucky*, 227). The marriage bond, however, clearly states, "there is a marriage shortly intended to be solemnized between the above bound John McKinley and Julia Bryan." In the *Bench and Bar of St. Louis*, John McKinley's wife is referred to as Julia Ann Bryan (68). In 1915 the Alabama historian Thomas McAdory Owen definitively clarified the issue when he recorded the following from the McKinley family cemetery in Florence, Alabama: "To the memory of Mrs. Julianna McKinley—wife of Mr. John McKinley, who died 22d October 1822. Aged 30 years, 1 mon and 18 days." The confusion stems from the apparent common use of the shortened version of her name. See Thomas McAdory Owen, Surname Files, Alabama Department of Archives and History, Montgomery, n.d. In both Kentucky and Alabama, "Julia" appears on every public record and newspaper reference where her name is given.

Incidentally, family lore mistakenly lists the marriage date of John McKinley and Julia Bryan as 1812, as evidenced in a brief family history written by Elizabeth A. McKinley, a granddaughter, sometime after 1928 when she was in her eighties. See Elizabeth A. McKinley, "The Star-Spangled Banner," unpublished manuscript, 1928, Pope-Humphrey Family Papers, Filson Historical Society, Louisville, KY.

76. *Kentucky Gazette*, June 27, 1814, vol. 5, no. 26.

77. This is discussed in more detail in chapter 4 relative to McKinley's elections in Alabama, but this account from the *Kentucky Gazette* provides an interesting perspective from one voter during an 1810 campaign: "[The candidate] asked me to drink some grog, and took me to a Booth, and there I was saluted with a hearty shake of the hand from all the candidates, who seemed to be as much my friends as if they

had known me all their lives. Soon after the candidates began to speak, and they all promised a great deal of good things to us people if we would elect them." Quoted in Kerr, *History of Kentucky*, 477. According to the *Gazette*, the voter was shortly thereafter approached by a friend who, referring to the candidates, questioned, "<u>Yes, he says so now,</u> but what was his conduct before the election came on? Did he then shake hands with every man he met, stop and talk with us, care about any man's affairs but his own, pull off his hat to everybody, enquire after our health and families, and endeavor to conciliate our good will?" Quoted in ibid.

78. *Kentucky Gazette*, August 8, 1814, vol. 5, no. 32.

79. *Literary Cadet and Saturday Evening Bulletin*, November 18, 1826, vol. 1, no. 31, p. 2.

80. Wickliffe held several prominent political offices in Kentucky and was one of the leaders of the Democratic-Republican Party in the state. A successful lawyer, he would go on to become Kentucky's largest slaveholder and one of the wealthiest men in the state.

81. Robert Wickliffe to Henry Clay, September 20, 1817, *Papers of Henry Clay*, ed. James F. Hopkins and Mary W. M. Hargreaves (Lexington: University Press of Kentucky, 1961), 2:382, emphasis in original.

82. The McKinleys' three children were Elizabeth (who married Donald Campbell in 1833), who died at a young age, Andrew (who married Mary Elizabeth Wilcox, the stepdaughter of Kentucky senator John J. Crittenden), and Mary (who married Alexander Pope Churchill). During the latter part of the nineteenth century, the existence of another McKinley son was reported, but that attribution appears to be due to sloppy journalism. In 1869 a Dr. Samuel McKinley, identified by the *New York Times* as the "son of Judge McKinley, formerly Judge of the Supreme Court of the United States," was the focus of a sensational custody hearing. See *New York Times*, January 2, 1869, p. 5.

There is no evidence for any relationship between John and Samuel McKinley. The latter appears on no family census records, in no family histories, and in no public records where John McKinley is mentioned. The elder McKinley also made no provisions for such a person in his will, and neither his second wife, Elizabeth, nor his children, Andrew and Mary, all of whom were alive at the time of the *New York Times* story, ever publicly acknowledged the existence of another sibling.

83. *Kentucky Gazette*, December 13, 1817, vol. 3, no. 50.

Chapter 3

Epigraph. *Daily National Intelligencer* (Washington, DC), May 8, 1818, issue 1652, col. B.

1. The eastern part of the state, roughly from the city of Wetumpka to the present border with Georgia, and from Union Springs in the south to Fort Payne in the north would not be ceded to the United States until the 1830s.

2. Thomas D. Clark and John D. W. Guice, *Frontiers in Conflict: The Old Southwest, 1795–1830* (Albuquerque: University of New Mexico Press, 1989), 161.

3. Malcolm J. Rohrbough, *The Land Office Business: The Settlement and Administration of American Public Lands, 1789–1837* (New York: Oxford University Press, 1968), 92.

4. "Between 1800 and 1830 cotton production doubled every decade. Indeed it increased more than twofold between 1814 and 1816" (ibid.). The growing volume of American cotton exports clearly reflected the demand. Approximately 83 million pounds were exported in 1815; just five years later total cotton exports reached nearly 130 million pounds. See Tony Allan Freyer, *Forums of Order: The Federal Courts and Business in American History* (Greenwich, CT: JAI Press, 1979), 3. Exports would reach 744 million pounds in 1840 and exceed one billion pounds in the 1850s.

5. Quoted in Theodore Henley Jack, "Sectionalism and Party Politics in Alabama, 1819–1842" (Ph.D. diss., University of Chicago, 1919), 8n31.

6. Albert B. Moore, *History of Alabama* (Tuscaloosa: Alabama Book Store, 1934), 75.

7. Thomas P. Abernethy, *The South in the New Nation, 1789–1819* (Baton Rouge: Louisiana State University Press, 1976), 471.

8. Ibid.

9. Michael Paul Rogin, *Fathers and Children: Andrew Jackson and the Subjugation of the American Indian* (New York: Alfred A. Knopf, 1975), 174.

10. Quoted in Gordon T. Chappell, "Some Patterns of Land Speculation in the Old Southwest," *Journal of Southern History* 15 (November 1949): 464.

11. Quoted in Rohrbough, *The Land Office Business,* 91, emphasis in original.

12. Ibid.

13. Quoted in Adam Rothman, *Slave Country: American Expansion and the Origins of the Deep South* (Cambridge, MA: Harvard University Press, 2005), 183.

14. *Carolina Observer* (Fayetteville), February 27, 1817, issue 37, col. C.

15. Ibid.

16. A Scottish newspaper in 1818 described the wave of people leaving European shores for America as "a spectacle without a parallel since the time of the crusades." Quoted in Abernethy, *The South in the New Nation,* 469.

17. Quoted in Frances C. Roberts, "Politics and Public Land Disposal in Alabama's Formative Period," *Alabama Review* 22 (July 1969): 166.

18. Marquis James, *The Life of Andrew Jackson* (New York: Bobbs-Merrill, 1938), 178. Given his ties to the land as both Indian fighter and land speculator, it was no exaggeration to credit Jackson, as another of his biographers did, with having "almost single-handedly . . . set in motion the beginnings of rapid American economic development." See Rogin, *Fathers and Children,* 177.

19. Payson Jackson Treat, *The National Land System, 1785–1820* (New York: E. B. Treat and Company, 1910), 173.

20. Rohrbough, *The Land Office Business,* 100.

21. Ramage, *John Wesley Hunt,* 86.

22. Turner Rice, "The Cypress Land Company: A Dream of Empire," *Journal of Muscle Shoals History* 3 (1975): 21. See also Ruth Ketring Nuermberger, *The Clays of Alabama* (Lexington: University of Kentucky Press, 1958), 7. A highly romanticized account of the origins of Cypress is offered in a children's history book that was used in Alabama schools during the 1920s. In her chapter titled "The Founding of Florence," Pitt Lamar Matthews writes: "It was not the Indians alone who felt the promise of the Tennessee Valley. The white men also fell under its spell. In 1818 three Tennesseans, traveling through what is now Lauderdale County, Alabama, told each other that some day a great city would be built at the foot of Muscle Shoals on the hill where Florence now stands. These three men were General John Coffee, who won fame in the Creek War and in the Battle of New Orleans; Judge John McKinley, who became a Supreme Court judge of the United States; and James Jackson, a wealthy planter and turfman, whose thoroughbred horses became known all around the world. They bought up all the land from the Indians for miles around and organized 'The Cypress Land Company.'" Pitt Lamar Matthews, *History Stories of Alabama* (Dallas: Southern Publishing Company, 1929), 289.

23. Quoted in Chappell, *Some Patterns of Land Speculation,* 467.

24. Rohrbough, *The Land Office Business,* 124.

25. Ibid., 121.

26. Moore, *History of Alabama,* 82–83.

27. Rohrbough, *The Land Office Business,* 124.

28. See Andrew Jackson, *The Papers of Andrew Jackson,* ed. Harold Moser and Daniel Feller (Knoxville: University of Tennessee Press, 1980–), 7:14n4.

29. Abernethy, *From Frontier to Plantation,* 271.

30. Coffee's familiarity with the land made him a fortune. Not only did he use his office to assist Cypress with his own land speculation activities, he also traded on his knowledge, refusing to give any information to prospective land buyers without a fee. In addition, he worked out an arrangement with the land office clerks where he would receive a full half of anything they were paid for any information they gave potential buyers. See Rogin, *Fathers and Children,* 175.

31. Jackson would later purchase land there himself, independently of Cypress. Several accounts record that he was able to purchase his land at the government's minimum price of $2 an acre because no one dared bid against him at public auction. See James, *Life of Andrew Jackson,* 277, and Rogin, *Fathers and Children,* 176.

32. See *McKinley v. Irvine,* 13 Ala. 681 (1848), 1848 Ala. LEXIS 151.

33. *Daily National Intelligencer,* May 8, 1818, issue 1652, col. B.

34. Quoted in Chappell, *Some Patterns of Land Speculation,* 470.

35. Ibid.

36. Abernethy relates the account of a Mobile man who very much regretted the disappointment new settlers would feel when they learned that the "Alabama Terri-

tory contained good lands with transportation easily accessible but that twenty bushels of corn was a good yield, rather than the reported hundred bushels." See *The South in the New Nation*, 472.

37. As Gordon Chappell has written, while land speculators were motivated by sheer profit and did, in fact, take advantage of willing, if unwise, investors, they played an important role in bringing government land to market and encouraging the settlement of the frontier. See Chappell, *Some Patterns of Land Speculation*, 477.

38. Daniel Dupre, *Transforming the Cotton Frontier: Madison County, Alabama, 1800–1840* (Baton Rouge: Louisiana State University Press, 1997), 60.

39. Ibid.

40. Quoted in Nuermberger, *The Clays of Alabama*, 7.

41. Quoted in Hugh C. Bailey, *John Williams Walker: A Study in the Political, Social and Cultural Life of the Old Southwest* (Tuscaloosa: The University of Alabama Press, 1964), 157.

42. Abernethy, *From Frontier to Plantation*, 225.

43. Ibid.

44. *Wisconsin Democrat* (Green Bay), May 5, 1849, issue 18, p. 3.

45. Ramage, *John Wesley Hunt*, 87.

46. William Warren Rogers, Robert David Ward, Leah Rawls Atkins, and Wayne Flynt, *Alabama: The History of a Deep South State* (Tuscaloosa: The University of Alabama Press, 1994), 54. The focal point of this growth was Madison County. The *Western Gazetteer* of 1817 reported, "[T]he settlement of Madison County is probably without parallel in the history of the Union. In 1816 it had 14,200 out of a population of 33,287 for the Territory." Quoted in Abernethy, *The South in the New Nation*, 469.

47. Roberts, "Politics and Public Land Disposal," 173.

48. King was elected in 1852 along with President Franklin Pierce, but served just forty-five days before dying in office. He holds the distinction of being the only vice president to be sworn in on foreign soil, having received the oath of office in Cuba where he had gone in a futile attempt to regain his health.

49. Roberts, "Politics and Public Land Disposal," 173.

50. Ibid., 174.

51. Moore, *History of Alabama*, 114.

52. Ibid., 79.

53. Crawford filled the same post during the latter part of the Madison administration. He also served for a short time as Madison's secretary of war. He would be a candidate for the presidency himself in 1824.

54. Roberts, "Politics and Public Land Disposal," 168–69. Crawford was responsible for bringing John Coffee's name to the attention of the president for the newly created surveyor general position in the northern district of the cession lands.

55. Abernethy, *From Frontier to Plantation*, 52.

56. Roberts, "Politics and Public Land Disposal," 172.

57. Quoted in Moore, *A History of Alabama*, 115.

58. Royall, *Letters from Alabama,* 242, emphasis in original. Her use of the word "Republican" refers to the party of Jefferson, which was known as the Democratic-Republican Party but also by the interchangeable terms of "republican" and "democrat." It eventually embraced just the latter and is the forerunner of the modern Democratic Party. The modern Republican Party was formed as an anti-slavery party in 1854.

59. Jack, "Sectionalism and Party Politics in Alabama," 21.

60. Andrew Jackson and the presidential election of 1824 would introduce another element with which Alabama politicians and voters would align themselves: personality.

61. Moore, *A History of Alabama,* 115.

62. The Popes were so well-known and powerful in the Broad River area that they were known as the "Royal family." See Bailey, *John Williams Walker,* 31. The "royal" appellation would follow them to Alabama, where it was used in a derogatory manner by their political opponents.

63. Dorothy Scott Johnson, comp., *Madison County Deed Books, 1810–1819* (Huntsville, AL: Johnson Historical Publications, 1976), 60.

64. Pauline Jones Gandrud, *Alabama Records* (Easley, SC: Southern Historical Press, 1980), 207:65.

65. Ibid., 35:1. The Alabama state legislature held its first session at the Huntsville Inn in October 1819 while Huntsville was serving as the first capital of Alabama.

66. Justus Wyman, "A Geographical Sketch of the Alabama Territory," *Transactions of the Alabama Historical Society* 3 (1899): 107–28.

67. Martin, "John McKinley: Jacksonian Phase," 8.

68. "Register of Gubernatorial Appointments—Civil and Military," *Alabama Historical Quarterly* 6, no. 2 (1944): 176.

69. Quoted in Gatell, "John McKinley," 769.

70. "Until the General Assembly shall otherwise prescribe, the powers of the supreme court shall be vested in, and its duties shall be performed by, the Judges of the several circuit courts, within this state." Alabama Constitution of 1819, Article 5, Section 3.

71. *Journal of the House of Representatives* (December 14, 1819), 172–73, http://www.legislature.state.al.us/misc/history/acts_and_journals/House_Journal_1819_Oct_25-Dec_17/Page44_Dec14.html (accessed August 22, 2007). Richard Ellis moved to Texas fifteen years later and served as the president of the 1836 Texas constitutional convention that created the Republic of Texas.

72. John McKinley to John Coffee, December 21, 1819, Robert Dyas Collection of John Coffee Papers, Tennessee Historical Society, Tennessee State Library and Archives, Nashville (hereafter Coffee Papers [Dyas]; available on microfilm at Ralph Brown Draughon Library, Auburn University). Coffee's election is recorded in *Alabama House Journal,* December 15, 1819, 188.

73. Ibid. He would later chide Coffee for not paying attention to the machinations

in Lauderdale County in the selection of its representatives to the statehouse. "If you do not take more interest in your elections," McKinley warned, "your county will be ruined." See John McKinley to John Coffee, November 16, 1820, John Coffee Papers, Alabama Department of Archives and History, Montgomery (hereafter Coffee papers [ADAH]).

Chapter 4

Epigraph. James Birney to Henry Clay, February 20, 1826, *Papers of Henry Clay*, 5:119.

1. "Register of Gubernatorial Appointments—Civil and Military," 327.

2. Harry Toulmin, *A Digest of the Laws of the State of Alabama* (Cahawba, AL: Ginn and Curtis, 1823), 22.

3. Joseph G. Baldwin, *The Flush Times of Alabama and Mississippi: A Series of Sketches* (1853; reprint, Gloucester, MA: Peter Smith, 1974), 174. Although written primarily as satire, Baldwin's description of the courtroom efforts of both lawyers and judges during the early years of Alabama and Mississippi has been recognized for its significant historical value as well. Baldwin would later serve on the Supreme Court of California.

4. Ibid., 173.

5. Ibid.

6. Ibid.

7. Paul M. Pruitt Jr., "The Life and Times of Legal Education in Alabama, 1819–1897," *Alabama Law Review* (Fall 1997): 284.

8. Quoted in Tony A. Freyer, Paul M. Pruitt, Timothy W. Dixon, and Howard P. Walthall, "Alabama's Supreme Court and Legal Institutions: A History" (unpublished manuscript, n.d.), 22, provided to the author by Paul M. Pruitt.

9. As published in a Mobile newspaper later that year, these requirements included the following: "In every cause before the court, for trial, the counsel for the plaintiff must read the papers and open his cause; he will be answered by the counsel for the defendant; who will be replied to by the counsel for the plaintiff, and this will end all discussion. . . . No authority shall be read in the conclusion of an argument, which was not read in the opening, unless to rebut authority introduced by the opposite counsel, or by leave of the court. . . . The counsel in every cause shall file with the clerk a brief of the case and a reference to the authorities on which he intends to rely, at least one day before the cause shall be heard." See *Mobile (AL) Gazette and General Advertiser*, August 10, 1820, issue 6, col. D.

10. Baldwin, *The Flush Times*, 175.

11. Ibid.

12. *Thomas Logwood v. President, Directors, Etc. of the Planters' and Merchants' Bank of Huntsville*, Minor 23 (1820).

13. "The Charter in question is then a contract, whose obligation the Legislature

is restrained from impairing. The Legislature cannot alter, control, or abridge the Charter, without the consent of the individuals composing the Corporation." Minor 25 (1820).

14. Ibid.

15. See *Olive v. O'Riley*, Minor 410 (Ala. 1826) and *Adams v. Ward*, 1 Stew. 42 (Ala. 1827). Several times his own interests, including transactions involving his property, slaves, and matters related to Cypress, also came before the court.

16. Charles S. Sydnor, *Gentlemen Freeholders: Political Practices in Washington's Virginia* (Chapel Hill: University of North Carolina Press, 1952), 39.

17. Daniel Dupre, "Barbecues and Pledges: Electioneering and the Rise of Democratic Politics in Antebellum Alabama," *Journal of Southern History* 60 (August 1994): 483.

18. One of the more curious horsemanship skill events at these barbecues was the gander pull. After having its neck plucked and greased, a male goose would be tied by its feet to a bar several feet above the ground. A rider would then start for the gander at a dead run, slowing his horse just in time to reach up and wrench the bird's neck several times before his momentum carried him past. Subsequent riders would do the same thing until one successfully removed the gander's head.

19. *Democrat* (Huntsville, AL), June 27, 1827, vol. 4, p. 3. This particular issue carried announcements for eight separate political barbeques in the area.

20. Quoted in Dupre, "Barbecues and Pledges," 483.

21. Ibid., emphasis in original.

22. Ibid.

23. Quoted in ibid., 492–93.

24. Near present-day Selma, Alabama, Cahaba was the state capital of Alabama until 1826 when the capital was moved to Tuscaloosa.

25. *Alabama House Journal,* November 6, 1820, 3–4.

26. Ibid., November 7, 1820, 4.

27. Ibid., November 9, 1820, 8.

28. John McKinley to John Coffee, November 16, 1820, Coffee Papers (Dyas).

29. *Alabama House Journal,* December 7, 1820, 79.

30. Quoted in Bailey, *John Williams Walker,* 105.

31. *Alabama House Journal,* December 20, 1820, 126–27.

32. Ibid., June 4, 1821, 5.

33. Ibid., June 15, 1821, 49–52.

34. Of the fifty members of the Alabama House who served with McKinley during the 1820 legislative session, only twelve returned the following year.

35. *Alabama House Journal,* December 19, 1821, 237.

36. McKinley would serve just two years of his three-year term, submitting his resignation to Governor Israel Pickens in December 1823. See *Alabama Senate Journal,* December 8, 1823, 57.

37. Quoted in Richard W. Griffin, "Athens Academy and College: An Experi-

ment in Women's Education in Alabama, 1822–1873," *Alabama Historical Quarterly* 20 (Spring 1958): 7. See also Thomas McAdory Owen and Marie Bankhead Owen, *History of Alabama and Dictionary of Alabama Biography*, vol. 1 (Chicago: S. J. Clarke Publishing Company, 1921), 67.

38. See *Encyclopedia of Alabama*, s.v. "John McKinley," by Robert Saunders, Jr., http://www.encyclopediaofalabama.org (accessed November 17, 2009). It has also been reported that the second school in the city of Florence was initially held in the basement of the McKinley home. Julia McKinley was said to have personally recruited a Miss James from her home state of Pennsylvania to open a regular school in Florence for children over the age of ten.

William McDonald, an amateur historian and native of Florence, Alabama, spent forty years chronicling the history of the city. Much of his research came from interviews with longtime residents. While he offers additional information about Justice McKinley, much of it is anecdotal and cannot be corroborated independently. McDonald reports that McKinley was said to have imported a teacher from France for his children and that they only spoke French in the home. He states further that the McKinleys permitted a brick cow shed on their property to be used as a school for the children of slaves who were taught by local black ministers. See McDonald, *A Walk through the Past*, 50–52.

39. Moore, *History of Alabama*, 82.

40. Royall, *Letters from Alabama*, 227.

41. *Cadet and Statesman* (Providence, RI), November 18, 1826, vol. 1, no. 31, p. 2.

42. McKinley was ecumenical in his business dealings, selling part of his land in downtown Athens to a group who erected a one-room Baptist church on the site. Athens First Baptist held meetings at the site until 1949, and still uses the building for church functions. See "A Condensed History of First Baptist Church of Athens, Alabama, 1820–2009," http://www.fbcathens.org/content/condensed-history-first -baptist-church-athens-alabama-1820-2009 (accessed August 16, 2010).

43. He was elected a trustee of the church in 1837, just prior to joining the Supreme Court. See Doris (Mrs. Thurman M.) Kelso, *A History of the First Presbyterian Church Florence, Alabama* (privately published, 1968), 66, 74.

44. See Aleathea Thompson Cobb, *Presbyterian Women of the Synod of Alabama* (Mobile, AL: privately published, 1935), 212.

45. *Boston Courier,* June 11, 1838, issue 1035, col. B.

46. Royall, *Letters from Alabama*, 229–30.

47. McKinley was commissioned a captain in the Second Division, Fifth Brigade, Thirty-Fourth Regiment of the Alabama state militia on October 24, 1821, by Governor Thomas Bibb. See "Register of Gubernatorial Appointments—Civil and Military," 286.

48. In 1918, ninety-two-year-old James Simpson offered this explanation for McKinley's military rank when recalling his memories of early Florence to the *Florence (AL) Times:* "I do not know where he [McKinley] got the military title, but he was a promi-

nent lawyer. He came here from Kentucky and all the Kentuckians are colonels, you know." James Simpson, "Recollections of Florence," *Florence Times*, August 8, 1918.

49. Royall, *Letters from Alabama*, 230.

50. Laura C. Hood, Sara M. Hood, Hugh M. Hood, and Jack B. Hood, *Alabama Historical Association Markers*, 2nd ed. (Bloomington, IL: AuthorHouse Publishing, 2006), 132. Coulter's home is now known as the Coulter-McFarland Home and is on the National Register of Historic Places. There is a similar lack of detail with regard to how McKinley cultivated his plantations on the outskirts of Florence or his other extensive property holdings. Letters from McKinley make particular reference to cotton, of course, but to little else. A glimpse of at least one additional usage of his land is glimpsed in an 1828 letter from McKinley to John Wesley Hunt in Kentucky. Writing from Washington, McKinley told Hunt that he was "obliged to have the race track sown in meadow or lose the benefits of the track. I have therefore ordered the ground to be prepared and the seed to be sown." See John McKinley to John Wesley Hunt, December 15, 1828, William Pope Papers, Pope-Humphrey Papers, Filson Historical Society, Louisville, KY (hereafter Pope Papers).

51. There is no record of Elizabeth's birth, but it probably occurred around 1815. An unidentified free white female between the ages of fifteen and nineteen is listed on McKinley's 1830 federal census (only heads of families were named in this particular census). The *Florence Gazette* later identified her as the "eldest daughter of Col. John McKinley" when she married Donald Campbell on September 11, 1833, in Florence. See Pauline Jones Gandrud, *Marriage, Death, and Legal Notices from Early Alabama Newspapers, 1819–1893* (Easley, SC: Southeastern Historical Press, 1981), 594. There is virtually no other reference to the couple other than Campbell's 1834 effort to sell property in Limestone and Marengo counties. However, in 1853 the Alabama Supreme Court considered a case involving an indebted Donald Campbell who took his slaves to Ohio and then Indiana and later freed them upon his return to Florence prior to departing for California in 1848. His creditors brought suit against the local sheriff for failing to seize Campbell's slaves to satisfy the debt. The sheriff maintained that he could not because, having been manumitted, they were no longer the property of Campbell, to which the Alabama Supreme Court agreed. See *Union Bank of Tennessee v. Benham*, 23 Ala. 143 (1853). Campbell's trip west with a group of men from Florence is described in Edward M. Steel, *A Forty-Niner from Tennessee: The Diary of Hugh Brown Heiskell* (Knoxville: University of Tennessee Press, 1998).

With no record of Elizabeth on any census after 1830 and no mention of her in Justice McKinley's will, it is reasonable to conclude that she preceded her father in death. For what it is worth, when his oldest daughter was born in 1848, Andrew McKinley named her Elizabeth, perhaps in tribute to both his stepmother and sister.

52. Royall, *Letters from Alabama*, 230.

53. Ibid.

54. See, for example, Gandrud, *Alabama Records*, 197:21.

55. Gandrud, *Marriage, Death, and Legal Notices from Early Alabama Newspapers,*

434. In 1915 the Alabama historian Thomas McAdory Owen visited the McKinley family cemetery in Florence. He described the brick enclosure and brick tombs that had been erected there, including an elaborate arch and monument, all of which had fallen into serious disrepair. He found three inscriptions for children and a fourth stone slab, which read as follows: "To the memory of Mrs. Julianna McKinley—wife of Mr. John McKinley, who died 22d October 1822. Aged 30 years, 1 mon and 18 days." Julia's grave was excavated at full depth according to Owen, but it is not known when her body was taken or where it was reinterred. The entire lot was razed in the 1970s to make room for the Florence Alabama Police Department. See Owen, Surname Files.

56. Walker died the following April just a few months shy of his fortieth birthday.

57. *Alabama House Journal,* December 2, 1822, 47.

58. Ibid., 46.

59. Sam Houston to Andrew Jackson, January 19, 1823, *Correspondence of Andrew Jackson,* ed. John Spencer Bassett (Washington, DC: Carnegie Institute of Washington, 1926–35), 6:479.

60. Members of the U.S. Senate were elected by their respective state legislatures until 1913 when the Seventeenth Amendment was ratified, which provided for the popular election of senators.

61. *Alabama Senate Journal,* December 12, 1822, 30. Thirty-nine legislators voted for Kelly, thirty-eight for McKinley.

62. *Niles Weekly Register* (Baltimore, MD), January 11, 1823, vol. 23, no. 19, p. 291.

63. Sam Houston to Andrew Jackson, January 19, 1823, *Papers of Andrew Jackson,* 5:241.

64. Sam Houston to Andrew Jackson, January 19, 1823, *Correspondence of Andrew Jackson,* 6:479, emphasis in original.

65. Andrew Jackson to Richard K. Call, February 3, 1823, *Correspondence of Andrew Jackson,* 3:186.

66. Andrew Jackson to John Coffee, February 17, 1823, *Papers of Andrew Jackson,* 5:249.

67. Ibid.

68. *Acts of Alabama* (1823), 66.

69. Elizabeth, Andrew, and Mary lived to maturity, but there may have been other children in the McKinley family. In 1915 Thomas McAdory Owen found the graves of three other children buried next to Julianna Bryan McKinley in the family cemetery in Florence. Unfortunately, he failed to record their headstone inscriptions. See Owen, Surname Files.

70. *Village Messenger* (Fayetteville, TN), March 17, 1824, vol. 2, no. 2.

71. Some evidence of the Armistead family's wealth is found in the marriage contract that McKinley witnessed between Elizabeth's sister Mary and Willis Pope, son of LeRoy Pope, in 1827. The contract listed some 250 acres in Loudon County, money, and slaves that she brought into the marriage. See Gandrud, *Alabama Records,* 71:59.

72. "Armistead Family" (continued from vol. 6, p. 226), *William and Mary College*

Quarterly Historical Magazine 7, no. 1 (July 1898): 23. Elizabeth Armistead was born February 11, 1800, to Robert Armistead and Margaret Ellzey (ibid.). In 1891 a Chicago newspaper conveyed the following wire report: "Louisville, Ky., Feb. 11—Mrs. Elizabeth McKinley, wife of Justice McKinley, of the United States Supreme Court, died here today on the ninety-first anniversary of her birth." *Daily Inter Ocean*, February 12, 1891, vol. 19, no. 324, p. 2.

73. The McKinleys lived in the home until 1829.

74. See Gandrud, *Alabama Records,* 161:51. See also John McKinley to Henry Clay, January 9, 1826, *Papers of Henry Clay,* 5:18. A lifelong supporter of Henry Clay, Hopkins was also particularly vocal in his opposition to Andrew Jackson. This opposition would cost him in 1836 when he lost his race against McKinley for a seat in the U.S. Senate.

75. For example, McKinley and Hopkins served as opposing counsel in *Pope and Hickman v. John Nance and Co.,* Minor 299 (1824), 1824 Ala. LEXIS 44.

76. See, for example, *Standefer v. Chisholm,* 1 Stew. & P. 449 (1832), 1832 Ala. LEXIS 15.

77. See *McKinley v. Irvine,* 13 Ala. 681 (1848), 1848 Ala. LEXIS 151.

78. James E. Saunders, *Early Settlers of Alabama* (New Orleans: L. Graham and Son, 1899), 44.

79. William Birney, *James G. Birney and His Times* (New York: D. Appleton and Company, 1890), 45–46.

80. James Birney to Henry Clay, February 20, 1826, *Papers of Henry Clay,* 5:119, emphasis in original.

81. Senator Chambers was a client of McKinley's, a fellow member of the Georgia Faction, and a close friend. Before he died, he made McKinley and Arthur Hopkins the executors of his will as well as the guardians of his children. See Gandrud, *Alabama Records,* 111:29–30.

82. The original commissioners of the bank were LeRoy Pope, John P. Hickman, David Moore, Benjamin Cox, John M. Taylor, Thomas Fearn, Jesse Searcy, Clement C. Clay, and John W. Walker. See Edward C. Betts, *Early History of Huntsville, Alabama, 1804–1870* (Montgomery, AL: Brown Printing Company, 1916), 32.

83. Martin, "John McKinley: Jacksonian Phase," 8.

84. Thomas P. Abernethy, *The Formative Period in Alabama* (Montgomery, AL: Brown Printing Company, 1922), 111.

85. See Moore, *History of Alabama,* 118.

86. On December 21, 1820, in response to the financial crisis that was made worse by the struggles of private banks, the legislature established the Bank of the State of Alabama and designated several men in ten cities to oversee the collection of subscriptions toward the bank. John McKinley, Lemuel Mead, Nicholas Hobson, Frederick James, and Stephen Ewing were the superintendents of the branch office at Huntsville. They were tasked with raising $150,000 in subscriptions. Although this initial effort to create a state bank was unsuccessful, a second attempt three years later succeeded. See *Acts of Alabama* (1820), 20.

87. Abernethy, *The Formative Period in Alabama*, 53. Congressional passage of the Relief Act of 1821 allowed debtors to return parcels back to the government and extended credit for up to eight years depending on the amount the debtor owed.

88. Quoted in Ruth Ketring Nuermberger, "The 'Royal Party' in Early Alabama Politics," *Alabama Review* 6 (April 1953): 94.

89. *Alabama House Journal*, December 19, 1826, 130.

90. Robert J. Dinkin, *Campaigning in America: A History of Election Practices* (New York: Greenwood Press, 1989), 34.

91. Ibid.

92. Moore, *History of Alabama*, 118.

93. Dupre, "Barbecues and Pledges," 487.

94. J. Mills Thornton III, *Power and Politics in a Slave Society* (Baton Rouge: Louisiana State University Press, 1978), 19.

95. Ibid.

96. John McKinley to Henry Clay, June 3, 1823, *Papers of Henry Clay*, 3:428.

97. Ibid.

98. Ibid.

99. Ibid.

100. John McKinley to Henry Clay, September 29, 1823, *Papers of Henry Clay*, 3:490–91. In a foreshadowing of the charges that would subsequently be leveled against him, McKinley went on to discuss the shifting political allegiances of Alabama's congressional delegation. He described Senator William Kelly as "like St Paul 'All things to all men.'" Congressman George Owen "pretends to be for General Jackson but is in reality for Adams." Congressman Gabriel Moore "is a man in whom little confidence can be placed. He declared himself for Mr. Calhoun first, then for Mr. Adams, but finding neither suited his constituents he pretends now to be for Jackson."

101. McKinley to Clay, September 29, 1823, *Papers of Henry Clay*, 3:490–91, emphasis in original.

102. Moore, *History of Alabama*, 120.

103. Ibid., 123.

104. *Emancipator & Republican* (Boston), December 12, 1850, vol. 15, no. 33, p. 1.

105. See Jackson, *The Papers of Andrew Jackson*, vol. 6, ed. Andrew Jackson, Sam B. Smith, Harold D. Moser, J. Clint Clifft, Harriet Fason Chappell Owsley, and Wyatt C. Wells (Knoxville: University of Tennessee Press, 2002), 88, 166, 235.

106. Andrew Jackson to John Coffee, March 1, 1821, *Papers of Andrew Jackson*, 5:14. Other members of the extended Jackson family apparently held McKinley in considerably lower esteem. In February 1821, Jackson received the following letter from his nephew Stockley D. Hutchins in which the latter proudly declared, "Dear Uncle I am . . . confined in the Common Jaoll [*sic*] . . . for an assault on John McKinley in which I displayed the patriotism which should be engrafted in the bosom of every free born American." Quoted in James, *Life of Andrew Jackson*, 303–4.

107. Thornton, *Power and Politics in a Slave Society*, 16–17.

108. Moore, *History of Alabama*, 119.

109. Gatell, "John McKinley," 770, emphasis in original.

110. Of Adams's party loyalties, historian Richard Hofstadter has written, "He was never a good Federalist, and after his conversion he never became a good [Democratic-] Republican. . . . One finds in him a throwback to eighteenth-century views of party, which suited the headstrong independence of his temperament. Thinking of himself not as a party politician but as the custodian and spokesman of the whole nation [as president], he never saw any way of reconciling these two roles." See Hofstadter, *The Idea of a Party System*, 231.

111. John McKinley to Henry Clay, January 9, 1826, *Papers of Henry Clay*, 5:18.

112. Always sensitive to public criticism, McKinley would have been mortified to learn that his inquiry had been circulated. A decade later it would find its way into a highly critical piece on McKinley that was reprinted in newspapers nationwide. See the *Boston Courier*, June 11, 1838, issue 1035, col. B.

113. See *Papers of Henry Clay*, 5:119, 122. Several years earlier McKinley had been instrumental in securing from the state legislature a position for Birney as solicitor of the fifth circuit. Birney would later become an early and noted champion of the abolitionist movement. He ran for president in 1844 on the Liberty Party ticket, and the sixty thousand votes he received probably cost his old friend Henry Clay the presidency that year.

114. Henry Clay to James Birney, September 22, 1826, *Papers of Henry Clay*, 5:702.

115. Quoted in Ruth Ketring Nuermberger, "The 'Royal Party' in Early Alabama Politics (Part II)," *Alabama Review* 6 (July 1953): 204.

116. Clay would later serve as governor of Alabama from 1835 to 1837 and succeed McKinley in the U.S. Senate after the latter's elevation to the Supreme Court.

117. Andrew Jackson to Sam Houston, December 15, 1826, *Papers of Andrew Jackson*, 6:243.

118. *Southern Advocate* (Huntsville, AL), November 3, 1826, vol. 2, p. 2.

119. *Southern Advocate*, December 15, 1826, vol. 2, no. 33, p. 3.

120. Ibid., emphasis in original.

121. Ibid.

122. Ibid.

123. Ibid.

124. In January 1827, by a four-to-one margin (with two judges not participating), the Alabama Supreme Court rejected the claims of the debtors. See *Jones v. Watkins*, 1 Stew. 81 (Ala. 1827). On the basis of that ruling, three of the four Supreme Court judges in the majority were subjected to a trial in the Alabama Senate in 1829 to determine if they should be removed from office. Former senator William Kelly, the man who defeated McKinley in his first bid for the U.S. Senate in 1822, was the primary force behind the effort to oust the judges and acted as prosecutor during the hearing. Kelly had previously served as counsel for the debtors in the *Jones v. Watkins* case, offering his legal services on a contingency basis; his fee would be 50 percent of any amount refunded. See Nuermberger, "The 'Royal Party' in Early Alabama Poli-

tics (Part II)," 202. His financial interest in the affair may be found in his memorial to the Alabama legislature seeking removal of the judges in which he made the following rather remarkable admission: "Under a belief that they [the judges] would abide by the principles settled and sanctioned by themselves, I made contracts that I could have complied with, if they had met the expectation generated by their own decisions, but which I had no means to meet when they departed from their decisions and dismissed my cases. Nay, I was by that unexpected event plunged into a state of embarrassment, little short of hopeless irretrievable ruin." See Henderson M. Somerville, "Trial of the Alabama Supreme Court Judges in 1829," in *Proceedings of the Twenty-Second Annual Meeting of the Alabama State Bar Association, Montgomery, Alabama, June 16–17, 1899* (Montgomery, AL: Brown Printing Company, 1899), 68. After the trial, the Senate voted overwhelmingly to reject the resolution calling for the judges' removal.

125. Quoted in Abernethy, *The Formative Period in Alabama*, 114.

126. Ibid.

127. *Democrat,* October 27, 1826, vol. 4, p. 3, emphasis in original.

128. *Democrat,* December 8, 1826, vol. 4, p. 2.

129. Ibid.

130. *Democrat,* October 27, 1826, vol. 4, p. 3. See also the *Literary Cadet and Saturday Evening Bulletin,* November 18, 1826, vol. 1, no. 31, p. 2.

131. *Literary Cadet and Saturday Evening Bulletin,* November 18, 1826, vol. 1, no. 31, p. 2.

132. Ibid.

133. *Democrat,* January 19, 1827, vol. 4, p. 2.

134. In addition to Clay, McKinley's opponents originally included Nicolas Davis of Lauderdale, Richard Ellis of Franklin, Thomas W. Farrar of Jefferson, and his business partner with Cypress, James Jackson, also of Lauderdale. *Daily National Journal* (Washington, DC), Friday, December 1, 1826, issue 715, col. A.

135. *Democrat,* January 19, 1827, vol. 4, p. 2.

136. *Tuscumbian,* December 6, 1826, typewritten transcript in Owen, Surname Files.

137. *United States Senate Journal,* 19th Cong., 2nd Sess., December 27, 1826, 55.

138. *U.S. Telegraph and Commercial Herald* (Washington, DC), December 20, 1826, issue 275, col. B.

Chapter 5

Epigraph. *Baltimore Patriot,* February 3, 1830, vol. 35, issue 39, p. 2.

1. Henry Clay to Francis T. Brooke, December 23, 1826, *Papers of Henry Clay,* 5:1023.

2. Andrew Jackson to Sam Houston, December 15, 1826, *Correspondence of Andrew Jackson,* 3:324.

3. Ibid.

4. Sam Houston to Andrew Jackson, January 5, 1827, *Papers of Andrew Jackson,* 6:257, emphasis in original.

5. *U.S. Telegraph and Commercial Herald,* January 1, 1827, col. A.

6. Ibid.

7. *United States Senate Journal,* 19th Cong., 2nd Sess., 172.

8. Ibid., 66. The first order of business for this committee were petitions of landowners in areas recently acquired by the United States who argued that they held title to their lands because such had been recognized by the foreign governments that previously controlled the territory.

9. *Register of Debates,* 19th Cong., 2nd Sess., 50. In future years, McKinley's health would be an ongoing topic of discussion both on and off the bench.

10. *Register of Debates,* 19th Cong., 2nd Sess., 143–44. He also used this occasion to take the Supreme Court to task for its 1819 opinion in *Sturges v. Crowninshield* (17 U.S. 122), which struck down a New York state law discharging bankruptcy debt. Praising Chief Justice John Marshall as "one of the ablest Judges in the world," McKinley questioned if "still he might have been in error." The fact that the Court had engaged in "judicial legislation" to foist its will upon New York demonstrated to McKinley "that the powers of the Federal Government [might be used] to overshadow State powers, and render them almost contemptible." See ibid., 142–43.

11. Ibid.

12. *Democrat,* January 19, 1827, vol. 4, p. 2.

13. Ibid.

14. *Register of Debates,* 19th Cong., 2nd Sess., 309.

15. Ibid., 315.

16. Ibid., 316.

17. Ibid. Congress subsequently approved the land grant during this session for what would later be known as the Wabash and Erie Canal.

18. *Literary Cadet and Saturday Evening Bulletin,* September 8, 1827, vol. 2, no. 42, p. 2.

19. *Daily National Intelligencer,* August 17, 1827, issue 4542, col. A.

20. *Literary Cadet and Saturday Evening Bulletin,* September 8, 1827, vol. 2, no. 42, p. 2.

21. *U.S. Telegraph and Commercial Herald,* August 11, 1827, issue 272, col. D.

22. *Literary Cadet and Saturday Evening Bulletin,* September 8, 1827, vol. 2, no. 42, p. 2.

23. *Baltimore Sun,* July 26, 1852, issue 60, pg. 1.

24. *Register of Debates,* 20th Cong., 2nd Sess., 480.

25. *Register of Debates,* 20th Cong., 1st Sess., 454.

26. Ibid., 457.

27. Ibid., 519.

28. Ibid.

29. Ibid.

30. Ibid.

31. Ibid., 454.

32. Ibid., 508,

33. See *Speech of Mr. McKinley, of Alabama, on the Bill to Graduate the Price of Public Lands. Delivered in the Senate of the United States, March 26, 1828* (Washington, DC: Green and Jarvis, 1828).

34. Quoted in the *U.S. Telegraph and Commercial Herald*, June 24, 1828, issue 105, col. D, emphasis in original. In addition to land-related issues, McKinley was also comfortable raising and answering constitutional questions about government authority. In February 1828, there was extensive debate in the Senate as to whether the vice president, exercising his constitutional role as president of that body, could call another member to order. The feeling among some in the Senate was that only a fellow senator selected from that body to preside should be granted that privilege. McKinley made it very clear where he stood on the issue: "The argument appears to be grounded on the fact that the Senate does not elect him. We complain that we do not elect him—that he is not a member—but against whom do we complain? Against the People of the United States. They elect him; and they, by the Constitution, declare that he shall preside over the deliberations of the Senate. I say, then, . . . it is the Vice President to whom the powers naturally belonging to a presiding officer should be accorded." See *Register of Debates,* Senate, 20th Cong., 1st Sess., 297.

35. John McKinley to John Wesley Hunt, January 1, 1828, Pope Papers.

36. John McKinley to John Wesley Hunt, February 8, 1828, Pope Papers.

37. Ibid.

38. John McKinley to John Coffee, May 25, 1828, Coffee Papers (ADAH).

39. John McKinley to John Coffee, October 26, 1828, Coffee Papers, (ADAH).

40. See, for example, *Bennett v. Black,* 1 Stew. 494 (Ala. 1828); *Bell and Wife v. Hogan,* 1 Stew. 536 (Ala. 1828); and *Thompson v. Jones,* 1 Stew. 556 (Ala. 1828).

41. John McKinley to John Wesley Hunt, November 12, 1828, Pope Papers.

42. Ibid.

43. *Register of Debates,* 20th Cong., 2nd Sess., 43. The king determined the boundary in 1831, but the state of Maine refused to recognize his decision. The dispute persisted until 1842.

44. John McKinley to John Wesley Hunt, March 26, 1829, Pope Papers.

45. Ibid.

46. Jackson, *Papers of Andrew Jackson,* 7:105.

47. *U.S. Telegraph and Commercial Herald,* January 3, 1829, issue 2, col. E.

48. *Register of Debates,* 21st Cong., 1st Sess., 416.

49. Daniel Dupre, "Ambivalent Capitalists on the Cotton Frontier: Settlement and Development in the Tennessee Valley of Alabama," *Journal of Southern History* 56 (May 1990): 225–26.

50. *Register of Debates,* 21st Cong., 1st Sess., 415–16.

51. Ibid.

52. The American System was Henry Clay's vision of a strong, unified country under the guidance of the federal government. Under this vision, the government would direct the placement and construction of internal improvements such as roads and canals to improve transportation and facilitate commerce. It would also regulate the sale of public lands and levy tariffs to protect selected domestic industries.

53. Henry W. Farnam, *Chapters in the History of Social Legislation in the United States to 1860* (Baltimore, MD: Waverly Press, 1938; reprint, Union, NJ: Lawbook Exchange, 2000), 136 (page references are to reprint edition).

54. *Register of Debates,* 21st Congress, 1st Sess., 15.

55. Ibid.

56. Ibid., 21.

57. Ibid., 435.

58. *Baltimore Patriot,* February 3, 1830, vol. 35, issue 39, p. 2, emphasis in original.

59. Ibid.

60. *Daily National Journal,* April 30, 1830, issue 1998, col. C.

61. *Register of Debates,* 21st Cong., 1st Sess., 384.

62. Ibid.

63. *U.S. Telegraph and Commercial Herald,* April 17, 1830, issue 91, col. B, emphasis in original.

64. *Virginia Free Press & Farmers' Repository* (Charlestown, WV), May 5, 1830, issue 10, col. D.

65. John McKinley to John Coffee, February 5, 1830, Coffee Papers (Dyas).

66. Ibid.

67. Ibid.

68. Ibid.

69. John McKinley to John Coffee, February 25, 1830, Coffee Papers (Dyas). In an interesting postscript to this letter, McKinley wrote: "I have written this in the Senate Chambers while a debate is going on. [Y]ou must therefore excuse any defects you may find in it."

70. Ibid.

71. Ibid.

72. Ibid.

73. *Democrat,* June 17, 1830, vol. 7, p. 3.

74. *Southern Advocate,* June 4, 1830, vol. 5, p. 3.

75. *Democrat,* July 8, 1830, vol. 7, p. 3.

76. *Southern Advocate,* September 18, 1830, vol. 5, pp. 1–2.

77. See Martin, "John McKinley: Jacksonian Phase," 18–20.

78. *Democrat,* November 25, 1830, vol. 8, p. 3.

79. See Andrew Jackson to John Coffee, December 28, 1830, *Correspondence of Andrew Jackson,* 4:215–16.

80. Ibid.

81. Ibid.

82. Ibid., emphasis in original.

83. Ibid.

84. Quoted in Dupre, "Barbecues and Pledges," 504.

85. *Southern Advocate,* January 25, 1830, vol. 5, p. 3.

86. Ibid.

87. *Southern Advocate,* December 11, 1830, vol. 6, p. 1.

88. Ibid.

89. Ibid.

90. Ibid.

91. Ibid.

92. Ibid.

93. Ibid.

94. Charles Savage to John Coffee, February 5, 1831, Coffee Papers (Dyas).

95. *Democrat,* December 23, 1830, vol. 5, p. 3.

96. Ibid., emphasis in original.

97. *Daily National Journal,* January 1, 1831, vol. 7, issue 4006, p. 3.

98. Ibid.

99. Quoted in *U.S. Telegraph and Commercial Herald,* January 10, 1831, issue 8, col. D.

100. Ibid.

101. Ibid.

102. John McKinley to John Coffee, February 21, 1831, Coffee Papers (Dyas).

103. Ibid.

104. Andrew Jackson to John Coffee, December 28, 1830, *Correspondence of Andrew Jackson,* 4:215–16.

105. John McKinley to John Coffee, January 2, 1831, Coffee Papers (Dyas).

106. Ibid.

107. *U.S. Telegraph and Commercial Herald,* June 9, 1831, issue 137, col. A.

108. Ibid., emphasis in original.

109. Ibid.

110. Learning of Van Buren's defeat, Senator Thomas Hart Benton of Missouri is said to have commented to Senator Gabriel Moore of Alabama, "You have broken a minister and elected a Vice President." "Good God," Moore replied. "Why didn't you tell me that before I voted?" Quoted in James, *Life of Andrew Jackson,* 595.

111. Andrew Jackson to John Coffee, December 28, 1830, *Correspondence of Andrew Jackson,* 4:402.

112. Ibid.

113. *Globe* (Washington, DC), February 2, 1832, issue 199, col. D.

114. *Globe,* September 29, 1832, issue 93, col. F.

115. Martin, "John McKinley: Jacksonian Phase," 26.

116. Quoted in the *Globe,* September 29, 1832, issue 93, col. F, emphasis in original.

117. Ibid. Prior to the passage of the Twelfth Amendment, the Constitution pro-

vided that in the event of a tie between the second highest number of electoral votes, the Senate would chose the vice president by ballot.

118. See Andrew Jackson to John Coffee, April 9, 1833, *Correspondence of Andrew Jackson*, 5:56.

119. Clement C. Clay to James K. Polk, August 19, 1833, *Correspondence of James K. Polk*, ed. Herbert Weaver (Nashville, TN: Vanderbilt University Press), 2:100.

120. Quoted in the *Globe*, September 5, 1833, issue 72, col. E. It is unclear if the Mobile paper's phrasing of "just weight" was in any way a pun referring to the nearly five-hundred-pound Dixon Lewis.

121. Donald R. Kennon and Rebecca M. Rogers, *The Committee on Ways and Means: A Bicentennial History 1789–1989, House Document 100-244* (Washington, DC: GPO, 1989), 99.

122. Charles G. Sellers Jr., *James K. Polk, Jacksonian, 1795–1843* (Princeton: Princeton University Press, 1957), 213.

123. Ibid.

124. *Nashville Banner*, July 29, 1834, vol. 22, no. 1275, p. 3.

125. *Paul Pry* (Washington, DC), August 9, 1834, no. 37, p. 3.

126. John McKinley to James K. Polk, August 13, 1834, *Correspondence of James K. Polk*, 2:445.

127. James K. Polk to Levi Woodbury, February 27, 1835, *Correspondence of James K. Polk*, 3:118.

128. John McKinley to James K. Polk, March 31, 1835, *Correspondence of James K. Polk*, 148.

129. *Globe*, August 27, 1834, issue 65, col. C.

130. *Globe*, September 4, 1834, issue 72, col. E.

131. Ibid.

132. *Globe*, October 21, 1834, issue 112, col. A.

133. Ibid.

134. *Congressional Globe*, 23rd Cong., 2nd Sess., 1–2.

135. *New Hampshire Statesman*, April 1, 1835, issue 48, col. F.

136. Huebner, *The Taney Court*, 74.

137. Quoted in the *Globe*, June 2, 1835, issue 303, col. D

138. Ibid.

139. Moore, *History of Alabama*, 171.

140. The other electors were Thomas D. King, William R. Pickett, John S. Hunter, Robert H. Watkins, and William R. Hallett. See *Arkansas Gazette* (Little Rock), December 29, 1835, issue 2, col. E.

141. *Globe*, December 23, 1835, issue 166, col. B. Although White was denied the Democratic nomination, he ran as a Whig in the 1836 election and received 26 electoral votes.

142. *Globe*, December 28, 1835, issue 169, col. A.

143. Henry J. Abraham, *Justices and Presidents: A Political History of Appointments to the Supreme Court*, 3rd ed. (New York: Oxford University Press, 1992), 104.

144. Huebner, *The Taney Court*, 74.

145. Quoted in the *Globe*, August 31, 1836, issue 68, col. B.

146. John A. Campbell to Henry Goldthwaite, November 20, 1836, Campbell Family Papers, Southern Historical Collection, Manuscripts Department, Wilson Library, University of North Carolina, Chapel Hill (hereafter Campbell Family Papers).

147. See, for example, the *Globe*, February 25, 1832, issue 218, col. A.

148. *Globe*, March 2, 1832, issue 223, col. C.

149. Brian G. Walton, "Elections to the United States Senate in Alabama before the Civil War," *Alabama Review* 27 (January 1974): 19.

150. *Fayetteville (NC) Observer*, November 24, 1836, issue 1016, col. C.

151. Ibid.

152. John A. Campbell to Henry Goldthwaite, November 20, 1836, Campbell Family Papers.

153. Ibid.

154. *Raleigh (NC) Register*, December 6, 1836, issue 4, col. B.

155. John A. Campbell to Henry Goldthwaite, November 27, 1836, Campbell Family Papers.

156. Ibid.

157. *Pensacola (FL) Gazette*, December 3, 1836, issue 39, col. A.

158. *New York Spectator*, December 12, 1836, col. B.

159. Quoted in the *Democrat*, December 13, 1836, vol. 13, p. 3.

160. It is not known why McKinley never took the oath of office for his second term as senator. A contemporary account from March 1837 states that "every Senator from every State in the Union, except one (Mr. McKinley of Alabama)" was present on Inauguration Day to be sworn in by the new vice president, Richard M. Johnson. See *Boston Courier*, March 12, 1837, issue 906, col. F.

161. See Curtis Nettels, "The Mississippi Valley and the Federal Judiciary," *Mississippi Valley Historical Review* 12 (September 1925): 202–26. See also Schmidhauser, "Judicial Behavior and the Sectional Crisis of 1837–1860," 627.

162. Quoted in Nettels, "The Mississippi Valley and the Federal Judiciary," 218.

163. While Article III of the Constitution sets forth the duties of the judicial branch, it makes no mention of the number of members required for the Supreme Court, leaving that up to congressional discretion. The Judiciary Act of 1789 had created just six seats for the new Supreme Court. Between 1789 and 1863, however, Congress would eventually expand the Court to ten seats. Congress reduced the number of seats on the Supreme Court to nine in 1869, where it has remained ever since.

164. These were not new criteria. George Washington was the first to emphasize geography by ensuring that the six justices who comprised the first Supreme Court

equally represented the North and South. Political considerations arose in the appointment of other early justices, but none more so than in John Adams's appointment of John Marshall. Thus, politics and geography were factors in Supreme Court appointments for at least three decades prior to McKinley's nomination.

165. James K. Polk to Andrew Jackson, March 3, 1837, *Correspondence of James K. Polk,* 4:73.

166. Ibid.

167. Smith was confirmed 23–16, while Catron's nomination was secured by a vote of 28–15. See Lee Epstein, Jeffrey A. Segal, Harold J. Spaeth, and Thomas A. Walker, *The Supreme Court Compendium: Data, Decisions, and Developments* (Washington, DC: Congressional Quarterly, 1994), 284. Smith considered it something of a badge of honor to have been the first person to decline a seat on the Court after confirmation. He penned a public letter in April 1837 that was published in newspapers across the country. Such a public response was necessary, he wrote, to answer the frequent inquiries put to him as to "why [he] would decline a very dignified office, of light labors, and a permanent salary of $5000, a year." Contrary to rumors that had broadly circulated, he said his health was fine, his legal abilities sharp, and his regard for the Court as an institution still high. His stated reason for declining the seat was that he feared his ability to remove himself from discussions of political issues (in the still fevered political environment that Jackson had left behind) that might yet come before the Court. Rather than "place [himself] in a delicate situation, and, in public estimation, cast a blot upon the sacred ermine," he declined the seat. See *Kentucky Gazette,* May 11, 1837, issue 19, p. 2; and Kentuckian Digital Library, http://kdl.kyvl.org/ (accessed June 17, 2010). Smith died three years later.

168. Governor Clement C. Clay resigned his seat and won a special election in the legislature on June 19, 1837, to replace McKinley in the Senate.

169. John McKinley to James K. Polk, May 5, 1837, *Correspondence of James K. Polk,* 4:114. Chapman and Martin were members of Alabama's congressional delegation.

170. Ibid., 115.

171. John McKinley to James K. Polk, February 10, 1836, *Correspondence of James K. Polk,* 3:491.

172. John McKinley to James K. Polk, February 10, 1836, *Correspondence of James K. Polk,* 3:491–92.

173. John McKinley to James K. Polk, March 31, 1836, *Correspondence of James K. Polk,* 3:569.

174. Ibid., 491.

175. Holmes Alexander, *American Talleyrand: The Career and Contemporaries of Martin Van Buren, Eighth President* (New York: Russell and Russell, 1968), 335.

176. Arthur M. Schlesinger Jr., *The Age of Jackson* (Boston: Little, Brown, and Company, 1953), 218.

177. Anthony E. Kaye, *Joining Places: Slave Neighborhoods in the Old South* (Chapel Hill: University of North Carolina Press, 2007), 98.

178. John McKinley to Andrew Jackson, April 14, 1827, Andrew Jackson Papers, Library of Congress, Washington, DC.

179. John McKinley to William Pope, April 25, 1837, Pope Papers.

180. John McKinley to William Pope, June 12, 1837, Pope Papers.

181. Ibid.

182. Ibid.

183. Quoted in Gerald T. Dunne, *Justice Joseph Story and the Rise of the Supreme Court* (New York: Simon and Schuster, 1970), 373.

184. Ibid., 376.

185. Quoted in James McClellan, *Joseph Story and the American Constitution* (Norman: University of Oklahoma Press, 1971), 292n79.

186. Ibid., emphasis in original.

187. "Register of Gubernatorial Appointments—Civil and Military," 176.

188. Although some judicial experience is normally thought to be a requirement for service on the Supreme Court, some of the Court's most eminent members had never previously served as a judge, including Joseph Story, Louis Brandeis, Felix Frankfurter, and William Douglas. Influential members such as Hugo Black, Thurgood Marshall, and Antonin Scalia had a *combined* total of nine years' judicial experience prior to joining the Court. Six of the seventeen men (through John Roberts) who have served as chief justice of the Supreme Court had just one to five years of judicial experience prior to their appointment. Eight chief justices, including most recently William Rehnquist, had none. See Abraham, *The Judicial Process,* 58–60.

189. Indeed, not until 1957 would all nine members of the Court be law school graduates.

190. Quoted in Dunne, *Justice Joseph Story,* 373.

191. *Daily Pittsburgh Gazette,* May 11, 1837, vol. 4, no. 292, col. E; quoted in Nettels, "The Mississippi Valley and the Federal Judiciary," 226.

192. John Catron to James K. Polk, May 8, 1837, *Correspondence of James K. Polk,* 4:116.

193. John McKinley to William Pope, June 12, 1837, Pope Papers. Actually, in 1882, Roscoe Conkling became the last person to reject a Supreme Court appointment after being confirmed by the Senate.

194. John McKinley to James K. Polk, May 5, 1837, *Correspondence of James K. Polk,* 4:115.

195. McKinley's official appointment read: "To all who shall read these presents. Greetings: Know ye, that, reposing a special trust and confidence in the wisdom, uprightness, and learning of John McKinley of Alabama, I have nominated, and by and with the advice and consent of the Senate, do appoint him one of the Associate Justices of the Supreme Court of the United States, and do authorize and empower him to execute and fulfill the duties of that office according to the Constitution and laws of the United States and to hold the said office, with all the powers, privileges and emoluments to the same of rights appertaining, unto the said John McKinley, dur-

ing his good behavior. 25 September 1837, Martin Van Buren." See *Engrossed Minutes of the Supreme Court of the United States,* January 9, 1838 (microfilm, M-215).

Chapter 6

Epigraph. *Congressional Globe,* 30th Cong., 1st Sess., appendix 588.

1. See http://www.supremecourtus.gov/about/justicecaseload.aspx.

2. In 1844 Congress extended the term of the Court by a month, requiring it to convene the first Monday in December beginning later that year.

3. James Sterling Young, *The Washington Community, 1800–1828* (New York: Columbia University Press, 1966), 76, 87.

4. Quoted in Elizabeth Urban Alexander, *Notorious Woman: The Celebrated Case of Myra Clark Gaines* (Baton Rouge: Louisiana State University Press, 2001), 156.

5. Young, *The Washington Community,* 77.

6. Justices Smith Thompson and John McLean were apparently the first to begin this practice. See Swisher, *The Taney Period,* 45, 48.

7. In 1850, for a variety of reasons, the justices abandoned the practice of boarding with each other. During the Court's term that year, four justices took up residence in District hotels, while the other five were located in separate boardinghouses. See Samuel C. Busey, *Pictures of the City of Washington in the Past* (Washington, DC: W. Ballantyne and Sons, 1898), 315.

8. Catherine Allgor, *Parlor Politics* (Charlottesville: University Press of Virginia, 2000), 110.

9. Busey, *Pictures of the City of Washington in the Past,* 314.

10. Dana, *The Journal,* 245.

11. Ibid.

12. Ibid.

13. Alexander H. Stephens to Linton Stephens, December 2, 1844, Alexander H. Stephens Collection, Manhattanville College, Purchase, NY.

14. Ibid. Taney would later move to Washington, becoming the first justice to take up permanent residence there. See David M. O'Brien, *Storm Center: The Supreme Court in American Politics,* 8th ed. (New York: W. W. Norton, 2008), 113.

15. Alexander H. Stephens, *Recollections of Alexander H. Stephens: His Diary Kept When a Prisoner at Fort Warren, Boston Harbour, 1865,* ed. Myrta Lockett Avary (New York: Doubleday, 1920; reprint, New York: Da Capo Press, 1971), 49 (pages are to reprint edition).

16. Swisher, *The Taney Period,* 18.

17. See McClellan, *Joseph Story and the American Constitution,* and Dunne, *Justice Joseph Story.*

18. Other notable founding officers included former chief justice of the Supreme Court John Jay and Associate Justice Bushrod Washington.

19. Swisher, *The Taney Period,* 211–12.

20. Charles Warren, *The Supreme Court in United States History* (Boston: Little, Brown, and Company, 1937), 2:269–70.

21. Paul Finkelman, "John McLean: Moderate Abolitionist and Supreme Court Politician," *Vanderbilt Law Review* 62 (March 2009): 532.

22. Quoted in Swisher, *The Taney Period*, 47. John Quincy Adams confided in his diary that Justice McLean "thinks of nothing but the Presidency by day and dreams of nothing else by night" (Finkelman, "John McLean," 525).

23. Campbell, *Four Score Forgotten Men*, 149.

24. The Court's reporter at the time, Richard Peters, revealed, "I have heard in one day not less than five persons . . . say 'he is crazy.' . . . He sits in his room for three or four hours in the dark—jumps up and runs down into the judges' consultation room in his stocking feet, and remains in that condition while they are deliberating." Quoted in G. Edward White and Gerald Gunther, *The Marshall Court and Cultural Change, 1815–35* (New York: Macmillan, 1988), 302.

25. Swisher, *Roger B. Taney*, 360.

26. Swisher, *The Taney Period*, 52. Baldwin's death in 1844, incidentally, occasioned the longest vacancy in Supreme Court history as the Senate sparred with President John Tyler and then President James K. Polk over his replacement. Twenty-seven months after his death, the Senate finally confirmed Robert Grier to succeed Baldwin.

27. His son, Henry C. Wayne, was a brigadier general in the Confederate Army.

28. The others who would serve with McKinley during his tenure on the Supreme Court were Peter Daniel of Virginia, who sat on the bench from 1842 to 1860, Samuel Nelson of New York, who sat from 1845 to 1872, Levi Woodbury of New Hampshire, 1845 to 1851, Robert Grier of Pennsylvania, 1846 to 1870, and Benjamin Curtis of Massachusetts, who sat from 1851 to 1857.

29. For example, in the spring of 1824, the American Colonization Society, which helped establish the African country of Liberia as a settlement for freed slaves, invited all the members of Congress and the Supreme Court as well as "all of the distinguished men now in this city" to the Court's chambers to discuss the business of the organization. See the *Daily National Intelligencer,* March 5, 1824, issue 3473, col. E.

30. The Court occupied the basement room until 1860 when it moved to the Senate's former chambers when that body moved to its present wing in the Capitol. The room was later used as a library and for storage but was fully restored in 1975. Modern-day visitors to the Capitol can tour the Old Supreme Court Chamber and, even with the benefit of guides and modern lighting, can appreciate the faithfulness of the depictions offered by nineteenth-century courtroom spectators.

31. Quoted in Warren, *Supreme Court in United States History*, 1:460–61.

32. Thomas Hamilton, *Men and Manners in America*, vol. 2 (Edinburgh: William Blackwood, 1833; reprint, New York: Augustus M. Kelley Publishers, 1968), 127 (pages to reprint edition).

33. See Swisher, *Roger B. Taney*, 358.

34. Charles Lanman, *Bohn's Handbook of Washington* (Baltimore: Murphy and Company, 1852), 35.

35. Harriet Martineau, *Retrospect of Western Travel,* ed. Daniel Feller (Armonk, NY: M. E. Sharpe, 2000), 61.

36. Quoted in Warren, *Supreme Court in United States History,* 2:177.

37. Dana, *The Journal,* 241.

38. Ibid.

39. William Allen Butler, *A Retrospect of Forty Years, 1825–1865* (New York: Charles Scribner's Sons, 1911), 50.

40. From an 1827 account quoted in Warren, *Supreme Court in United States History,* 1:469. This cry, incidentally, has scarcely changed over the past two centuries. Each session of the current Supreme Court begins with the marshal proclaiming, "Oyez, Oyez, Oyez! All persons having business before the Honorable, the Supreme Court of the United States, are admonished to draw near and give their attention, for the Court is now sitting. God save the United States and this Honorable Court."

41. The Supreme Court also paid deference to its female spectators, as indicated in this 1845 account from a North Carolina correspondent: "On a pleasant day . . . when squads of ladies, with their whiskered attendants, are moving about the Capitol, gliding from the House to the Senate Chamber and thence down to the Supreme Court room, . . . the few cushioned seats [there] are filled. Attention and politeness are here enjoined by law and custom. Servitors employed by the Government pay special attention to the ladies, always directing them, if necessary, to seats, and never failing to clear the seats of the sterner sex, if they are wanted for the ladies." *Weekly Raleigh Register and North Carolina Gazette,* February 14, 1845, issue 19, col. E.

42. *Weekly Herald* (New York), January 29, 1842, issue 19, col. D.

43. There were obvious challenges for those who appeared before the Court while also serving in the executive and legislative branches. At the start of the Court's 1850 term, for example, Daniel Webster had to beg off arguing several cases that had been docketed because his duties as secretary of state had not allowed him proper time to prepare without the assistance of other counsel who were not yet in Washington. See the *New Hampshire Statesman,* December 27, 1850, issue 1544, col. E.

44. *Cleveland Daily Herald,* February 26, 1841, issue 145, col. A.

45. *Gibbons v. Ogden,* 19 U.S. 448 (1821); *U.S. v. Libellants of Schooner Amistad,* 40 U.S. 518 (1841). See David C. Frederick, *Supreme Court and Appellate Advocacy* (St. Paul, MN: Thompson West, 2003), 18, 23. In a January 1847 letter, Daniel Webster commented, "This is the 6th day of the argument in the Lexington cause [*New Jersey Steam Navigation Company v. Merchants Bank,* 47 U.S. 344 (1848)]. I have been sitting here, for that number of days, 4½ hours per day." Daniel Webster to Franklin Haven, January 29, 1847, Daniel Webster, *The Papers of Daniel Webster—Correspondence,* ed. Charles M. Wiltse (Hanover, NH: University Press of New England, 1974–84), 6:206.

46. Arguing against an 1848 congressional proposal to limit oral arguments, Mary-

land senator Reverdy Johnson, himself a frequent advocate before the Court, defended lengthy oral arguments from a lawyer's perspective: "[C]ase after case occurs, in which three, four, five, six, or even ten or eleven hours have been exhausted in argument strictly pertinent, in a strain of eloquence directly bearing upon the point at issue, no part of which could have been omitted without spoiling, in some measure, the effect of the whole. Who is to determine when the argument is irrelevant? . . . [W]ho can tell what course of argument will succeed with each one of the nine judges? That which would be sufficient if you were addressing a single judge would be thrown away as entirely useless, if addressed to some other judge." *Congressional Globe,* 30th Cong., 1st Sess., appendix 587 (1848).

47. Quoted in Warren, *Supreme Court in United States History,* 1:467.

48. Beveridge, *Life of John Marshall,* 4:82–83.

49. In 1849, over the dissent of Justices Wayne and Woodbury, the Court adopted Rule 53, which ordered that "no counsel will be permitted to speak, in the argument of any case in this court, more than two hours, without the special leave of the court." By this rule, the Court also required for the first time that written briefs be filed to consist of "a printed abstract of the case . . . , together with the points intended to be made, and the authorities intended to be cited in support of them arranged under the specific points." 48 U.S. iv (1849).

50. Casper and Posner, *Workload of the Supreme Court,* 13.

51. Quoted in Swisher, *The Taney Period,* 277.

52. Ibid.

53. Quoted in O'Brien, *Storm Center,* 116.

54. Ibid.

55. Baldwin, *The Flush Times,* 179.

56. Quoted in John R. Schmidhauser, *The Supreme Court: Its Politics, Personalities, and Procedures* (New York: Holt, Reinhart, and Winston, 1960), 115. The original reference is Justice John Archibald Campbell's eulogy of Justice Benjamin Curtis, 87 U.S. x (1874).

57. Ibid.

58. See White, "The Internal Powers of the Chief Justice," for discussion of the lack of opinion circulation on the Taney Court.

59. McClellan, *Joseph Story and the American Constitution,* 42n146.

60. A complete listing of these cases can be found in appendix 1.

61. White, "The Internal Powers of the Chief Justice," 1476.

62. See Blaustein and Mersky, *The First One Hundred Justices,* 142–43.

63. Ibid.

64. In modern practice, the chief justice, if in the majority, assigns the writing of the majority opinion. If he is not, then the senior-most member of the Court in the majority assigns the opinion. Data compiled by Epstein et al. demonstrate that the number of dissents and concurrences, as a proportion of the total number of cases

where an opinion was rendered, was generally very low from the Court's 1800 term until well into the twentieth century. See Epstein et al., *Supreme Court Compendium*, 149–58.

65. Finkelman, "John McLean," 524.

66. William Domnarski, *In the Opinion of the Court* (Urbana: University of Illinois Press, 1996), 32.

67. Benjamin R. Curtis Jr., *A Memoir of Benjamin Robbins Curtis* (Boston: Little, Brown, and Company, 1879), 2:341.

68. White, "The Internal Powers of the Chief Justice," 1481.

69. Epstein et al. (*Supreme Court Compendium*, 515) estimate that McKinley participated in 793 cases during his fourteen terms on the bench. This figure is too high because it does not factor in the five full terms he missed. Those omissions notwithstanding, he still participated in several hundred cases as a member of the Supreme Court.

70. *Congressional Globe,* 30th Cong., 1st Sess., appendix 588 (1848).

71. Ibid.

72. Warren, *Supreme Court in United States History,* 1:61.

73. Casper and Posner, *Workload of the Supreme Court,* 12.

74. R. Kent Newmyer, *Supreme Court Justice Joseph Story: Statesman of the Old Republic* (Chapel Hill: University of North Carolina Press, 1985), 319.

75. Ibid.

76. Freyer, *Forums of Order,* xviii–xix.

77. Tachau, *Federal Courts in the Early Republic,* 12.

78. Hall, *Oxford Companion to the Supreme Court of the United States,* 145.

79. Warren, *Supreme Court in United States History,* 1:58.

80. Quoted in *The Supreme Court of the United States: Its Beginnings and Its Justices, 1790–1991* (Washington, DC: Commission on the Bicentennial of the United States Constitution, 1992), 17.

81. See White and Gunther, *The Marshall Court and Cultural Change,* 164–65 for a further discussion of these methods.

82. Ibid., 174.

83. Finkelman, "John McLean," 540.

84. Maeva Marcus, "The Earliest Years (1790–1801): Laying Foundations," in *The United States Supreme Court: The Pursuit of Justice,* ed. Christopher Tomlins (New York: Houghton Mifflin, 2005), 32.

85. Quoted in Warren, *Supreme Court in United States History,* 1:88.

86. Ibid., 89.

87. Associate Justices James Blair Jr., John Rutledge, and Thomas Johnson and Chief Justice John Jay all resigned, citing the rigors of circuit riding and/or greater prestige in other state-level offices. See Artemus Ward, *Deciding to Leave: The Politics of Retirement from the United States Supreme Court* (Albany: State University of New York Press, 2003), 25–26.

88. See Felix Frankfurter and James M. Landis, *The Business of the Supreme Court: A Study in the Federal Judicial System* (New York: MacMillan, 1927), 44–48.

89. In 1911, after more than a century of protests from presidents and justices alike, Congress finally removed the circuit-riding responsibilities of the Supreme Court.

90. Christopher L. Tomlins, ed., *The United States Supreme Court: The Pursuit of Justice* (New York: Houghton Mifflin, 2005), 534–35.

91. The "expenses in attending [the circuit] courts alone will not be less than $1500 a year while other judges will not have to expend five hundred." John McKinley to James K. Polk, May 5, 1837, *Correspondence of James K. Polk,* 4:115.

92. Quoted in Frankfurter and Landis, *The Business of the Supreme Court,* 48n155.

93. Elizabeth Urban Alexander notes that litigants in New Orleans were represented by both English- and French-speaking attorneys. A translator rendered the evidence and charge to the jury in the jurors' native tongue, but not the attorneys' arguments. "If, for example, arguments opened in English, those in the jury who did not know the language withdrew from the jury box to the gallery; when these jurors returned to listen to the French counsel, the English-speaking jurors withdrew" (*Notorious Woman,* 136–37).

94. Justice Catron, for example, who was assigned to the Eighth Circuit (which included Missouri, Kentucky, and Tennessee), complained that the route from his residence in Tennessee to Washington and from thence to his circuit sites and back home took more than six months. See Swisher, *Roger B. Taney,* 355.

95. John L. Ringwalt, *Development of Transportation Systems in the United States* (Philadelphia: Railway World Office, 1888; reprint, New York: Johnson Reprint Corp., 1966), 77 (page references are to reprint edition). There were no railways in operation in Arkansas until after McKinley's death.

96. Ibid., 117. The railroad really started to come into its own during the decade following McKinley's death. Between 1850 and 1860, the total number of railway miles in the United States tripled.

97. Many European visitors to nineteenth-century America wrote detailed accounts of their travels throughout the country that made their way into newspaper columns, published journals, and guidebooks for emigrants. While the specific accounts refer only to the particular adventures of the authors, the uniformity of these and other descriptions with regard to the modes and dangers of travel in America gives historians some confidence as to both the accuracy of these accounts and their applicability to other travelers of the same era.

98. On May 6, 1839, the steamer *George Collier* exploded during passage from New Orleans to St. Louis. An Ohio paper reported the following: "For some time past the news of accidents to steamboats has multiplied in a frightful manner, among which the most terrible is that which happened to the *George Collier. . . .* At half past one o'clock [in] the morning . . . when within eighty miles of Natchez, the piston rod gave way, breaking the forward cylinder head, and carrying away part of the boiler stands. The steam which escaped scalded 45 persons, 26 of whom died in the course of the

day. . . . Five or six children have been so much injured that they are not expected to recover." Quoted in the *Newark (OH) Advocate,* May 25, 1839, issue 40, col. A.

99. Louis C. Hunter, *Steamboats on the Western Rivers: An Economic and Technological History* (New York: Octagon Books, 1969), 414.

100. Ibid., 416.

101. Alexander Graham Dunlop, *The New World Journal of Alexander Graham Dunlop, 1845,* ed. David Sinclair and Germaine Warkentin (Toronto: Dundurn Press, 1976), 11.

102. Quoted in Walter Brownlow Posey, "Alabama in the 1830s as Recorded by British Travelers," *Birmingham-Southern College Bulletin* 31 (December 1938): 25.

103. See ibid., 5.

104. Quoted in William D. Hoyt Jr., "Justice Daniel in Arkansas, 1851 and 1853," *Arkansas Historical Quarterly* 1 (June 1942): 160.

105. Ibid.

106. J. Winston Coleman Jr., *Stage-Coach Days in the Bluegrass* (Louisville: The Standard Press, 1936), 35.

107. Quoted in Posey, "Alabama in the 1830s," 19.

108. Henry D. Southerland Jr. and Jerry E. Brown, *The Federal Road through Georgia, the Creek Nation, and Alabama, 1806–1836* (Tuscaloosa: The University of Alabama Press, 1989), 62.

109. U.S. Congressional Serial Set Vol. No. 339, Session Vol. No. 2, 25th Cong., 3rd Sess., S.Doc. 50, p. 35.

110. Quoted in Coleman, *Stage-Coach Days in the Bluegrass,* 142.

111. Ibid., 106.

112. Quoted in Posey, "Alabama in the 1830s," 28–29.

113. See Swisher, *The Taney Period,* 265, and Hoyt, "Justice Daniel in Arkansas."

114. Coleman, *Stage-Coach Days in the Bluegrass,* 66.

115. For more information including a breakdown of annual yellow fever deaths by city, see John McLeod Keating, *A History of the Yellow Fever Epidemic of 1878* (Memphis: Howard Association, 1879), 86–88.

116. See Frankfurter and Landis, *The Business of the Supreme Court,* 49n163.

117. U.S. Statutes at Large, vol. 5, 24th Cong., 2nd Sess., Chapter 34, 1837, pp. 176–77.

118. Casper and Posner, *Workload of the Supreme Court,* 15.

119. John Catron to James K. Polk, May 8, 1837, *Correspondence of James K. Polk,* 4:116.

120. Swisher, *The Taney Period,* 265–66.

121. Quoted in Newmyer, *Supreme Court Justice Joseph Story,* 318.

122. For an account of the great diversity among the Taney Court justices relative to the publishing of their circuit opinions, see Swisher, *The Taney Period,* 262.

123. Ibid.

124. *Guard* (Holly Springs, MS), November 15, 1842, p. 1.

125. *The Iowa,* 54 U.S. 283 (1851), transcript of record, p. 262, *U.S. Supreme Court Records and Briefs, 1832–1978.*

126. Quoted in Swisher, *The Taney Period,* 262.

127. John P. Frank, *Justice Daniel Dissenting* (Cambridge, MA: Harvard University Press, 1964), 280.

128. Chief Justice Taney alluded to this fact in his eulogy to McKinley. See 55 U.S. iii (1852).

Chapter 7

Epigraph. *Congressional Globe,* 27th Cong., 2nd Sess., 392.

1. *Mississippian* (Jackson), December 1, 1837, issue 39, col. A.

2. John McKinley to Martin Van Buren, November 6, 1839, Martin Van Buren Papers, Manuscript Division, Library of Congress, Washington, DC (hereafter Van Buren Papers).

3. *United States Senate Journal,* 25th Cong., 2nd Sess., 30.

4. 37 U.S. 66 (1838).

5. Curtis, *A Memoir,* 341.

6. 37 U.S. 238 (1838) and 37 U.S. 102 (1838), respectively.

7. 31 U.S.C. Section 3713, emphasis added.

8. 37 U.S. 102, at 134.

9. Ibid.

10. Ibid.

11. Ibid., at 139. Story's opinion was joined by Justice McLean and, curiously, Justice Baldwin, who also concurred in the majority opinion.

12. 37 U.S. 657 (1838).

13. Ibid., at 726.

14. Ibid., at 752. As this decision established the Court's jurisdiction only over state boundary disputes, the actual border would come before the Court several more times before it was ultimately resolved.

15. 37 U.S. 524.

16. Ibid., at 613. Justices Catron and Barbour joined Chief Justice Taney in dissent. They agreed that there were limits on executive branch power, but questioned whether the circuit court was authorized to issue a writ of mandamus to Kendall.

17. Ibid.

18. See David P. Currie, "Miss Otis Regrets," *Green Bag* 7 (Summer 2004): 374–85.

19. Chief Justice Taney submitted the following on behalf of the Court to the House committee tasked with the funeral arrangements: "<u>Resolved,</u> that with every desire to manifest their respect for the House of Representatives and the committee of the House by whom they have been invited and for the memory of the lamented deceased, the Justices of the Supreme Court, cannot consistently with the duties they owe to the public, attend in their official characters, the funeral of one who has fallen

in a duel." Quoted in ibid., 384. Despite the official statement, Justice Baldwin apparently attended Cilley's funeral anyway. See Story, *Life and Letters of Joseph Story,* 2:290. Congress formally banned dueling in Washington the following year.

20. *New York Spectator,* March 26, 1838, col. A.

21. *Daily National Intelligencer,* February 19, 1838, issue 7806, col. E.

22. Ibid.

23. Ibid.

24. *Congressional Globe,* 25th Cong., 2nd Sess., 179.

25. *Daily National Intelligencer,* March 15, 1838, issue 7827, col. A.

26. Ibid.

27. *Congressional Globe,* 25th Cong., 2nd Sess., 247.

28. Ibid.

29. Ibid.

30. Ibid. As mentioned in chapter 6, yellow fever was an annual unwelcome visitor to New Orleans but it was far less deadly in the fall and winter months. Whether deliberately or not, Clay overstated its impact at that time of the year because the November 1837 circuit court in New Orleans *was* still held. U.S. District Judge Philip K. Lawrence convened the court and heard disputes through January 1838. See the *Arkansas Gazette* (Little Rock), December 5, 1837, issue 51, col. A.

31. Ibid.

32. Ibid., 250.

33. Ibid.

34. Ibid.

35. Justice Story, however, lamented the quality of the cases considered by the Court that term in a letter to Charles Sumner. "Our last term at Washington," Story grumbled, "was on the whole, dull, and dry, and tedious. There were few causes of general interest argued and still fewer which gave rise to very comprehensive researches into nice or recondite law." He expressed greater concern about the inefficiency of the Court, which he attributed to the newly enlarged bench. "The addition to our numbers had most sensibly affected our facility as well as rapidity of doing business," he complained to Sumner. "'Many men of many minds' requires a great deal of discussion to compel them to come to definite results; and we found ourselves often in long and very tedious debates. I verily believe, if there were twelve Judges, we should do no business at all, or at least very little." Joseph Story to Charles Sumner, March 15, 1838, *Life and Letters of Joseph Story,* 2:295–96.

36. Casper and Posner, *Workload of the Supreme Court,* 15.

37. 38 U.S. 519 (1839).

38. Quoted in Warren, *The Supreme Court in United States History,* 2:51.

39. These included "closing the courts to prevent adjudication of debtor-creditor controversies, making depreciated paper legal tender for debts, [and] allowing extensions of time to debtors through stay laws (which were virtual moratoriums)." Quoted in Freyer, *Forums of Order,* 11.

40. *New York Spectator*, May 3, 1838, col. D.

41. *Daily National Intelligencer*, May 30, 1838, issue 7892, col. F.

42. *Pensacola (FL) Gazette*, April 28, 1838, issue 8, col. C.

43. *Fayetteville (NC) Observer*, June 6, 1838, issue 1096, col. D.

44. *Philadelphia Inquirer and Daily Courier*, April 28, 1838, issue 101, col. E.

45. *New-Yorker*, June 23, 1838, vol. 5, no. 14, 217.

46. Quoted in Warren, *The Supreme Court in United States History*, 2:50.

47. Quoted in Swisher, *The Taney Period*, 109n27.

48. Quoted in Warren, *The Supreme Court in United States History*, 2:141.

49. *Madisonian* (Washington, DC), May 31, 1838, issue 113.

50. Quoted in Peleg Whitman Chandler, ed., *The Law Reporter* (Boston: Weeks, Jordan, and Company, 1838), 1:189.

51. Quoted in the *Fayetteville (NC) Observer*, June 6, 1838, issue 1096, col. D.

52. Quoted in Chandler, *The Law Reporter*, 1:189, emphasis in original.

53. Quoted in the *Daily National Intelligencer*, April 9, 1839, issue 8159, col. A, emphasis in original.

54. *Boston Courier*, June 11, 1838, issue 1035, col. B.

55. Ibid. The word "cute" is a shortened form of the word "acute" and was used in the nineteenth century to mean cunning or shrewd.

56. Ibid.

57. *New-Yorker*, June 23, 1838, vol. 5, no. 14, 217.

58. Ibid.

59. *Extra Globe* (Washington, DC), July 17, 1839, vol. 5, no. 11, p. 165.

60. *Mississippian*, June 8, 1838, issue 14, col B.

61. Ibid. The paper explained, "It is for the interest of all parties, that the payment of debts should be regularly enforced. And it is especially the interest of defendants, that they pay their debts while a sinking currency can be used for that purpose. The postponement of that evil day only adds fuel to the flame, and redoubled embarrassment to every interest."

62. For those with suits pending in the federal court, the resulting delay was a mixed blessing as the *Pensacola Gazette* explained at the time: "The defendants, no doubt, will be well pleased with the arrangement. There are on the docket of the Circuit Court 280 suits, brought by persons residing abroad, against those within the state. It will be, if it takes place, rather an onerous case for the plaintiffs, but *they must console themselves* with the hope that their turn will come by and by." *Pensacola (FL) Gazette*, June 9, 1838, issue 14, col. F.

63. *Daily National Intelligencer*, June 8, 1838, issue 7900, col. D.

64. Other justices experienced similar circuit court delays and cancellations due to the absence of key court personnel. See Swisher, *The Taney Period*, 267.

65. Quoted in the *Mississippian*, June 1, 1838, issue 13, col. F.

66. *Daily National Intelligencer*, June 8, 1838, issue 7900, col D.

67. *Arkansas Gazette*, July 4, 1838, issue 29, col. C.

68. U.S. Congressional Serial Set Vol. No. 339, Session Vol. No. 2, 25th Cong., 3rd Sess., S.Doc. 50, 38.

69. Ibid.

70. The same route today would require 4,863 miles.

71. U.S. Congressional Serial Set Vol. No. 339, Session Vol. No. 2, 25th Cong., 3rd Sess., S.Doc. 50, 4-5.

72. *Congressional Globe*, 25th Cong., 3rd Sess., 115.

73. U.S. Congressional Serial Set Vol. No. 351, Session Vol. No. 1, 25th Cong., 3rd Sess., H.Rpt. 272.

74. Ibid., 1. Consideration of the report was postponed until February 21, but with Congress nearing the end of its session at that point, no action was ever taken. See Serial Set Vol. No. 5184, Session Vol. No. 81, 59th Cong., 2nd Sess., H.Doc. 355, pt. 3, Section 2495, p. 994. Lawrence served until his death in 1841.

75. 38 U.S. 230 (1839).

76. Ibid., at 261.

77. Statutes at Large, or Public Law 25-36, 5 Stat. 322 (1839).

78. See *Arkansas Gazette,* June 12, 1839, issue 26, col. F.

79. See the *Extra Globe,* July 17, 1839, vol. 5, no. 11, p. 165.

80. See *Daily National Intelligencer,* April 9, 1839, issue 8159, col. A.

81. 38 U.S. 519, at 567.

82. Ibid.

83. See *Daily National Intelligencer,* April 9, 1839, issue 8159, col. A. In a January 1839 letter, Daniel Webster informed Nicolas Biddle (former president of the Second Bank of the United States) that Ingersoll had "volunteered to support the judge's [McKinley] decision, on account of his hearty coincidence of opinion, and his judgment in regard to the importance of the principles involved." Webster to Biddle, January 25, 1839, *Papers of Daniel Webster,* 4:343, emphasis in original.

84. 38 U.S. 519, at 579–80 (1839).

85. Ibid., 580.

86. *Newark (OH) Advocate,* April 6, 1839, issue 33, col. A.

87. Quoted in Swisher, *The Taney Period,* 210.

88. Swisher, *Roger B. Taney,* 385.

89. Schlesinger, *The Age of Jackson,* 328.

90. 38 U.S. 519, at 589-90.

91. Ibid., at 601.

92. Ibid., at 606.

93. Maurice G. Baxter, *Daniel Webster and the Supreme Court* (Amherst: University of Massachusetts Press, 1966), 193.

94. 38 U.S. 519, at 599 (1839).

95. Maltz, "Majority, Concurrence, and Dissent," 361.

96. 38 U.S. 519, at 601.

97. Maltz, "Majority, Concurrence, and Dissent," 361.

98. *Virginia Free Press & Farmers' Repository,* May 23, 1839, issue 17, col. F.

99. Quoted in the *Daily National Intelligencer,* June 1, 1839, issue 8205, col. D.

100. Ibid.

101. Quoted in William D. McCain, *The Story of Jackson: A History of the Capital of Mississippi, 1821–1851* (Jackson, MS: J. F. Hyer Publishing Company, 1852), 169.

102. Ibid., 170.

103. Quoted in the *Boston Courier,* June 6, 1839, vol. 13, no. 1578, p. 1.

104. *North American* (Philadelphia), May 30, 1839, vol. 1, no. 57, p. 2.

105. Ibid.

106. Quoted in the *Daily National Intelligencer,* June 1, 1839, issue 8205, col. D.

107. Kenneth S. Greenberg, *Honor and Slavery* (Princeton: Princeton University Press, 1996), 16.

108. *Daily National Intelligencer,* June 1, 1839, issue 8205, col. D.

109. Ibid.

110. *Boston Courier,* June 6, 1839, vol. 13, no. 1578, p. 1.

111. Ibid.

112. Quoted in ibid., emphasis in original. McKinley apparently put both Mississippi and the initial incident behind him. In early February 1841, Attorney General Henry D. Gilpen received Dixon's application for a presidential pardon of the $400 fine imposed on him by McKinley for contempt of court. Among the application materials was a letter from McKinley recommending that the fine be pardoned. In advising President Martin Van Buren, Gilpen stated that there was nothing to preclude the president in granting the pardon if he so chose. See U.S. Congress, *Message from the President of the United States, transmitting copies of opinions given by the Attorneys General, etc., which give construction to the public laws not of a temporary character. March 3, 1841,* 26th Cong., 2nd Sess., H.Doc. 123, Serial Set Vol. No. 387, Session Vol. No. 6, p. 1382. U.S. Congressional Serial Set, Record Number: 103DFDA759F06180.

113. *U.S. v. Price and Company* (1838) was apparently an unreported circuit decision. Quoted in the *Daily National Intelligencer,* June 11, 1839, issue 8213, col. C.

114. Statutes at Large, or Public Law 25-191, 5 Stat. 304 (1838).

115. Quoted in the *Daily National Intelligencer,* June 11, 1839, issue 8213, col. C.

116. Quoted in the *Cleveland Daily Herald,* June 17, 1839, issue 250, col. B.

117. Quoted in the *Pennsylvania Inquirer and Gazette* (Philadelphia), July 6, 1839, issue 5, col. H.

118. An interesting exchange between a steamboat captain and his passengers eager for a race was recounted by former U.S. senator and secretary of the interior Carl Schurz: "They crowded around the captain, a short, broad-shouldered and somewhat grumpy-looking man, who paced the 'hurricane deck' with an air of indifference. Would he permit the *Ocean Wave* [a rival ship] to get ahead? he was asked. 'Would you like to be blown up?' he asked in return. 'No,' was the answer, 'we would not like to be blown up, but we don't want the *Ocean Wave* to beat us, either.'" Quoted in Hunter, *Steamboats on the Western Rivers,* 406.

119. Quoted in the *Pennsylvania Inquirer and Gazette*, July 6, 1839, issue 5, col. H.

120. *Daily National Intelligencer*, June 19, 1839, issue 8220, col. A.

121. Statutes at Large, or Public Law 27-94, 5 Stat. 626 (1838).

122. John McKinley to Martin Van Buren, November 6, 1839, Van Buren Papers.

123. Ibid.

124. Ibid.

125. Ibid.

126. John T. Woolley and Gerhard Peters, The American Presidency Project, http://www.presidency.ucsb.edu/ws/?pid=29481 (accessed August 31, 2011).

127. Quoted in Swisher, *The Taney Period*, 254.

128. See *Engrossed Minutes of the Supreme Court of the United States*, March 14, 1843 (microfilm, M-215).

129. The first justice born in the nineteenth century was Benjamin Curtis (1809–74).

130. Writing to the newly appointed Nathan Clifford in 1858, Taney said, "It is usual where there is likely to be a difference of opinion upon an important constitutional question, to postpone it [the case], until we have a full court." Quoted in Swisher, *The Taney Period*, 292n69.

131. John McKinley to William Pope, March 22, 1840, Pope Papers.

132. *Congressional Globe*, 26th Cong., 2nd Sess., 93.

133. *Madisonian*, February 23, 1841, vol. 4, no. 63, p. 3.

134. Newmyer, *Supreme Court Justice Joseph Story*, 366.

135. *U.S. v. Libellants of Schooner Amistad*, 40 U.S. 518 (1841).

136. Newmyer, *Supreme Court Justice Joseph Story*, 368.

137. John Quincy Adams, *The Memoirs of John Quincy Adams*, ed. Charles Francis Adams (Philadelphia: J. B. Lippincott and Company, 1876; reprint, New York: AMS Press, 1970), 10:437.

138. 40 U.S. 449 (1841).

139. Quoted in Swisher, *The Taney Period*, 366.

140. Newmyer, *Supreme Court Justice Joseph Story*, 367.

141. 40 U.S. 449, at 517.

142. Swisher, *The Taney Period*, 368. John Quincy Adams also noted in his journal that McKinley was present and offered his dissent verbally.

143. Quoted in Swisher, *The Taney Period*, 367.

144. Ibid.

145. 40 U.S. 449, at 510, emphasis added.

146. Ibid., at 512–13.

147. *Congressional Globe*, 26th Cong., 2nd Sess., 212.

148. Warren, *The Supreme Court in United States History*, 2:78.

149. Smith may have exaggerated the support of the Court for the proposed changes. Swisher notes that Chief Justice Taney balked at the prospect of having to ride circuit from Maryland to western Virginia in the new circuit. Justice Catron im-

mediately provided the solution: "Judge McKinley *must* take it, or do anything else to obtain relief—so that this trifle should not for a moment stand in the way of an arrangement, to last with slight alterations for forty years." See Swisher, *The Taney Period*, 255n20, emphasis in original. There is no record of what the long-suffering McKinley thought about a circuit stretching from the Gulf of Mexico to the central Appalachians.

150. *Congressional Globe*, 26th Cong., 2nd Sess., 213.

151. Ibid., 215.

152. Ibid.

153. B. W. Godfrey to Joseph Story, April 25, 1841, Joseph Story Papers, Phillips Library, Peabody Essex Museum, Salem, MA (hereafter Joseph Story Papers).

154. Jefferson Davis, *Jefferson Davis Constitutionalist: His Letters, Papers, and Speeches*, ed. Dunbar Rowland (Jackson: Mississippi Department of Archives and History, 1923), 2:184.

155. Godfrey to Story, April 25, 1841.

156. Judith K. Schafer, *Slavery, the Civil Law, and the Supreme Court of Louisiana* (Baton Rouge: Louisiana State University Press, 1994), 13.

157. Charles Payne Fenner, "The Jurisprudence of the Supreme Court of Louisiana," *Louisiana Historical Quarterly* 4 (1921): 76.

158. An 1843 Mississippi Supreme Court case invoked McKinley's devotion to state court precedent where applicable. "Judge McKinley . . . decided in conformity to the principles laid down in the case of Stamps v. Brown; and that when the cases relied on to support the contrary rule, found in Tennessee, New York and other reports, were cited, the judge very properly remarked, that if he were presiding in the courts in those state, or in cases which happened there, he would be governed by those decisions; but that as he was sitting in a case which arose under our laws and usages, the decision of our supreme court as to those laws and usages would govern him." *Hogatt v. Bingaman*, 8 Miss. 565 (1843).

159. *Fleitas v. Richardson*, 147 U.S. 538, at 545 (1893).

160. *Weekly Herald*, January 29, 1842, issue 19, col. D.

161. 41 U.S. 1 (1842).

162. Newmyer, *Supreme Court Justice Joseph Story*, 334–35.

163. 1 U.S. Statutes at Large 92.

164. 41 U.S. 1, at 19.

165. Ibid.

166. *Swift* was overturned in 1938 by *Erie Railroad Co. v. Tompkins*, 304 U.S. 64. Writing for a 6–2 majority, Justice Louis Brandeis declared, "[I]n applying the [Swift] doctrine this Court and the lower courts have invaded rights which in our opinion are reserved by the Constitution to the several states." 304 U.S. 64, at 80.

167. Freyer, *Forums of Order*, 87.

168. 41 U.S. 539 (1842).

169. Ibid., at 622.

170. Quoted in Swisher, *The Taney Period*, 543.

171. 41 U.S. 539, at 611.

172. Quoted in Newmyer, *Supreme Court Justice Joseph Story*, 376.

173. Ibid., 378.

174. Maltz, "Majority, Concurrence, and Dissent," 361–62.

175. *Congressional Globe*, 27th Cong., 2nd Sess., 213.

176. U.S. Congressional Serial Set Vol. No. 402, Session Vol. No. 2, 27th Cong., 2nd Sess., H.Doc. 95.

177. Ibid., 1.

178. Ibid.

179. Ibid., 2.

180. Ibid. McKinley still maintained business interests in Kentucky. Swisher asserts that McKinley was still an active partner in the "firm of Clark, Churchill and Company, manufacturers of hemp bagging and rope." Swisher, *The Taney Period*, 67.

181. U.S. Congressional Serial Set Vol. No. 402, Session Vol. No. 2, 27th Cong., 2nd Sess., H.Doc. 95.

182. See Walker Lewis, *Without Fear or Favor: A Biography of Chief Justice Roger Brooke Taney* (Boston: Houghton Mifflin Company, 1965), 250–68.

183. Newmyer, *Supreme Court Justice Joseph Story*, 281.

184. U.S. Congressional Serial Set Vol. No. 402, Session Vol. No. 2, 27th Cong., 2nd Sess., H.Doc 95, 2–3.

185. Ibid., 3.

186. Ibid., 3–4.

187. Adams, *Memoirs*, 11:125.

188. Pope's nephew, Alexander Pope Churchill, married McKinley's daughter Mary in 1839.

189. *Congressional Globe*, 27th Cong., 2nd Sess., 392.

190. Ibid.

191. Ibid.

192. Ibid.

193. Ibid.

194. Ibid.

195. *New York Herald*, May 21, 1842, issue 424, col. E.

196. McKinley's presence at circuit court in Jackson was noted in the *Mississippian*, May 6, 1842, issue 1, col. C.

197. Quoted in McCain, *The Story of Jackson*, 133.

198. *Daily National Intelligencer*, June 18, 1842, issue 9154, col. F.

199. *American* (Baltimore, MD), May 19, 1842, issue 13150, p. 4.

200. *Congressional Globe*, 27th Cong., 2nd Sess., 514.

201. Ibid., 877.

202. *Guard*, November 15, 1842, p. 1, http://marshallcountyms.org/articles/images4/1842-11-15-1.pdf (accessed March 22, 2010).

203. *Vermont Gazette* (Bennington), November 29, 1842, vol. 13, p. 3.

Chapter 8

Epigraph. Dumas Malone, ed., *Dictionary of American Biography*, index 3 (New York: Charles Scribner's Sons, 1933), 105.

1. See Henry Morton Woodson, *Historical Genealogy of the Woodsons and Their Connections* (Memphis: self-published, 1915), 539, and Logan U. Reavis, *Saint Louis: The Future City of the World* (St. Louis: Gray, Baker, and Co., 1875), 847. Andrew would later return to Missouri where he became a successful real estate developer who spearheaded the creation of St. Louis's outstanding Forest Park.

2. Quoted in Swisher, *The Taney Period*, 304n48.

3. See Warren, *The Supreme Court in United States History*, 2:106–7.

4. John McKinley to Richard Peters, June 6, 1843, Richard Peters Collection, Historical Society of Philadelphia.

5. Ibid.

6. Quoted in Swisher, *The Taney Period*, 258. Taney would live until 1864, Daniel until 1860, and McKinley until 1852.

7. See Frank, *Justice Daniel Dissenting*.

8. Ibid., 281.

9. 42 U.S. 89 (1843).

10. *The Woodrop Sims*, High Court of Admiralty, 2 Dods. Adm 83 (1815).

11. *The Louisville v. Strout*, 15 F. Cas. 987, at 988 (1839).

12. *Merchants Magazine and Commercial Review* (New York), July–December 1848, vol. 19, p. 187.

13. *Pensacola (FL) Gazette*, April 29, 1843, issue 5, col. C.

14. *Daily National Intelligencer*, May 5, 1843, issue 9427, col. C.

15. *Daily Atlas* (Boston), May 8, 1843, issue 264, col. G.

16. *Daily National Intelligencer*, May 5, 1843, issue 9427, col. C.

17. *Daily Scioto Gazette* (Chillicothe, OH), July 18, 1844, issue 15, col. D. "Locofoco" had originally been used to describe a small, radical group of New York Democrats in the 1830s, but the Whigs quickly applied the derisive term against the entire opposition party. In the months before the election, Whig newspapers would print long lists of names of those who had purportedly abandoned Van Buren and the Democrats for Clay. Under the heading "Renunciations of Locofocoism," a Vermont newspaper listed several prominent men; the first on the list was "Mr. McKinley, of Alabama, Judge of U.S. Supreme Court." See *Vermont Watchman and State Journal* (Montpelier), July 26, 1844, issue 47, col. A.

18. Swisher, *The Taney Period*, 277.

19. The most significant case of the term was *Louisville, Cincinnati and Charleston Railroad v. Letson*, 43 U.S. 497 (1844). Oral arguments had been held the previous year

in McKinley's absence and he did not participate in the Court's decision. In fact, only five justices were present to rule that corporations could be included within the meaning of the word "citizen" in diversity-of-state citizenship cases arising under Article III of the Constitution. This and similar rulings opened the floodgate for corporate litigation in the federal courts.

20. 43 U.S. 127, at 133 (1844).

21. Quoted in Warren, *The Supreme Court in United States History*, 2:128–29.

22. 43 U.S. 127, at 197.

23. Dana, *The Journal*, 256–57.

24. John C. Calhoun to Francis Wharton, May 19, 1844, *The Papers of John C. Calhoun,* ed. Clyde N. Wilson (Columbia: University of South Carolina Press, 1988), 18:557.

25. Swisher, *The Taney Period*, 279.

26. Chandler, *The Law Reporter*, 6:472.

27. Story, *Life and Letters of Joseph Story*, 2:509.

28. *Ex Parte Christy*, 44 U.S. 292 (1845).

29. Ibid., at 325.

30. Ibid., at 312.

31. Story, *Life and Letters of Joseph Story*, 2:509.

32. 44 U.S. 212 (1845).

33. Ibid., at 221.

34. Ibid., at 222.

35. 41 U.S. 367 (1842).

36. 44 U.S. 212, at 235.

37. Mark A. Graber, "Resolving Political Questions into Judicial Questions: Tocqueville's Thesis Revisited," *Constitutional Commentary* 21 (2004): 529.

38. Martin Siegel, *The Taney Court: 1836–1864* (Millwood, NY: Associated Faculty Press, 1987), 151.

39. *Marbury v. Madison*, 5 U.S. 137 (1803); *Dred Scott v. Sandford*, 60 U.S. 393 (1857).

40. 44 U.S. 212, at 233.

41. Mark A. Graber, "Naked Land Transfers and American Constitutional Development," *Vanderbilt Law Review* 53 (January 2000): 103.

42. *U.S. v. William Picher* (unreported decision), May 1845.

43. 1 Stat. 627, 668 (1799).

44. *New York Herald*, May 27, 1845, issue 144, col. E.

45. William Wood, *Autobiography*, vol. 2 (New York: J. S. Babcock, 1895), 53.

46. Ibid., emphasis in original.

47. Ibid., 54.

48. See Frankfurter and Landis, *The Business of the Supreme Court*, 50n165, 52n178.

49. *Congressional Globe*, 29th Cong., 1st Sess., 261.

50. "Judge McKinley continues sick," wrote a correspondent with the *New York Tribune*. Quoted in *Daily Atlas*, February 27, 1846, issue 206, col. G.

51. 37 U.S. 657 (1838).

52. 45 U.S. 591 (1846).

53. The Court upheld Missouri's claim in *Missouri v. Iowa*, 48 U.S. 660 (1849).

54. Quoted in Warren, *The Supreme Court in United States History*, 2:151.

55. *Engrossed Minutes of the Supreme Court of the United States*. Among the important cases McKinley missed during this time were *Jones v. Van Zandt* (46 U.S. 215 [1847]), which heightened tensions over slavery when the eight justices present unanimously upheld the Federal Fugitive Slave Act of 1793, and the *License Cases* where the Court upheld state commercial regulations (46 U.S. 504 [1847]).

56. McKinley's return to circuit is noted in the *Tri-Weekly Flag and Advertiser* (Montgomery, AL), April 20, 1847, issue 43, col. E.

57. Lewis, *Without Fear or Favor*, 314. Justice Daniel was also absent when that term began. See *North American and United States Gazette* (Philadelphia), December 8, 1847, issue 16, p. 185, col. C.

58. Daniel Webster to Franklin Haven, February 25, 1847, Webster, *Papers of Daniel Webster*, 6:211. The *Lexington* case was the shortened name for *New Jersey Steam Navigation Company v. Merchants Bank*, 47 U.S. 344 (1848), whose oral arguments occupied over two weeks during the 1846 and 1847 terms. Woodbury did indeed side with the majority for the bank, rendering McKinley's presence and opinion on the matter moot.

59. *Daily Atlas*, February 23, 1848, issue 202, col. C. The paper was frustrated by the two-term absence of McKinley and its impact on the resolution of the *Luther v. Borden* (48 U.S. 1 [1848]) case, which was on the Court's docket in 1847. The case would be argued again the following term, but only six justices participated in the decision, as the others—including McKinley—had not attended any of the oral arguments.

60. See Senator William Allen's comments in the *Congressional Globe*, 30th Cong., 1st Sess., appendix 584.

61. Ibid., 351.

62. Ibid., 352.

63. *Congressional Globe*, 30th Cong., 1st Sess., 640.

64. *Congressional Globe*, 30th Cong., 1st Sess., appendix 588.

65. *Congressional Globe*, 33rd Cong., 2nd Sess., 213.

66. *Arkansas State Democrat* (Little Rock), June 2, 1848, issue 3, col. E.

67. Ibid., June 9, 1848, issue 4, col. D.

68. 48 U.S. 283 (1849). These cases were formally known as *Smith v. Turner* and *Norris v. City of Boston*.

69. Quoted in Warren, *The Supreme Court in United States History*, 2:178.

70. Ibid., 168–71.

71. Quoted in Charles Fairman, "The Retirement of Federal Judges," *Harvard Law Review* 51, no. 3 (January 1938): 407.

72. *Engrossed Minutes of the Supreme Court of the United States*.

73. Daniel Webster to Edward Curtis, January 3, 1849, *Papers of Daniel Webster*, 6:310.

74. Quoted in Warren, *The Supreme Court in United States History*, 2:178–79.

75. Ibid. Given the five seriatim opinions, the bewildered court reporter could only declare in the syllabus to the case, "<u>Inasmuch as there was no opinion of the court, as a court,</u> the reporter refers the reader to the opinions of the judges for an explanation of the statutes and the points in which they conflicted with the Constitution and laws of the United States" (emphasis added). See *Smith v. Turner* and *Norris v. City of Boston*, 48 U.S. 281 (1849).

76. *Daily Atlas*, February 12, 1849, issue 190, col. F. The paper noted that McKinley did make some remarks from the bench the following day just before the remaining dissents were read.

77. Quoted in Warren, *The Supreme Court in United States History*, 2:179.

78. 48 U.S. 283, at 453 (1849).

79. Ibid., at 444.

80. Ibid., at 445, emphasis added.

81. Ibid.

82. *Daily Atlas*, February 12, 1849, issue 190, col. F. Shortly after their decision in the *Passenger Cases*, the members of the Court were briefly profiled in a newspaper report that was circulated throughout the country. Only Justices McLean, Woodbury, and Grier earned favorable treatment from the writer, who described the Court and its members while observing a session. Of McKinley, the writer noted that he possessed a "tall, but not striking appearance" and compared him to John Catron as one who was "probably not of the most eminent attainments, though he might rank among the 'respectable.'" *Cleveland Daily Herald*, February 17, 1849, issue 40, col. C.

83. *Natchez (MS) Semi-Weekly Courier*, March 27, 1849, issue 26, col. B.

84. *Bangor (ME) Daily Whig and Courier*, May 8, 1849, issue 263, col. C. Long used in Europe for a variety of ailments, hydrotherapy had become a popular and lucrative treatment in America by the mid-1840s.

85. See *North American and United States Gazette*, July 4, 1849, issue 16, p. 665 col. C; *Daily National Intelligencer*, July 16, 1849, issue 11, p. 356, col. D; and *Natchez (MS) Semi-Weekly Courier*, July 3, 1849, issue 54, col. E.

86. Swisher notes a curious conflict of interest in the case: Judge Monroe's brother was lead counsel for Samuel Morse in the dispute. See *The Taney Period*, 490.

87. 9 Stat. 403 (1849).

88. *Natchez (MS) Semi-Weekly Courier*, July 3, 1849, issue 54, col. E.

89. Ibid.

90. Ibid., emphasis in original. The dispute erupted in federal courts in several other states as well including Massachusetts, New York, Ohio, and Pennsylvania. The Supreme Court settled the issue five years later, granting Morse an injunction against O'Reilly's devices because they infringed upon the former's patent. However, the Court also stated that Morse could neither lay claim to nor patent the force of electromagnetism. See *O'Reilly v. Morse*, 56 U.S. 62 (1854).

91. 49 U.S. iii (1850).

92. *North American and United States Gazette*, January 11, 1850, issue 16, p. 826, col. F.

93. In an April 1841 letter to Justice Story, B. W. Godfrey of New Orleans wrote, "Judge McKinley has been listening, for the last few days, to arguments of counsel in the case of Mrs. Gaines, and the distinguished lawyers engaged on both sides of the question, have made the case the most interesting of any before the Court." Godfrey to Story, April 25, 1841, Joseph Story Papers.

94. The most comprehensive treatment of Gaines's life and legal efforts is Alexander's *Notorious Woman*.

95. *Patterson v. Gaines*, 47 U.S. 550 (1848). Gaines knew the importance of cultivating relationships with the people who would ultimately determine the fate of her claim. With her second husband, General Edmund Pendleton Gaines—a heroic figure of both the War of 1812 and several Indian wars—she entertained the justices at their home in Washington. She related one such incident in January 1843 that occurred while the Court was sitting: "Several of the Judges of the Supreme Court of the U.S. have called. I playfully observed to them that I fully expected the Decision upon the merits of my case would be given this term, what they had so promised last winter. In the same tone they replied, 'Did we indeed? Well, well, we shall certainly do something about it.'" Myra Clark Gaines to General Joshua Whitney, January 14, 1843, Joshua Whitney Papers, Broome County Historical Society, Binghamton, NY.

96. 47 U.S. 550, at 602–3.

97. *North American and United States Gazette,* January 11, 1850, issue 16, p. 826, col. F.

98. Alexander Walker, *The Great Gaines Case* (New Orleans: Office of the Daily Delta, 1850), 4.

99. Ibid., 59.

100. Ibid., 58.

101. Ibid., 41.

102. Ibid., 73.

103. Ibid.

104. *North American and United States Gazette,* March 4, 1850, issue 16, p. 870, col. B.

105. *The Iowa,* 54 U.S. 283 (1851), Transcript of Record, *Supreme Court Records and Briefs, 1832–1978,* 262, Gale, Cengage Learning, Robert Crown Law Library, Stanford Law School.

106. Samuel Taylor, *Memoir of Roger Brooke Taney, LLD* (Baltimore: John Murphy and Company, 1872), 471.

107. *Milwaukee Daily Sentinel and Gazette,* November 14, 1850, issue 494, col. A.

108. Ibid.

109. *Emancipator and Republican,* December 12, 1850, issue 33, p. 1.

110. *New Hampshire Statesman,* December 27, 1850, issue 1544, col. E.

111. 51 U.S. 82 (1850).

112. Ibid., at 93–94.

113. 60 U.S. 393 (1857).

114. *New York Daily Times,* December 4, 1851, p. 2. Only Taney, McLean, Catron, Nelson, and Curtis were present.

115. Curtis, *A Memoir,* 165.

116. *New York Daily Times,* February 5, 1852, p. 3. In May 1852 Webster was seriously hurt in a carriage accident, and though he largely recovered from his injuries, his health began to decline sharply. He died the following October.

117. *Gaines v. Relf,* 53 U.S. 472 (1852).

118. Ibid., 539. The following day, again with McKinley absent, the Court announced its decision in one of the most significant commerce clause cases of the era: *Cooley v. Board of Wardens of the Port of Philadelphia,* 53 U.S. 299 (1852).

119. *Daily Scioto Gazette,* April 14, 1852, issue 115, col. A.

120. *Engrossed Minutes of the Supreme Court of the United States.*

121. *New York Daily Times,* April 8, 1852, p. 3.

Chapter 9

Epigraph. 55 U.S. iii, at v (1852).

1. Calendar of Early Jefferson County Kentucky Wills, box 2, no. 4, p. 218, Filson Historical Society, Louisville, KY.

2. Dr. Robert Sahr of Oregon State University has created a conversion chart that estimates the approximate value of the U.S. dollar over time. See http://oregonstate .edu/cla/polisci/sites/default/files/faculty-research/sahr/inflation-conversion/pdf /value-in-dollars.pdf (accessed August 25, 2010).

3. Calendar of Early Jefferson County Kentucky Wills, box 2, no. 4, p. 220.

4. John McKinley Churchill died February 24, 1852, and John McKinley died May 17, 1852. Both have headstones beside their grandfather's in Louisville's Cave Hill Cemetery, but cemetery records now list John McKinley Churchill's as a "false" grave.

5. Siegel, *The Taney Court,* 273.

6. McKinley's grave can be found in Section I, Lot 71, Part Range, Grave 1A of Louisville's Cave Hill Cemetery. His second wife, Elizabeth, is interred beside him and the graves of his daughter, son-in-law, and grandsons sit immediately behind his monument. Each is covered with a well-tended patch of ivy.

7. *Baltimore Sun,* July 21, 1852, vol. 31, no. 56, p. 2.

8. *Adams Sentinel and General Advertiser* (Gettysburg, PA), July 26, 1852, vol. 52, no. 38, p. 4.

9. The Supreme Court continues this practice to this day with the chief justice and other officers of the Court offering condolences and memorializing on behalf of a recently departed justice.

10. In addition to the summer passing of Clay and McKinley, Webster died on October 24, 1852, and Sergeant died a month later on November 23, 1852. The Court's memorials were printed at the beginning of the U.S. Reports (55 U.S. iii–v), and a copy was made available for reprinting in local newspapers. See *Daily National Intelligencer,* December 11, 1852, issue 12, p. 418, col. C.

11. An additional personal connection between the two was made when Crittenden married his third wife, Elizabeth Moss Wilcox, in 1853. His new stepdaughter, Mary, was already married to Justice McKinley's son, Andrew.

12. 55 U.S. iii (1852).

13. Senator Solomon Downs of Louisiana and John Archibald Campbell of Alabama were the group's chairman and secretary, respectively, and had been commissioned with presenting the resolutions to the attorney general for the memorial service.

14. 55 U.S. iii, at iv–v.

15. One of his biographers notes that the congenial relationship between the chief justice and the other justices, including McKinley, was fostered by the meals they took together in their boardinghouse and the sitting room that they shared. See Lewis, *Without Fear or Favor*, 291.

16. 55 U.S. iii, at v (1852).

17. More than two decades after his death, McKinley was remembered by William B. Wood, an Alabama circuit judge who had resided in Florence for most of his life. Forty years younger than McKinley, Wood had no professional association with the justice as he was not even admitted to the Florence bar until after the latter had moved to Louisville. It is not clear if he knew him personally at all. Still, in his July 4, 1876, address to the citizens of Florence, Wood stated, "The one who attained the highest honors of any one citizen, was John McKinley. He was a man of talent and indomitable will. He would bear no contradiction; was very imperious, and often so overbearing as to make bitter enemies. It is astonishing how he ever succeeded as a politician. Only by the force of ability and strong partisanship can his success be accounted for. He was an ardent supporter of General Jackson, and aided materially in his elevation to the Presidency. He was elected to the U.S. Senate, and whilst senator, was rewarded for his zeal in the support of Gen. Jackson with the appointment of Judge of the Supreme [C]ourt of the United States." "Historical Address of Hon. Wm. B. Wood, July 4, 1876," *Florence (AL) Gazette* (July–September 1876, p. 3), http://www.rootsweb.ancestry.com/~allauder/history-wood-1876-3.htm (accessed November 2, 2009).

18. 99 U.S. 496 (1878).

19. *Sherry v. McKinley*, 99 U.S. 496 (1878), Transcript of Record, *U.S. Supreme Court Records and Briefs, 1832–1978*, 2–3.

20. See also *De Treville v. Smalls*, 98 U.S. 517 (1878), and *Keely v. Sanders*, 99 U.S. 441 (1878).

21. *Sherry v. McKinley*, *U.S. Supreme Court Records and Briefs, 1832–1978*, 18.

22. *Morning Oregonian* (Portland), February 28, 1897, issue 9, p. 4, col. E.

23. John Gorley Bunker, *Liberty Ships: The Ugly Ducklings of World War II* (Annapolis, MD: Naval Institute Press, 1972), 246.

24. This effort to honor McKinley was initiated in 1996 by William E. Smith Jr., former president of the McKinley Young Lawyers of the Shoals (also named in honor of the justice), and several northern Alabama historical societies.

25. Public Law 105-299. The renamed building was officially dedicated on May 4, 1999. Two years later, as part of its statewide legal history program, the Alabama State Bar erected an Alabama Legal Milestone Marker on the site to honor McKinley. That marker reads: "Named for Alabama's first United States Supreme Court Justice, John McKinley made his home in Florence, Alabama, from 1821 to 1842. Born May 1, 1780, in Culpepper County, Virginia, he died July 19, 1852, and is buried in Louisville, Kentucky. McKinley was an early settler of Huntsville, Alabama, and resided in the Howard Weeden Home. As a member of the Cypress Land Company, he was one of the seven founders of Florence in 1818. McKinley helped establish one of Florence's first schools and its first church, First Presbyterian Church. McKinley was an early benefactor of public education in Alabama by donating land for the current Athens States University and serving on the original Board of Trustees for the University of Alabama. As a local lawyer, he gained regional status as an Alabama legislator and national status in both the U.S. House and Senate. His work in Congress on the first Florence Canal establishes him as the 'Spiritual Father of the TVA.' While a resident of Florence in 1838, McKinley was sworn in as the 23rd Associate Justice of the United States Supreme Court where he served until his death." See http://www .hmdb.org/marker.asp?marker=28930 (accessed April 22, 2009).

26. See http://www.florenceal.org/2008_Inductees_Walk_of_Honor.pdf (accessed April 22, 2009). McKinley's plaque reads: "First serving as a member of the U.S. Senate (1826–30), John McKinley was appointed to the U.S. Supreme Court by President Van Buren, becoming the first justice from Alabama."

27. Gatell, "John McKinley," 777.

28. The Marshall Court did so through such landmark rulings as *Marbury v. Madison*, 5 U.S. 137 (1803); *Martin v. Hunter's Lessee*, 14 U.S. 304 (1816); *McCulloch v. Maryland*, 17 U.S. 316 (1819); *Gibbons v. Ogden*, 22 U.S. 1 (1824); and *Martin v. Mott*, 25 U.S. 19 (1827).

29. John R. Schmidhauser, *The Supreme Court as Final Arbiter in Federal-State Relations, 1789–1957* (Chapel Hill: University of North Carolina Press, 1958), 50.

30. Ibid., 51.

31. The seven justices and the year they resigned are as follows: Justice Thomas Johnson (1793), Chief Justice John Jay (1795), Justice John Blair (1796), Chief Justice Oliver Ellsworth (1800), Justice John Rutledge (1800), Justice Alfred Moore (1804), and Justice Gabriel Duval (1835). See Abraham, *The Judicial Process*, 414–15.

32. Dana, *The Journal*, 256–57.

Bibliography

Cases

Adams v. Ward, 1 Stew. 42 (Ala. 1827).

Bank of Augusta v. Earle, 38 U.S. 519 (1839).

Beaston v. Farmers' Bank, 37 U.S. 102 (1838).

Bell and Wife v. Hogan, 1 Stew. 536 (Ala. 1828).

Bennett v. Black, 1 Stew. 494 (Ala. 1828).

Cooley v. Board of Wardens of the Port of Philadelphia, 53 U.S. 299 (1852).

De Treville v. Smalls, 98 U.S. 517 (1878).

Dred Scott v. Sandford, 60 U.S. 393 (1857).

Erie Railroad Co. v. Tompkins, 304 U.S. 64 (1938).

Ex Parte Christy, 44 U.S. 292 (1845).

Ex Parte Hennen, 38 U.S. 230 (1839).

Fleitas v. Richardson, 147 U.S. 538 (1893).

Gaines v. Relf, 53 U.S. 472 (1852).

Gibbons v. Ogden, 19 U.S. 448 (1821).

Gibbons v. Ogden, 22 U.S. 1 (1824).

Groves v. Slaughter, 40 U.S. 449 (1841).

Hogatt v. Bingaman, 8 Miss. 565 (1843).

Iowa, the, 54 U.S. 283 (1851).

Jones v. Van Zandt, 46 U.S. 215 (1847).

Jones v. Watkins, 1 Stew. 81 (Ala. 1827).

Keely v. Sanders, 99 U.S. 441 (1878).

Kendall v. United States ex rel. Stokes, 37 U.S. 524 (1838).

Lessee of Pollard v. Hagan, 44 U.S. 212 (1845).

License Cases, 46 U.S. 504 (1847).

Louisville, Cincinnati and Charleston Railroad v. Letson, 43 U.S. 497 (1844).

The Louisville v. Strout, 15 F. Cas. 987 (1839).

Luther v. Borden, 48 U.S. 1 (1848).

Marbury v. Madison, 5 U.S. 137 (1803).

Martin v. Hunter's Lessee, 14 U.S. 304 (1816).

Martin v. Lessee of Waddell, 41 U.S. 367 (1842).

Martin v. Mott, 25 U.S. 19 (1827).

McCulloch v. Maryland, 17 U.S. 316 (1819).

McKinley v. Irvine, 13 Ala. 681 (1848).

Missouri v. Iowa, 48 U.S. 660 (1849).

M'Kinney v. Carroll, 37 U.S. 66 (1838).

New Jersey Steam Navigation Company v. Merchants Bank, 47 U.S. 344 (1848).

Olive v. O'Riley, Minor 410 (Ala. 1826).

O'Reilly v. Morse, 56 U.S. 62 (1854).

Patterson v. Gaines, 47 U.S. 550 (1848).

Pope and Hickman v. John Nance and Co., Minor 299 (Ala. 1824).

Rhode Island v. Massachusetts, 37 U.S. 657 (1838).

Rhode Island v. Massachusetts, 45 U.S. 591 (1846).

Sherry v. McKinley, 99 U.S. 496 (1878).

Smith v. Turner and *Norris v. City of Boston*, 48 U.S. 283 (1849).

Stamps v. Brown, 2 Miss. 526 (1832).

Standefer v. Chisholm, 1 Stew. & P. 449 (Ala. 1832).

Strader v. Graham, 51 U.S. 82 (1850).

Strout v. Foster, 42 U.S. 89 (1843).

Sturges v. Crowninshield, 17 U.S. 122 (1819).

Swift v. Tyson, 41 U.S. 1 (1842).

Thomas Logwood v. President, Directors, Etc. of the Planters' and Merchants' Bank of Huntsville, Minor 23 (Ala. 1820).

Thompson v. Jones, 1 Stew. 556 (Ala. 1828).

Union Bank of Tennessee v. Benham, 23 Ala. 143 (1853).

U.S. v. Libellants of Schooner Amistad, 40 U.S. 518 (1841).

U.S. v. Price (unreported decision, 9th Circuit), (1838).

U.S. v. William Picher (unreported decision, 5th Circuit), May 1845.

Vidal et al. v. Philadelphia, 43 U.S. 127 (1844).

White v. Turk, 37 U.S. 238 (1838).

The Woodrop Sims, High Court of Admiralty, 2 Dods. Adm 83 (1815).

Primary and Secondary Sources

Abernethy, Thomas P. *The Formative Period in Alabama*. Montgomery, AL: Brown Printing Company, 1922.

———. *From Frontier to Plantation in Tennessee: A Study in Frontier Democracy*. Tuscaloosa: The University of Alabama Press, 1967.

———. *The South in the New Nation, 1789–1819*. Baton Rouge: Louisiana State University Press, 1976.

Abraham, Henry J. *The Judicial Process*. 7th ed. New York: Oxford University Press, 1998.

———. *The Judiciary: The Supreme Court in the Governmental Process.* 10th ed. New York: New York University Press, 1996.

———. *Justices and Presidents: A Political History of Appointments to the Supreme Court.* 3rd ed. New York: Oxford University Press, 1992.

Adams, John Quincy. *Memoirs of John Quincy Adams.* Ed. Charles Francis Adams. 11 vols. Philadelphia: J. B. Lippincott and Company, 1876. Reprint, New York: AMS Press, 1970.

Alexander, Elizabeth Urban. *Notorious Woman: The Celebrated Case of Myra Clark Gaines.* Baton Rouge: Louisiana State University Press, 2001.

Alexander, Holmes. *American Talleyrand: The Career and Contemporaries of Martin Van Buren, Eighth President.* New York: Russell and Russell, 1968.

Allgor, Catherine. *Parlor Politics.* Charlottesville: University Press of Virginia, 2000.

"Armistead Family." *William and Mary College Quarterly Historical Magazine* 7, no. 1 (July 1898): 17–24.

Atkinson, David N. *Leaving the Bench: Supreme Court Justices at the End.* Lawrence: University Press of Kansas, 1999.

Bailey, Hugh C. *John Williams Walker: A Study in the Political, Social and Cultural Life of the Old Southwest.* Tuscaloosa: The University of Alabama Press, 1964.

Baldwin, Joseph G. *The Flush Times of Alabama and Mississippi: A Series of Sketches.* 1853. Reprint, Gloucester, MA: Peter Smith, 1974.

Baxter, Maurice G. *Daniel Webster and the Supreme Court.* Amherst: University of Massachusetts Press, 1966.

Beckner, Lucien. "History of the County Court of Lincoln County, VA." *Register of the Kentucky State Historical Society* 20 (January 1922): 170–90.

Bench and Bar of St. Louis, Kansas City, Jefferson City, and Other Missouri Cities. Chicago: American Biographical Publishing Company, 1884.

Betts, Edward C. *Early History of Huntsville, Alabama, 1804–1870.* Montgomery, AL: Brown Printing Company, 1916.

Beveridge, Albert J. *The Life of John Marshall.* 4 vols. Boston: Houghton Mifflin, 1916–19.

Birney, William. *James G. Birney and His Times.* New York: D. Appleton and Company, 1890.

Biskupic, Joan, and Elder Witt. *The Supreme Court and the Powers of the American Government.* Washington, DC: Congressional Quarterly, 1997.

Blaustein, Albert P., and Roy M. Mersky. *The First One Hundred Justices.* Hamden, CT: Archon Books, 1978.

Brenner, Saul. "The Chief Justices' Self Assignment of Majority Opinions in Salient Cases." *Social Science Journal* 30 (1993): 143–50.

Brewer, Willis. *Alabama: Her History, Resources, War Record, and Public Men from 1540 to 1872.* Montgomery, AL: Barrett and Brown, 1872. Reprint, Tuscaloosa, AL: Willo Publishing Company, 1964.

Bunker, John Gorley. *Liberty Ships: The Ugly Ducklings of World War II.* Annapolis, MD: Naval Institute Press, 1972.

Busey, Samuel C. *Pictures of the City of Washington in the Past.* Washington, DC: W. Ballantyne and Sons, 1898.

Butler, William Allen. *A Retrospect of Forty Years, 1825–1865.* New York: Charles Scribner's Sons, 1911.

Calhoun, John C. *The Papers of John C. Calhoun.* Ed. Robert L. Meriwhether, William Hemphill, and Clyde N. Wilson. 28 vols. Columbia: University of South Carolina Press, 1959.

Campbell, Tom W. *Four Score Forgotten Men.* Little Rock: Pioneer Publishing Company, 1950.

Carson, Hampton L. *The History of the Supreme Court of the United States.* Philadelphia: P. W. Zeigler and Company, 1902.

Casper, Gerhard, and Richard A. Posner. *The Workload of the Supreme Court.* Chicago: American Bar Association, 1976.

Chandler, Peleg Whitman, ed. *The Law Reporter.* Boston: Weeks, Jordan, and Company, 1838–44.

Chappell, Gordon T. "Some Patterns of Land Speculation in the Old Southwest." *Journal of Southern History* 15 (November 1949): 463–77.

Clark, Thomas D., and John D. W. Guice. *Frontiers in Conflict: The Old Southwest, 1795–1830.* Albuquerque: University of New Mexico Press, 1989.

Clay, Henry. *The Papers of Henry Clay.* Ed. James F. Hopkins, Mary W. M. Hargreaves, et al. 11 vols. Lexington: University Press of Kentucky, 1959–92.

Cobb, Aleathea Thompson. *Presbyterian Women of the Synod of Alabama.* Mobile, AL: privately published, 1935.

Coleman, J. Winston, Jr. *Stage-Coach Days in the Bluegrass.* Louisville: The Standard Press, 1936.

Collins, Lewis. *Historical Sketches of Kentucky.* Cincinnati: J. A. and U. P. James, 1848. Reprint, New York: Arno Press, 1971.

Conkwright, Bessie Taul. "A Sketch of the Life and Times of General Benjamin Logan." *Register of the Kentucky State Historical Society* 14 (January 1916): 21–35.

Cook, Bettie Cummings, comp. *Kentucky Federal Court Records, District and Sixth Circuit Order Books, 1804–1815.* Vol. 2. Evansville, IN: Cook Publications, 1995.

Cook, Michael L., ed. *Lincoln County Kentucky Records.* Vol. 2. Evansville, IN: Cook Publications, 1988.

Cook, Michael L., and Bettie A. Cook, eds. *Kentucky Court of Appeals Deed Books.* Vols. 2 and 4. Evansville, IN: Cook Publications, 1985.

Cresap, Bernarr. "History of Lauderdale County, Historical Address." *Journal of Muscle Shoals History* 5 (1977): 61–85.

Currie, David P. "The Constitution in the Supreme Court: Article IV and Federal Powers, 1836–1864." *Duke Law Journal* 4 (September 1983): 695–747.

———. "Miss Otis Regrets." *Green Bag* 7 (Summer 2004): 374–85.

———. "The Most Insignificant Justice: A Preliminary Inquiry." *University of Chicago Law Review* 50 (1983): 466–80.

Curtis, Benjamin R., Jr. *A Memoir of Benjamin Robbins Curtis*. 2 vols. Boston: Little, Brown, and Company, 1879.

Dana, Richard Henry. *The Journal*. Ed. Robert F. Lucid. Cambridge, MA: Belknap Press of Harvard University Press, 1968.

Davis, Jefferson. *Jefferson Davis Constitutionalist: His Letters, Papers, and Speeches*. Ed. Dunbar Rowland. 10 vols. Jackson: Mississippi Department of Archives and History, 1923.

Dinkin, Robert J. *Campaigning in America: A History of Election Practices*. New York: Greenwood Press, 1989.

Dollar, John M. "John McKinley: Enigmatic Trimmer." Master's thesis, Samford University, 1981.

Domnarski, William. *In the Opinion of the Court*. Urbana: University of Illinois Press, 1996.

Dunlop, Alexander Graham. *The New World Journal of Alexander Graham Dunlop, 1845*. Ed. David Sinclair and Germaine Warkentin. Toronto: Dundurn Press, 1976.

Dunne, Gerald T. *Justice Joseph Story and the Rise of the Supreme Court*. New York: Simon and Schuster, 1970.

Dupre, Daniel. "Ambivalent Capitalists on the Cotton Frontier: Settlement and Development in the Tennessee Valley of Alabama." *Journal of Southern History* 56 (May 1990): 215–40.

———. "Barbecues and Pledges: Electioneering and the Rise of Democratic Politics in Antebellum Alabama." *Journal of Southern History* 60 (August 1994): 479–512.

———. *Transforming the Cotton Frontier: Madison County, Alabama, 1800–1840*. Baton Rouge: Louisiana State University Press, 1997.

Easterbrook, Frank H. "The Most Insignificant Justice: Further Evidence." *University of Chicago Law Review* 50 (1983): 481–503.

Ellet, E. F. *The Court Circles of the Republic*. Hartford, CT: Hartford Publishing Company, 1869.

Epstein, Lee, Jeffrey A. Segal, Harold J. Spaeth, and Thomas A. Walker. *The Supreme Court Compendium: Data, Decisions, and Developments*. Washington, DC: Congressional Quarterly, 1994.

Fairman, Charles. "The Retirement of Federal Judges." *Harvard Law Review* 51, no. 3 (January 1938): 397–443.

Farnam, Henry W. *Chapters in the History of Social Legislation in the United States to 1860*. Baltimore, MD: Waverly Press, 1938. Reprint, Union, NJ: Lawbook Exchange, 2000.

Feibelman, Herbert U. "John McKinley of Alabama—Legislator, U.S. Congressman, Senator, Supreme Court Justice." *Alabama Lawyer* 22 (October 1961): 422–26.

Fenner, Charles Payne. "The Jurisprudence of the Supreme Court of Louisiana." *Louisiana Historical Quarterly* 4 (1921): 71–80.

Finkelman, Paul. "John McLean: Moderate Abolitionist and Supreme Court Politician." *Vanderbilt Law Review* 62 (March 2009): 519–65.

Foote, Henry S. *The Bench and Bar of the South and Southwest.* St. Louis: Soule, Thomas, and Wentworth, 1876.

Frank, John P. *Justice Daniel Dissenting.* Cambridge, MA: Harvard University Press, 1964.

Frankfurter, Felix, and James M. Landis. *The Business of the Supreme Court: A Study in the Federal Judicial System.* New York: MacMillan, 1927.

Frederick, David C. *Supreme Court and Appellate Advocacy.* St. Paul, MN: Thompson West, 2003.

Freyer, Tony Allan. *Forums of Order: The Federal Courts and Business in American History.* Greenwich, CT: JAI Press, 1979.

Freyer, Tony A., Paul M. Pruitt, Timothy W. Dixon, and Howard P. Walthall. "Alabama's Supreme Court and Legal Institutions: A History." Unpublished manuscript, n.d.

Gandrud, Pauline Jones. *Alabama Records.* 245 vols. Easley, SC: Southern Historical Press, 1981.

———. *Marriage, Death, and Legal Notices from Early Alabama Newspapers, 1819–1893.* Easley, SC: Southern Historical Press, 1981.

Gatell, Frank Otto. "John McKinley." In *The Justices of the United States Supreme Court, 1789–1969: Their Lives and Major Opinions,* ed. Leon Friedman and Fred L. Israel. 1:769–92. New York: Chelsea House, 1969.

"Genealogical Queries." *William and Mary Quarterly,* 2nd ser., 10, no. 1 (January 1930): 87–96.

Graber, Mark A. "The Jacksonian Makings of the Taney Court." http://digitalcommons .law.umaryland.edu/cgi/viewcontent.cgi?article=1004&context=fac_pubs (accessed September 9, 2010).

———. "Naked Land Transfers and American Constitutional Development." *Vanderbilt Law Review* 53 (January 2000): 73–121.

———. "The New Fiction: *Dred Scott* and the Language of Judicial Authority." *Chicago-Kent Law Review* 82, no. 1 (2007): 177–208.

———. "Resolving Political Questions into Judicial Questions: Tocqueville's Thesis Revisited." *Constitutional Commentary* 21 (2004): 485–545.

Green, Thomas Marshall. *Historic Families of Kentucky.* Cincinnati: Robert Clarke and Company, 1889.

Greenberg, Kenneth S. *Honor and Slavery.* Princeton: Princeton University Press, 1996.

Griffin, Richard W. "Athens Academy and College: An Experiment in Women's Education in Alabama, 1822–1873." *Alabama Historical Quarterly* 20 (Spring 1958): 7–26.

Hall, Kermit, ed. *The Oxford Companion to the Supreme Court of the United States.* New York: Oxford University Press, 1992.

Hall, Timothy L. *Supreme Court Justices: A Biographical Dictionary.* New York: Facts on File, 2001.

Hamilton, Thomas. *Men and Manners in America*. Vol. 2. Edinburgh: William Blackwood, 1833. Reprint, New York: Augustus M. Kelley Publishers, 1968.

Hay, Robert Pettus. "A Jubilee for Freemen: The Fourth of July in Frontier Kentucky, 1788–1816." *Register of the Kentucky Historical Society* 64 (July 1966): 169–95.

Hicks, Jimmie. "Associate Justice John McKinley: A Sketch." *Alabama Review* 28 (July 1965): 227–33.

Hockensmith, Charles D. *The Millstone Quarries of Powell County*. Jefferson, NC: McFarland and Company, 2009.

Hofstadter, Richard. *The Idea of a Party System: The Rise of Legitimate Opposition in the United States, 1780–1840*. Berkeley: University of California Press, 1969.

Hood, Laura C., Sara M. Hood, Hugh M. Hood, and Jack B. Hood. *Alabama Historical Association Markers*. 2nd ed. Bloomington, IL: AuthorHouse Publishing, 2006.

Hoyt, William D., Jr. "Justice Daniel in Arkansas, 1851 and 1853." *Arkansas Historical Quarterly* 1 (June 1942): 158–62.

Huebner, Timothy S. *The Taney Court: Justices, Rulings, and Legacy*. Santa Barbara, CA: ABC-CLIO, 2003.

Hunter, Louis C. *Steamboats on the Western Rivers: An Economic and Technological History*. New York: Octagon Books, 1969.

Jack, Theodore Henley. "Sectionalism and Party Politics in Alabama, 1819–1842." Ph.D. diss., University of Chicago, 1919.

Jackson, Andrew. *Correspondence of Andrew Jackson*. Ed. John Spencer Bassett. 7 vols. Washington, DC: Carnegie Institute of Washington, 1926–35.

———. *The Papers of Andrew Jackson*. Ed. Harold Moser and Daniel Feller. 7 vols. to date. Knoxville: University of Tennessee Press, 1980.

James, Marquis. *The Life of Andrew Jackson*. New York: Bobbs-Merrill, 1938.

Johnson, Dorothy Scott, comp. *Madison County Deed Books, 1810–1819*. Huntsville, AL: Johnson Historical Publications, 1976.

Kaye, Anthony E. *Joining Places: Slave Neighborhoods in the Old South*. Chapel Hill: University of North Carolina Press, 2007.

Keating, John McLeod. *A History of the Yellow Fever Epidemic of 1878*. Memphis, TN: Howard Association, 1879.

Kelso, Doris (Mrs. Thurman M.). *A History of the First Presbyterian Church, Florence, Alabama*. Florence, AL: privately published, 1968.

Kennon, Donald R., and Rebecca M. Rogers. *The Committee on Ways and Means: A Bicentennial History, 1789–1989, House Document 100-244*. Washington, DC: GPO, 1989.

Kerr, Judge Charles, ed. *History of Kentucky*. Vol. 1. New York: American Historical Society, 1922.

Lanman, Charles. *Bohn's Handbook of Washington*. Baltimore: Murphy and Company, 1852.

Levin, H., ed. *The Lawyers and Lawmakers of Kentucky.* Chicago: Lewis Publishing Company, 1897.

Lewis, Walker. *Without Fear or Favor: A Biography of Chief Justice Roger Brooke Taney.* Boston: Houghton Mifflin, 1965.

Lomask, Milton. *Aaron Burr: The Conspiracy and Years of Exile, 1805–1836.* New York: Farrar, Straus, and Giroux, 1982.

MacKinnon, Ann Pennington, Peggy Selby Galloway, and Michael C. Watson, comps. *Lincoln County, Virginia/Kentucky Deed Abstracts, 1781–1795.* Harrodsburg, KY: MGW Publications, 1998.

Malone, Dumas, ed. *Dictionary of American Biography.* Index 3. New York: Charles Scribner's Sons, 1933.

Maltz, Earl M. "Majority, Concurrence, and Dissent: *Prigg v. Pennsylvania* and the Structure of Supreme Court Decisionmaking." *Rutgers Law Journal* 31 (Winter 2000): 345–98.

Marcus, Maeva. *The Documentary History of the Supreme Court of the United States, 1789–1800.* Vol. 3, *The Justices on Circuit.* New York: Columbia University Press, 1990.

———. "The Earliest Years (1790–1801): Laying Foundations." In *The United States Supreme Court: The Pursuit of Justice,* ed. Christopher Tomlins. New York: Houghton Mifflin, 2005.

Marengo County Heritage Book Committee. *The Heritage of Marengo County, Alabama.* Clanton, AL: Heritage Publishing Consultants, 2000.

Martin, John M. "John McKinley: Jacksonian Phase." *Alabama Historical Quarterly* 28 (Spring 1966): 7–31.

———. "The Senatorial Career of Gabriel Moore." *Alabama Historical Quarterly* 26 (Spring 1964): 249–81.

Martineau, Harriet. *Retrospect of Western Travel.* Ed. Daniel Feller. Armonk, NY: M. E. Sharpe, 2000.

Matthews, Pitt Lamar. *History Stories of Alabama.* Dallas: Southern Publishing Company, 1929.

McAdams, Mrs. Harry Kennett. *Kentucky Pioneer and Court Records.* Lexington, KY: Keystone Printery, 1929. Reprint, Baltimore: Genealogical Publishing, 1975.

McCain, William D. *The Story of Jackson: A History of the Capital of Mississippi, 1821–1851.* Jackson, MS: J. F. Hyer Publishing Company, 1952.

McClellan, James. *Joseph Story and the American Constitution.* Norman: University of Oklahoma Press, 1971.

McDonald, William L. *A Walk through the Past: People and Places of Florence and Lauderdale County, Alabama.* Killen, AL: Heart of Dixie Publishing, 1997.

Melton, Buckner F., Jr. *Aaron Burr: Conspiracy to Treason.* New York: John Wiley and Sons, 2002.

Moore, Albert B. *History of Alabama.* Tuscaloosa: Alabama Book Store, 1934.

Morgan, Robert. *Boone: A Biography.* Chapel Hill, NC: Algonquin Books, 2007.

Nettels, Curtis. "The Mississippi Valley and the Federal Judiciary." *Mississippi Valley Historical Review* 12 (September 1925): 202–26.

Newmyer, R. Kent. Review of *History of the Supreme Court of the United States: The Taney Period,* by Carl B. Swisher. *Stanford Law Review* 27 (May 1975): 1373–79.

———. *Supreme Court Justice Joseph Story: Statesman of the Old Republic.* Chapel Hill: University of North Carolina Press, 1985.

Nuermberger, Ruth Ketring. *The Clays of Alabama.* Lexington: University of Kentucky Press, 1958.

———. "The 'Royal Party' in Early Alabama Politics." *Alabama Review* 6 (April 1953): 94–98.

———. "The 'Royal Party' in Early Alabama Politics (Part II)." *Alabama Review* 6 (July 1953): 198–212.

O'Brien, David M. *Storm Center: The Supreme Court in American Politics.* 8th ed. New York: W. W. Norton, 2008.

Owen, Thomas McAdory, and Marie Bankhead Owen. *History of Alabama and Dictionary of Alabama Biography.* Vol. 1. Chicago: S. J. Clarke Publishing Company, 1921.

Perrin, William H. *The Pioneer Press in Kentucky.* Filson Club Publications. Louisville, KY: John P. Morton and Company, 1888.

Polk, James K. *Correspondence of James K. Polk.* Ed. Herbert Weaver. 10 vols. Nashville, TN: Vanderbilt University Press, 1969.

Posey, Walter Brownlow. "Alabama in the 1830s as Recorded by British Travelers." *Birmingham-Southern College Bulletin* 31 (December 1938): 1–47.

Pruitt, Paul M., Jr. "The Life and Times of Legal Education in Alabama, 1819–1897." *Alabama Law Review* (Fall 1997): 281–321.

Ramage, James A. *John Wesley Hunt: Pioneer Merchant, Manufacturer, and Financier.* Lexington: University Press of Kentucky, 1974.

Ranck, George W. *History of Lexington, Kentucky: Its Early Annuals and Recent Progress.* Cincinnati: Robert Clarke and Company, 1872. Reprint, Bowie, MD: Heritage Books, 1989.

Reavis, Logan U. *Saint Louis: The Future City of the World.* St. Louis: Gray, Baker, and Co., 1875.

"Register of Gubernatorial Appointments—Civil and Military." *Alabama Historical Quarterly* 6, no. 2 (1944): 121–328.

Rice, Turner. "The Cypress Land Company: A Dream of Empire." *Journal of Muscle Shoals History* 3 (1975): 21–35.

Ringwalt, John L. *Development of Transportation Systems in the United States.* Philadelphia: Railway World Office, 1888. Reprint, New York: Johnson Reprint Corp., 1966.

Roberts, Frances C. "Politics and Public Land Disposal in Alabama's Formative Period." *Alabama Review* 22 (July 1969): 163–74.

Rogers, William Warren, Robert David Ward, Leah Rawls Atkins, and Wayne Flynt.

Alabama: The History of a Deep South State. Tuscaloosa: The University of Alabama Press, 1994.

Rogin, Michael Paul. *Fathers and Children: Andrew Jackson and the Subjugation of the American Indian.* New York: Alfred A. Knopf, 1975.

Rohrbough, Malcolm J. *The Land Office Business: The Settlement and Administration of American Public Lands, 1789–1837.* New York: Oxford University Press, 1968.

Rothman, Adam, *Slave Country: American Expansion and the Origins of the Deep South.* Cambridge, MA: Harvard University Press, 2005.

Royall, Anne Newport. *Letters from Alabama: 1817–1822.* Tuscaloosa: The University of Alabama Press, 1969.

Saunders, James. E. *Early Settlers of Alabama.* New Orleans: L. Graham and Son, 1899.

Schachner, Nathan. *Aaron Burr: A Biography.* New York: A. S. Barnes and Company, 1961.

Schafer, Judith K. *Slavery, the Civil Law, and the Supreme Court of Louisiana.* Baton Rouge: Louisiana State University Press, 1994.

Schlesinger, Arthur M., Jr. *The Age of Jackson.* Boston: Little, Brown, and Company, 1953.

Schmidhauser, John R. "Judicial Behavior and the Sectional Crisis of 1837–1860." *Journal of Politics* 23 (November 1961): 615–40.

———. *The Supreme Court: Its Politics, Personalities, and Procedures.* New York: Holt, Reinhart, and Winston, 1960.

———. *The Supreme Court as Final Arbiter in Federal-State Relations, 1789–1957.* Chapel Hill: University of North Carolina Press, 1958.

Sellers, Charles G., Jr. *James K. Polk, Jacksonian, 1795–1843.* Princeton: Princeton University Press, 1957.

Siegel, Martin. *The Taney Court: 1836–1864.* Millwood, NY: Associated Faculty Press, 1987.

Simpson, James. "Recollections of Florence." *Florence Times,* August 8, 1918.

Somerville, Henderson M. "Trial of the Alabama Supreme Court Judges in 1829." In *Proceedings of the Twenty-Second Annual Meeting of the Alabama State Bar Association, Montgomery, Alabama, June 16–17, 1899,* 59–86. Montgomery, AL: Brown Printing Company, 1899.

Southerland, Henry D., Jr., and Jerry E. Brown. *The Federal Road through Georgia, the Creek Nation, and Alabama, 1806–1836.* Tuscaloosa: The University of Alabama Press, 1989.

Speech of Mr. McKinley, of Alabama, *on the Bill to Graduate the Price of Public Lands. Delivered in the Senate of the United States, March 26, 1828.* Washington, DC: Green and Jarvis, 1828.

Steel, Edward M. *A Forty-Niner from Tennessee: The Diary of Hugh Brown Heiskell.* Knoxville: University of Tennessee Press, 1998.

Stephens, Alexander H. *Recollections of Alexander H. Stephens: His Diary Kept When a Prisoner at Fort Warren, Boston Harbour, 1865*. Ed. Myrta Lockett Avary. New York: Doubleday, 1920. Reprint, New York: Da Capo Press, 1971.

Story, William W., ed. *Life and Letters of Joseph Story*. Vol. 2. Boston: Little and Brown, 1851.

The Supreme Court of the United States: Its Beginnings and Its Justices, 1790–1991. Washington, DC: Commission on the Bicentennial of the United States Constitution, 1992.

Sutherland, James F., comp. *Early Kentucky Landholders, 1787–1811*. Baltimore: Genealogical Publishing, 1986.

Swisher, Carl Brent. *Roger B. Taney*. New York: Macmillan, 1935.

———. *The Taney Period, 1836–64*. Vol. 5 of *History of the Supreme Court of the United States*. New York: Macmillan, 1974.

Sydnor, Charles S. *Gentlemen Freeholders: Political Practices in Washington's Virginia*. Chapel Hill: University of North Carolina Press, 1952.

Tachau, Mary K. Bonsteel. *Federal Courts in the Early Republic: Kentucky, 1789–1816*. Princeton: Princeton University Press, 1978.

Talbert, Charles G. *Benjamin Logan: Kentucky Frontiersman*. Lexington: University of Kentucky Press, 1962.

Taylor, Samuel. *Memoir of Roger Brooke Taney, LLD*. Baltimore: John Murphy and Company, 1872.

Thornton, J. Mills, III. *Power and Politics in a Slave Society*. Baton Rouge: Louisiana State University Press, 1978.

Tomlins, Christopher L., ed. *The United States Supreme Court: The Pursuit of Justice*. New York: Houghton Mifflin, 2005.

Toulmin, Harry. *A Digest of the Laws of the State of Alabama*. Cahawba, AL: Ginn and Curtis, 1823.

Treat, Payson Jackson. *The National Land System, 1785–1820*. New York: E. B. Treat and Company, 1910.

Walker, Alexander. *The Great Gaines Case*. New Orleans: Office of the Daily Delta, 1850.

Walton, Brian G. "Elections to the United States Senate in Alabama before the Civil War." *Alabama Review* 27 (January 1974): 3–38.

Ward, Artemus. *Deciding to Leave: The Politics of Retirement from the United States Supreme Court*. Albany: State University of New York Press, 2003.

———. "The 'Good Old #3 Club' Gets a New Member." *Journal of Supreme Court History* 33 (March 2008): 110–19.

Warren, Charles. *A History of the American Bar*. Boston: Little, Brown, and Company, 1911.

———. *History of the Harvard Law School and of Early Legal Conditions in America*. Clark, NJ: Law Book Exchange, 2008.

———. *The Supreme Court in United States History*. Vols. 1–2. Boston: Little, Brown, and Company, 1937.

Watlington, Patricia. *The Partisan Spirit*. New York: Atheneum, 1972.

Webster, Daniel. *The Papers of Daniel Webster—Correspondence*. Ed. Charles M. Wiltse. 7 vols. Hanover, NH: University Press of New England, 1974–84.

Weld, Theodore Dwight. *American Slavery as It Is: A Testimony of a Thousand Witnesses*. New York: American Anti-Slavery Society, 1839.

Whatley, George C. "Justice John McKinley." *Journal of Muscle Shoals History* 12 (1988): 27–30.

Wheeler, Russell R., and Cynthia Harrison. *Creating the Federal Judicial System*. 3rd ed. Washington, DC: Federal Judicial Center, 2004.

White, G. Edward. "The Internal Powers of the Chief Justice: The Nineteenth Century Legacy." *University of Pennsylvania Law Review* 154 (2006): 1463–1510.

White, G. Edward, and Gerald Gunther. *The Marshall Court and Cultural Change, 1815–35*. New York: Macmillan, 1988.

Wigdor, Alexandra K. *The Personal Papers of Supreme Court Justices*. New York: Garland, 1986.

Wilson, Dona Adams, comp. *Woodford County, Kentucky Marriage Bonds and Consents, 1789–1830*. Lexington, KY: Lynn Blue Print, 1998.

Wilson, Samuel M. "The Court Proceedings of 1806 in Kentucky against Aaron Burr and John Adair." *Filson Club Historical Quarterly* 10, no. 1 (1936): 31–40.

Wood, William. *Autobiography*. Vol. 2. New York: J. S. Babcock, 1895.

Woodson, Henry Morton. *Historical Genealogy of the Woodsons and Their Connections*. Memphis: self-published, 1915.

Woolley, John T., and Gerhard Peters. The American Presidency Project, Santa Barbara, CA. http://www.presidency.ucsb.edu/ws/?pid=29481 (accessed August 31, 2009).

Wyman, Justus, "A Geographical Sketch of the Alabama Territory." *Transactions of the Alabama Historical Society* 3 (1899): 126.

Young, James Sterling. *The Washington Community, 1800–1828*. New York: Columbia University Press, 1966.

Newspapers

The Ralph Brown Draughon Library at Auburn University and the Robert Crown Law Library at Stanford University provided access to nearly all of the following historic newspapers through the following databases: News Archive, Newsbank "America's Historical Newspapers," Infotrac "Nineteenth Century U.S. Newspapers," and Proquest Historical Newspapers. The Ralph Brown Draughon Library at Auburn University and the Alabama Department of Archives and History in Montgomery, Alabama, provided access to both original and microfilm copies of Huntsville's *Southern Advocate* and *Democrat* newspapers.

Adams Sentinel and General Advertiser (Gettysburg, PA)
American (Baltimore, MD)
Arkansas Gazette (Little Rock)

Arkansas State Democrat (Little Rock)
Baltimore Patriot
Baltimore Sun
Bangor (ME) Daily Whig and Courier
Boston Courier
Cadet and Statesman (Providence, RI)
Carolina Observer (Fayetteville, NC)
Cherokee Phoenix and Indian's Advocate (Georgia)
Cleveland Daily Herald
Daily Atlas (Boston)
Daily Herald and Gazette (Cleveland, OH)
Daily Inter Ocean (Chicago)
Daily National Intelligencer (Washington, DC)
Daily National Journal (Washington, DC)
Daily Pittsburgh Gazette (Pittsburgh, PA)
Daily Scioto Gazette (Chillicothe, OH)
Democrat (Huntsville, AL)
Emancipator & Republican (Boston)
Fayetteville (AR) Observer
Fayetteville (NC) Observer
Florence (AL) Times
Globe (Washington, DC)
Guard (Holly Springs, MS)
Kentucky Gazette
Literary Cadet and Saturday Evening Bulletin (Providence, RI)
Madisonian (Washington, DC)
Milwaukee Daily Sentinel and Gazette
Mississippian (Jackson)
Mobile (AL) Gazette and General Advertiser
Morning Oregonian (Portland)
Nashville Banner
Natchez (MS) Semi-Weekly Courier
Newark (OH) Advocate
New Hampshire Statesman
New York Daily Times
New York Herald
New York Spectator
New York Times
New Yorker
Niles Weekly Register (Baltimore, MD)
North American (Philadelphia)
North American and United States Gazette (Philadelphia)

Paul Pry (Washington, DC)
Pensacola (FL) Gazette
Pennsylvania Inquirer and Gazette (Philadelphia)
Philadelphia Inquirer and Daily Courier
Raleigh (NC) Register
Scioto Gazette (Chillicothe, OH)
Southern Advocate (Huntsville, AL)
Tri-Weekly Flag and Advertiser (Montgomery, AL)
Tuscumbian (Tuscumbia, AL)
U.S. Telegraph and Commercial Herald (Washington, DC)
Vermont Gazette (Bennington)
Vermont Watchman and State Journal (Montpelier)
Village Messenger (Fayetteville, TN)
Virginia Free Press and Farmers' Repository (Charlestown, VA [now WV])
Weekly Herald (New York)
Weekly Raleigh Register and North Carolina Gazette
Western World (Frankfort, KY)
Wisconsin Democrat (Green Bay)

Collected Papers

Campbell Family Papers. Southern Historical Collection, Manuscripts Department, Wilson Library, University of North Carolina, Chapel Hill.

John Coffee Papers. Alabama Department of Archives and History, Montgomery, AL.

Robert Dyas Collection of John Coffee Papers. Tennessee Historical Society, Tennessee State Library and Archives, Nashville. (Available on microfilm at Ralph Brown Draughon Library, Auburn University.)

Andrew Jackson Papers. Library of Congress, Washington, DC. (Available on microfilm at Ralph Brown Draughon Library, Auburn University.)

Kentucky Papers of the Lyman C. Draper Collection. (Available on microfilm at Ralph Brown Draughon Library, Auburn University.)

Richard Peters Collection. Historical Society of Philadelphia.

Pope-Humphrey Papers. Filson Historical Society, Louisville, KY.

Alexander H. Stephens Collection. Manhattanville College, Purchase, NY.

Joseph Story Papers. Phillips Library, Peabody Essex Museum, Salem, MA.

Martin Van Buren Papers. Manuscript Division, Library of Congress, Washington, DC.

Joshua Whitney Papers, Broome County Historical Society, Binghamton, NY.

Index